The Irish in the Italian Campaign, 1943–45

Also available by Richard Doherty:

Wall of Steel: The History of 9th (Londonderry) HAA Regiment, RA (SR); North-West Books, Limavady, 1988

The Sons of Ulster: Ulstermen at war from the Somme to Korea; Appletree Press, Belfast, 1992

Clear the Way! A History of the 38th (Irish) Brigade, 1941–1947; Irish Academic Press, Dublin, 1993

Irish Generals: Irish Generals in the British Army in the Second World War; Appletree Press, Belfast, 1993

Only the Enemy in Front: The Recce Corps at War, 1940–46; Spellmount, Staplehurst, 1994

Key to Victory: The Maiden City in the Second World War; Greystone Books, Antrim, 1995

The Williamite War in Ireland, 1699–1691; Four Courts Press, Dublin, 1998

A Noble Crusade: The History of Eighth Army, 1941–1945; Spellmount, Staplehurst, 1999

Irish Men and Women in the Second World War; Four Courts Press, Dublin, 1999

Irish Winners of the Victoria Cross (with David Truesdale); Four Courts Press, Dublin, 2000

Irish Volunteers in the Second World War; Four Courts Press, Dublin, 2001

The Sound of History: El Alamein 1942; Spellmount, Staplehurst, 2002

The North Irish Horse: A Hundred Years of Service; Spellmount, Staplehurst, 2002

Normandy 1944: The Road to Victory; Spellmount, Staplehurst, 2004

Ireland's Generals in the Second World War; Four Courts Press, Dublin, 2004

The Thin Green Line: A History of the Royal Ulster Constabulary GC, 1922–2001; Pen & Sword, Barnsley, 2004

None Bolder: A History of 51st (Highland) Division, 1939–1945; Spellmount, Staplehurst, 2006

The British Reconnaissance Corps in World War II; Osprey Publishing, Oxford, 2007

Eighth Army in Italy 1943–45: The Long Hard Slog; Pen & Sword, Barnsley, 2007

The Siege of Derry 1689: The Military History; Spellmount, Stroud, 2008

Only the Enemy in Front: The Recce Corps at War, 1940–46 (revised p/bk edn); Spellmount, Stroud, 2008

Ubique: The Royal Artillery in the Second World War; Spellmount, Stroud, 2008

Helmand Mission: With the Royal Irish Battlegroup in Afghanistan 2008; Pen & Sword, Barnsley, 2009

In the Ranks of Death: The Irish in the Second World War; Pen & Sword, Barnsley, 2010

The Humber Light Reconnaissance Car 1941–45; Osprey Publishing, Oxford, 2011

Hobart's 79th Armoured Division at War: Invention, Innovation and Inspiration; Pen & Sword, Barnsley, 2011

British Armoured Divisions and Their Commanders 1939–1945; Pen & Sword, Barnsley, 2013

Victory in Italy: 15th Army Group's Final Campaign 1945; Pen & Sword, 2015

Churchill's Greatest Fear: The Battle of the Atlantic - 3 September 1939 to 7 May 1945; Pen & Sword, 2015

El Alamein 1942: Turning Point in the Desert; Pen & Sword, 2017

Monte Cassino: Opening the Road to Rome; Pen & Sword, 2018

Aspects of Arnhem: The Battle Re-examined (with David Truesdale); Pen & Sword, 2023

The Irish in the Italian Campaign, 1943–45

Men and Women of Ireland in one of the Second World War's Toughest Theatres

Richard Doherty

Pen & Sword
MILITARY

First published in Great Britain in 2025 by
Pen & Sword Military
An imprint of Pen & Sword Books Limited
Yorkshire – Philadelphia

ISBN 978 1 03612 408 3

A CIP catalogue record for this book is available from the British Library.

Typeset by Mac Style
Printed in the UK by CPI Group (UK) Ltd, Croydon, CR0 4YY.

MIX
Paper | Supporting responsible forestry
FSC www.fsc.org FSC® C013604

The Publisher's authorised representative in the EU for product safety is Authorised Rep Compliance Ltd., Ground Floor, 71 Lower Baggot Street, Dublin D02 P593, Ireland.
www.arccompliance.com

For a complete list of Pen & Sword titles please contact

PEN & SWORD BOOKS LIMITED
47 Church Street, Barnsley, South Yorkshire, S70 2AS, England
E-mail: enquiries@pen-and-sword.co.uk
Website: www.pen-and-sword.co.uk
or
PEN AND SWORD BOOKS
1950 Lawrence Road, Havertown, PA 19083, USA
E-mail: uspen-and-sword@casematepublishers.com
Website: www.penandswordbooks.com

Contents

For all those men and women from the island of Ireland who served in Italy during the Second World War, especially those who never came home. And for the people of Italy who welcomed them into their hearts 'even when we destroyed their crops to build gunsites'.

Map 1: The Italian Campaign.

Map 2: Operation HUSKY, the landings in Sicily, 10 July 1943.

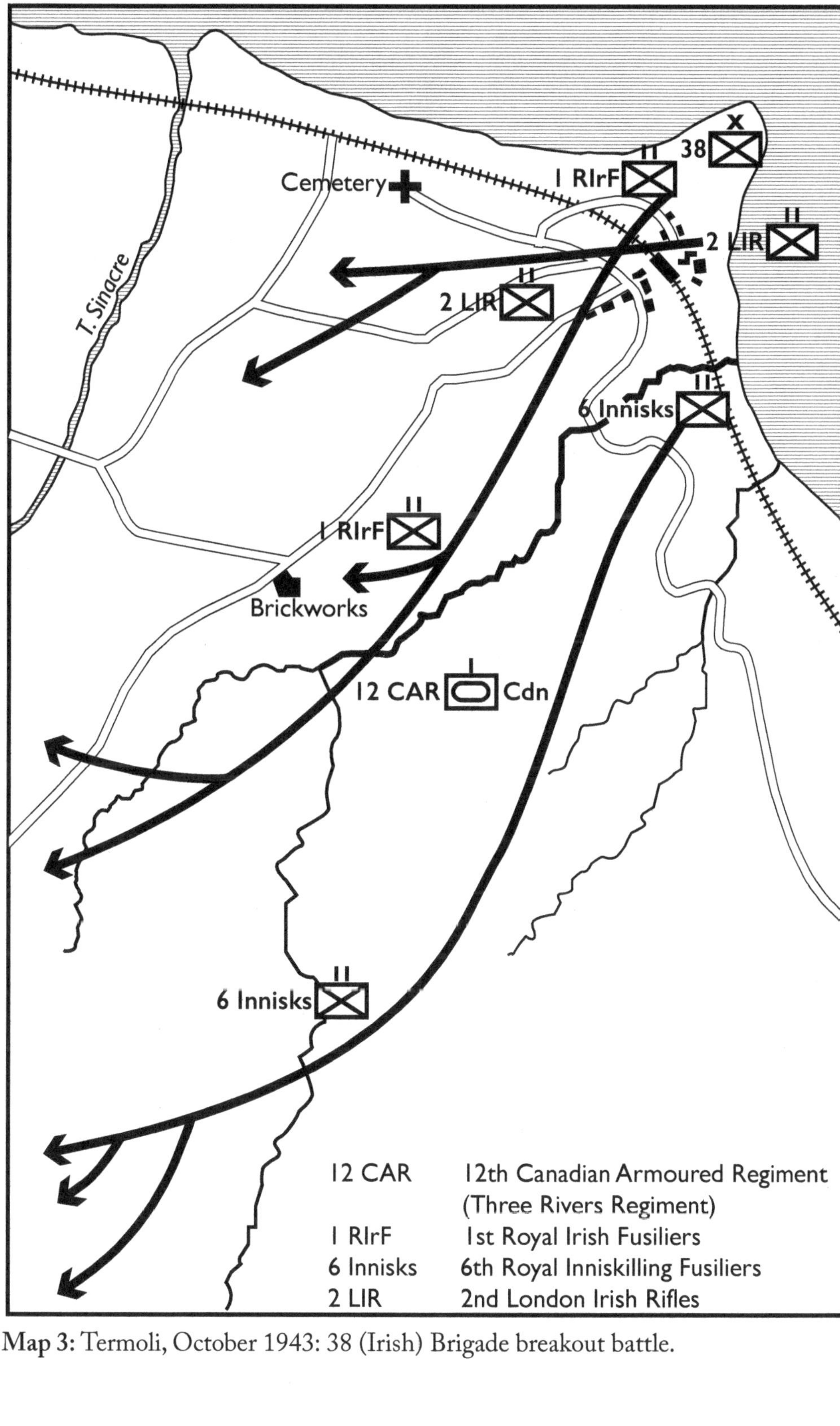

Map 3: Termoli, October 1943: 38 (Irish) Brigade breakout battle.

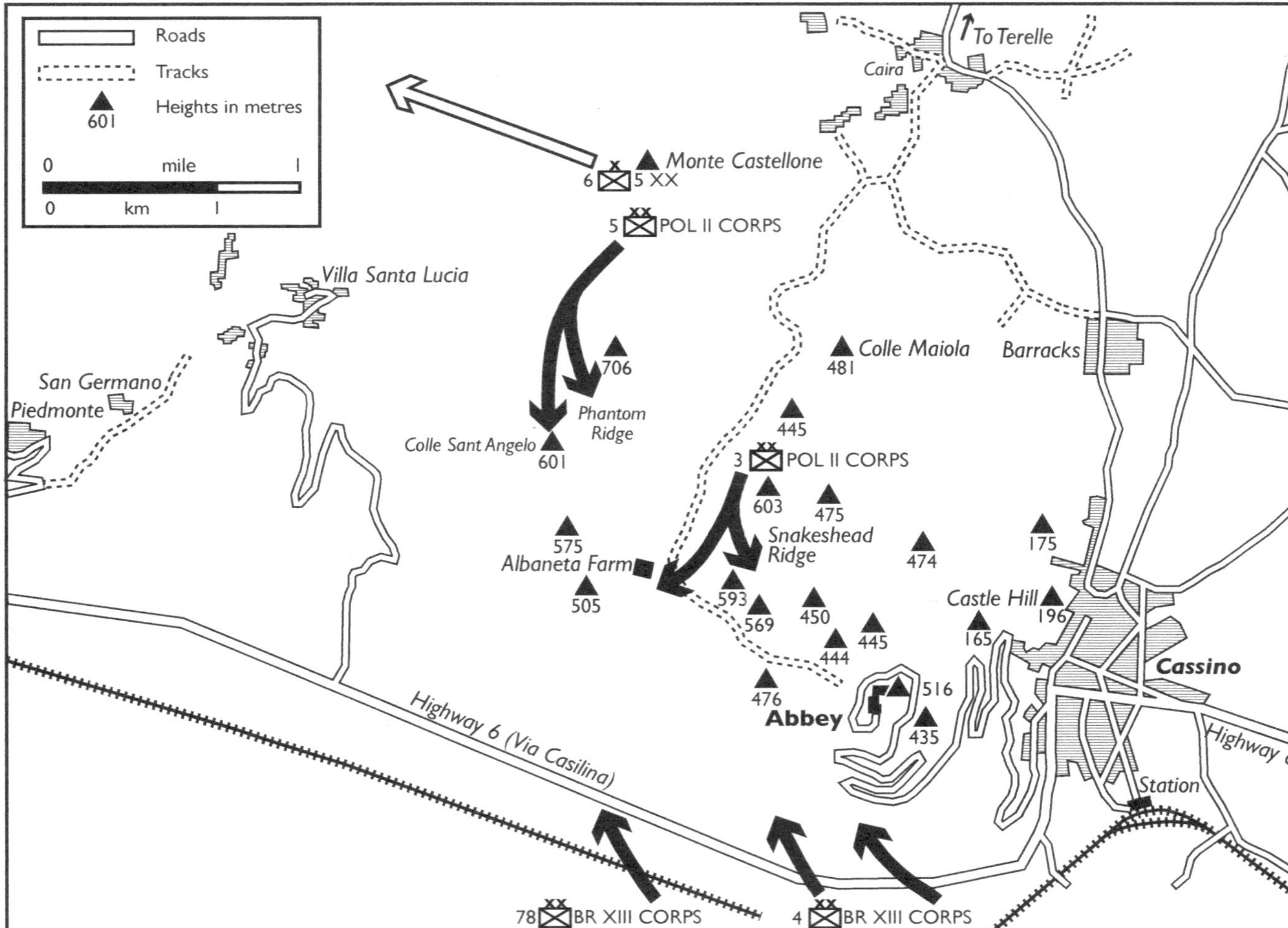

Map 4: Operation HONKER – Eighth Army's Offensive at Cassino 11–17 May 1944.

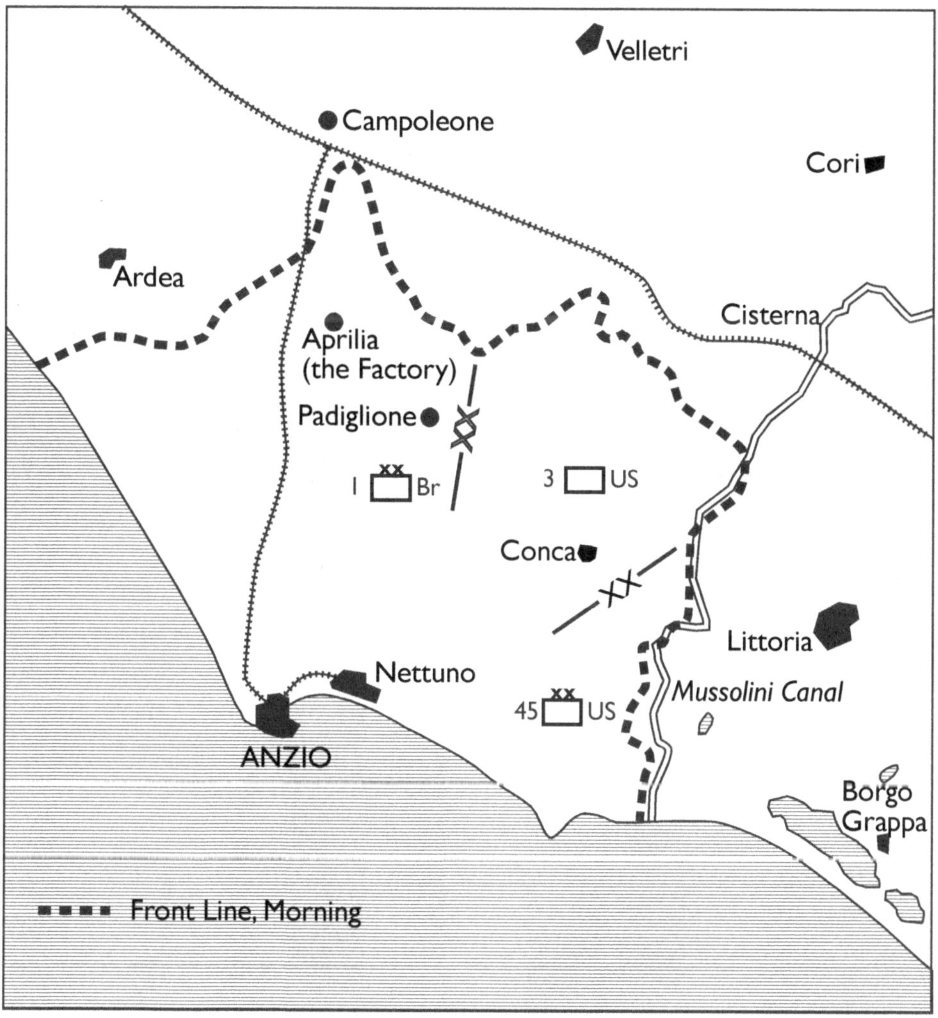

Map 5: Anzio Beachhead – 1 February 1944.

Map 6: Northern Italy 1944–45.

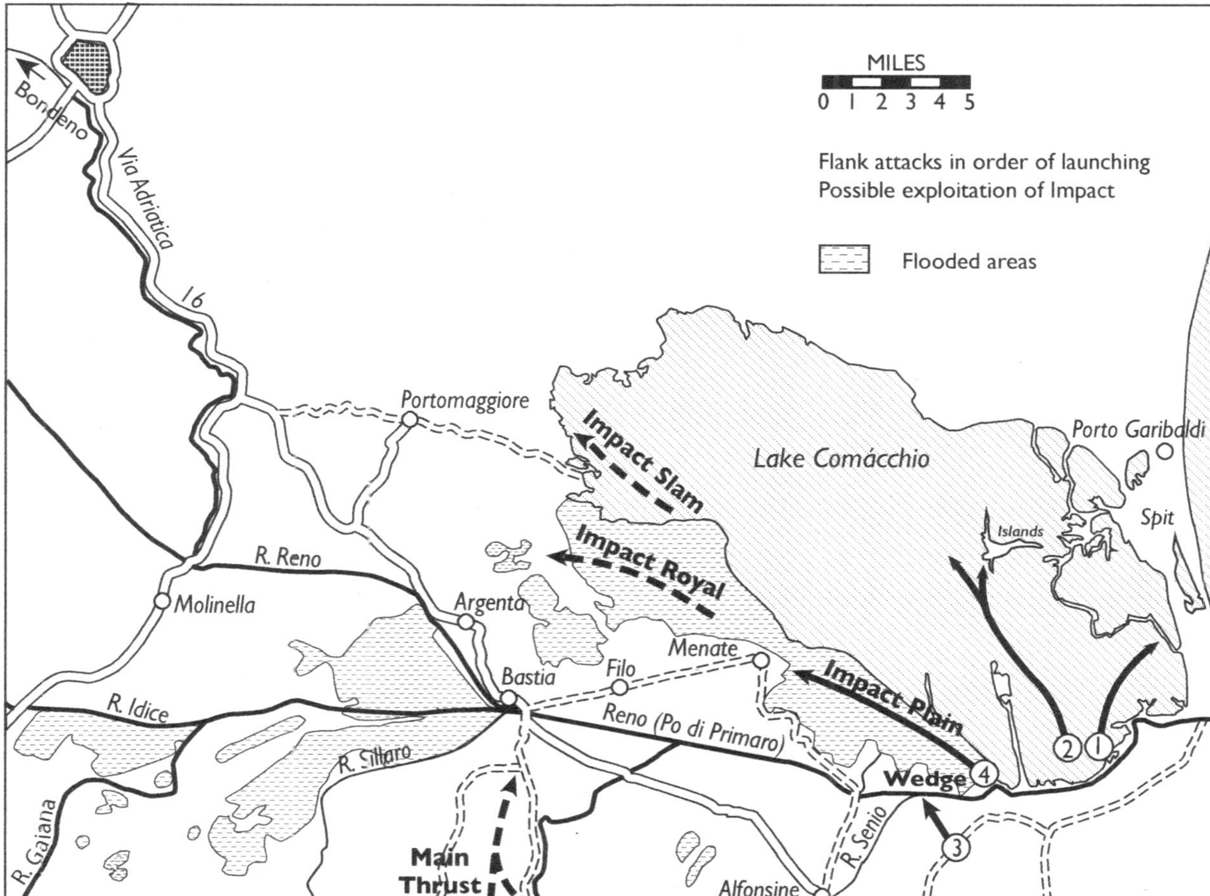

Map 7: THE ARGENTA GAP, V Corps plan for April 1945.

Acknowledgements

It is both an oxymoron and a truth to state that writing a history book is a solo task that involves many people. While an author may shape the book and write the text, many others will have helped take the work to that stage. This has certainly been the case with this account of Irish service personnel and civilians in the Italian campaign. Although most of the book was written during 2024, its 'DNA' dates back to when I was at school and, arguably, even before I started school.

My interest in Italy and the Italian campaign goes back to childhood days in the 1950s. Our neighbouring Radcliffe and McFeely families had fathers who, like mine, had served in Italy while Joe Radcliffe had married an Italian girl, Lucia Bedeschi. My father had stories of Italy that might have been holiday reminiscences, had there not been a war raging. In hindsight, I realised that he had a real affection for Italy and its people and, obviously, I owe a debt to him. Later I became aware of veterans of the Italian campaign in neighbouring streets, two of whom, Tommy McCready and John Logue, feature in the pages that follow.

When I wrote my first book, published in 1988, I had the assistance of many veterans of the Italian campaign who had served with my father. Writing and presenting BBC Radio Ulster's 'Sons of Ulster' series the following year put me in touch with more veterans, including Lieutenant Colonel Desmond Woods MC*. I had also worked alongside many veterans, including a number who served in Italy, one of them being Joe Robinson.

As the reader will appreciate, it would be impossible to list all who contributed to this book. However, it is right to record the names of those whose contributions were significant: Capt. E.H. 'Sonny' Babington ERD MiD, Bobby Baxter BEM, Bill Black, Maj. Gen. H.E.N. 'Bala' Bredin CB DSO** MC*, Jim Canning, Eddie Cassidy, Col Kendal Chavasse DSO* MiD, Lt Col Brian Clark MC GM, Dermot Clarke, Bertie Cuthbert, Jim Dinsmore, Maj. John Duane MC, Henry Elwood, Maj. Desmond Fay MC, Lt Col Val ffrench-Blake DSO, R.J. Hamilton MM, Robert Hamilton, Jack Hassard MiD, Col John Horsfall DSO MC*, Willie Hunter, George Lapsley, John Ledwidge, John Logue, Sam McAughtry, Col John McCann CBE TD, Maj. Ernie McClure,

Col Sir Basil A.T. McFarland CBE ERD MiD, George McCallion, Jimmy McFeely, Jack McIlmoyle, Joe McIlmoyle, Johnnie McMahon, Tom Moore, Col A.J. 'Tony' Morris OBE MC KM, Lt Col M.J.F. 'Murphy' Palmer DSO, John J. Ormsby, Capt. A.G. Parsons MC, Tom Patton, Jim Peoples, Joe Robinson, Capt. R.J. 'Robbie' Robinson DCM, Joe Russell, William Sherrard, Eamon Simms, William 'Billy' Smyth, Jimmy Soutar, Miles Stott BEM, Alex Taylor, Fred Taylor, John Taylor, Col P.J.C. 'Jim' Trousdell OBE, Victor Webb, Eric Wilson, Col A.D. Woods MC* and Walter Wray.

Many veterans' families have given me support and information over the years for which I am very grateful. Joe Radcliffe's family – his wife Lucia Bedeschi, daughter Marina and son Danilo – have been especially helpful, as was Marina's late husband, Paolo Petri. The family of Sergeant 'Rex' Doherty MM MiD were also very helpful, as were John Logue's family, and many others. Alwyn Buchanan, a nephew of Fusilier Alex Carlin, provided photos of his late uncle and Anthony Babington, son of Captain E.H. 'Sonny' Babington was generous in his support. The late Bob McCreery, son of Lieutenant General Sir Richard McCreery GCB KBE DSO MC, Eighth Army's last commander, gave me invaluable assistance.

I am especially grateful to regimental museums for their enthusiastic support. Maeve Cadden of The Inniskillings Museum has been most helpful, giving me access to war diaries and images; Colonel Mark Scott, Chairman of the Trustees, provided an account of the Anzio campaign written by his late father, Colonel Bobby Scott, who commanded 2nd Inniskillings. Caroline Corvan of the Royal Irish Fusiliers Museum has provided support and information and I am grateful to her and to Brigadier Adrian Naughten MBE, Chairman of the Trustees. The Reverend Michael Keaveny, whose alma mater was the Pontifical Irish College in Rome, provided information on Monsignor Hugh O'Flaherty and post-war life in Rome while the Reverend Aidan McGrath OFM first told me of the experiences of his aunt, Eveline McGrath of the QAs, over dinner in Rome in 2016 and then introduced me to his cousin, Dr Paul Stewart, who has written a biography of Eveline, his mother, a remarkable lady who died at the age of 100. Over the past three decades, James Durney has been a mine of information on the service of Irishmen and women, especially from County Kildare, and once again I thank him for his assistance and valuable information.

In Italy I have had the help of many individuals. The wonderful Lucia Bedeschi provided a vivid picture of the Italy of her childhood and youth, and of wartime Rome. Guidance around the battlefields of the Cassino campaign was provided by my good friend Damiano Paravano who also introduced me to Enrico Canini who led us on a detailed tour of much of the Anzio battleground. Over many years Alessandro Teti has given me much information on southern Italy and the fighting there, especially around Campobasso; in return I was pleased to assist him with information on the Decima MAS attack on Alexandria harbour. In northern Italy I enjoyed the expertise, and artistic ability, of Piero Compagni and his colleague Sanzio Guerrini of the Senio Line Museum in Alfonsine. Dottore Pier Paolo Battistelli and Professore Piero Crociani were generous with their time and knowledge; both are highly-respected historians who have been published in both English and Italian. *Tenente Colonello* Filippo Cappellano welcomed me to the *Archivo dell'Ufficio Storico dello Stato Maggiore Esercito* in Rome when he was in charge; he, too, is a published military historian.

Other institutions which have helped include the National Army Museum, Chelsea, the Imperial War Museum, London; the National Archives, Kew, Surrey; the RAF Museum, Hendon; the Australian War Memorial; the National Library of Ireland, Dublin; the Public Records Office of Northern Ireland, Belfast; the Linen Hall Library, Belfast and Derry Central Library, Londonderry.

As ever, Tim Webster has done an excellent job on the maps in this book. It would be impossible to provide maps that cover every action mentioned but some significant actions covered are included in the map section.

I have never been disappointed in the work of the Pen and Sword team. Philip Sidnell, my commissioning editor, has been a tower of strength while production manager Matt Jones has an unbeatable work ethic matched only by his professionalism. Dominic Allen has created a fine jacket that does justice to those who served in Italy.

To anyone whom I may have omitted, please accept my apologies.

None of this would have been possible without the support of my family: Carol, my wife, our children Joanne, James and Catríona, our sons in law Steven McCurdy and Olivier Baillache, and our grandchildren Cíaran, Katrina, Josh, Sophie, Hannah, Élias and Emilia. My thanks to you all.

Richard Doherty
Muchea, Western Australia
and
Co. Londonderry
2024

Prologue

During 2024 it was almost impossible to miss media coverage of the 80th anniversary of Operation OVERLORD, the Normandy landings, or, as much of the print and broadcast media proclaimed, D Day. Thus, much of the population may be excused for believing that the term D Day relates only to a single day in France: 6 June 1944. In reality, every military operation began on D Day and at H Hour.

In late-1944 Nancy Astor MP, the first woman to take her seat in the House of Commons, referred to a letter that she had received from a soldier in Italy who had signed himself 'D Day Dodger'. Often accused, wrongly, of creating the description, Astor unwittingly popularized it in much the same way as 'Old Contemptibles' had become a badge of honour in 1914.

Rather than being D Day Dodgers, those who served in Italy experienced many D Days but 2024 brought fewer commemorations for them and even less publicity. The battles of Cassino and Anzio were marked and a Papal audience reflected one granted to Irish personnel in 1944. That gathering of Irish personnel in the Vatican in June 1944 pointed to a considerable Irish presence in the UK forces in Italy. In fact, that Irish presence in Italy was much greater than in any other theatre of war. It was formed by an Irish armoured regiment, an Irish infantry brigade, three Irish infantry battalions in other formations, an Irish heavy anti-aircraft regiment, two Irish light anti-aircraft regiments, an armoured regiment with a part-Irish history and many Irish individuals in the forces as well as VADs from St John Ambulance and the Red Cross.

The purpose of this book is to tell at least some of their story. It cannot hope to tell the complete story but, hopefully, it will spark interest in that story and draw attention to the part the Irish played in liberating Italy. That part was not confined to soldiers, sailors and airmen but also included civilians, such as the courageous Monsignor Hugh O'Flaherty and the singer Delia Murphy and her daughter, Blon.

Growing up in the 1950s I was aware that both our next-door neighbours were, like our father, former soldiers who had served in Italy. In streets nearby were others who had done likewise. However, it was many years later when I realised just how strong had been the Irish presence in Italy. This then is my small tribute to all of those Irish men and women.

Chapter 1

Sicily

Allied victory in Tunisia was followed by debate about what should follow. Having earlier planned (twice) to invade Sicily, British commanders proposed further operations in the Mediterranean, including seizing Sicily or Sardinia, followed by landings on mainland Italy. Initially, American planners disagreed, arguing for concentration on a campaign in north-west Europe. However, General George C. Marshall, US Army Chief of Staff, accepted that seizing Sicily would assist Allied shipping in the Mediterranean without diverting forces from the intended landings in France. Agreeing to the Sicily operation, he was adamant that that did not imply the US would support further Mediterranean operations.

The Combined Chiefs of Staff appointed a commander for what was codenamed Operation HUSKY, General Dwight D. Eisenhower who had held the equivalent post for operations in French North-West Africa. HUSKY, scheduled for the July moon, would be preceded by capturing the island of Pantellaria, about seventy miles from Sicily.

Two Allied armies would deploy: General Sir Bernard Montgomery's Eighth Army and Lieutenant General George S. Patton's Seventh, both under command of General Sir Harold Alexander's 15 Army Group. 'Alex' had commanded 18 Army Group in Tunisia and was also Eisenhower's deputy. The original Chiefs of Staff plan was for dispersed landings in the south, south-east and north-west area of Sicily to neutralize Axis airfields and seize the main ports. However, Alexander, Montgomery and Patton were not involved in that planning since all three were prosecuting the campaign in Tunisia. When they were able to comment, changes were made, largely on Montgomery's insistence, although both the naval commander, Admiral Sir Andrew Cunningham, and air commander, Air Chief Marshal Sir Arthur Tedder, felt that Montgomery's plan would leave over a dozen airfields in Axis hands, thus presenting significant threat to the Allied invasion fleet. Eisenhower then brought Cunningham, Montgomery and Tedder together, at which point Montgomery proposed concentrating the effort in south-eastern Sicily and seizing the ports there. Alexander joined them next day, 3 May 1943, as discussion continued. Eventually, Montgomery's proposals were accepted: it was considered that maintaining invading formations over open beaches was a lesser risk than the original plan's broad dispersal of effort. Thus, Montgomery had his way and the plans were modified. Although his argument was sound, his attitude to his fellow commanders led to ill feeling, especially with Patton and Tedder.

* * *

It so happened that a new vehicle made landing supplies across beaches much simpler than ever before: the DUKW was a six-wheeled amphibious lorry with a watertight body, capable of carrying men or equipment from ship to shore and thence to supply dumps.[1] (DUKW was the General Motors' designation: D indicated year of introduction, 1942; U a Utility vehicle; K all-wheel drive; and W tandem rear axles, both driven.) Used by the US Marine Corps on Guadalcanal in 1942, Operation HUSKY saw its debut in Europe. In his 1948 *Despatches*, Alexander commented that it was 'not too much to say that the DUKW revolutionized the problem of beach maintenance'.[2]

Cunningham's staff planned the invasion force's move from ports along the north African coast, Malta and the UK: 1st Canadian Division arrived from British ports. Protecting the force from attack by ships, submarines and aircraft fell to Cunningham and his staff as did its support by naval gunfire during the landings. The Rathmines-born admiral was equal to the task: appointed Commander-in-Chief, Mediterranean Fleet in June 1939, he ensured that the fleet was prepared for Italy's inevitable entry into the war, which occurred a year later. He inflicted serious losses and setbacks on the *Regia Marina*, although Italian special forces damaged seriously his last two battleships, HMSs *Queen Elizabeth* and *Valiant*, in Alexandria harbour in December 1941. By subterfuge, Cunningham disguised the fact that both had been 'sunk' and were resting on the harbour bed until temporary repairs enabled them to sail from the Mediterranean for repair.

Cunningham had also ensured the evacuation of much of the Commonwealth force from Greece and Crete in 1941 and the maintenance of the besieged port of Tobruk that same year. In late-1942 he became Naval Commander, Allied Expeditionary Force under Eisenhower who admired his 'absolute selflessness, energy, devotion to duty, knowledge of his task, and in understanding of the requirements of allied operations'. The role included Operation TORCH, the landings in French North-West Africa, in which he commanded the fleet protecting and supporting the landings. Thus, Cunningham had a deep understanding of the requirements of expeditionary warfare which he brought to the planning of HUSKY and subsequent landings in mainland Italy. In February 1943, he returned to his role of C.-in-C., Mediterranean Fleet, having been promoted to admiral of the fleet on 21 January. With Axis armies facing defeat in Tunisia in May 1943, Cunningham ordered that there should be no 'Dunkirk' escape for von Arnim's *Heeresgruppe Afrika*. Such were their losses since the final battle of El Alamein in late 1942 that Germans referred to the defeat in Tunisia as 'Tunisgrad', reflecting a casualty total that paralleled Stalingrad.

With ground troops in two task forces, Cunningham did likewise for his naval elements. Montgomery's Eighth Army's leading formations were designated Eastern Task Force, or Task Force 545; Patton's Seventh Army equivalents were Western Task Force, or Task Force 343. The Mediterranean Fleet formed Eastern Naval Task Force, under Admiral Sir Bertram Ramsay, who had planned DYNAMO, the Dunkirk evacuation, and would go on to plan NEPTUNE, the naval aspect of the Normandy landings in 1944. Western Naval Task Force was formed by the US Navy's Eighth Fleet under Admiral Kent Hewitt who had overseen the US Navy's role in TORCH. Although overshadowed by the Normandy landings of June 1944, HUSKY was the largest seaborne invasion in history.

* * *

One assault force of three landing ships, infantry (LSIs), carrying 231 Independent Brigade Group, was commanded by Captain Lord Ashbourne in the LSI HMS *Keren*. Edward Russell Gibson, third baron Ashbourne, was the nephew of William Gibson, the second baron, a Gaelic enthusiast who wore Irish dress and spoke in Irish in the House of Lords. For his part in HUSKY, Gibson was appointed DSO.[3] Having sailed from Egypt in convoy MWF36, Ashbourne's group reached their release position in 'Bark East' sector and, despite rough seas, the infantry were soon heading to the shore 'though in somewhat ragged formation' where they 'touched down nearly on time'.[4] Some idea of sea conditions may be gleaned from the fact that sailors, as well as soldiers, suffered from seasickness, one man of 1st Black Watch dying.[5]

Operation HUSKY included a major effort by Allied air forces in North Africa and Malta with the overall air component Mediterranean Air Command (MAC) under Tedder. Lieutenant General Carl Spaatz commanded Tunisia-based Northwest African Air Forces (NAAF), with groups from the Royal Air Force and US Ninth and Twelfth Air Forces to provide air support. The RAF had developed the close air support concept in North Africa, using fighter aircraft with bombs or cannon to deal with enemy armour while in radio contact with ground forces; rockets would later be added to their inventory and air-ground communication became more sophisticated. The US Army Air Forces, having studied Desert Air Force (DAF) operations, were adopting similar tactics. Aircraft from Malta, under Air Vice-Marshal Sir Keith Park, of Battle of Britain fame, were also involved in the air plan, as were groups from US Ninth Air Force under Major General Lewis H. Brereton, an officer with an undistinguished record, described by one USAF College academic as 'the worst military commander in history'.[6] As soon as practically possible, it was intended that medium bombers and tactical fighters would occupy Sicilian airfields to provide close, effective support to ground forces.

In preparation for HUSKY, Allied air forces had deployed strategic bombers from North Africa, the Middle East and UK against airfields in Sardinia, Sicily and southern Italy, industrial targets in southern Italy and the ports of Messina and Palermo in Sicily, Cagliari in Sardinia, and Naples. Bombing of targets in northern Italy by Bomber Command aircraft was increased; Greece was bombed by aircraft from the Middle East. That broad spread of bombing was designed to confuse the Axis about the Allies' true objective. Seven days before D Day, the bombers concentrated on Sicilian airfields and communications between the island and the Italian mainland. However, to maintain confusion over where landings would be made, no beach defences were attacked.

Only two airfields were operational on D Day, the majority of Axis aircraft having moved to the mainland. Between mid-May and 10 July, Allied aircrews flew 42,227 sorties, in which 323 Luftwaffe and 105 *Regia Aeronautica* aircraft were destroyed. Allied losses were 250 aircraft, mostly shot down by anti-aircraft fire over Sicily.[7] Among those involved in such operations were Irish personnel such as Wing Commander Anthony (Tony) Lovell, Squadron Leader Robert W. Turkington and Squadron Leader Brian B. Considine, each decorated and with combat experience.

Also included in the air element were airborne forces, including paratroopers, glider-borne infantry, artillery and engineers. Two divisions were assigned: 1st British Airborne, under Major General George Hopkinson, supported Eighth Army by seizing critical bridges and high ground. Hopkinson's division would deploy its airlanding brigade and a parachute brigade in the first major British airborne deployment.

Major General Matt Ridgway's US 82nd Airborne Division was held in reserve in Tunisia, but its 505th Parachute Regimental Combat Team (RCT), under Colonel James 'Jumpin' Jim' Gavin, was dropped on Sicily in the US Army's first operational regimental combat parachute mission. Gavin, born to Irish immigrant parents in New York, was placed in an orphanage some two years later from which he was adopted by Martin and Mary Gavin from Pennsylvania.[8]

* * *

Two operations were planned for 1st Airborne Division: LADBROKE, preceding the seaborne landings, with 1 Airlanding Brigade, under Brigadier Philip 'Pip' Hicks, landing south of Syracuse to seize the Ponte Grande bridge, a coast artillery battery and key points around Syracuse. All objectives were to be in British hands before the first landing craft beached on the morning of 10 July. Codenamed *Waterloo*, Ponte Grande bridge carried the main Syracuse-Cassibile road over the Anapo river and nearby canal. The glider assault was in two phases, a *coup de main* with two infantry companies and Royal Engineers landing close to the objective in eight Airspeed Horsa gliders at 2315 on the 9th, followed by the main body in 136 Waco gliders landing at 0115 on the 10th. Operation FUSTIAN would follow on the 12th with Brigadier Gerald Lathbury's 1 Parachute Brigade dropping all three battalions to seize Primosole bridge carrying the Syracuse-Catania road over the Simeto river.[9]

The Prussian general and military theorist Carl von Clausewitz opined that military operations are subject to frictions, which was certainly true of both airborne operations. A shortage of British transport aircraft and glider tugs forced 1 Airlanding Brigade to rely on USAAF Douglas C-47 Skytrains (Dakotas in British service). Unfortunately, many Skytrain pilots had little experience and had never seen action. Gliders were to be cast off about 3,000 yards from the coast to avoid anti-aircraft fire but high winds meant that the weather was not ideal. By the evening of 9 July, wind strength had increased to Force 6 (25–31mph)[10] and, with many pilots unused to night flying, gliders were cast off much farther out when enemy and 'friendly' fire greeted the aerial armada.

The results were tragic. Seventy-eight gliders crashed into the sea. Those that reached Sicily were dispersed over some twenty-five square miles rather than their planned landing zones (LZs). Many died as gliders hit the waves and broke up, although some survived to be picked up. Among the dead was Lieutenant Michael Bourke Connell of the Glider Pilot Regiment. Born into an Irish family in India, Connell had been commissioned in the Royal Irish Fusiliers on 1 July 1939 and served with the 1st Battalion in France in 1940. Nicknamed 'Crow' by a fellow officer, due to 'an attractive touch of beakiness' and a habit of shrugging his shoulders 'just like an old hoodie flapping', he had earned the respect of his fellow officers and soldiers in France.[11] In 1943,

'Crow' Connell transferred to the Glider Pilot Regiment and was piloting glider No.58 when he was lost with his co-pilot, Sergeant Albert Hill.[12]

The airlanding brigade's battalions were 1st Border Regiment, 2nd South Staffordshire Regiment and 7th King's Own Scottish Borderers; the KOSB did not deploy. The chaplain of 2nd South Staffords, Alan Buchanan, born in Fintona, County Tyrone and ordained in the Church of Ireland, had been commissioned in the Royal Army Chaplains' Department in 1942 and posted to 2nd South Staffords. His glider came down in Italian lines. He and the others aboard were captured by an Italian officer with excellent English. Buchanan persuaded the Italian to surrender to the South Staffords since the area was surrounded by British troops and the officer, after speaking with his men, agreed. The group set out in search of Allied forces. The first they encountered, assuming the Italians were the captors, opened fire, but the situation was resolved quickly by the chaplain. In September 1944, Padre Buchanan was captured by the Germans at Arnhem.[13]

Of the *coup-de-main* group's eight Horsas, only two reached the target area, one being lost when enemy fire struck it on landing, detonating its Bangalore-torpedo cargo. The surviving Horsa carried a South Staffords' platoon which, supported by others of the battalion and some from 1st Border, seized the bridge, holding it against furious Italian attack until most defenders had been killed and ammunition exhausted. The bridge changed hands again when 2nd Royal Scots Fusiliers evicted the Italians after a brief engagement.

Operation FUSTIAN also ran foul of the frictions of war. Approaching the coastline, the paratrooper-carrying C-47s and sixteen glider-tug combinations came under fire from Allied warships. Some pilots simply turned back. Others carried on against AA fire from friend and foe. Only thirty-nine C-47s reached the drop zones (DZs). Four dozen dropped their paratroopers up to a half-mile away. The first six gliders were lost to the sea, six crashed on land and seven made safe landings some distance from their LZs. Only four landed on assigned LZs. Among those lost and whose bodies were never recovered was Captain Hubert Greeves, a medical officer with 181st Airlanding Field Ambulance. From Moy in County Tyrone, he is commemorated on the Cassino Memorial.[14]

Horsa 127A was another loss. Flown by Astley John 'Babe' Cooper AFC, a native of Tipperary, and Sergeant Morgan, 127A carried the Royal Artillery commander and his staff. Closing on the LZ, AA fire hit the tug, forcing Cooper to cast off at 500 feet. The Horsa went out of control, skimmed the river and hit the far bank, killing all onboard.

The C-47s carrying paratroopers were also engaged by defending AA guns. As men of 1st Parachute Battalion began jumping, the gunners found their range. Corporal Jack Fryer, formerly Royal Ulster Rifles, found his C-47 illuminated by a searchlight beam that allowed the guns to concentrate on the aeroplane, which was hit, starting a fire. Only four jumped, Fryer being the last, before the transport began its death plunge. He injured his back as he hit the ground. Separated from his 'stick', he sought cover in some rocks where, hearing a noise to his front, he cocked his Sten and called the challenge 'Red Berets'. The response should have been 'Kill Italians'. Instead, Fryer heard an Irish voice enquire, 'Is that you, Corporal Fryer?' It was Cork-born Major Mervyn Dennison, another Royal Ulster Rifles' veteran.[15] Such were the frictions encountered in FUSTIAN that only twelve officers and 283 other ranks answered the brigade roll call: 1,856 had embarked.[16]

Other Ulster Rifles personnel were among those of 1 Parachute Brigade, including Lieutenant Bryan Woods, whose family came from Malahide (his older brother Desmond had earned the MC in Palestine in 1938 and would earn a Bar at Cassino), Sergeant John Bermingham from Dublin, Privates Cecil Newell, Hugh Adamson, from County Down, and Boyde Alexander Black from County Antrim. From the Royal Irish Fusiliers were Privates David McLoughlin from Belfast, Leslie McNeice from County Antrim and James McFadden from County Tyrone.[17] Their experiences were varied. Wounded in the leg and captured, Boyde Black was later repatriated by the Germans. Cecil Newell recalled being fired at by 'Yanks', British and Italians with the Germans joining in 'for good measure' during the landing. Later, at Catania, he remembered Frank Lyons 'from the south of Ireland' dealing with a German sniper: Lyons

> took the anti-tank rifle and waited. When the German fired, Frank aimed at the flash. That night a patrol was sent out, and they found the sniper. Frank had hit the barrel of the German's rifle and had split the barrel and the German in half.[18]

A survivor of 3rd Parachute Battalion, Private Lawrence Lee from County Mayo fought at Primosole Bridge alongside 1st Battalion men and was among those who returned to Tunisia.[19]

In spite of all that had gone wrong, airborne forces had achieved much in preparation for the seaborne landings.

* * *

Tied in with the airborne operation was a Special Raiding Squadron (SRS) seaborne assault on coast artillery positions at Capo Murro di Porco. Those and similar positions had already been attacked by RAF bombers. USAAF bombers had also struck the Axis headquarters and communications centre. Commanding the SRS was former Irish and Lions' rugby international Major Robert Blair Mayne from Newtownards, County Down who had been appointed DSO for operations with 1st Special Air Service in North Africa; he would receive a Bar for Sicily. His squadron was twenty minutes late in arriving at its beach while No.3 Commando grounded on its beach 'almost on time'.[20]

* * *

British seaborne landings were led by 5th and 51st (Highland) Divisions, the former from Lieutenant General Miles Dempsey's XIII Corps, the latter from Lieutenant General Sir Oliver Leese's XXX Corps. Dempsey had Irish roots although the family had moved to England by the early nineteenth century.[21] XIII Corps was on the right flank in the Gulf of Noto to take Syracuse, Augusta and Catania while XXX Corps was to protect its left flank, contact Seventh Army and, if necessary, assist in taking Catania.[22] Overall, XIII Corps' plan included a landing south of Syracuse, for which the airborne operation was to hold open the route to Syracuse via Ponte Grande bridge; neutralization of coast defence batteries at Capo Murro di Porco and other locations by a commando assault; and a two-divisional advance to secure a beachhead. The second division, 50th (Northumbrian), was to seize Avola, thus securing the plateau overlooking the coast and protecting the beachhead from the west.[23]

Fifth Division, traditionally the Army's reserve division, included a 'Union' brigade: 13 Brigade had a Scottish battalion, 2nd Cameronians (Scottish Rifles); an Irish battalion, 2nd Royal Inniskilling Fusiliers; and an English battalion, 2nd Wiltshire Regiment (Duke of Edinburgh's). Of the other brigades, 15, a Yorkshire formation, included the 1st Battalions of the Green Howards, King's Own Yorkshire Light Infantry (KOYLI) and York and Lancaster Regiment. The Green Howards had a tradition of recruiting in the west of Ireland while in 1st King's Own Yorkshire LI an Irish officer, Major Arthur Francis McCausland Riggs, would assume command in battle. (The regiment's 2nd Battalion had served in the retreat from Burma in 1942, during which the CO, Christopher Keegan, another Irish man, had earned the DSO.) Commanding 2nd Inniskillings in 13 Brigade was Lieutenant Colonel Patrick Joseph O'Brien-Twohig, from Cork.

Although recruited largely in the Scottish Highlands, 51st (Highland) Division included Irish personnel in its Highland infantry battalions and supporting units with one of its artillery regiments commanded by an Irishman,

Lieutenant Colonel William Anthony Sheil DSO, who would earn a Bar to his DSO in Sicily.

The wind also affected the assault, slowing the already slow landing craft and creating 'a short steep sea' that drove them to leeward.[24] Although Montgomery and Cunningham later wrote that the enemy was not expecting an assault due to wind and sea conditions, the Italian commander, General Alfredo Guzzoni, had his garrison stand to in the early evening of the 9th while, ninety minutes before midnight, German Naval Command confirmed that the Allied invasion had begun.[25]

Mention has already been made of the use of DUKWs in HUSKY, their first use in Europe. Developed as a military amphibious vehicle by the US National Defense Research Council, the design had been standardized in October 1942. Based on a standard 2.5-ton six-wheel-drive truck, it used those wheels on land but on water was driven by a propeller and steered through a combination of the front wheels and a rudder. The DUKW required a skilled driver, especially in a difficult sea.[26]

Among Royal Army Service Corps (RASC) drivers on D Day was John Logue, from County Londonderry, a former Inniskilling Fusilier, a member of a specialized beachhead commando. Each DUKW also carried a Pioneer Corps soldier, among whose duties was holding the vehicle steady during loading from a ship. As Driver Logue was taking his DUKW back to sea, his Pioneer colleague informed him that the vehicle was leaking. Logue knew he could cure the problem by adjusting a pump in the bilges, but the other soldier did not know how to steer the DUKW at sea. Logue gave him a hurried familiarization, emphasizing the need for a steady course, before descending to adjust the pump.

> I don't know how long I was there ... but the first thing I knew was the thump as the DUKW hit what I thought ... was a rock but turned out to be a spike on the beach, one of those big anti-invasion spikes.

With the vehicle holed, the duo had no option but to get out and walk. There was no sign of anyone else on the beach.

> Then I heard a strange sound and I knew that he had stepped on a mine. I tried to push him out of the way but it was too late; the mine had popped up and exploded. He was hurt, there was a lot of blood and I started to carry him. After a while I saw an officer, one of the beach organization blokes. He asked us how we got there and I told him the Pioneer Corps lad was pretty badly hurt.

The officer pointed out that Logue had also been injured. Although unaware of it, he had been wounded in the thigh. The pair had walked through a minefield and were fortunate to survive. 'About an hour later, I knew that I had been hurt when my leg started to stiffen up.' Evacuated to North Africa, he returned to his unit in time for the Salerno landings.[27]

* * *

Major General Sidney Kirkman's XIII Corps' included 50th (Northumbrian) Division, composed of 151 and 69 Brigades with 168 Brigade 'on loan' from 56th (London) Division, bringing 1st London Irish Rifles into the picture: the commanding officer, Dubliner Lieutenant Colonel Ian Henry Good, would be appointed DSO as would be his counterpart in 8th Durham Light Infantry, Lieutenant Colonel Robert Peysley Lidwill. In 5th Division, Major Arthur Francis McCausland Riggs would assume command of 1st King's Own Yorkshire LI when the CO was wounded south of Villasmundo while the CO of 2nd Inniskillings, Pat O'Brien-Twohig, would be decorated with the DSO for the action at the Simeto river. There would be a second DSO to the 'Lumps', as 2nd Inniskillings were known, awarded to a young subaltern from Belfast, Lieutenant Harry Christie, also at the Simeto. As the campaign continued, further commanding officers would be appointed DSO while there would be awards of the Military Cross, Military Medal and Mentions in Despatches. The DSOs were not restricted to infantry officers since a Gunner, Lieutenant Colonel Richard Goodbody, from Limerick, commanding 11th (Honourable Artillery Company) Royal Horse Artillery, and a senior medical officer, Lieutenant Colonel Ian Fraser, would also be honoured with the award.

The poor weather also assisted enemy resistance, as did the nature of many beaches. Major General Douglas Wimberley, 51st (Highland) Division, chose not to use the 'seemingly excellent' beach in Portopalo Bay since it was too obvious, instead selecting more difficult beaches where resistance was lighter.[28] His assaulting brigade was soon on its objective. Captain Lord Ashbourne split HMS *Keren*, as well as the HMTs *Strathnaver* and *Otranto*, from the main body of MWF36 to land 231 Brigade's first elements on time and on the intended beach.[29] Gaining almost total surprise, by noon the brigade was on its final objective, the northbound road from Pachino.

Neither division's leading elements had straightforward landings although, by evening, 17 Brigade had secured Syracuse. The Northumbrians' first assaulting units faced a confusing situation with landing craft scattered, landings in wrong locations and 6th Durhams finding a company of 1st King's Own Yorkshire LI joining them as they approached Avola railway station.

Nonetheless, both divisions made progress as the defenders ceded ground. One Durham battalion, 8th, commanded by Robert Lidwill, was in reserve with orders to assist wherever possible. Although 8th should have landed on Jig-Green beach, it found itself on How-Amber, a 5th Division beach. Initial landings were all made in darkness but units found themselves in the wrong places even after the sun had risen. The Northumbrians' historian noted that:

> As it became light, however, two things became apparent: first, ... the transports were very much farther offshore than they should have been. One estimate was that they were twelve miles offshore instead of seven. This to some extent accounted for the lack of news, as many wireless sets would be at the extreme limit of their range. Secondly, there was no enemy coast-defence artillery fire.[30]

For 2nd Royal Inniskilling Fusiliers, the Sicily landings are summed up in the regimental history which notes that 5th Division landed near Syracuse (captured within twenty-seven hours) before the division turned north towards Messina. Initially, only Italian troops who 'were more inclined to surrender than to fight' were encountered.[31]

For any Italian or German observer overlooking Avola, the sea must have appeared crammed with ships of all sizes. Landings continued and Avola soon changed ownership. The observers would also have noticed tanks and artillery disembarking to support the infantry, in small numbers at first. However, the threat was clear and, meanwhile, naval gunfire pummelled targets on land. Among the first guns ashore were the Priests of B Battery, 11 RHA, attached to 23 Armoured Brigade. 'Priest' was the name given to the US M7 howitzer motor carriage by the Royal Artillery which had begun the practice of bestowing ecclesiastical names on self-propelled artillery (the M7 mounted a 105mm howitzer on an M3 tank chassis). B Battery was ashore by 0600, with 50th Royal Tank Regiment's first tanks spearheading 23 Armoured Brigade. By late morning, 11 RHA was complete with Lieutenant Colonel Richard Goodbody, the CO, demonstrating the level of leadership and support for other arms that would earn him the DSO.[32]

* * *

Of course, there had been casualties with sailors, soldiers and airmen killed or wounded. While no field hospitals could be established onshore, a hospital ship, HMHS *Saint David*, lay offshore. Onboard, Lieutenant Colonel Ian Fraser, in charge of the penicillin team (antibiotics were still in their infancy), was charged with treating casualties on the beaches. Soon after the first landings, Fraser volunteered to go ashore at Capo Passero to collect wounded

> in spite of heavy and continuous divebombing and shellfire. He operated … continuously for the next 48 hours, in face of many enemy attacks. Although exhausted he donated a pint of his own blood to one of his patients, thereby saving his life. By his gallant, fearless and devoted action, regardless of personal risk and safety, this officer, a brilliant and experienced surgeon, not only set an inspiring example of coolness under fire but, by employing a new technique for the first time in forward surgery, has established a new and most valuable wound treatment.[33]

Ian Fraser was appointed DSO for his work off Sicily. Subsequent service in Operation AVALANCHE, the main landings in Italy in September, was included in the citation.

As Allied forces increased their beachhead strength, they pushed the enemy back. When battle honours were awarded in the 1950s, the first for Sicily was 'Landing in Sicily', covering from 9 to 12 July. The next, 'Primosole Bridge', marked the initial seizure of the bridge by airborne troops in FUSTIAN, the fighting around it and its recapture by 8th Durhams. Although the small airborne force, no more than two companies, that first captured the bridge had been forced off, they withdrew only a short distance, harassing the Axis troops who had evicted them. It was then the turn of the Durhams under Robert Lidwill to present the Axis defenders with their marching orders. On the night of 15/16 July, Lidwill attacked and captured a bridgehead over the Simeto at the bridge; an earlier attack by 9th Durhams had been repelled.

At 0730 on the 15th an attack was launched, supported by two field artillery regiments. Doughty Fallschirmjäger resistance saw several Durham platoons that had crossed the Simeto forced back. As the battle raged, tanks moved in but were countered by 88mm guns firing over open sights. Several attempts by German engineers to demolish the bridge were stopped by small-arms fire. A renewed assault was planned, supported by four field regiments and a battery of medium guns; it was hoped that two more field regiments could be in action by H Hour. The fresh assault was that involving Lidwill's battalion which

> held the bridgehead during the next day when further troops could be sent over the river Simeto to enlarge the bridgehead – and his complete disregard for his personal safety during the whole of this period was an inspiration to all … . The position held by his battalion was continually under heavy MMG fire and occasional heavy shellfire and in very close

> contact with the enemy, who were eventually only driven out … by our own Sherman tanks. Lt Col Lidwill's conduct … in Sicily up to date has been of the highest order and an example to all.[34]

The Durhams' success in securing the bridgehead assisted in opening the road to Catania and Lidwill was appointed DSO.

The overall plan called for No.3 Commando to re-embark and land north of Augusta, move inland and secure the Ponte dei Malati over the Lentini river, holding it until units of 50th Division arrived. Once again, grit entered the works as, from landing, the commando met opposition but reached the objective which was held until early on the 14th. Although the commandos pulled back, they continued harassing the enemy, ensuring that the bridge was not demolished before 50th Division's leading troops arrived. No.3 Commando suffered no fewer than 153 casualties. One of their dead, a young officer from Lisnaskea, County Fermanagh, Lieutenant Anthony Butler, had served in the North Irish Horse; he died on 14 July.[35]

Ian Good's 1st London Irish Rifles were in 168 Brigade with 50th Division with the battalion in action for the first time on the night of 17/18 July in a 'silent attack' (without artillery support) on the line of the Fosso Bottacetto. Although support from the divisional artillery plus another field regiment, a medium regiment and two regiments of self-propelled artillery (ninety-six field guns, sixteen mediums and forty-eight 105mm howitzers) was planned, thirty minutes before H Hour it was decided to put down fire only if requested.[36]

On the left of the brigade advance, 1st London Irish came under heavy enfilade fire from machine guns, mortars and artillery with the bitter and confused fighting making it difficult to establish the leading companies' true situations.

> With a complete disregard of danger, … Good went forward over very open and bullet-swept ground, discovered the exact situation and reported it.
>
> Later, … when ordered to withdraw his battalion and take up a defensive position some 400 yards in rear, he extricated his companies with great skill, [although] they were disorganized, due to heavy and confused fighting and that there was only a short period of darkness left. Due to Lt Col Good's untiring efforts, the battalion had re-organized, was digging in in the position by daylight and was ready and eager to continue the fight despite its heavy losses.[37]

During that fighting, Lieutenant Michael Power, a Royal Irish Fusilier seconded to the London Irish, was killed leading his platoon. Also killed were Lieutenants Austin Orr and Thomas Coghlin. All three were Irish born: both Power and Coghlin had English wives; Coghlin was an older officer at 36. Another platoon commander, Lieutenant Arthur Crampton, had a bullet pass through the rim of his steel helmet, grazing his scalp. Although dazed, he recovered, carried on and earned the MC.[38]

The struggle for the Fosso Bottacetto was the battalion's first battle, from which lessons were learned at battalion and higher levels. Later, Good issued a special order of the day to his battalion:

> We have taken part in our first battle of this war as a fighting team after a long period of waiting and training. It was a hard battle, entered into after hard marching, and was that hard and most exacting operation of war – a night attack. It was followed by several days in the line under exhausting conditions.
>
> I should like you to know that in my opinion, and that opinion is shared by others, the battalion has proved itself a successful fighting team. In that team I include our affiliated battery of 90th Field Regiment Royal Artillery.[39]

* * *

While 1st London Irish fought at the Fosso Bottacetto, 2nd Inniskillings were in action along the Simeto. After a speedy advance, with Italian posts taken in skirmishes, the battalion reached the high ground above Catania, one machine-gun post being captured by Corporal Stephen Hughes of D Company who turned its gun on the retreating foe; he received the DCM. An Inniskilling patrol under Major R.C. Thompson reached the south bank to find a concrete bridge intact, albeit prepared for demolition. Codenamed 'Lemon', it became the focus of a brigade attack, in which the Inniskillings were to establish a bridgehead. On the afternoon of 18 July, Major Owen Meade led C Company towards 'Lemon' against strong resistance. Meade deployed a platoon across the Simeto, east of the bridge, to attack from the rear while his other two platoons kept the defenders engaged; he also had a platoon of B Company attached. The outflanking manoeuvre succeeded and 'Lemon was our fruit'.[40] However, the customary German counter-attack arrived with customary fury. The Lumps on the north bank were not fooled by a group of Germans calling 'Don't fire, this is the Jocks', the platoon commander, Lieutenant Harry Christie, challenging them. When the correct response was not given, he 'directed fire to the place where the sporrans ought to be'.[41] Fighting continued through the night, Christie playing a major role. Meade 'handled his company with outstanding ability' against determined enemy pressure which caused many casualties and the loss of three Brens. Although wounded by machine-gun fire, Meade refused to leave until Lieutenant Colonel O'Brien-Twohig ordered him to do so, since he was almost unable to stand due to loss of blood. Meade was awarded the MC. Succeeding Meade as C Company commander was Captain Thomas McCabe, who had been commissioned from the Irish Guards, but he was killed.[42]

In a final effort to gain the bridge, the CO ordered B Company to counter-attack across the Simeto. Commanding B Company was Captain Robert 'Bob' Alexander. A Royal Ulster Constabulary policeman and graduate of Queen's University, Belfast, Alexander had represented Ireland at cricket and rugby and had been in the Lions' South Africa squad in 1938. David Cole wrote that Alexander 'led his company over the river and, despite the most heroic onslaught, they were immediately cut down by withering German machine-gun fire. … Bob died amongst his leading platoons.'[43] Alexander's prowess in sport was probably not known to the Inniskillings' historian who failed to note his death in his account of the battle for Lemon bridge.[44]

'Pat' O'Brien-Twohig was decorated with the DSO for his leadership. Although a counter-attack by his battalion, supported by tanks, prompted an enemy withdrawal, that was not immediately obvious and O'Brien-Twohig personally reconnoitred the bridge area. Finding it clear, he ordered his battalion forward to consolidate the position. The citation for his DSO noted that there was no doubt that the success of the operation was 'very largely due to the conduct of Lieutenant Colonel O'Brien-Twohig whose courage, determination and leadership … inspired all who saw him'.[45]

Another DSO appointment to 2nd Inniskillings went to Lieutenant Harry Christie from Belfast. It was quite unusual for an officer below the rank of major to be appointed DSO but Christie, a teacher in civilian life, deserved it. Not only had he countered the German attack mentioned above, but he fought off another seven, four of them very strong, and supported by heavy machine-gun fire. When Germans penetrated Inniskilling positions, he took command of the survivors of another platoon to fight them off. Not only did his soldiers repel further attacks, but they also followed up the retreating Germans with the bayonet. At all times, Christie displayed 'leadership and personal courage of [the] very highest order' and 'continued to direct the defence with great vigour'.[46] Although Cole suggested that Christie had been recommended for the Victoria Cross, this is not borne out by surviving paperwork.[47]

In mainland Italy, General Montgomery visited the battalion and presented the ribbon of the DSO to both the CO and Lieutenant Christie. He also addressed the ranks, 'congratulated us on the speed of our Calabrian advance and gave us a brief account of how his plans were working out'. As Monty prepared to leave, Pat O'Brien-Twohig called for three cheers for the 'General from Donegal' which 'seemed to please Monty'.[48]

The Intelligence Officer, Captain Jim Bradley, earned the MC for maintaining communications between elements of the battalion, especially during the hours of darkness:

> he moved everywhere under heavy fire, sometimes at ranges of 40 yards, without regard to his own safety. On two occasions when part of 14 Platoon was penetrated and gave ground, he personally led them back and counter-attacked with bomb and bayonet, [throwing] the enemy back in hand-to-hand fighting, and re-established them in position.[49]

Bradley had been born into the Inniskillings, his father having served in the regiment and achieved warrant rank.

Fusilier Thomas Moore, one of two brothers, was awarded the Military Medal (MM). The driver of a Bantam car, he was towing a 2-pounder anti-tank gun which he repositioned in darkness under heavy fire. From its new position, the gun could more effectively engage enemy tanks. On the morning of the 20th, in the battle's final phase, he was

> engaged in handling and towing A/Tk guns … and he carried out this work in an exemplary manner in very testing circumstances. When not towing guns he made several successful runs to the RAP with wounded. … [He] personally was responsible for saving at least one gun and his conduct throughout was an inspiration … .[50]

Relieved by the Cameronians, the Lumps rested briefly south of the river as other units expanded the bridgehead they had created. Then came a move to Sferro, some fifteen miles away, and also on the Simeto, where Wimberley's Highlanders had carved out a bridgehead and, unable to expand it, dug in. The battalions of 13 Brigade were to support the Highlanders as they prepared for a fresh assault, the Inniskillings undertaking 'vigorous and useful patrol work'.[51]

Returning to 5th Division, the Inniskillings carried out sweeping-up operations on the slopes of Monte Etna, Mongibello to Sicilians, where the other Moore brother, William, was driving a carrier on protective duty on the Paterno-Belpasso road for an anti-tank gun troop which came under heavy shellfire. An ammunition lorry was hit, causing a major fire and Fusilier Moore realized that a nearby portee (a 6-pounder on a lorry) was in danger of going on fire. He 'unhesitatingly and with complete disregard of the exploding ammunition, drove forward to the portee and towed it to safety. ... [when] the camouflage net in the carrier caught fire and Fus. Moore successfully cut it free.' Three days later, a similar act of bravery occurred during an ambush when the Bren gunner in his carrier dismounted and was wounded. William Moore dashed to his aid, while also covering the carrier commander, and brought the casualty back. Since another two German machine guns had opened fire, the carrier was ordered to withdraw. 'Moore, still firing from the hip, withdrew to the carrier and successfully drove [it] out of action'.[52] That second act of courage took place on the day the Inniskillings took Tremonte, a success that brought congratulations from corps and divisional commanders. Fox commented that 'The entire Allied line from Paterno to the sea could now swing forward'.[53]

The battalion had suffered considerably since landing in Sicily. While some wounded would return after treatment, others would be unfit for further service or be downgraded from infantry duties. The latter category included Fusilier Eamon Simms, a Derry man who had enlisted early in the war. In the Madagascar campaign, he contracted Blackwater Fever, a serious complication of malaria that could be fatal. Fusilier Simms sustained a head wound at Francofonte; a bullet pierced his steel helmet, grazing his skull. He required hospital treatment and, subsequently, was transferred to the RASC as a driver.[54]

Francofonte was also where Lieutenant Colonel William Anthony Sheil DSO, CO of 128th (Highland) Field Regiment, earned a Bar to the DSO he had been awarded at El Alamein. Responsible for organizing artillery support for an attack by 152 (Seaforth and Camerons) Brigade, Sheil had to deal with Fallschirmjäger who 'were offering very stubborn resistance, were sniping very accurately and were attempting to regain the initiative'. Completely oblivious to his own safety, he went forward to reconnoitre the enemy positions, pinpointed exact locations and observed 128th Field Regiment's fire on several strongpoints. When those proved impossible targets for the 25-pounders, Sheil manhandled anti-tank guns, 6-pounders and a 17-pounder, into action and directed their fire, thus overcoming the strongpoints. 'His leadership and inspiring example were a considerable contributing factor to the successful issue of a hard-fought fight.'[55]

* * *

While Lieutenant Colonel Sheil commanded a Scottish field regiment, the first of two Irish artillery regiments was already operational in Sicily: 66th Light Anti-Aircraft (LAA) Regiment was formed in June 1940 in Northern Ireland. Initially, it included 175 and 176 LAA Batteries, formerly of 102nd Heavy AA (HAA) Regiment, the first complete Territorial Army unit raised in Northern Ireland. A third battery, 251, joined in March 1941, only to be replaced by 276 LAA Battery. After service at home, 66th LAA Regiment deployed to Egypt in preparation for HUSKY. Disembarking from the HMT *F10* at Port Tewfik in early May, following the long voyage around Africa, the regiment received twelve Bofors 40mm light AA guns per battery, plus some vehicles. Following training at Agami, near Alexandria, it came under command of 2 AA Brigade, assigned to HUSKY.[56]

In early June, guns and equipment were shipped to the Levant while personnel entrained for Suez. On the 30th, 175 and 176 Batteries embarked on the HMTs *Empire Trooper* and *Duchess of Bedford*. The regiment's other elements, including RHQ and 276 Battery, boarded the HMT *Orbita*. All sailed to Alexandria where the gunners enjoyed four days' leave before joining a convoy for Sicily. Since 66th LAA Regiment was not involved in the first landings, its gunners were spectators at the naval bombardment of Syracuse, home of Archimedes, on D Day. After that city's capture on 11 July, the regimental reconnaissance party landed to establish locations for gunsites. On the 13th, 176 Battery disembarked with twelve guns to defend the port. They were in action that night when enemy aircraft attacked the port and shipping.[57]

After 13 July, 66th LAA Regiment was involved in the AA defence of Syracuse throughout the campaign. Additional guns landed on D plus 4 engaged intruders that night and the following night, firing some 3,000 rounds on each occasion. With the complete regiment ashore, the guns were integrated fully into the defensive barrages planned for Syracuse. On that night 10,000 rounds were loosed off at enemy aircraft, including bombers dropping parachute mines in the harbour.[58]

With Eighth Army advancing northward and liberating Augusta, pressure on the AA defence of Syracuse diminished, although the defenders never relaxed. Nonetheless, 276 Battery deployed a troop to protect HQ Eighth Army. On the night of 24/25 July a ship was set on fire during one attack. Fw.190s later harassed vessels in the harbour in daylight dive-bombing raids. August was spent at Syracuse defending against occasional attacks. The Germans had executed a masterly evacuation from Sicily so that, by the 17th, the ground campaign was over. AA gunners remained on alert since Luftwaffe raids on Sicily, particularly its ports, continued in anticipation of an Allied crossing of the strait of Messina.

The second LAA regiment was a re-roled infantry battalion. Originally 8th Royal Ulster Rifles, 117th (RUR) LAA Regiment came into being on 1 January 1942 when AA units were at a premium.[59] The Rifles retained their distinctions, including their distinctive Harp-and-Crown badge and, by March 1943, the regiment, with 383, 384 and 385 LAA Batteries, was in action in Tunisia. It deployed to Malta before embarking for Sicily on 8 August.

Following miscalculations in loading ships, 117th LAA Regiment was among a number of units without transport in 73 AA Brigade, which had six regiments ashore but sufficient vehicles only for a regiment and a half. Combing out units in rear areas helped Brigade HQ move batteries where they were needed. Sent to defend airfields at Lentini, the Ulster gunners were strafed by Bf.109s en route.[60]

By mid-September, with Sicily in Allied hands and Eighth Army landing in mainland Italy, 117th LAA Regiment deployed under 73 AA Brigade to protect the embarkation port and ferries at Milazzo in northern Sicily.

* * *

As the advance continued, both armies were reinforced by follow-up formations. Eighth Army welcomed 78th Division, known as the Battleaxe Division, although, having been in First Army, the division was unenthused about joining Montgomery's 'lot'. It deployed 11, 36 and 38 (Irish) Brigades As well as 1st Royal Irish Fusiliers, 6th Royal Inniskilling Fusiliers and 2nd London Irish Rifles, the brigade included artillery, engineers, medical and other units in which many Irish served. The affiliated field artillery regiment, 17th Field, later adopted the entirely unofficial, and unapproved, title of 17th Field Regiment Royal Hibernian Artillery. One CO, Rupert Lecky from County Carlow, would defend his regiment's claim to the title.

The Irish Brigade was commanded by Brigadier Nelson Russell DSO MC, a Faugh (pronounced 'Fog'), or Royal Irish Fusilier. A veteran of the First World War who had earned the MC as a young officer, he was the brigade's second commander, having succeeded Brigadier The O'Donovan, another Faugh, when the formation was assigned to what became First Army. Russell knew his brigade and his Irish soldiers well and had been an inspiring leader in Tunisia.[61]

After an uncomfortable voyage, Russell's brigade landed on 25 July before travelling about ninety miles to a concentration area near Syracuse. Shortly after arriving there, Captain Brian Clark, the Faughs' adjutant, noticed 'a most obnoxious smell', caused by a dead mule. That introduction to the heat and smells of Sicily as an operational battlefield was amplified when one Faugh decided to cremate the mule with a homemade incendiary device that, in Clark's words, increased threefold 'the operational radius of the smell'. Veterans would later recall the smell of Etna, the heat, the dust, liquid bully-beef and the prevalence of malaria. The Simeto valley, in particular, was remembered as being mosquito-infested with light aircraft spraying the breeding grounds. Belfast man Bobby Baxter, of 2nd London Irish, remembered Sicily as 'a land of heat and smelly socks'. All of that was before a re-match with the Germans, including Fallschirmjäger whom the Irish Brigade had encountered in Tunisia.[62]

By 28 July, objectives had been set for 78th Division in Operation HARDGATE, the attack on the German Etna Line. While 11 Brigade held positions north of Catenanuova, 36 Brigade would seize Centuripe, atop a hill some 2,000-feet high, plus two hills roughly two miles to the north. The Irish Brigade would pass through, force a crossing of the Salso river and, if the going was good, the Simeto, some few miles beyond. However, there is an old military axiom that no plan survives first contact. This was a classic case of its truth. All seemed to be going well, perhaps too well; 11 Brigade moved so smoothly to a covering position that the divisional commander, Major General Evelegh, decided to bring the main attack forward by a day to disrupt any enemy attempt to reinforce Centuripe.

An unexpected attack by Fallschirmjäger on 36 Brigade upset the plan. By the afternoon of 2 August, the Centuripe attack had been brought to a standstill although 11 and 36 Brigades had gained several locations suitable for an assault by fresh troops. A revised plan for a two-phase silent night attack, with divisional artillery on call, was made. In the first phase, Inniskillings and Faughs reconnoitred in force to place both battalions within striking distance of their objectives. The Inniskillings would seize Point 640 and gain contact with the Germans at Point 704, thus uncovering more of the road to Centuripe. Meanwhile, the Faughs would push forward to between Points 698 and 603 and determine who held Points 611, 703 and 704. Should the going be good, both battalions, appraised of Phase B, would be ready to move on. (The actions were fought over the August Bank Holiday weekend, then at the beginning of the month. It changed to the present arrangement in the late 1960s, except for Scotland.)

Once again, grit was encountered. With C Company in the van, all four Inniskilling rifle companies advanced in single file along mule tracks, three-yard gaps between individuals. Facing a climb of over 2,000 feet during the four-mile march, each man carried only his own equipment. Without mules, heavier equipment, weaponry, food and water were left behind. The war diary notes: 'The Faughs were advancing along the main road on our left.'

By 0845, C Company was on Point 640, under heavy fire, including mortars, from Point 708 and the ridge south-east of Centuripe. With Battalion HQ to C Company's right rear, recce patrols were deployed.[63]

Nelson Russell was familiar with the defenders' laydown: Centuripe and both flanks were firmly in German hands, as were Points 611, 703 and 704. An attack by the westward route was impossible. With the Faughs also held up by machine-gun fire, and the Inniskillings being assailed by the Germans on Point 708, a daylight frontal assault via the final steep slopes would be madness. When an attempt to seize Point 664 failed, Russell decided on two attacks late in the day, allowing some daylight for the inevitable street fighting.

The Rifles would make the first attack on Points 703, 704 and 611 with Inniskillings and Faughs attacking when the Rifles were firm on their objectives. All the divisional artillery, seventy-two 25-pounders, would support the Rifles before switching to the Fusilier battalions. However, the Inniskillings, seemingly unaware of the details, moved forward at 1630. With the soldiers baked in the heat, little water and an apparent lack of orders, an Inniskilling attack was launched. With German fire on C Company having reduced, and the spur to their front apparently deserted, it was decided that Centuripe would be entered 'by the front door'. The Inniskillings' CO, Lieutenant Colonel Neville Grazebrook, was following Admiral Nelson's example. Choosing the cool of the late afternoon, he launched C Company at the front door.[64]

To kick in that door, C Company had to scale a 100-foot-high cliff. They had some artillery support, but A Company, who followed, had none and suffered machine-gun fire from both flanks. Major George 'Hobo' Crocker from Cork, still under enemy fire, re-organized his men to pass through C Company into Centuripe where they met typical German resistance, including a Panzer III. In the subsequent close-quarter fighting with Fallschirmjäger, Crocker was wounded but remained with his soldiers until they were established in the town square. The citation for Crocker's MC noted that he displayed 'conspicuous gallantry and leadership and conducted the battle with the greatest skill'.[65] Lieutenant Samuel Morrow, Éire-born but living in Killyleagh, County Down, was also wounded and subsequently died.

The assault led to several other gallantry decorations for 6th Inniskillings, including a Bar to the MC Lieutenant Johnnie McClinton had earned in Tunisia. Ordered to seize the ridge commanding the eastern flank, McClinton led his platoon's attack on a farmhouse on Point 664, the key to the ridge. In spite of heavy fire, he succeeded, 'undoubtedly due to [his] personal courage and power of leadership'.[66] Another platoon commander, Lieutenant Ernest Hewitt, took command of A Company when the company commander was wounded, organizing the defence of the town square throughout the evening and night and repelling all attacks. Sergeant Robert Phillips of A Company, originally of the Welch Regiment, assumed command of his platoon when the platoon commander was wounded, continued the attack and gained the main square, subsequently repelling a counter-attack that isolated his platoon. He received the MM.[67] Lance Corporal Robert Apling also earned the MM during the attack on the eastern ridge, having led his section against a machine-gun post manned by an enemy platoon and prevailed; he also fought off a counter-attack.[68]

While both 1st Royal Irish Fusiliers and 2nd London Irish fought in the battle, and took their objectives, Russell recorded that 'chief credit was due to The Royal Inniskilling Fusiliers, who bore the brunt of the fighting'.[69] Both Faughs and Rifles fought with determination. Within an hour of crossing their start lines, Points 704 and 611 had been taken by the Rifles' G and F Companies respectively; H Company was held up by machine-gun fire from Point 703 and both flanks. The ground was extremely difficult, as recalled many years later by Bobby Baxter who told the author that the terrain was so bad 'that it was possible to wear out a pair of army boots in one day'.[70] He spoke from personal experience.

Russell then launched the Faughs to avoid having to fight in the dark. Even so, dusk was falling as D Company, under Captain Billy Hanna from Armagh, moved off. In preparation for the attack, a small feature on the battalion front, described in the war diary as a pimple, was doused with mortar fire, and occupied by a platoon to support the advance. However, as D Company passed the 'pimple', machine guns opened fire. Billy Hanna was hit and killed almost immediately and Sergeant Robbie Robinson wounded. When a radio message to Battalion HQ reported that Captain Hanna had been wounded, Captain Brian Clark said, 'No, he's dead.' During the CO's briefing before the attack, Clark had looked across at Billy Hanna and 'saw a man who was going to die; he had death on his face'. Others had also noticed Hanna's face and were not surprised that he had been killed.[71] A further attack, by a fighting patrol of C Company, was ordered and the objective was reached – it was 'a shambles, littered with dead bodies of Boche and the bones of long-deceased Sicilians blown from their [last] resting places' – and found no enemy present. Meanwhile, Major Paddy Proctor, from County Donegal, moved forward with A Company. By 0300 on the 3rd, Proctor's company was on its objective. The Faughs had secured Points 718, 685 and 702 and moved into Centuripe in the morning. Before long, carrier-borne Faugh patrols were probing towards the next objective.[72]

Centuripe would live long in the memories of those present. One observer, a veteran of Tunisia, recalled it as 'the strongest defensive position I have seen'. General Alexander later described the defenders as men who fought with 'fanatical vigour'. They were also fighting to gain time for the German withdrawal into the north-eastern corner of Sicily, from which they would cross to mainland Italy and continue the fight. Even so, Centuripe had fallen earlier than the Germans anticipated. A rapid follow-up was essential to keep them off balance.

In their usual fashion, the Germans strove to delay pursuit by cratering the narrow, twisting road down from Centuripe and bombarding it with mortars and artillery. Equally thoroughly, Royal Engineers toiled twelve hours to restore that road before moving heavy equipment forward to repair a bridge across the Salso. Since the river was all but dry, infantry had no need for the bridge, but it was essential for vehicles. To protect the engineers, infantry crossed to secure the far bank. D Day for the infantry crossing was 4 August, with 1500 as H Hour. The field guns of 78th Division provided support, in concert with those of 51st (Highland) Division, including William Sheil's 128th Field Regiment, plus medium guns from corps.[73]

The Faughs led the way, securing their bridgehead within two hours with relatively light casualties from snipers and machine guns. With the Rifles also across, patrols deployed towards the Simeto while the Inniskillings held the Salso bridgehead. For the Faughs and Rifles, the main task was clearing up any enemy between the Salso and Simeto before, if possible, creating a bridgehead across the Simeto that night. That bridgehead was secured by the Faughs' C and D Companies who led the advance from the Salso. Both had crossed the Simeto, which was flowing fast as it passed through a gorge, and were across by 0500. However, both company commanders had been wounded and two D Company platoons had been forced back to the south bank. While not precarious, the bridgehead was not secure. To the Faughs' left, the Rifles were also on the south bank and the Inniskillings were moving up from the Salso. The Faughs' A Company had also crossed the river to support their comrades.

Although the Simeto's northern bank was honeycombed with caves, of which the Germans made full use, artillery fire was brought down on individual enemy positions as they were identified, compelling their occupants to withdraw. In return, the Germans bombarded the Faughs with shells and mortars. The bombardment was not constant, but one mortar round killed Major Charles O'Farrell, Support Company's commander, a loss Nelson Russell regarded as 'probably the greatest ... incurred by the Faughs since the beginning of the war'. Perhaps O'Farrell's death prompted Russell's order to enlarge the bridgehead with a brigade attack.[74] Both Faughs and Rifles constituted the bulk of the attacking force with an Inniskillings' company attached to the latter; another joined later.

At 1530 the attack began with divisional artillery support and four batteries of medium guns, plus two platoons of 4.2-inch mortars from 1st Kensington Regiment, 78th Division's support battalion. Five objectives were assigned to the Faughs and three to the Rifles; some were stout stone houses which made excellent strongpoints. Fighting was intense with Fallschirmjäger exhibiting their usual dogged determination. The struggle lasted several hours before the Irish Brigade prevailed. The last two strongpoints to fall were the Casino and the Palace, both eventually knocked out by Faugh anti-tank guns and a Rifles' PIAT. During the battle, C Company 6th Inniskillings joined the Faughs, taking the village of Macaioni with several prisoners and earning praise from the Faughs' CO, Lieutenant Colonel Beauchamp Butler, himself an Inniskilling.[75]

During the battle, the officer commanding 11 Platoon of the Rifles was killed as his platoon neared an enemy machine-gun post. Lance Sergeant Hugh Donaghy immediately handed the platoon over to the next senior NCO and stalked the post which he wiped out with grenades. Donaghy then came under fire from another machine gun to his flank which he also attacked and neutralized. Hugh Donaghy was awarded the MM for conduct which 'was an inspiration to his Company and showed a complete disregard for his own safety'.[76]

That night, Inniskillings' stretcher-bearer Lance Corporal Charles Shaw also earned the MM, going forward to collect wounded 'with complete disregard for his own safety in the face of continual sniping'. Shaw established an advance RAP and organized carrier parties across the Simeto. The citation noted that he 'generally displayed a high degree of initiative and devotion to duty and was responsible for saving the lives of many seriously wounded men'.[77]

Lieutenant Colonel Beauchamp Butler joined the ranks of Irish COs appointed DSO. His award, for the Simeto crossing, also referred to the Salso crossing and the Centuripe battle. The citation noted that he

> led his battalion with great gallantry. Throughout a hard day's fighting he was tireless in his efforts to ensure success – personally directing the fire of his anti-tank guns and mortars …; launching attacks and never giving a desperate and determined enemy any loophole.
>
> Colonel Butler was under continuous and accurate short-range MG and rifle fire and mortar fire for many hours, but his complete disregard of danger and his inspiring example to his Battalion inspired the success of the operation.
>
> This officer had also rendered distinguished service in the attack on Centuripe and the crossing of the river Salso.[78]

Beauchamp Henry Butler, a native of Rathvilly, County Carlow, had married a Tyrone woman in Clogher Cathedral before the war.[79] He was not to see his home again, falling at the head of his Faughs in Italy.

During the night of 5/6 August, there was a tragic loss when Major Peter Savage of the Rifles was shot accidentally and died of his injuries. He had been Mentioned in Despatches.[80]

The Irish Brigade was given a brief respite after five days' sustained operations in which its soldiers had advanced twenty-five miles, fighting three battles. Naturally, the infantry had not been alone: Russell was generous in his praise for the gunners who, as ever, gave excellent service and the sappers who had sent out recce parties, bulldozed roads, filled craters and constructed bridges, all under heavy fire. He summed up the sappers' work as 'magnificent'.[81] In the respite thus allowed 38 Brigade, the other brigades of 78th Division took up the running.

* * *

Meanwhile, Richard Goodbody's 11 RHA continued working with 23 Armoured Brigade, whose commander, Brigadier George W. Richards was to become Brigadier Royal Armoured Corps at Eighth Army HQ, handing over to Brigadier Arkwright. Before moving on, Richards recommended that Goodbody be appointed DSO. The citation referred to the Limerick man's skilful command of his regiment since the opening hours of HUSKY.

> During the whole of this period his regiment was constantly in action, often covering a very wide front. Colonel Goodbody never spared himself and was constantly well forward, often under heavy shellfire, selecting new battery areas. His support and advice were a tremendous help to me. Wherever the trouble was Colonel Goodbody would be found reconnoitring for good OPs and ordering FOOs forward to occupy them. ... the brigade was never without artillery support when required.
>
> At Vizzini on the 13th July and again on the river Dittaino on the 19th July Colonel Goodbody showed great gallantry and leadership in reconnoitring suitable gun areas and OPs. ... [82]

Richards had commanded 23 Armoured Brigade since July 1942, his tenure including the final battle of El Alamein. With lengthy experience in the North African campaign, he was clearly showing his appreciation for outstanding support from Goodbody's regiment.

* * *

The Irish Brigade returned to the fray on 11 August as the campaign was winding down. That, however, did not mean the Germans were any less determined. All three battalions met tough resistance. With 36 Brigade taking Maccarone to cover the Irish battalions' forward assembly areas, the Faughs set out for Capella and Monte Maletto before liberating Maletto while the Rifles made for Sperina with the Inniskillings in reserve. Capella and Monte Maletto were soon in Faugh hands, C Company under Lieutenant Paul Hamilton and A Company under Major Paddy Proctor leading the advance. Counter-attacks were beaten off next day, aided by 3-inch mortars and medium machine guns brought forward on mules. D Company also had a tight fight in Maletto on the 12th: Second Lieutenant Fielding not only evicted the defenders but, with six Faughs, pursued and captured several fleeing Germans in spite of enemy rifle and machine-gun fire.[83]

The Rifles were unable to take their objective in darkness, only a company and a half making a lodgement on Monte Sperina. A battalion attack, supported by the Inniskillings attacking Monte La Nave and an 'Uncle' target by the divisional artillery, left the feature in Rifles' hands by 1700. The cost was several losses, including 39-year-old Major Peter Fitzgerald MC, a solicitor from Brackenstown, County Dublin, F Company's commander, and Sergeant Leo McCrory, 'a first-class man and a very good platoon commander'.[84] Lieutenants John White and Henry Seymour showed 'dash and courage' in leading their platoons, Seymour receiving the MC; White would earn one at Termoli in October.[85]

With the Germans abandoning their positions, the Irish Brigade pursued them in the darkness over almost six miles, diverting somewhat to avoid American artillery. The campaign was all but over for the Brigade. It was also over for 2nd Inniskillings, the regimental history noting that 'On 11 August these Inniskillings rested awhile'. Of their thirty-two days in Sicily, all but four had been in close contact with the enemy.[86]

* * *

Ian Good's 1st London Irish had advanced with 168 Brigade from Catania through difficult country where stone-wall-flanked narrow roads protected rearguards, and occasional snipers. Near San Giovanni di Galermo, mortar bombs assailed the Rifles. D Company, attempting a flanking move, encountered 'heavy trouble', A and C Companies were held up, but B made some progress. Several casualties were sustained but a plan was made to seize the next village which the Germans were defending. An artillery bombardment smote the Germans but when Rifles' patrols probed forward they hit thin air: the enemy had gone.

Near Gravina a D Company patrol was ambushed with three killed and several wounded. With one of the wounded in serious condition, Corporal James Byrne got him to a comfortable and safe location before returning to company HQ, bringing back two stretcher-bearers to take him to safety. The trio were also ambushed with one stretcher-bearer, Rifleman Staines, wounded in the arm. However, they reached the casualty but, to avoid enemy fire, had to remain in cover for thirty minutes. After breaking through a wall and crawling with the stretcher, they reached their own lines. Corporal Byrne was awarded the MM.[87]

Marching in the heat of the day and resting each night, the battalion followed the retreating Germans northward. 'Some enemy fire was encountered, but it dwindled in power. The weather continued very hot and fatigue began to show itself.' With the absence of roads causing 168 Brigade to be 'squeezed out', 69 Brigade took over the pursuit and 1st London Irish rested at Giarre, some twenty miles north of Catania. For the first time in three weeks, the riflemen enjoyed a good night's rest. Not long after reaching Giarre, they heard that the Americans were in Messina. The campaign on the island of 'heat and smelly socks' was over. But Italy lay ahead. German resistance in Sicily was a foretaste of what would happen in Italy, a country that was a defender's dream and an attacker's nightmare.[88]

Chapter 2

Italy: Tough Old Gut

Eighth Army's landing in Italy, Operation BAYTOWN, was executed by Dempsey's XIII Corps deploying 5th Division, under Major General Gerard Bucknall, and Major General Guy Simonds' 1st Canadian Division, both battle-hardened formations. Although Montgomery had earlier objected to BAYTOWN, opining that AVALANCHE, at Salerno six days later, should be the main effort, he acquiesced but, when landing craft and naval support were switched to AVALANCHE, renewed his objections. Nonetheless, BAYTOWN went ahead with D Day on 3 September, the fourth anniversary of the UK's declaration of war on Germany.

Dempsey's force crossed to Reggio di Calabria under a heavy artillery bombardment from Sicily while aircraft from the Desert Air Force (a title retained until the end of the war although it had officially become First Tactical Air Force) provided air cover from Sicily. Eighth Army was to tie down enemy forces in Calabria, creating a lodgement in Italy's 'toe'. That assumed that enemy forces were willing to be tied down there. Field Marshal Kesselring thought differently.

Kesselring had won the argument over German defences in Italy, triumphing over Rommel who preferred a line north of Rome. Kesselring proposed a belt of lines across Italy between Naples and Rome which Hitler preferred.[1] Accepting that the Allies would land in Italy, Kesselring ordered LXXVI Panzerkorps, part of General Heinrich von Vietinghoff's Tenth Army, to pull back from the forces landing in Calabria, which he did not consider the main Allied landing. He identified Salerno, an area north of Naples, or even somewhere closer to Rome as locations for the principal Allied effort.[2] All that remained in Calabria of German forces was a regiment deployed to support the Italian 211th Coastal Division. However, following the announcement of the armistice of Cassibile, that division surrendered to XIII Corps, leaving only 185th Nembo Parachute Regiment to resist. Resistance ended on the Aspromonte massif five days after the landings.

The Calabrian terrain and demolitions of bridges, cratering or blocking of roads impeded Eighth Army's progress. Italy's most heavily wooded region was ideally suited to such blocking tactics.

In addition to BAYTOWN, Eighth Army's V Corps landed at Taranto in Operation SLAPSTICK. It included 1st Airborne Division, whose commander, Major General George Hopkinson, accepted the garrison's surrender before advancing northward. Elements of 1st Fallschirmjäger Division were positioned to ambush their British counterparts. On 9 September, at Castellaneta, a Fallschirmjäger block was attacked by 10th Parachute Battalion. In the ensuing engagement, Hopkinson was killed.

Events in Calabria showed that Montgomery had been correct: Eighth Army had not tied down any enemy forces but had been slowed by nature with more than a little help from German engineers. On the day Hopkinson died at Castellaneta, Fifth Army under General Mark W. Clark began landing at Salerno in Operation AVALANCHE.

* * *

Operation AVALANCHE, the Allied landings in the Gulf of Salerno, began on 9 September. Since Eisenhower had announced Italy's armistice with the Allies, there was uncertainty about what lay ahead. However, the Germans had earlier occupied Italy rapidly and ruthlessly and neutralized the *Regia Escercito*, Italy's Royal Army. Hoping to achieve tactical surprise, Clark and his planning team chose not to have a major naval gunfire bombardment at Salerno. It was a false hope. Kesselring had realized the area was a likely site for an Allied landing and Cunningham's team had advocated a heavy naval bombardment.

Three divisions, two from Richard McCreery's X Corps, and one American from Ernest Dawley's VI Corps, provided the main landing force. A group of British commandos and US rangers under Orlando Darby landed on the bay's northern coast to secure northward passes in the Amalfi and Chietri areas. US 82nd Airborne Division was held in reserve for the operation.

The 'Black Cats' of 56th (London) Division (the divisional symbol, Dick Whittington's black cat, was the origin of the nickname) were in the assault waves for AVALANCHE with 169 (Queen's) Brigade to the fore. (The brigade included 2/5th, 2/6th and 2/7th Battalions Queen's Royal Regiment.) At about 1430 hours on D Day, a company of 2/6th Queen's came under heavy machine-gun fire with several men wounded badly. Stretcher-bearer Private Patrick McCormack, from Cork, reacted promptly:

> Quite regardless of heavy machine-gun fire, … he immediately moved forward, dressed their wounds, collected them and stayed with them all through the night, and brought them in [next morning]. The casualties

> subsequently survived, ... entirely due to Private McCormack's action. This had a very great moral effect on ... the company in view of the difficulty of evacuating casualties during this operation.[3]

Patrick McCormack received an immediate award of the MM, one of the first Irishmen decorated for gallantry in mainland Italy. Five months later, McCormack, then a corporal, earned a Bar to the MM in similar circumstances.[4]

Private Christopher Joyce, 79 Company, Pioneer Corps, earned the DCM on D Day. In 21 Beach Group, Joyce, nicknamed 'Jackdaw', from Athlone, County Westmeath, was a member of the Irish Travelling community. He was probably the first Irish recipient of a gallantry award in mainland Italy since his citation begins with him, on his own initiative, attacking a German machine-gun post at 0500 on D Day. Bayonet fixed, he charged the post, capturing the gun and its four-man detachment at bayonet point. Joyce had been first to spot the post.

> Throughout the rest of the day [Private Joyce] engaged on the extremely important task of laying Sommerfeld track* on Amber Beach under continuous mortar fire. This soldier continuously set a fine example of energy and courage which was of immense value.[5]

Joyce's award began as a recommendation for a periodic MM before being upgraded. It was also unusual in being one of only four DCM awards to Pioneer Corps personnel.** (The only George Cross awarded to the Pioneer Corps went to Irishman George Scully.)

Another early Irish recipient of a gallantry award in Italy, Sergeant Richard O'Brien, from Newcastle West, County Limerick held the DCM for his actions during Operation MUSKETOON, a commando raid in Norway in October 1942. Originally in the Royal Berkshire Regiment, O'Brien was with No.2 Commando, part of the force landed along the northern shoreline of the gulf of Salerno. His citation, written by Captain the Duke of Wellington, refers to the 'Gulf of Salerno, 9–19 Sep 43' before noting that:

---

* Sommerfeld track was light wire netting reinforced by metal rods used to create temporary airstrips. Ironically, it was the work of a German engineer domiciled in the UK. It was supplied to the US forces on reverse Lend-Lease.

** The Pioneer Corps began life as the Auxiliary Military Pioneer Corps in October 1939, becoming the Pioneer Corps the following year, although it remained an auxiliary organization until 1950 when it became part of the Regular Army.

> At the Battle of Salerno 10–11th Sep 43 and Dragone Hill, 13 Sep and [Piegolelle], 15–18 Sep, this NCO showed complete disregard for personal safety.
>
> On the morning of 10 Sep 43 he went forward to contact a missing section under heavy fire and lead them to safety. Later, in the battle of [Piegolelle] after his Troop leader had been killed, he led a patrol in daylight through enemy lines and brought back valuable information and a prisoner. He then took charge of the Troop after all four of his officers had become casualties.[6]

He received the MM.

(Piegolelle is misspelt 'Piegolette' in the original citation.)

* * *

In Libya the gunners of 9th (Londonderry) Heavy AA Regiment, the 'Derry Boys', had trained intensively in loading, embarking and disembarking from LSTs (landing ships, tank) although initial sessions had involved nothing more than manoeuvring gun tractors, guns and equipment over areas of ground marked out to represent ships. Training included both 'dry-shod' and 'wet-shod' disembarkation. Although they had prepared for any eventuality in terms of getting weapons and equipment to Italy, elsewhere, a serious error occurred. Those arranging passage of 131 (Queen's) Brigade, 7th Armoured Division's infantry brigade, had blundered. The 'Desert Rats' landed only with their armoured brigade. In the prevailing situation, infantry units were critical.

With three LSTs arriving to unload a heavy AA regiment, the expedient of converting gunners to infantry was adopted. It was a shock to men who had expected to be recce'ing, and establishing, gun positions. Bombardier Robert Hamilton, 24 HAA Battery, summed it up when he described being converted to infantry 'at the stroke of a pen'.[7] In darkness, the gunners paraded to be told that they had become infantry. German pressure on the beachhead was intense with Kesselring determined to push Fifth Army into the sea. Mark Clark proposed evacuating his command. That was vetoed by Cunningham. Clark's superior, General Sir Harold Alexander, also held fast against the proposal, but informed Clark that he would assign elements of 82nd Airborne Division to support Fifth Army. In the meantime, gunners became infantrymen.

With Queen's Royal Regiment officers assigned as 'infantry advisers', 24, 25 and 26 Batteries became A, C and D Companies 1/6th Queen's and were 'lorried' to the Incarto area. Deployed in darkness to locations near the front, most had no idea what to expect.[8] Robert Hamilton recalled that 'there [were] some old regular soldiers there ... but we weren't right for fighting the Germans at that time as infantry'.[9] Sergeant John Taylor, also 24 Battery, commented that 'A lot of the boys hadn't a clue what was happening. We were just handed a rifle and so many rounds of ammunition.' Taylor was later sent out with a patrol which advanced under cover of an embankment. 'We went down along that, and the first thing I heard was the rattle of a machine gun. Everybody dived, and I'm sure my impression is still on that bank after all these years.'[10] Some had a more relaxed attitude. Sergeant Jim Canning, 25 Battery, recalled that some gunners began a kickabout with a football not far from the German positions. An RA officer arrived and admonished the footballers, only to be assured by 'Pop' Lapsley, 'don't worry sir, we'll not touch them.' When Canning's men were told to hold a crossroads, there was some concern. 'I had a Tommy gun and the rest had rifles, three-o-threes. What good's that, Lee-Enfields against tanks?' However, he was assured by the presence nearby of a battery of 25-pounders and approached the battery commander who was confident that he would stop any tanks.

> just at dawn, two tanks broke through and came down and, do you know?, I thought that was a brave man. He waited until they were about a hundred yards away before he opened fire and he just stopped them in their tracks. There was no more breakthrough that morning at all. That finished it.[11]

Although the personnel of 1/6th Queen's arrived on the 17th, 9th (Londonderry) wasn't relieved of its infantry role but was re-assigned to 5th Royal Tank Regiment, remaining under overall command of 7th Armoured Division. However, for 25 Battery, the infantry interlude ended that afternoon when the battery was ordered to deploy with its 3.7s for the AA defence of the beaches under command of 100th HAA Regiment. Both 24 and 26 Batteries stayed with 5 RTR until early on the 18th when they came under command of the Royal Scots Greys. Next morning, at 0830, the ad hoc rifle companies were disbanded and the gunners returned to their own role.[12]

The gunsites on the beaches had been selected by Lieutenant Colonel 'Bob' Aitken, the Derry Boys' CO, who was also AA Defence Commander (AADC), Salerno. Already 25 Battery had engaged hostile aircraft as the Luftwaffe harassed the beaches. Messerschmitt Bf.109s made strafing attacks on the 20th, 21st and 22nd, although enemy air activity was not as intense as expected. Meanwhile, 26 HAA Battery, defending an RAF landing-strip in the beachhead, engaged Focke Wulf 190s which strafed and bombed the landing-strip, several bombs landing close to the guns. On the 21st, a 190 that had been fired at by AA guns and Bren LMGs crashed into the hills around the bay and exploded. Early next morning, 190s made a low-level 'tip-and-run' raid on Montecorvino airfield before departing at high speed.[13]

While 26 Battery remained in the AA role, both 24 and 25 Batteries re-deployed to fire in a counter-battery role against German artillery. When he had taken command of the regiment, Aitken, himself a field gunner, had trained his batteries in field gunnery, ensuring their proficiency in the role. The first rounds in the counter-battery programme were fired in the early hours of 23 September as part of X Corps' 'neutralization programme' to silence German artillery. For its part, 24 Battery was firing seven rounds per gun per minute, discharging 566 rounds altogether, 398 of them from B Troop's guns. There was retaliation in which some men were injured and a gun limber and Bantam car damaged. Meanwhile, 25 Battery put down harassing fire on six specific targets, including artillery and armoured vehicles, at ranges between 11,300 and 14,400 yards.[14] The fire proved effective.

Having moved to a new position on the 25th, heavy fire caused A Troop 25 Battery to abandon the site and return to its previous position; there were no casualties. B Troop moved without interference while 24 Battery came under fire with heavy rounds falling across B Troop's positions. The rounds were from 170mm guns, a German counter-battery weapon. Tommy McCready of 24 recalled that they had little effect.[15]

There were instances of high humour even as shells fell around them. German guns were firing airburst rounds which exploded above the target, showering it with a rain of bullets. Slit trenches had been dug for shelter in such cases, but one gunner refused to dive into a trench, explaining, loudly, that it was pointless since 'they follow you in'. Another gunner who dived into a slit trench chose the wrong one. Emerging from a latrine trench which had not been filled in, he commented 'Any port in a storm' but found others avoiding his presence.[16]

During the night of 26/27 September both batteries were in action, laying down counter-battery fire; 24 Battery fired almost 500 rounds while 25 Battery unleashed 238 rounds at six specific targets. Before dawn the guns ceased firing. The Germans were withdrawing. The battle of Salerno was over. In a special order of the day, X Corps' commander, Major General Richard McCreery, wrote that, after ten days of heavy fighting the corps had:

> forced the enemy on to the defensive and on our right he is carrying out a big withdrawal. His object was to drive us back on to our beaches ... He has failed – thanks to the courage, endurance and splendid fighting spirit

> of you all. You have inflicted very heavy losses on the enemy and he has lost much equipment.[17]

On the 26th the battery commanders (BCs) learned that their next task was the AA defence of Naples, designated Fifth Army's main re-supply port. When battery sites were allocated from a map, Jack McVeigh, BC 26 Battery commented that any recce of the sites would 'be a bit difficult': the Germans were still in Naples. In the meantime, the regiment was ordered to the little harbour of Torre Annunziata, spending only hours there before being sent into Naples. By noon on 1 October that move was complete: 9th Regiment occupied six four-gun sites with RHQ in the Observatory and Bob Aitken again in the role of AADC. Snipers remained active in the city as the Derry Boys moved guns and instruments into position. Booby traps had also been left across the city, one exploding in the main post office on 7 October with much loss of life. In the early days, 215 HAA and 195 LAA Batteries were added to the defences, plus a US Army smoke company.[18]

The many casualties at Salerno included Irishmen, one of whom was a chaplain, the Reverend Gough Quinn MC. Padre to 3rd Coldstream Guards, Quinn was killed by a mortar round on 23 September. He had earned his MC with 5th Hampshires in France in 1940. An academically distinguished Belfastman, he was the son of a clergyman and one of three Irish chaplains to die in Italy. The others were George Levis, from Dun Laoghaire, County Dublin and Cecil Bingham, from Newry, County Down. The Reverend Levis, who succeeded Quinn as padre of 3rd Coldstream, died on 4 December 1943 while the Reverend Bingham died on 31 August 1944.[19]

* * *

With Eighth Army established on the 'toe' of Italy, both 66th and 117th LAA Regiments remained on Sicily. On 17 September, 276 Battery of 66th moved to defend Messina but was later sent back to Augusta. The war having moved on, the regiment turned its attention to training, including anti-tank practice, a role to which the Bofors gun was suited, while rear parties and transport finally arrived from Egypt. Mobile training was carried out in November, by which time the regiment was under command of the Royal Marines' Mobile Naval Base Defence Organization (MNBDO). When the MNBDO closed down at the end of the year 66th LAA Regiment passed to 73 AA Brigade and was re-deployed, with 175 LAA Battery covering Gerbini airfield, 176 in Syracuse and 276 at Catania airfield: RHQ and the REME workshop moved from Syracuse to Catania.[20]

On moving to Italy, 66th LAA Regiment was to join the defence of Naples but, instead, was sent to the airfield complex at Foggia. The need for AA defences diminishing in Italy, the regiment re-roled as a transport unit in September 1944 and deployed to Greece.[21]

* * *

As 9th Regiment drove into Naples, 38 (Irish) Brigade was preparing for its first action on mainland Italy. Their parent division, 78th, as part of XIII Corps, was assigned to Eighth Army's right sector. A light mobile force had been formed under Major Marcus Hartland-Mahon, Kendal Chavasse's second-in-command and another Irishman, to advance quickly while the main force stayed near Bari. Hartland-Mahon's grouping was absorbed into A Force, under Brigadier John Currie's 4 Armoured Brigade, which secured the Foggia plain airfields. Termoli on the east coast, with its small harbour, was the next objective.

Lest Termoli become the eastern anchor for a German defensive line, it was intended to seize the port quickly, a task given to 78th Division which also had the support of 4 Armoured Brigade and a Commando brigade (1 Special Service Brigade of 3 Army Commando, 40 Royal Marine Commando and Mayne's Special Raiding Squadron). Montgomery allocated the landing craft still at his disposal to support the operation. In Operation DEVON, the Commando brigade would land from the sea, oust the garrison and hold Termoli until 78th Division's main body arrived, some overland, the remainder also from the sea; the 'remainder' were 36 Brigade and 38 (Irish) Brigade.[22]

Air support to disrupt Luftwaffe operations and assist ground troops was also planned. However, Clausewitz's frictions appeared again as the early onset of autumn rains caused rivers to flood, inundating roads. Most aircraft were grounded temporarily, many bridges had been demolished by the Germans and the ground was sodden. But the plan went ahead: 1 Special Service Brigade landed and overwhelmed the garrison. German reports considered that Termoli harbour and town had fallen with hardly a shot fired by *Kampfgruppe* Rau, a motley of administrative personnel under Major Rau who, unusually among German field officers, lacked the ability to create a fighting force from such material. The few Fallschirmjäger present were insufficient to make a difference.[23]

Although 36 Brigade was to dock before long, the road-bound elements of 78th Division encountered many difficulties: from Germans, waterlogged terrain, overflowing watercourses and lack of bridges. Nonetheless, RHQ and B Squadron 56 Recce reached the Biferno river, the last major obstacle before

Termoli, 'by many and devious detours' by the 3rd. But, until sappers could build a pontoon bridge, the river was impassable. In spite of those conditions, and Luftwaffe intervention, RHQ and B Squadron crossed shortly before midnight to harbour about two miles south of Termoli. Next morning they drove through Termoli and recce'ed along the main road to Vasto. Some three miles from Petacciato, they withdrew to Termoli which they had passed through *before* the commandos landed, returning shortly after their arrival. A patrol had captured a German motorcyclist near Petacciato who informed his captors that he was from 16th Panzer Division, then on the move to Termoli.[24]

Kesselring had 'happened to be at Tenth Army headquarters when the reports [of the landings] came in, and immediately ordered the 16th Panzers to be rushed there with the mission of throwing the invaders back into the sea.' His sense of urgency was not shared by either the army or 16th Panzer's commanders. The formation deployed in penny packets, reducing its operational effectiveness. Allied air attacks at Isernia also slowed movement. In his *Memoirs*, Kesselring was scathing about Tenth Army's commander 'shilly-shallying while I was under the illusion that [16th Panzer] was racing to Termoli'. Noting that 'Tenth Army headquarters bungled the whole thing and lost the chance of an assured success', he added that the 'incident was a lesson' that was 'taken to heart at the time of the Anzio landings'.[25]

Elements of 36 Brigade were already ashore with 8th Argylls advancing towards San Giacomo, about five miles from Termoli, until the battalion ran up against the Germans, suffering considerable losses in spite of a screen of anti-tank guns. Other battalions also encountered 'the furious firepower' of 16th Panzer.[26] Meanwhile, 38 (Irish) Brigade was sailing towards Termoli on what Nelson Russell had anticipated might be 'a pleasant peacetime cruise' but which 'did not go according to plan'.[27] That was an understatement.

Termoli had strategic value for the Germans since Kesselring's forces were holding the Viktor Line, along the Volturno, against Fifth Army across the Apennines. With their lateral supply route running from Capua, also west of the mountains, via Campobasso to Termoli, losing the port would mean withdrawal to a new line. Hence the fury in which the Irish Brigade would be immersed.

The German assault broke the line held by 6th Royal West Kents of 36 Brigade, reducing the battalion to about eighty men, before turning on 5th Buffs, although Brigadier Howlett steadied them and their line held.[28] Also under severe pressure was the line held by a force under Kendal Chavasse DSO. Chavasseforce, which covered a significant part of the perimeter on the Argylls' flank, included RHQ and B Squadron 56 Recce, No.3 Commando, an SRS troop and a battery of anti-tank guns. With tanks attacking the Commando and SRS positions, B Squadron under heavy shellfire and out of contact with RHQ (its wireless vehicle had been destroyed) and a farm to the left occupied by Germans, the situation looked dire.[29] It seemed that the SRS had been overrun. They had actually abandoned their positions without permission. Chavasse ordered evacuation of all vehicles except the wireless recce cars. B Squadron was ordered to withdraw by the Argylls' CO, leaving only Chavasse's RHQ and 3 Commando. At that point 56 Recce's CO informed his men that they 'had an all-round shoot'. It was getting dark

> and we could hear the voices of enemy infantry, through the shelling. The order to withdraw came to me from Divisional HQ. I remember walking through the olive grove, with bullets whistling, to contact the CO of the Commando to tell him to withdraw. Then came the problem of getting our vehicles out. I got on to Division ... and asked for as much *noise* as possible so that the enemy would not hear the engines starting up. I remember having to talk in a soft tone, as if I could hear their voices in the dark they could hear mine! I also remember the gunner saying to me that he had never been asked for 'noise' before. Anyway, they gave it, and plenty of it too, and we slipped away unnoticed to behind the firmer line ... established behind us.[30]

That firmer line was held by 2nd Lancashire Fusiliers, through whom Chavasse's men withdrew by 0245 on 6 October as the Irish Brigade was disembarking at Termoli. Brigadier Russell was taken to meet Durnford Slater, his commando counterpart, and learned the tactical situation: the Germans were on the edge of Termoli while 'all that was between him and the sea were some very depleted Commandos, the Lancashire Fusiliers and perhaps – if still in existence – some of the Recce'. However, some good news was available: nine tanks had crossed the Biferno although four had later been disabled.[31]

The Irish Brigade was arriving in the front line, 300 men at a time, due to the small jetty. However, Russell's battle-hardened battalions had street-fighting experience from Sicily. He felt that, since the Germans did not usually attack at night, an immediate assault was unlikely.[32] As for his soldiers, the Great War veteran and military historian Eric Linklater wrote:

> The Irish had already shown a very soldierly competence in rapidly disembarking under heavy fire, and in darkness and an unknown town, taking position on its perimeter; when it came to fighting they were brilliantly successful.[33]

Nelson Russell then attended an O Group held by 78th Division's commander. He learned that tanks were expected to cross the Biferno in strength by early morning, that a Bailey bridge had been built across the river and air support had become available with US tactical aircraft supporting the Desert Air Force in harassing 16th Panzer Division. A battle plan was laid, in readiness for which all three battalions deployed in the Termoli perimeter for the planned attack. H Hour was 1100.[34]

But the tanks were delayed and Evelegh asked if the Irish Brigade could undertake their operation supported by a single squadron. The answer was positive. At 1130, both Fusilier battalions advanced with Three Rivers Regiment tanks, while the Rifles held a firm base. The operation was 'brilliantly successful', as Linklater described it, Canadian tankmen and Irish infantry co-operating as if they had worked together for months.[35]

Although, initially, the Faughs' A Company did not have a leading role, the flow of battle changed circumstances as the forward companies were held up. Major Paddy Proctor seized the initiative and A Company, with Canadian tanks, pressed forward on the right against strong opposition from infantry and tanks to seize their objective, the brickworks. Following a brief re-organization, he led A Company forward again at the head of the advance, overcame resistance from tanks and machine guns and reached Point 161, the final objective. Proctor was awarded the MC for his inspiring leadership and courage.[36]

Termoli has come to be regarded as a commando operation with writers on special forces attributing its success to 1 SS Brigade. Some even claim that 56 Recce's personnel were 'green' and abandoned their anti-tank guns.[37] Such comments indicate poor research: 56 Recce was the most experienced Reconnaissance Corps regiment with considerable experience in Tunisia and Sicily.[38] Since none of 56 Recce's anti-tank guns were with RHQ and B Squadron at Termoli, it is difficult to see how the regiment could have abandoned them. It is worth pointing out that Recce troopers assisted others, including the Argylls' CO, in manning the Argylls' weapons. It was probably an Argylls' gun that Trooper Albert Ives of 56 Recce was manning when he was killed by a round from a German tank. Trooper Ives, from Armagh City, was a 36-year-old former Royal Ulster Rifleman who had been butler to the Knight of Glynn and a footman to Lord Dunleath.[39]

* * *

For the next two weeks the Irish Brigade remained astride the coast road outside Termoli in contact with the Germans while 36 Brigade seized

Guglionesi and 11 Brigade rested. For Russell's men, the next objective would be Petacciato, to where the Germans were withdrawing. Meanwhile, 2nd Inniskillings and 1st Irish Rifles were also on mainland Italy, the Rifles' 168 Brigade having returned from 50th Division. The battalions were in different corps and armies, 5th Division in Dempsey's XIII Corps of Eighth Army and 56th in McCreery's X Corps of Fifth US Army.

The Lumps landed close to Reggio in Calabria where, to their surprise, they found themselves hailed as liberators. They were not sure about being addressed as 'Inglesi' but accepted it in good humour. Three days later, on 6 September, they were at sea in landing craft, 'jumping' forward to locate the enemy. However, sea conditions caused problems when the landing craft tried to run ashore. It was decided to disembark using lifelines but some men were swept from the lines. Lieutenant Norman 'Jock' Crawford, a champion swimmer, rescued four men, including one in danger of having his head smashed against the rudder. The padre, Father Power, also played a part in the rescues. For his endeavours, Crawford was awarded the George Medal. He was a son of the regiment: both his father and grandfather had commanded Inniskilling battalions.[40]

Not until late-October did 2nd Inniskillings meet the enemy in any significant strength. By that time 5th Division was in V Corps in the central Apennines nearing the city of Isernia, the approach to which was held in strength by units of 26th Panzer Division. For their part, the Inniskillings used battle patrols to assess enemy locations and strengths. Pat O'Brien-Twohig deployed small patrols led by Captains Duane, Christie DSO, Hingston and Crawford GM.[41] As a result of his endeavours, Crawford would earn the MC, but all four brought back useful information, prompting higher command to commend the Inniskillings' 'bold and skilful patrolling'. Crawford's patrol had identified enemy OPs and engaged the enemy, putting two patrols to flight, returning with valuable information. It was due to Crawford's 'leadership, personal courage and in particular his determination to carry out his task in spite of enemy opposition that the patrol was notably successful'.[42]

D Day for the subsequent operation was 4 November. The CO added another element, sending Lieutenant Lang with a D Company patrol over the hills. Included in Lang's patrol was a pioneer, armed with paint and a brush. The patrol reached Isernia at 0400. Four hours later, a 2nd Wiltshire patrol and a US patrol reached the town to find Isernia marked liberally with the Castle of Inniskilling. Lang returned with three British soldiers who had escaped enemy custody.[43]

Meanwhile, 1st Rifles, temporarily commanded by Major Monty Stopford, had crossed from Sicily, encamped at Salerno and moved to Caserta where 168

Brigade HQ and 10th Royal Berkshires were ensconced in the royal palace. Finally, came a move to rejoin the main body of 56th Division across the Volturno. The division included 201 Guards Brigade as well as 167, 168 and 169 Brigades and had a new GOC in Major General Gerald Templer, a Royal Irish Fusilier, an Irishman and an outstanding soldier. Taking over a forward position near Calvi Vecchia, the plan was for 1st Rifles to move into a gully under cover of darkness before attacking next morning through 201 Brigade's Scots Guards. The attack hit thin air. Following a heavy artillery bombardment, the Germans had withdrawn. The battalion moved into reserve.[44]

The next task was to capture high ground overlooking Teano, through which another battalion would advance towards Roccamonfina. While reconnoitring a road fork on Highway 6, a patrol was bombed by USAAF dive-bombers who had, apparently, mistaken the feature for another thirteen miles away. (The Lumps had also received unwanted attention from American airmen, prompting a German PoW to comment that 'When British bombers fly over, we duck, when German bombers fly over, you duck, when American bombers fly over we both duck'.)[45] Eventually, the Rifles reached the high ground overlooking Teano from east and north, capturing some of the German rearguard en route. The London Scottish found Teano abandoned and the Wiltshires liberated Roccamonfina. However, Rifles Tactical HQ had been bombarded by mortars, a 37mm *Vierzwilling* anti-aircraft gun and machine guns but carried on regardless. An OP supporting the battalion was also shelled, with the 37mm AA gun among the assailants. Captain Leslie Crocker of 408 Battery directed fire on the enemy, silencing the AA gun and mortars. Recommended for an immediate DSO, Crocker received the MC.[46]

Progress was slow, the terrain assisting the enemy who used valleys, hills and rivers to advantage. Against a determined foe and ground made for defence, not only was progress slow, but it cost many casualties. Such was the experience of 1st London Irish as the battalion left Roccamonfina to take Sipicciano on Monte San Croce's northern slopes. B and C Companies dispersed German rearguards as the Rifles trekked along a mountainside path. With the overall situation unclear, Lieutenant Colonel Good called a brief halt. However, a planned five-minute rest for battalion HQ became a month-long stay.[47]

The Rifles were in mountainous country in the shadow of Monte Camino with, to the left, the Gari river and, beyond that, Monte Cassino, topped by its historic abbey, with Monte Cairo looming over it. 'The whole panorama was one of bold grandeur, and no one then knew that they were looking at what became one of the bloodiest battlefields of the war, where many thousands of brave men died.'[48] There lay the Germans' Gustav Line, with Monte Camino the outer bastion. All this the Rifles saw while learning that Italy is not always sunny and that autumn Italian rainfall is heavier than that at home.

While on the high ground, the Rifles continued active patrolling to gain information for the next operation. One officer, in particular, was extremely active. Captain John Strick had trained X Platoon in England in anticipation of possible cross-channel raids, had been wounded in Sicily and, on returning to the battalion, was given command of the Carrier Platoon before being selected to form a battle patrol for which he chose survivors of X Platoon. The valuable information Strick brought back helped planning and provided targets for the divisional artillery.[49]

The experiences of 2nd Inniskillings were similar with a high level of patrolling, described as 'vigilant, adventurous, continuous', such that it earned the divisional commander's 'highest praise'. Prominent among patrol leaders were Harry Christie DSO, Geoff Cocksedge, John Duane, Norman Crawford MC GM and Lance Corporal Marsh. Christie's patrol on 12 November was engaged by German troops in San Vincenzo, at which time Christie was with a Sapper party reconnoitring the road. Hearing the shooting, he returned to the main body of his patrol, assumed command and withdrew it from the danger zone where they were outnumbered considerably. Realizing that five men were missing, he took a small group to search for them but, failing to do so, arranged with an American unit to attack San Vincenzo. Supported by a US company, he did so and liberated the village, driving eighteen Germans into American hands. The missing men were found but three were dead and one wounded. The citation for his MC notes that Christie 'displayed the greatest coolness [while] his disregard of his personal safety and the offensively determined way in which he handled his command was the reason why the patrol took the initiative from an enemy in better positions and much closer to support'.[50]

* * *

As the infantry battalions faced into a severe winter across the peninsula, both LAA regiments were crossing from Sicily to the mainland where 9th (Londonderry) Heavy AA Regiment was part of the defences of Naples. An additional heavy battery, 215 from 57th (Wessex) HAA Regiment, was assigned to 9th while four LAA batteries were added to the AADC's command, as were three smoke companies, including two American. All had joined by 14 October. Until then, all had been quiet over Naples, the Derry Boys' guns having fired only once – 187 rounds at an unidentified aircraft on the 8th. Although the Luftwaffe was much weakened in the Mediterranean, it remained a threat. Commanding *Luftflotte 2*, Field Marshal Wolfram Freiherr von Richtofen, a kinsman of the Great War's 'Red Baron', believed his bombers could best be used against supply ports. Naples was an obvious target. No one doubted that it would be bombed.[51]

All doubt was removed by the drone of unsynchronized aero engines on the night of 21 October. Sergeant Billy Smyth was at the command post at the sports stadium, N9 site, when first reports of approaching aircraft were received. He ordered a telephonist to notify the operations room. All detachments were already at full alert with some off-duty personnel making for gunsites to help, including Gunners John Ormsby and Aubrey 'Ginger' Evans, who were under twenty yards from 25 Battery's No.2 gun at N11 gunsite. Gunner Ormsby was certain the alarm had not been sounded, although the noise of enemy aircraft was almost overhead. No.3 gun opened fire without waiting for the alarm. The others followed suit, putting up a 'harbour barrage', one of a number of pre-planned barrages. It was later estimated that some fifty bombers were attacking.[52]

When No.3 gun had a firing-handle problem, Lance Bombardier Miles Stott left the gun-pit to collect replacement parts, held at No.2. At much the same time, Ginger Evans was making for No.2 to act as an additional ammunition number while John Ormsby, on his way to the command post, could hear a diving aircraft. Nos1 and 4 guns were firing as rapidly as possible.

En route to the command post, Ormsby was suddenly aware of a surge of heat as the ground before him erupted. Miles Stott, partway between two guns, was thrown into the air and back from whence he had come. Ormsby, at least, heard no sound. One Luftwaffe bomber was dive-bombing rather than bombing in a straight-and-level run. In all likelihood, only a single bomb landed in No.2 gun's pit but the effects were devastating. The ten-man detachment died instantly, blown to fragments. Ammunition stored in the gun-pit, over 100 rounds, exploded and the gun was destroyed, its carriage embedded in the remains of the pit while the barrel and breech penetrated an embankment to the depth of four feet. Splinters and fragments swept out with many striking the command post, killing two of the predictor team. Billy Peoples died instantly. Bobby Hamilton was dead within minutes. Caught in the shower of metal, Sergeant Jim Peoples' No.1 gun was struck. His detachment kept firing even though several men, including Peoples, were wounded. Then the gun itself 'died' as the breech-block slid back and refused to return. A metal splinter had penetrated its gravity tank and the recuperator's hydraulic fluid escaped. Although out of action, the weapon yielded up the parts to bring No.3 back into action. Despite No.4 gun also being hit and damaged, the detachment continued firing and put up 111 rounds.[53]

The medical officer, Captain Ronnie Cunningham, gave sterling service treating the wounded while 25 Battery's commander, Major Sir Basil McFarland, did much to maintain his gunners' morale. The raid lasted about forty minutes. When it ended, 25 Battery personnel turned to recovering what remained of their comrades and clearing the site. Fourteen gunners had died with another five wounded, Jim Peoples' condition being critical for some time. Of the dead, ten were Basuto soldiers who had been transferred in while the regiment was in Tripoli in a process known as 'dilution'; the African soldiers replaced British gunners who formed cadres for a number of new HAA regiments.[54]

Robert Hamilton, 24 Battery, remembered a plane darting around the barrage towards 25 Battery's position. Added to Ormsby's recollection of the sound of an aeroplane *diving*, this suggests that the attack on No.2 gun of A Troop 25 Battery was a calculated one rather than a random bomb hitting the gun-pit.[55]

Luftflotte 2 paid a heavy price. Two-four Battery, noting the bombers' reluctance to enter the gun defended area, believed that only about a third of the aircraft pressed home their attacks. Four were shot down, two being credited to the guns and, although some bombs fell in the harbour area, only slight damage occurred. Some fell in a troop concentration area, claiming some lives, including a Gunner who is buried alongside 25 Battery's men in Naples war cemetery.[56]

The dead were buried next day. The attack was 9th (Londonderry) HAA Regiment's single greatest loss of the war. Four of the dead were original members of the regiment: Lance Sergeant Jim Gilmour, Lance Bombardier Bobby Hamilton, Bombardier Dougie Mark and Lance Bombardier Billy Peoples.[57]

Two nights later, *Luftflotte 2* returned to Naples with some thirty bombers. They tried to outskirt the barrage and, for about seventy-five minutes, 9th Regiment's guns maintained their fire with one intruder claimed as a 'probable' by 24 Battery. Although a ship in the harbour was set alight, no major damage was done. There were incursions by single reconnaissance aircraft before October ended and more activity on the ground as 59th (The Essex Regiment) HAA Regiment arrived to increase the defences and 24, 25 and 26 Batteries concentrated in single sites, 59th's batteries occupying their vacated positions.[58]

A Ju.88 flying over Naples during the afternoon of 1 November was identified as a reconnaissance aircraft, heralding a raid. Some two dozen bombers arrived that evening. A brisk thirty-two-minute engagement followed with flares dropped, the smoke companies laying a smoke-screen, the guns firing barrage after barrage and searchlights probing the sky for intruders, at least two of which were 'coned' and engaged by 24 Battery. In all, 1,819 heavy rounds were fired by four batteries, all but 103 by 24, 25 and 26 Batteries. A

Troop 26 Battery reported a new development in Luftwaffe tactics: their first use of 'Window', or *Düppel.* (Bomber Command had first used Window, strips of aluminium foil intended to 'clutter' radar returns including the gun-laying (GL) radar of the AA defences and the airborne interception (AI) radar of the night-fighters, over Hamburg in July.) It 'caused little interference' during the Naples raid.[59]

Further raids followed during November: one on the 5th caused a fire that burned for an hour and during which a bomber 'disappeared' from radar screens, presumably shot down. Most intruders were turned away. Five days later, in the early morning, about a dozen bombers attacked but, again, with little effect. One aircraft, engaged at 5,600 feet, was shot down and crashed at Herculaneum; the wireless operator, who was captured, confirmed that heavy AA fire had brought it down. On the 26th, a recce Ju.88 was engaged by all three batteries before being downed by an RAF Spitfire. That evening a raid by at least twelve bombers was fought off with no damage to ships in the harbour. It was 9th's last engagement with the Luftwaffe at Naples. On Christmas Eve, the regiment received orders to move from Naples.[60]

* * *

Meanwhile the Luftwaffe had been taking 'a keen interest in Bari, mounting a series of low-intensity raids in November'. On the east coast, Bari was Eighth Army's main re-supply port, although US ships also unloaded there. Dubliner Dermot Clarke, a radio officer on the SS *Director*, a merchantman carrying petrol in jerrycans, which docked in Bari at the beginning of December, noted a similarity between Bari and Dun Laoghaire harbours. That was significant since *Director* was moved from the main harbour to the equivalent of Dun Laoghaire's coal harbour. At their first berth, Clarke saw a minesweeper hit a mine and start sinking, followed by a major rescue operation. Later, having moved to another berth, *Director* had just tied up when a raid began.[61]

On that Sunday evening Kesselring had authorized a raid by a large force of Ju.88s following a recce overflight by an Me.210. The raid began with three aircraft circling from the north and dropping large clouds of *Düppel.* In the RAF's GCI (ground-controlled interception) station, operators were 'blinded' by the effect. Believing that 'targets' were passing to the north, they failed to see a raid following behind. That was compounded by a command-and-control breakdown as the 'normal reporting line from sector operations to the AAOR' failed with no alternative established. Thus, no fighters were scrambled to intercept and AA fire was not authorized immediately, defensive fire beginning only as bombs started falling. The Ju.88 crews' task was made easier since the harbour was illuminated fully.[62] Bombs struck the US Liberty ship *John Harvey* which, unknown to port authorities, carried mustard-gas bombs. Dermot Clarke recalled that most of the water was blown out of the harbour: 'Could you imagine an explosion that would blow all the water out of Dun Laoghaire harbour?'[63]

The mustard-gas bombs exploded, as did ammunition on another US ship, the *John L. Motley*. Some two dozen vessels, mostly merchantmen, were sunk, with others damaged beyond repair. The death toll has never been calculated accurately. Over 300 died on the ships with many other casualties on shore. More would die before American authorities revealed that *John Harvey* had carried mustard gas. At least 1,000 are believed to have perished. Author Myles Dungan claimed that 'the British had stored [mustard gas] on one of their ships' and that the Americans 'only discovered the truth when their own experts found out the cause of the deaths'.[64] Since *John Harvey* was an American ship, that argument fails. The cargo had been authorized by Roosevelt with the British kept in the dark.[65]

Also in Bari that evening was Lieutenant Eveline McGrath from County Down. Serving in Queen Alexandra's Imperial Military Nursing Service, the QAs, on the staff of 98th General Hospital in Bari, she was having dinner with other nursing officers, three artillery officers and a medical officer when the bombing started. Just after the soup course a huge explosion rocked the room, smashing windows. However, 'Heavy red velvet curtains, billowing inwards, saved the group from injury from the flying glass as the general alarm sounded.' The head waiter helped them leave through the kitchen and back door. The gunners headed for the harbour, the nurses and doctor uphill to the hospital as bombs fell nearby. They were soon busy with casualties, Lieutenant McGrath spending hours preparing patients for surgery before getting a few hours' sleep and returning to duty next morning. Treating a Scandinavian seaman's injuries, she realized that burns on his body had been caused by mustard gas which she had been trained to identify. However, the harbour authorities, when contacted by the surgeon in charge, had no inkling of such a cargo. Officially, not until the arrival of American Lieutenant Colonel Stewart Alexander, who also recognized the garlic smell of the mustard-gas rash, was the cause of the burns known. It seems that an Irish nurse made the correct diagnosis hours before the doctor arrived.[66]

December was almost over before Bari harbour was back in use. By then, both Allied armies had come up against the stoutest element of the German 'Winter Line', the Gustav Line, which ran through the town of Cassino and included the mountain above it, Monte Cassino, on which stood the mother house of the Benedictine Order and the cradle of western monasticism.

Chapter 3

The Slog Continues

Winter in Italy came as a shock to many who had believed that the term 'Sunny Italy' applied to every month. In 1943 winter came early. British personnel found that winter in Italy could be as unpleasant, sometimes even more so, as at home while being at war made everything worse.

In the autumn and early winter, 78th Division, including 38 (Irish) Brigade, was committed to XIII Corps' advance on the Adriatic side of the peninsula while 2nd Inniskillings and 1st Irish Rifles were to the left of 78th Division; 5th Division, including the Lumps, was also in XIII Corps while 56th Division, with 1st Rifles, was in X Corps in Fifth US Army.

We left 2nd Inniskillings at Isernia where 'demolitions and other damage ... were so severe that the divisional Sappers had to employ all their resources, before the advance ... continued'.[1] The Inniskillings made their mark by installing outside the battalion HQ a full-length mirror bearing the legend 'Do you look like a victorious British soldier *now*?' The Lumps' panache was much admired by the neighbouring Americans.[2] On 7 December the battalion deployed to the isolated village of Castel di Sangro, liberated by 1st Canadian Division, where patrolling and harassing German outposts was again undertaken. Lieutenant Geoff Cocksedge earned the MC for his leadership of a patrol which crossed the in-spate Sangro river and, when engaged by a German machine-gun post, attacked and overcame it before locating others and assaulting one of them, putting the occupants to flight. Cocksedge then withdrew his patrol, outwitting an enemy party trying to cut him off, before getting his patrol, including a wounded man, back across the Sangro. His 'determination and coolness', as well as 'personal courage and skill' led to much valuable information being obtained. Fox also noted that Lieutenant Crawford was again prominent in patrolling.[3]

The battalion's time at Castel di Sangro was brief. On 12 December 5th Division sidestepped right to take part in an advance towards Pescara on the Adriatic coast, leaving Castel di Sangro to the 6th Battalion. Taking over positions from 2nd New Zealand Division and coming under temporary command of the Kiwis, Christmas was spent in scattered outposts, but

Christmas dinners were served. Patrol work, aided by Italian partisans, was undertaken. Patrols under Geoff Cocksedge and Captain Bill Vincent* cleared a village of Germans at bayonet point, capturing prisoners and material. Captain John Duane earned the MC for patrol work on 28 December and again on the 31st. On the 28th the Galway man led a patrol 3,000 yards behind enemy lines, returning with 'valuable and detailed information' on enemy dispositions. Although passing German outposts as closely as 150 yards, his patrol remained undetected. Three nights later, he led a thirty-man raiding party to attack locations identified in his earlier patrol. Although Duane got his party into position, they were thwarted by weather as a very severe blizzard began which lasted until the next evening. Duane sent a contact patrol back to cancel planned artillery support for the attack before bringing his men in under extreme conditions and through German positions manned by troops equipped and trained for winter warfare. His citation noted that it was no exaggeration to state that without his 'leadership, personal courage and soldierly qualities,' the party would 'almost certainly have suffered severe, if not total, casualties between the enemy and the weather'.[4]

The heavy snowstorm that forced John Duane's group to withdraw also wrote *finis* to a 'much wider enterprise' and, for a time, the Lumps were kept busy maintaining communications and supplies. As the worst of the storm subsided, 5th Division received orders transferring it to Mark Clark's Fifth Army, joining 56th (London) Division in McCreery's X Corps, putting both 2nd Inniskillings and 1st London Irish under the same commander. The transfer also meant moving to the other side of Italy's mountainous spine and a new battleground.[5] Montgomery had left Italy to take over planning for the Normandy landings in 1944. His grand plan for the Italian campaign had not worked out as anticipated. In November he had written about unleashing the New Zealanders in a right hook towards Rome, following which he expected to be exhausted and would need some leave and 'probably write a book "Alamein to Rome"'.[6]

In 5th Division's 17 Brigade the Catholic chaplain, Father Patrick Bluett, was a native of Limerick and priest of the archdiocese of Middlesbrough. On 24 November, while visiting soldiers in the Alfedena area, he met Corporal Vincent Vokes, a catholic, of the Intelligence Corps, attached to 2nd Royal Scots Fusiliers. Vokes was observing the area through binoculars, trying to locate a German StuG which was harassing the Fusiliers' area. Borrowing

* Referred to as Willy Vincent in David Cole's *Rough Road to Rome*, the author knew him as Bill.

Vokes's binoculars to 'have a look', Bluett remarked that an Italian flag was being flown inverted from a house below them. When Vokes studied the building, he realized that the flag was hanging from the gun of an AFV concealed in the house. Corporal Vokes radioed back the co-ordinates of the building and advised Father Bluett to leave the area before the artillery engaged the target. Unwittingly, the chaplain had exceeded his brief not to become involved in combat.

Bluett then learned that the forward company in Alfedena, which had been cut off, had suffered casualties who could not be evacuated until darkness fell. He chose to go to the company, down a forward slope across open ground.

> after he had gone a short distance the enemy shelled and machine-gunned his route. Undeterred by enemy fire, he made his way to the company and administered to the casualties such comfort as he was able and then returned … in daylight. His action and disregard of danger had a most invigorating effect on the company and greatly assisted in sustaining its high morale during the period for which it was isolated.

Father Bluett was awarded the MC.[7]

* * *

Captain John Strick's battle patrol of 1st London Irish had excelled in recce missions in the mountains, even in extremely difficult conditions, on one occasion discovering a strong, well-camouflaged German position on which they directed a divisional artillery bombardment.

November 1943 was very wet and the Rifles lived in bivouacs exposed to the elements. Late in the month the battalion learned that 56th Division was to participate in a further attack on Monte Camino at much the same time as US and Canadian troops assaulted its twin, Monte la Difensa. (The latter operation included the Canadian/US 1st Special Service Force.) Some mountain-warfare equipment was available while sappers worked wonders to improve local tracks and the RASC ensured adequate supplies of ammunition, food and water, all brought forward by jeep convoys. For the attack on Monte Camino, 1st London Irish came under 167 Brigade command. Strong artillery support was available, described as 'the biggest' bombardment since El Alamein with Royal Navy ships offshore adding support. The effect on the Germans, described by 56th Division's historian as 'terrifying', was salutary. Small areas were targeted, each struck by eleven tons of explosive per minute from the guns of 46th and 56th Divisions, some American batteries and units from an AGRA (Army Group Royal Artillery). Mark Clark later commented that Monte Camino was the 'Million Dollar Mountain' since so many shells were fired at it. It was estimated that the tonnage was 1,300, roughly 'equivalent to a major air raid on Berlin or other large German city'.[8] As for the enemy, 'In places they ran away; where there was cover they held on, but invariably emerged with their nerves in shreds and their morale at a very low level.'[9]

The battle for Monte Camino and its monastery lasted eight days. A Company 1st London Irish captured Formelli, a hamlet on the track to Rocca d'Evandro, the enemy supply artery. Captain D.A. Gibson directed fire from the mortars of four battalions, including the Rifles, in an effort to silence the enemy. Although the Germans returned fire, 'the men at the mortars remained steady and their accurate shooting added to the gradual demoralization of the enemy'.[10]

Finally, the Germans abandoned their positions. The London Scottish advanced to Rocca d'Evandro while the London Irish withdrew, 'very wet, tired and dirty after an eight days' gruelling attack'. The Rifles suffered some eighty casualties, a relatively low number in the circumstances. Among the dead was Bermuda-born Lieutenant Terence Barry 'a capable and gallant officer' who had been Mentioned in Despatches.[11] With Monte Camino in Allied hands, re-organization began: 56th Division handed over to 46th Division and moved to the coastal sector, close to the Garigliano river. By then 1st London Irish had reverted to 168 Brigade which came out of the line for the first time in two months. There was even the luxury of billets in Cascano village where the Rifles enjoyed Christmas, including a show presented by the *Liricals*, their concert party, during which the party leader, representing the Spirit of Monte Camino, sang a song entitled 'They've put S mines at the bottom of my garden'.[12]

Irishmen were serving in other units of 56th Division, including 7th Oxfordshire and Buckinghamshire LI, 167 Brigade, which had played a major part in the Monte Camino battles. Among that battalion's dead was Private Joseph Simms from Londonderry, killed on 11 November during a bayonet attack to relieve the survivors of 6th Grenadier Guards who had held Point 819 against all German efforts for four days in foul conditions of heavy rain and intense cold. Joseph Simms, who was married, had earlier served in the East Surreys; his widow lived in Surrey.[13] A brother of Eamon Simms, 2nd Inniskillings, who had been wounded in Sicily, another brother, Matthew, serving in the Royal Irish Fusiliers, had died of septicaemia in September 1940.[14]

Also advancing with X Corps west of the Apennines was 46th Division, a Territorial Army formation which included 128 (Hampshire) Brigade, composed of three Hampshire Regiment battalions. One was 5th Hampshire, a company of which was ordered to capture a position some half-mile north of the Volturno on the night of 15/16 October. When the company commander, Kildare man Captain Patrick Mordaunt, reported the position unoccupied, his CO ordered him to advance to the line of a canal three miles ahead. Mordaunt did so, crossing the canal to dig in on the far side. At dawn on the 16th his company was shelled by German artillery and attacked by infantry and a tank. Very heavy mortar fire forced another company, deployed in support, to withdraw. A third company, given the same task, could not get within two miles of the beleaguered company. Mordaunt, cut off completely, was in real danger of being overrun, in spite of which he held the position

> until the CO of his Bn was able to re-group at nightfall. During the night Capt. Mordaunt's company was again heavily counter-attacked but he did not withdraw … until his position had become quite untenable and the Commanding Officer was satisfied that the remainder of the Battalion's positions were secure. When he did eventually withdraw across the canal in the face of heavy enemy opposition, Capt. Mordaunt personally supervised the withdrawal, which was carried out in an excellent manner.[15]

Throughout the action, Patrick Mordaunt's courage and example, showing disregard for his own safety, provided inspiration to his soldiers. He was awarded the MC.

On 14 November, command of 128 (Hampshire) Brigade passed to Pat Scott, a Royal Irish Fusilier who had commanded 1st Royal Irish Fusiliers and 2nd London Irish Rifles in 38 (Irish) Brigade. He would remain in post until breaking an ankle in late-January 1944. His relief, Brigadier Douglas Kendrew, was one of the most decorated officers of the war, whose wife was Norah Harvey of Malin Hall, County Donegal.[16]

* * *

We left 38 (Irish) Brigade just north of Termoli as other brigades of 78th Division and 1st Canadian Division continued Eighth Army's advance, the Canadians, on the left, pushing into the foothills of the Matese mountains towards Vinchiaturo. The front had widened with 8th Indian Division joining 78th Division in V Corps while the Canadians and 5th Division were in XIII Corps; 4 Armoured Brigade was included in V Corps with 1 Canadian Armoured Brigade in XIII Corps.

Following the Termoli battle, 38 (Irish) Brigade held San Giacomo ridge and patrolled between there and Petacciato. Since skirmishes with German patrols ended with the Irish Brigade having the better of the engagements, Brigadier Russell considered that his brigade should secure Petacciato ridge from which it would be easier to assess the next obstacle, the Trigno river. Russell's proposal was approved but limited to a single-battalion operation, a task assigned to the Rifles. D Day was 19 October. Reconnaissance was carried out and artillery support arranged from 17th Field Regiment.[17]

The attack went as planned with close support from a squadron of 44th Royal Tanks and the Faughs' battle patrol, the last dealing with a machine-gun post on the right while 17th Field's bombardment ensured that the defenders took cover. F and G Companies led the attack; E joined them in the small hours of the 20th. Petacciato village was in Rifles' hands by dawn. The attackers had no casualties but the Germans lost men and equipment, including nineteen captured. It was a classic small-scale operation with artillery, infantry and armour working in harmony. As a result, HQ 78th Division allowed Russell to move the Faughs onto Petacciato ridge while 6th Inniskillings remained as a backstop at San Giacomo. The ridge would be the jumping-off point for the Irish Brigade's next operation, crossing the Trigno some three miles away. Although sixty-feet wide, the water in the middle was only about eighteen inches deep. Both banks were steep and high, between fifty and eighty feet, although much lower where the coast road and Petacciato-San Salvo road crossed.[18]

In preparation, two patrols deployed to check for German positions close to the Trigno. It was known that the river line was not held in depth, nor was the next line at the Sangro, the main defensive positions being some three miles behind the latter. However, there would be German positions close to both rivers. Leading the first patrol was Captain Desmond Woods MC who had just become H Company commander. Under cover of darkness, he led his platoon-strength patrol to a farmhouse from which he could observe the river in daylight. He was to ascertain if the bridge was intact, how much water was in the river and the gradients of the banks. He had

> the most marvellous view of the bridge .... It was intact and ... the banks weren't too steep, the level of the water ... was fairly low and should the bridge be blown it would be perfectly feasible to make a diversion for the tanks on either side ... it was absolutely incredible that during that morning I hardly saw any movement by Germans at all – they were very good at lying low by day and not giving their position away. ... they were a great deal better than we were.[19]

Shortly after noon, Woods was ordered to return to battalion HQ as soon as possible to report on the state of the river and the bridge. He left his platoon in hiding, taking only a few men with him, making part of the return journey in the bottom of a farm cart which had earlier been transporting manure.[20]

The Rifles' second patrol, including a Royal Engineer party, ventured onto the bridge to check for demolition preparations. Inevitably, there was a clash with Germans but, after a brisk fight, the patrol returned to report that there were no demolition charges. At brigade HQ Nelson Russell doubted that, although divisional HQ was happy to accept it. Russell ordered a company to move up to keep German engineers away and the gunners were asked to 'plaster' the area around the bridge throughout the day to discourage any engineers who might approach.[21]

At 1400 Major General Evelegh arrived with orders: the Irish Brigade was to 'capture the bridge intact and forthwith'. Russell protested that 'the ruddy thing will go up' but Evelegh insisted. With the Rifles occupying a ridge to the right of the bridge the Faughs would take it and, with three companies, create a bridgehead across the Trigno. At much the same time the Inniskillings would move to Petacciato ridge.

Although the plan initially worked well, Russell was proved right. As Major Tommy Wood's C Company, in the van, reached the bridge, 'it went up like Vesuvius at the top of her form', in Russell's words. C and D Companies waded across and formed the bridgehead. Sappers began work on a new crossing but came under fire, as did the Faughs in the bridgehead, which was in a wooded area. German shelling hampered taking food and supplies across and the flat open ground beyond the bridgehead was dominated by fire.[22]

The next phase was to take San Salvo on a ridge some 4,000 yards away. As plans for the attack were finalized the Inniskillings occupied Montenero, a village left of the bridgehead. San Salvo was to be the objective for the Rifles while the Faughs seized a defended feature left of the town on the night of 27/28 October. On the Rifles' right, 2nd Lancashire Fusiliers of 11 Brigade, having created a second bridgehead closer to the coast, would attack San Salvo railway station. Rain made matters more difficult for those in the bridgeheads while breaks in the clouds allowed enemy aircraft to strafe the areas.

Due to heavy rain on the afternoon of the 27th, Brigadier Russell asked for a postponement. He was overruled. Faughs and Rifles advanced, supported by an artillery bombardment. Some machine-gun posts escaped being shelled and those weapons, plus mortars and artillery, pinned the Faughs down. B Company's commander, Major William 'Dennis' Dunn, a Belfast man, was killed and his platoon commanders wounded. Paddy Proctor MC and his platoon commanders died when a mortar round fell in their midst as they planned the attack on the final ridge. Beauchamp Butler moved forward to rally and encourage his men but was killed by a machine-gun round. The London Irish historian described him as 'that quiet little man with an indomitable spirit who was greatly liked throughout the brigade'. The Rifles fared no better: F Company's leading platoon was pinned down between a minefield and defensive fire; the platoon commander, Lieutenant Michael Marmorstein, and most of his men perished in an attack on an MG post. Both Rifles' company commanders were wounded. The attack was called off and both battalions pulled back to the bridgehead. Next morning, while supervising re-supply, the Rifles' second-in-command, Major Kevin O'Connor, was killed by an enemy shell. The temporary cross placed on his grave described him as 'A Gallant Gentleman'.[23]

The Inniskillings relieved the Faughs, allowing them to return to San Giacomo to rest, refit and re-organize. Nelson Russell visited the battalion, finding their morale good despite the ordeal. The general feeling was that 'everybody buys it once and often twice. We've never bought it before – so it must have been about our turn, but, wasn't it a pity about the wee colonel – we'll have to square all that.' The visit to the Faughs left Russell confirmed in the belief 'that a good Regiment is always a good Regiment – in fair weather or foul'.[24] In place of Beauchamp Butler, James Dunnill DSO became the Faughs' CO.[25]

San Salvo was taken by 11 and 36 Brigades with 6th Inniskillings involved in the first phase of the operation. A complete armoured regiment, 46th Royal Tanks, gave support while a second, 50 RTR, was on call.[26] However, the Inniskillings suffered losses, including Major Hobo Crocker who was killed, as was Lieutenant Basil Hewitt. If there was any consolation for the battalion, it came in the award of the DCM to Company Sergeant Major Robert Stevenson of Crocker's A Company who, with all company officers killed, immediately took command and led the company to its objective, including through an attack by enemy armour while they crossed open ground.[27]

The battles to cross the Trigno and liberate San Salvo had seen considerable involvement of German aircraft. Luftwaffe fighters had strafed troops while Irish Brigade HQ had been bombed twice during the day. More casualties had been sustained from the bombing than in the San Salvo battle.

The Trigno/San Salvo episode was an indicator of what was to come in the campaign. Italy's hard mountain spine was funnelling the advancing armies to the coastal regions, but those were cut through with rivers and streams which were frequently flowing fast and high during the winter months and into early spring. Italy was made for defensive soldiering. Not for nothing did Napoleon comment that, since the peninsula is shaped like a boot, it should be entered from the top. Albert Kesselring was taking advantage of the country's many natural features, improving on them with concrete, steel and effective weaponry. Both armies had encountered elements of what German prisoners were calling the Winter Line. Rather than being a single line, it was a series of lines crossing Italy, the first the Viktor Line on the Volturno, already encountered by Fifth Army.

Awaiting both armies was the line crossing Italy from the Gulf of Gaeta on the west coast to near Ortona on the east. Known as the Bernhardt Line and initially intended as a delaying line, due to Hitler's insistence that the Allies be stopped on the Gaeta-Ortona line it was strengthened considerably. A switch line of the Bernhardt, known as the Gustav Line, including the Cassino massif, would become one of the most famous battlegrounds in European history. A second switch from the Bernhardt, intended to close the Liri valley to the Allies, was dubbed the Hitler Line.

The next river obstacle was the Sangro, on which the Germans had expended considerable effort. Facing Montgomery's men, the German LXXVI Panzerkorps of five divisions under General Herr against Eighth Army's eight had the advantages of terrain and strong defensive positions. However, Herr's command had given ground when 78th Division had pushed forward after San Salvo and by 9 November all German troops were north of the Sangro, allowing 78th Division to dominate the plain on either side. For almost a week Herr's men were confined to an escarpment north and west of the Sangro, providing little hindrance to 78th Division recce'ing the plain and river line.[28]

On the 15th the weather chose to hinder 78th Division's operations: the heavens opened, the Sangro widened and deepened and its speed increased. Expanding fourfold from its 100-foot width, its depth rose to chest height and the flow made crossing impossible while allowing the Germans breathing space to lay new minefields and strengthen defences. Once the river was again passable, sappers cleared new paths through those minefields. Corps HQ had decided that the renewed attack would include 8th Indian Division, 78th Division and 4 Armoured Brigade with the Indian Division securing high ground around Mozzagrogna to allow 78th, reinforced by 4 Armoured Brigade, to pass through, turn right towards the coast, roll up the German defensive lines and then swing left on the coast road. However, the Germans had used the interval afforded by poor weather to consolidate their defences. When the Gurkhas of 17 Indian Brigade attacked on 28 November they were beaten off by flamethrower tanks, the first appearance of such weapons in Italy.[29]

Charles Allfrey, commanding V Corps, Evelegh, Brigadier John Currie of 4 Armoured Brigade and Nelson Russell conferred at Currie's HQ. The new plan was based on arguments put forward by Currie and Russell that 'when we took a place we knew we had it'. Both had worked together before and were confident that they could achieve success, especially since their squadrons and companies had trained together and knew each other well; they had practised what became known as 'battlegroup' tactics.[30]

At 0630 on the 29th B and D Companies of 6th Inniskillings advanced supported by 44th Royal Tanks. Although mines impeded the tanks and machine-gun fire harassed the Inniskillings, the infantry fought through to their objective, the top of the Li Colli ridge. Three junior NCOs of D Company, which had the tougher fight, Corporal John Chatburn, Lance Corporal Patrick Madden and Lance Corporal John Powell, made singlehanded attacks on MG posts, eliminating them. All three received the MM.[31] With B and D Companies on the ridge, A Company advanced between them with 44 RTR tanks and the ridge was secure by 1500. Thus, the Inniskillings and 44 RTR had secured the base line for the next phase. Before that, 8th Argyll and Sutherland Highlanders, temporarily under Nelson Russell's command, relieved the Inniskillings so that the complete Irish Brigade could deploy in the next phase which required it to take Fossacesia.[32]

Supported by tanks of 3rd County of London Yeomanry (CLY), also known as the Sharpshooters, and 44 RTR, the Irish Rifles swept down the ridge, many mounted on tanks, and took Fossacesia. Major Desmond Woods' H Company was 'married' with B Squadron of the Sharpshooters and he recalled that

> we continued on until we'd finished our part of the attack and then another company passed through and we very successfully got onto our objective at a place called Fossacesia. We took quite a number of prisoners; they'd been taken completely by surprise.[33]

The Rifles lost only two dead and eight wounded.

The flanking attack by tanks and infantry had knocked the defences completely off balance. In the words of the Rifles' history, 'It was a triumph for planning and organization'.[34] Taking over from the Rifles, the Faughs, with two tank squadrons, made for the coast, took all their objectives and fifty prisoners and completed 'rolling up' the German defences. Both Faughs and Rifles stopped their advances at nightfall. For the Faughs there had earlier been an experience described by Captain Brian Clark, the adjutant, as his worst of the war. While 8th Indian Division was still fighting, the Faughs' CO, James Dunnill, had called an O Group in a gully with the commanders of B and C Companies. Clark ordered both company runners to 'fetch your Sunrays'. However, the message was misunderstood and instead of the Sunrays

– company commanders – both companies entered the gully just as a StuG dropped two shells into it, killing nineteen and injuring another twenty-three. The dead included Londonderry-born Lieutenant Alex 'Swinger' Smyth while Hunter Lang, the Medical Officer, died of wounds two weeks later.[35]

Next day the Rifles took Rocca before moving across country to a valley the Faughs had encountered the previous evening. That day the Faughs probed northwards near the coast while 6th Inniskillings, supported by armour, protected the brigade flank between Rocca and Lanciano.

When Nelson Russell asked James Dunnill to send a force to probe forward across high ground to the north, he set in motion a remarkable chain of events. Major Jimmy Clarke was allotted A and D Companies to investigate ground between the main road to San Vito and the sea, establish enemy strength and see if pressure there would prompt a withdrawal from positions on the main road which were impeding the Rifles. Clarke moved forward some four miles to about a half-mile from a ravine close to the road into San Vito. As well as his infantrymen, he had Captain Douglas Evans of 17th Field Regiment and a wireless operator to direct fire on the road. Establishing his force in a fallback position that night, Clarke decided to send a volunteer patrol into the town in daylight while the main body deployed around an abandoned house that served as his HQ. The patrol, led by Lieutenant John Day, received a warm reception from the inhabitants who greeted the Faughs as liberators, their celebratory sounds carrying to Clarke on the high ground. Some two dozen shocked Germans became prisoners. However, the sounds of celebration died down as the sounds of battle erupted. Two German armoured cars attacked Day's patrol with the young subaltern being wounded fatally. Although eight Faughs were captured, the others obeyed Day's last order: hide in the town. One, Fusilier John Toland, led some of his comrades to the town's northern end and created mayhem with a Bren. With two bursts, Toland killed two German motor-cyclists before opening fire on a convoy of horse-drawn carts, firing three magazines into the leading vehicles. As well as creating confusion, the attack brought heavy fire onto Toland's little group. His No.2 on the Bren was shot in the head and Toland and the remaining Faugh burst into a house, took cover in the cellar, and emerged again and again, engaging the Germans before hiding another time. While John Day was recommended unsuccessfully for the Victoria Cross, Toland was awarded a Russian gallantry medal.[36]

The Germans tried flushing Clarke's men out of their locations but were resisted doughtily while Douglas Evans called down effective artillery fire on enemy movement along the road. Nelson Russell wrote of Clarke's commando:

> They kept saying how comfortable they were and what a good time they were having – though looking at the mortars falling in their part of the world I wouldn't have called it great comfort myself. However, it's very hard to resist such appeals as 'we got a ruddy Hauptmann last attack' or 'We've added five MGs to the establishment. So I let 'em be, for the present anyway, for the effect they were producing ... must have been astonishing. Two hundred Faughs – six miles behind the Bosche – killing and blazing at everything.[37]

After dark, Clarke and his men pulled back while staying close to San Vito where they had done much to break the German hold.

That hold was broken completely next day when Inniskillings and Sharpshooters, after a nocturnal march via Fossacesia and Santa Maria, attacked from the Treglio ridge at first light. The remaining Faughs joined Clarke's force south of San Vito which was in Allied hands by 1600. The Germans fought tenaciously in the streets and the Inniskillings suffered casualties, including a company commander killed, while junior NCOs again demonstrated outstanding leadership. Lance Corporal David Milligan earned the MM for his courage and initiative while Patrick Madden repeated his earlier feats. Faughs and Rifles moved north to the Feltrino to prepare for a nocturnal crossing en route to the next major river obstacle, the Moro.[38]

Advancing to the Moro was not simple. Enemy posts had to be dealt with while 38 (Irish) Brigade was the spearpoint of Eighth Army with its left flank exposed. The Inniskillings deployed to protect that flank as the other battalions pushed on, the Faughs meeting strong opposition in their sector with casualties including Major Tommy Wood MC, who was killed. Desmond Woods' H Company of the Rifles reached the high ground over the Moro. He was ordered to attack the bridge, which was intact but, having sent a patrol to reconnoitre, he reported that it was mined and well defended. Nelson Russell arrived to check the ground and concluded that a brigade-strength attack would be required. Before that attack, however, 78th Division was withdrawn. The Irish Brigade, the only element of 78th Division still in the line, needed a rest after seven days and nights of hard fighting. Since landing in Italy, the Brigade had lost thirty-six officers and over 800 other ranks – more than a battalion.[39]

Relief came in the form of 1 Canadian Brigade. Farley Mowat, a platoon commander in the Hastings and Prince Edward Regiment, the *Hasty Ps*, wrote:

> It was pelting rain when I went forward with the [Royal Irish] Fusiliers' intelligence officer .... Long lines of soaked and muddy Fusiliers wound

> their way past us, moving to the rear. Their faces were as colorless as paper pulp and they were so exhausted they hardly seemed to notice the intense shelling the coastal road was getting … .
>
> But I noticed, as I had never noticed before. The rancid taint of cordite seemed to work on me like some powerful and alien drug. My heart was thumping to no regular rhythm. It was hard to draw breath, and I was shivering spasmodically though I was not cold. Worst of all, I had to wrestle with an almost irresistible compulsion to stop, to turn about, to join those deathly-visaged men who were escaping from the battle that awaited me.[40]

Although it had been hoped that the Irish Brigade might enjoy Christmas out of the line, the Inniskillings were ordered to move into the upper reaches of the Sangro to Capracotta, close to Kendal Chavasse's 56 Recce. Not until mid-January would 6th Inniskillings rejoin the brigade.

Chapter 4

More Mountains, More Rivers – and Anzio

During December, General Alexander, recognizing that the best prospect of liberating Rome lay on Fifth Army's front, began re-organizing both armies. He chose to reinforce Fifth with formations from Eighth, commanded by Lieutenant General Sir Oliver Leese since Montgomery's departure, while feeding formations arriving in Italy into Eighth with one exception: 1st Division, which arrived from North Africa in early December, joined VI US Corps. As already mentioned, 5th Division moved to Fifth Army, joining McCreery's X Corps, which already included 56th Division. New arrivals included 5th Canadian Armoured Division (raising the Canadians to corps status), the initial division of II Polish Corps, 4th Indian Division and the French Expeditionary Corps (FEC), all but the French joining Eighth Army.[1]

Plans were being finalized for a seaborne hook to Fifth Army's next advance. While the main body of Clark's army – FEC, US II Corps and X British Corps – would continue advancing towards Rome, VI Corps would land at Anzio, thereby 'restoring momentum to the offensive and … reaching Rome during January 1944 or early February'.[2] The two-divisional landing at Anzio was seen as 'a powerful descent from the sea behind the German western flank' to unlock the stalemate, an optimistic assessment considering the rates of advance hitherto achieved in Italy. The UK *Official History* is critical of the Allied leaders, most of whom had Great War experience:

> the circumstances of the Italian campaign were coming to resemble those of static warfare on the Western Front a quarter of a century ago. Yet the leaders were now assuming that a rate of progress was possible in Italy that was unrealistic in the light of the experience of the earlier war.[3]

The initial effect on Irish units of Alexander's re-grouping placed both 2nd Inniskillings and 1st London Irish in Fifth Army, albeit in McCreery's British X Corps. However, they were subsequently transferred to VI US Corps, a formation in which 1st Irish Guards (24 Guards Brigade, 1st Division) also served. Having fought in Tunisia, the 'Micks' landed in Taranto on

7 December and moved to Monte Carrafa, 'a square medieval building' which was a comfortable enough location for celebrating Christmas. A move to Gragnano near Naples followed in preparation for embarkation for Operation SHINGLE, the Anzio landings.[4] By D Day for SHINGLE, 22 January, both 2nd Inniskillings and 1st Irish Rifles were positioned along the Garigliano river, once the border between the Papal States and the kingdom of Naples. The Rifles had entered the line there on New Year's Day, the Lumps a week later.

Initially, the Rifles carried out intensive patrolling with the redoubtable John Strick leading his battle patrol as a preliminary to a X Corps operation to coincide with the Anzio landings. All three divisions of X Corps would attack, 46th Division on the right, 56th in the centre and 5th on the left. Clark intended X Corps to draw German troops to their sector, thus preventing them moving to counter the Anzio landings. Fifth Army's other two corps were also involved, General Alphonse Juin's FEC attacking in the mountains to the north on the right flank and II US Corps in the centre, crossing the Gari at Sant'Angelo in Theodice, as well as the Rapido north of Cassino.

An assault crossing of the Garigliano required an array of specialists similar to those needed for an amphibious landing.

> Beach-masters, swimmers, boat-paddlers, tow-rope hauliers, all were carefully selected and made thoroughly familiar with what was expected of them. Sappers were allocated to each infantry battalion, to help in the actual crossing and afterwards to clear paths through whatever minefields that might be encountered on the other side.[5]

In 56th Division, 167 and 169 Brigades would execute the assault crossing. The German defences, some distance back on high ground, allowed good observation of the Allied line. With the lower ground seeded with minefields, there was little opportunity for a surprise attack by X Corps. Even so, when the attack was made, on the night of 17/18 January, 8th Royal Fusiliers crossed with little opposition although 9th Royal Fusiliers met determined resistance, with many casualties as assault boats were holed by machine-gun fire. The survivors pressed on to reach the far bank. Elsewhere, 169 Brigade, supported by Royal Marine commandos, had a successful crossing, 2/5th and 2/6th Queen's landing in succession; the former then liberated Sujo. With the assaulting brigades firm on the north bank, a bridgehead was established which attracted strong German reaction. Although von Vietinghoff, commanding Tenth Army, thought the attack might be a feint, Kesselring regarded it as 'the greatest crisis that we have so far experienced'.[6]

A German counter-attack on 22 January, D Day for SHINGLE, fell on 167 and 168 Brigades but failed to knock them off balance, although inflicting many casualties. Among 1st London Irish dead were Lance Corporals William Hamill and Patrick Thompson of Belfast and Rifleman Thomas Kirkland from Fermanagh.[7] Difficult fighting at Castelforte, San Lorenzo and Monte Damiano ensued with a series of engagements, in one of which Lance Corporal Eric Norman earned the DCM for continuing with his duties as a wireless operator although wounded. Norman crawled from trench to trench to find a working wireless set and, after treatment, assisted signals' personnel at HQ until wounded again by shell splinters, at which stage he was sent to hospital.[8]

The Inniskillings were also involved, crossing close to where the Garigliano flows into Gaeta Bay. They were

> to cross ... by boats, to clear the plain beyond of enemy outposts, to form up on a line in front of the main German entrenchments and wait there for the assisting barrage to open; then to assault. Assembly area was on the verge of the Appian Way, a little south of the river's bank.[9]

In spite of careful planning and preparation, a series of mishaps prompted improvisation. The boats for the crossing were delayed, only two arriving before H Hour and the supporting artillery bombardment, beginning as planned, alerted the Germans to the probability of a crossing. Captain Patrick Long used both boats to ferry a patrol across and establish a bridgehead. Engaged by an enemy machine gun, the patrol attacked the MG post, at a farmhouse called Epitaffio, overcoming the defenders. When more boats were brought up, Major Martin Grant of A Company took his leading platoons across, but with serious losses from drowning and shellfire. As A Company closed on its first objective, Massa Rossi farm, a mortar round killed Major Grant, a Belfast man, and some Germans captured by his company. The farm was taken in a bayonet charge led by Lance Sergeant Banton, the only other officer, Lieutenant Fleming, having been wounded. Banton's leadership and courage earned him the MM. Having taken Massa Rossi, the survivors of A Company formed a defensive perimeter before collecting the wounded, including Germans, for treatment.[10]

Well behind schedule, Major John Nixon's B Company crossed in Wiltshires' boats to be followed an hour later by C Company, Major Percy Blake, Battalion HQ, a mortar detachment and a machine-gun platoon. A much depleted battalion was on its line by 0530, at which time the supporting artillery fire was to begin. It was then that an enemy shell fell on the HQ group, killing Captain

Bradley MC, the MG officer, the artillery signallers, several battalion signallers and runners, and wounding others. Lieutenant Colonel O'Brien-Twohig DSO was wounded, a shell splinter ripping his neck. However, he refused to leave. Also injured, the signals officer, Captain David Cole, re-organized signallers, restored damaged equipment to working order and led a line party to re-establish contact with the forward companies.[11] Majors Nixon and Blake and Captain Cole were each awarded the MC. Although English-born, Cole's parents were from Ulster and he had requested to be commissioned in an Irish unit.[12]

B and C Companies advanced towards the railway line before the ridge marking the Gustav Line in that sector. B Company suffered seventeen casualties in a minefield, delaying its advance, but C made better progress, once again due to the resourcefulness of an NCO, Sergeant Robert Boak. The battalion pioneer sergeant, Boak had been ordered to take a fighting patrol ahead to identify minefields and, where possible, clear paths. Sergeant Boak, who was well ahead of the battalion, not only reconnoitred a route across the Ausente river, but, with great courage, remained in the riverbed during the bombardment, which fell in the river, to clear forward to the road ahead of the attacking troops.

> The night darkness was now giving way to dawn and the attack had to traverse a stretch every yard of which was under the fire of the interlocked German posts; and between them minefields and wire barriers. The importance of the instantaneous and effective response to the disaster at Battalion Headquarters was shown: the Battalion was working as a well co-ordinated machine; the protective barrage was perfect, keeping many of the enemy anxious to remain underground rather than come to the surface.[13]

C Company broke into the centre of the German position at noon and began adapting its trench system to meet the inevitable counter-attack. The Lumps had opened an 800-yard-long breach in the Gustav Line. From London, the BBC announced to the world that 'an important breach' has been made in the main defences of the Gustav Line. It was the first such rupture, proving that Kesselring's assessment had been correct.[14] Neither attack to the flanks of the Inniskillings had made much progress, although the Wiltshires had reached Tufo on the left.

That night an attack towards Minturno ridge was initiated, only to encounter a German counter-attack which fell largely on B Company. O'Brien-Twohig called for defensive fire, sending a runner to C Company asking for a supporting attack. The runner never got through and no attack materialized. B Company, although in a precarious position, continued a series of counter-attacks including one led by Sergeant Thomas Anderson who was acting as the company sergeant major, the latter having been wounded. Armed with a German machine gun, Anderson rushed the Germans, firing from the hip and killing several. The others fled. Later, he covered the company's withdrawal, again using his captured German weapon, before re-organizing the company in new positions. The citation for his MM concluded that 'but for the initiative and cool calculating bravery of this NCO, a great part of his Company would have been killed or captured'. The MM was also awarded to Fusilier John Stranex, a runner in 10 Platoon, B Company. When Germans overran a company post, Stranex organized the other two fusiliers at platoon HQ and made a bayonet charge, driving the enemy from the post they had just taken. But for Stranex's quick wits and courage, the remainder of 10 Platoon might have been captured.[15]

There were many other acts of bravery and many casualties were suffered. Battalion morale remained high, much of which was due to the leadership of Pat O'Brien-Twohig whose twin mottoes were 'Keep on attacking' and 'Keep the artillery going'. Not surprisingly, he was awarded a Bar to the DSO he had earned in Sicily.[16]

A major German counter-attack fell on 2nd Inniskillings in the early hours of the 19th. As enemy troops tried to enter the battalion positions, Major Blake called for an artillery bombardment on the front, ordering the guns to adjust their range until shells were falling immediately in front of his positions. Such 'danger-close' shelling inevitably caused 'friendly' casualties with both Blake and Captain Bill Vincent wounded. Lieutenant George Blythe, in a forward trench, was killed and Captain Exham was wounded while bringing ammunition forward. Blake refused to be evacuated until the situation was stabilized, at which point he handed over to John Nixon. Before long, the line was restored, many prisoners taken and some Inniskillings, earlier captured by the enemy, freed.[17]

German artillery continued targeting the battalion lines with one round killing two officers. One, who died immediately, was Captain Harry Christie DSO MC. Lieutenant Maurice Bell, wounded severely, died five days later. Both were from Belfast. Noting that Christie's death was mourned by all 'as of a brother-in-arms of exceptional gallantry and of friendly comradeship', Fox wrote:

> The Inniskillings had paid grievous price for their achievement. The measure of the casualties can be judged by the fact that fully a third of officer rank were killed or seriously injured.[18]

Inniskillings had held the centre of Wellington's line at Waterloo, suffering heavy losses but contributing significantly to that battle's outcome. The 1944 battle on the Garigliano may not have had the same import as Waterloo, but the gallantry of 2nd Inniskillings matched that of their predecessors. They remained in the line, coming under renewed attack. Active patrolling continued with O'Brien-Twohig overseeing the patrols. On 26 January, he was ordered to hospital for treatment of the wound sustained earlier but was back with the battalion before long.[19]

Fifth Division's success led to the Germans deploying 90th PanzerGrenadier Division to the Garigliano sector where, subsequently, it was involved in attacks on 2nd Inniskillings. Clark failed to build on the British success. He also failed to build on the success of the French on the northern flank, refusing to reinforce Juin's corps. Instead, he concentrated on II US Corps and sought to blame McCreery's corps for 36th (Texas) Division's failure to cross the Gari.

Clark's first offensive in the Cassino sector had failed. He was quick to launch another, with an extemporized New Zealand Corps of 2nd New Zealand and 4th Indian Divisions. Prior to their attack, the Monastery on Monte Cassino was bombed by USAAF aircraft and reduced to rubble, although the oldest part of the building was almost unscathed. Once again, the attack failed despite the attackers' courage. Among the units of 4th Indian Division was 1st/9th Gurkha Rifles, whose CO, Gilbert William Nangle from Moneymore, County Londonderry, ordered two companies to support a Rajputana Rifles' attack on Castle Hill, on the mountain's lower slopes. C Company, under Captain Michael Drinkall, seized the prominence known as Hangman's Hill, under 300 yards from the Monastery, one of the most remarkable actions of the Italian campaign. However, Nangle did not live to see Allied success at Cassino; he died on 2 March.[20]

* * *

On 22 January the first wave of VI Corps went ashore at Anzio. By then, most of the Allied forces in Italy were committed to liberating Rome, whether from Anzio or along the Via Appia or Via Casilina, the latter passing through Cassino under the shadow of Monte Cassino and Monte Cairo. Had 2nd Inniskillings and 1st London Irish been anticipating a reduction in German strength on their front, they were disappointed: enemy forces persisted in efforts to smash X Corps' line. Hard fighting continued for both battalions.

At San Lorenzo a few tanks, having crossed the Garigliano, arrived to support the defenders, their presence a boon to B and A Companies of 1st London Irish. When German tanks attempted to break through 'they got an unexpectedly warm welcome and were compelled to turn back'. Several days of fighting saw the German effort come to an end. Three bridgeheads spread over a front of seven miles were secure and expanded to a depth of two miles.[21] Having been unable to cross in their sector due to the height of the riverbanks there, 46th Division had been called on to provide fresh troops for the other divisions and 1st London Irish, which had lost about 192 all ranks, including a dozen officers, was relieved by a Hampshires' battalion. Lieutenant Colonel Ian Good commented that 'Now we must lick our wounds and get ready for the next bout as quickly as possible, making sure that we maintain and enhance the high name of the London Irish Rifles under all circumstances'.

With the battalion rested and back across the Garigliano, plans were being finalized for another attack on Castelforte when the CO learned that 56th Division was being withdrawn to join VI Corps at Anzio. Moving to Capua, the Rifles received reinforcements but had no time to let them settle in or train before embarking.[22]

As the Rifles prepared to leave the Garigliano sector, 2nd Inniskillings were returning there into positions on Monte Damiano's slopes. Although the Germans held the summit, Inniskilling patrols dominated much of the ground, finding many enemy outposts 'manned' by dead Germans. Three companies were close to the German line, in a 'very desolate position', with the fourth in reserve. With German artillery observers overlooking the Lumps' area, daylight movement was impossible and trench improvements had to be made at night. Re-supply was also nocturnal, mules and porters bringing essentials forward. On 22 February the battalion was relieved and 'passed on to the relieving unit a more secure and a slightly more comfortable position'.[23]

Tremonsuoli, a village about a mile from the sea, was the Inniskillings' new 'home'. Overlooking the Via Appia, the battalion patrolled actively with the principal danger being mines. In one incident, Lieutenant Norman Crawford MC GM was leading a patrol that was caught in a mine blast, killing one soldier and injuring Crawford and four others.[24]

On 29 February, Pat O'Brien-Twohig went to Salerno for a short spell of leave, returning a week later. However, on his return, he was ordered to hospital again, since his wound required further treatment. Although not then appreciated, it was his goodbye to the battalion he had led with such distinction. Lieutenant Colonel Peter Slane MC, a 25-year-old who had earned the MC with the Lumps in Sicily, succeeded him as CO. (O'Brien-Twohig recovered and was promoted to command a brigade in Italy, for which he was appointed CBE. Before that, he married Percy Blake's sister, a QA, in a 'picturesque' old Catholic church in Castellammare with Bill Vincent as best man and Percy Blake giving his sister away.)[25]

As with the Rifles, the Inniskillings, on departure from Tremonsuoli, learned that they were destined for Anzio with 5th Division. On 11 March the battalion embarked in Naples for the beachhead where VI Corps was besieged. The battalion's soldiers were not the first Inniskillings at Anzio, however. On D Day for SHINGLE at least two members of the regimental family had landed. Brigadier E.E.J. (Eric) Moore, commanding 2 Brigade, 1st Division, a veteran of the First World War had been appointed DSO for the capture of Pantellaria island, a prelude to HUSKY.[26] The other was Private John Logue RASC whom we 'met' in Operation HUSKY when he was wounded early in the operation.

> we didn't know we were going to Anzio; we were well up the coast before we realized ... [and] then they told us that we were going in behind the lines to make a landing at Anzio. ...
>
> I just got halfway up the beach when a shell landed. I noticed the smoke and everything but I didn't know at the time that the amphibian had been hit until I got onto the beach and went to get instructions as to what to do. I had an artillery piece on and some men, so I wanted to see what I was going to do with this; it had to be lifted off with a crane. And the sergeant said to me, 'Paddy, you'll not go very far, for there's a big hole in the front of your amphibian.' It was about two [feet] or so in diameter. But it didn't stop you. You got another one.[27]

He recalled that it was several days before his unit moved into Anzio town where it was to be stationed. The initial element of the overall plan had gone well and almost unopposed, with the Germans taken by surprise. The same was not true of Fifth Army's attack with deadlock setting in. Those in Anzio believed that the main force would be through in forty-eight hours, 'that [General] Alexander was going to make a big push along with us, synchronized like, as we landed at Anzio, that [Fifth]* Army would ... break through to us in forty-eight hours'. Recalling that he was wounded on 9 March, he reflected that 'they hadn't broken through then'.[28]

Brigadier Moore's 2 Brigade was in 1st Division, known as the Spearhead Division from its divisional badge, alongside 3 Brigade and 24 Guards Brigade. The last-named formation included 1st Irish Guards which thus became the first Irish unit in the beachhead. The Micks had served in the Tunisian

* In the original interview with the author John Logue referred to Eighth Army, a formation with which he would have been more familiar.

campaign, where one of their number had earned the Victoria Cross. They would suffer heavily at Anzio.

Fifth Army's plan required VI Corps to secure a beachhead in the area of Anzio and advance on Colli Lazioli. Three forces, one of three American regiments (the equivalent of British brigades), a British brigade group, plus two commandos and an American rangers group, were to form a seven-mile-deep bridgehead around Anzio, from which the entire force would cut both main roads some dozen miles south-east of Rome. The Irish Guards' history notes that a time for the establishment of the beachhead was not defined but it was believed that the Germans would counter-attack in divisional strength on D Day. To meet that strike, most of 1st Division, with a regiment of tanks and two artillery regiments, was held in reserve, to be joined by US 504th Parachute Regimental Combat Team, landing from the sea.[29]

Brigadier Murray, commanding 24 Guards Brigade, had believed that there would be hard fighting on D Day and D plus 1 but, if the landing achieved surprise, it should be exploited by launching both leading battalions, 5th Grenadier and 1st Irish, towards Albano where they could create chaos. However, no such orders were issued. As it turned out, both Highways 6 and 7 were busy with German staff cars

> beating it back to Rome bearing officers and men who considered that their presence so far south was no longer necessary. The Grenadiers and Irish could have picked up most of these military refugees and harried the others. The Germans at the front would have been looking over their shoulders instead of straight ahead.[30]

An opportunity had been missed. Moreover, there seemed to be 'delay and inaction' which 'caused unconcealed disquiet amongst the Battalion', the guardsmen having been keyed up for action which did not occur. Nor could they understand why 1st Division was not advancing. The regimental history describes D plus 1, 23 January, as 'a completely wasted day'.[31] But the Germans were not wasting time and, by the end of that day, had two divisions concentrating against the Allied lodgement; 29th and 104th PanzerGrenadier Regiments screened the beachhead while more troops concentrated in the Velletri area. Had the Allied command hoped that the landing would persuade Kesselring to pull back from the Gustav Line, or withdraw significant forces from there, they were shown to have miscalculated. Lloyd Clark notes that Kesselring 'had been decisive in his actions and visited the front personally'. He saw no need to withdraw, pointing out to General von Senger und Etterlin that the existing line was shorter than one that ran across Italy from 'in front of the gates of Rome'.[32]

At the same time, the Germans were attacking Fifth Army's main body (as both Inniskillings and London Irish had experienced). On the evening of the 23rd, as darkness fell, Luftwaffe bombers struck at Anzio harbour and the beaches. The destroyer HMS *Janus* was sunk, killing 150 men, including its captain. HMS *Jervis*, another destroyer, was damaged so badly that it had to sail to Naples, although with no loss of life. Both were hit by air-launched glider-bombs. The destroyer USS *Plunkett* was hit by a bomb after avoiding two glider bombs on the 24th but reached Naples with dead and injured crewmen. The USS *Prevail*, a minesweeper, also sustained major damage. Also on the 24th the hospital ship *Saint David* was attacked and sunk by a German bomber; the ship went down in five minutes. At the time HMHS *Saint David*, clearly marked and illuminated as a hospital ship, was about twenty-five miles south-west of the beachhead.[33]

The apparent lethargy within VI Corps reflected the corps commander's caution, especially as he had been advised to be careful by Clark before leaving Naples. (Major General John P. Lucas had succeeded Major General Ernest J. Dawley who had been relieved after the Salerno landings.) Lucas chose to secure his beachhead before committing his command to action. He had gifted the Germans a breathing space, of which they had taken full advantage. In Lloyd Clark's words, 'Lucas had not stuck his head out too far. He had not stuck it out at all.'[34]

Kesselring's reaction included ordering formations from as far away as Germany and Yugoslavia, as well as France and elsewhere in Italy, to move to counter the new threat. Fourteenth Army was deployed to seal off the beachhead and did so on the 24th. In the meantime, a motley of units initiated that task under Luftwaffe staff officer Lieutenant General Ernst Schlemmer. Schlemmer positioned infantry units in the Alban Hills as a reserve, rather than deploying them to block possible Allied axes of advance. Kesselring reacted quickly, removing Schlemmer and replacing him with General Alfred Schlemm, commander of I Fallschirmjäger Corps. Schlemm set about his task with a clear vision of what was needed. Lucas's procrastination ensured that the Germans could confine VI Corps to a limited lodgement. The opportunity to seize, at least, a much larger portion of ground could have been taken in the operation's early hours and days. Lucas's failure to do so condemned those in the beachhead to suffer in cold, wet conditions under constant observation from the enemy on higher ground.[35]

On the 24th, with the arrival of 179th US Regimental Combat Team (RCT), Lucas took 1st Division out of reserve, ordering it to probe towards Albano. A recce patrol from 5th Grenadier Guards found Aprilia defended heavily but brought back five prisoners from 3rd PanzerGrenadier Division. Aprilia, the 'Factory', would become a focus for 24 Guards Brigade.

A brief description of the beachhead is provided by 5th Division's historian, who wrote that the US divisions 'held the more open country from the sea to Nettuno following roughly the line of the Mussolini Canal to the area of Padiglione'. The British sector was from Padiglione to the main Campoleone-Anzio road 'at a point where a fly-over bridge of some prominence crossed it seven miles north of Anzio'. The road crossing that bridge then cut at 90 degrees to the main Anzio road, running from there to the sea. Dubbed the 'Lateral Road', it climbed gently to La Cogna, a small village dominating the enemy positions but which was, in turn, exposed to enemy fire. The road then descended to a junction with the coastal road. North of it were small valleys, dubbed 'wadis' by British troops, interspersed with some woods close to the sea.

> To the south of the lateral road lay open rolling farmland with here and there a young wood and valley. The junction of the Lateral and Coastal Roads took place at the hamlet of St Lorenzo, an extremely exposed place known appropriately as 'Stonk' Corner and only used by those with charmed lives, at least by day. From the woods … the front line ran across country in a north-westerly direction to where the Moletta River ran into the sea.[36]

Referring to the Anzio campaign, the authors of a history of the Irish Guards wrote:

> To veterans of that campaign in the Italian spring of 1944 the name recalls memories of death in appalling conditions of mud and cold, and of a battle so nearly lost. The Germans described it as the Allies' 'Epic of Bravery'.[37]

For 1st Irish Guards, the Anzio campaign lasted thirty-seven days, in which the battalion, rebuilt after heavy losses in Tunisia, suffered casualties worse than in Tunisia where 125 officers and men had been killed or died of wounds with another 245 wounded in fifty-four days. Anzio cost the Micks 129 killed or died of wounds and a further 227 wounded. The casualty total in Anzio was 746 all ranks killed, wounded or missing. (Father Brookes, the battalion chaplain, wrote that 1,080 all ranks had gone into Anzio but only 267 came back.)[38]

Following a recce by 5th Grenadiers, the three battalions deployed. The Grenadiers took Aprilia, a new town created by Mussolini and inhabited by people from northern Italy. The Micks were at the apex of a narrow salient, to the Grenadiers' left, with 1st Scots Guards behind, holding a railway station. A German regiment was close by. The entire front was overlooked by German positions on the high ground; the roads were also under observation. By dusk on the 25th the battalion was established in its positions, uncomfortable as they were. Not long after dawn on the 26th the Micks were in action. As the forward company, No.3, breakfasted, Captain Kennedy, its commander, reported German tanks less than a mile away. At much the same time, German artillery fired on the Micks.

As the tanks closed on the battalion front, No.3 Company's anti-tank guns, commanded by Captain Desmond Young, engaged them, hitting two before one gun was knocked out and most of the detachment perished; the second gun jammed. Then German infantry entered the fray. Kennedy called artillery fire down on them, breaking up the attack. Next into action were German machine guns and mortars which lashed both Nos1 and 2 Companies. The pattern for the day had been set. It proved to be the pattern for many of the Micks' days at Anzio. By the end of that day, 1st Irish Guards had lost 120 men to shelling alone, thirty of them dead.[39] Among the wounded was Regimental Sergeant Major McLoughlin, hit by splinters from a shell that had killed Guardsman Ayre and wounded others. McLoughlin had to be evacuated, much against his will, causing the adjutant, Captain Desmond Fitzgerald (who later wrote the history of the regiment in the Second World War), to comment, 'If such a thing were possible, I'd say the Sergeant Major is crying'.[40]

The regimental history records thirty dead, but the *Army Roll of Honour* shows only half that number, the former account presumably including those who later died of wounds. Since the history was written by the then adjutant, this seems most likely.[41] Of the fifteen recorded in the Roll of Honour for 26 January, six were born in Ireland (four in 'Éire' and two in Northern Ireland) and three had been born in Britain to Irish parents.[42] Of that day, the *Official History* notes that 'the Grenadier Guards and the Irish Guards repelled a counter-attack and 24 Guards Brigade then settled in to hold Aprilia'.[43]

The cautious Lucas faced an almost equally cautious German commander, Eberhardt von Mackensen, whose Fourteenth Army took responsibility for besieging VI Corps from 25 January. Next day, von Mackensen expressed the view that the Allies' most likely move would be to take the high ground at Velletri in a drive towards Valmontone, with a secondary thrust towards

Littoria. However, he hoped to initiate a counter-attack before that happened. Mackensen was also acutely aware that Hitler wanted the Allies prevented from expanding their holdings. Therefore, German forces established outposts from Cisterna to Campoleone, to be built on as the start line for an offensive or used as a defensive line.[44]

Fitzgerald devoted a chapter (27 pages) of his history of the Irish Guards in the Second World War to the fighting around Aprilia, under the title 'Carroceto' with the overall experiences of the 1st Battalion at Anzio narrated in 152 pages. It is a story of suffering, endurance and courage, the last illustrated by the many gallantry decorations awarded, a selection of which illustrates the battalion's achievements in a purgatory comparable to anything their forebears had endured on the Western Front a generation before.

Major Savill Young, Support Company commander, was appointed DSO. The son of an RIC officer who had been killed serving with the Micks in 1917, Young had been 'unceasingly occupied in the vital task of co-ordinating and siting all supporting arms ... in the recent actions' and had

> probably been exposed to more personal danger than any other man in the [battalion], but he continued about his duties with an aloof calmness that had an immense steadying and encouraging effect on all who saw him and all those under his command.[45]

On the morning of 26 January, during the German counter-attack, when four anti-tank guns had been knocked out, Young closed the gap by identifying new positions and emplacing other guns to meet the attackers, all while under enemy artillery fire. During the night attack on the 29th/30th, he advanced with the rifle companies to identify positions for the supporting arms, returning to the battalion's original positions although both available roads were controlled by the Germans, some of them between the forward positions and his destination. At one stage he crawled for about 500 yards to avoid machine-gun fire. Mortar rounds fell around him and he had to contend with snipers. Young then organized the move of 3-inch mortars and anti-tank guns to No.3 Company's positions, establishing the battalion's firm base. Moreover, he also organized US tank-destroyers to advance with Captain Kennedy at last light.

> This officer with his great experience and complete trustworthiness had been of the greatest help in the [battalion] during the last two campaigns and has the admiration of all ranks for his complete disregard of personal safety and high sense of duty.[46]

Another Young commanded the anti-tank guns in Support Company: Captain Desmond Young from County Donegal, although born in Ballymena in 1916, was commissioned in the Irish Guards in June 1940. He saw active service in Tunisia and was wounded badly but returned to the battalion in August 1943, taking command of Support Company's anti-tank guns and mortars. In those early German attacks, he fought his guns well, taking a sharp toll of the enemy, despite losing guns and men.[47] Fitzgerald, in a letter to Desmond's brother, wrote:

> It is difficult to pick out any particular incident on the beachhead at Anzio, because it was all so bloody, and there seemed to be so much happening the whole time. I do, however, very well remember him coming to see me the morning after the big German night attack. He was so tired that he could hardly stand up. He said all his guns had been smashed, and he wanted some more, please. We got him some more on that occasion, but these were smashed too, because, of course, he and his crew would insist on staying with the Infantry and protecting them against German tanks, which was just what we expected from him. When that second lot of guns was smashed, there were no more, and, anyway, what we then wanted was men on their two flat feet.[48]

On the night of 22/23 February, Desmond Young was searching for a comrade when he was hit by a burst of machine-gun fire. Fitzgerald described what happened:

> Desmond came up to the gully with the remnant of his gun crew to help John Kennedy. It was a filthy night and nobody knew where John Kennedy was, not even Kennedy himself. However, when I told Desmond this, he wasn't a bit worried and said he would find him all right. That was the last I saw of him. I heard the machine-gun burst shortly after that.[49]

After the Victoria Cross, the Distinguished Conduct Medal was the highest gallantry award for an 'other rank' until 1993. Several were awarded to NCOs and guardsmen at Anzio. Guardsman William Montgomery was in No.1 Company in the night attack on 29/30 January. Although the company reached its objective to the left of the main Anzio-Albano road, German tanks threatened its establishing defences, firing flares to illuminate and machine-gun the digging guardsmen. However, Guardsman Montgomery engaged the tanks with a Bren gun, forcing their crews to close hatches and visors. In doing so, Montgomery exposed himself to German machine-gun fire. When daylight broke, and no British tanks or supporting arms appeared, the company had to withdraw. Once again, Montgomery, assisted by Guardsman Taylor, took up position on a railway embankment to cover the remainder of the company withdrawing over 400 yards of open ground.

Montgomery's position meant that his head and shoulders were exposed. He was also liable to be shot from behind by German soldiers. Ignoring the risks, he

> left the cutting in the last party with his [Company Commander]. Twice on the way back across the stretch of open ground he halted to return the fire of enemy MGs, once engaging, whilst in a standing position, a concealed German MG 150 yards away and effectively silenced it. [His] outstanding courage, skill and coolness … greatly facilitated the withdrawal of his [Company] and there is no doubt that a great many of his comrades owe their lives to his complete disregard for his own safety.[50]

In the night action of 3/4 February, Montgomery was the first to engage and draw enemy fire when the Micks' right flank was exposed. Although captured, he fought his way out, shooting several of his guards before escaping in a carrier. Despite being wounded in the leg, he was back on duty on the night of the 4th. 'No personal danger could prevent this Guardsman from doing more than his duty and he earned the greatest admiration from all who saw him.'[51]

Guardsman Harry Taylor, who supported Montgomery on the night of 29/30 January, received the MM. Early in the night, Taylor cleared a house occupied by Germans who had threatened his company before supporting Montgomery in distracting German tank crews and in the company withdrawal. Also wounded in the leg, Harry Taylor made his way back with Guardsman Montgomery's help. The commanders of Nos1 and 2 Companies were

> emphatic that without the courage, skill and devotion to duty of this Guardsman the two companies would have suffered far heavier casualties than they did while crossing the open ground in the face of the enemy MG posts which were engaged by or turned their attention to this Guardsman.[52]

The first action rewarded with the DCM was that of Offaly man Sergeant Joseph Dunne, commanding 13 Platoon in No.3 Company on the battalion's left flank in Carroceto on 26 January. When the Germans launched their attack at 0800 they overran another platoon, knocking out anti-tank guns and a Vickers machine gun. Dunne quickly re-organized 13 Platoon and beat off two infantry attacks, showing no concern for his own safety. Three nights later, in the battalion's night attack, he led his platoon with the 'highest skill and determination' and, when held up by a machine gun firing on fixed lines, dashed forward alone and knocked it out.

When the battalion attacked with US tank destroyers next morning, Joseph Dunne was again at the head of 13 Platoon which destroyed three enemy posts with no losses. He was also in action on the morning of the 31st. Locating a German snipers' nest, he stalked and wiped it out, tracking down the last of six snipers that afternoon. When his company was overrun in the German assault on the night of 3/4 February, Dunne was wounded but fought his way back to his own lines. His DCM citation noted that:

> This NCO's record for skill, determination, marksmanship and personal courage during the whole of the Bn's action in the Anzio bridgehead is of the highest order and merits ... the immediate award of the DCM.[53]

Captain D.M. Kennedy, commanding No.3 Company, earned the MC over several days from the 26th. Although losing a platoon overrun and two anti-tank guns, he re-organized his company and repelled the attackers, inflicting heavy casualties on them. Before the subsequent night attack, he carried out reconnaissance patrols, gleaning good intelligence on enemy dispositions which proved invaluable. His citation emphasized his 'magnificent leadership' which 'undoubtedly kept up the morale of his fast dwindling company and resulted in his Battalion position being held against heavy odds'.[54]

Lance Sergeant George Banks, commanding a section in No.3 Company, also distinguished himself on the 26th. Holding the left forward position at Carroceto, he

> maintained complete control of his section, kept them hidden from the tanks, and engaged the enemy ... with devastating fire. By his control, steadfastness and personal example, he ensured that his platoon's and [company's] position remained firm.

George Banks was prominent in the night attack of the 29th/30th and subsequent sweep with US tank destroyers.[55] He was awarded the MM. On 18 February he was evacuated to hospital.

Perhaps the most remarkable award of the DCM was to Lance Corporal Maurice Moriarty, a stretcher-bearer in No.2 Company, in the attack on 29/30

January, during which the company suffered many casualties. Moriarty spent most of that night moving wounded to comparative safety, usually dragging them *under* the German machine-gun fire. He showed no concern for his own safety either then or during the attack on the night of 3/4 February. Ignoring heavy shellfire, he spent that night gathering wounded and taking them to the safest location he could identify, between an earth bank and some carriers. The position was overrun and the Germans ordered Moriarty to march to the rear as a prisoner. He refused and 'had not a German soldier fortunately been wounded at this moment he would probably have been shot'. Following that defiance, he remained with his patients, caring for them all through that day and night under heavy Allied shellfire. The next night, 'with remarkable resource and initiative', he and another soldier loaded the wounded on two carriers and drove away in a successful dash for the Scots Guards' lines. As his DCM citation noted:

> The tireless devotion of this Cpl to his wounded comrades and his complete disregard of his personal safety or the consequences to himself of his courageous actions are an exceptional example of gallantry, self-sacrifice and resource.[56]

Lance Corporal Alan Dodds, battalion Intelligence despatch rider during the first week in the beachhead,

> was entrusted with numerous tasks of responsibility and importance, all of which he carried out in an exemplary manner. He was constantly riding up and down roads under heavy shell fire and at all times he remained a model of coolness and willingness.[57]

On 2 February Dodds was promoted to be intelligence sergeant and thus was at battalion HQ when the Germans attacked on the night of the 3rd/4th. He displayed remarkable and constant courage and initiative as

> with Major D.M.L. Gordon-Watson and L/Cpl Cross, he fought his way out of Bn HQ when it was surrounded and with his Tommy-gun did great execution amongst the Germans who had infiltrated into the gullies in the rear. By a quick snap shot he disposed of a German who suddenly appeared from a culvert and following up his advantage he captured the remainder of the German section … in the culvert.[58]

Dodds then reported to the commanding officer at the new battalion position, a farm. Having found and repaired a derelict motorcycle, he helped guide parties of guardsmen to the new position, although he was the target for enemy machine-gunners and snipers. Dodds was awarded the MM, as was Lance Corporal Alfred Cross. In Cross's case, an earlier incident, when battalion HQ was behind the railway embankment at Aprilia, also featured. On that occasion, during a heavy bombardment, a 5th Grenadiers' ammunition lorry had been hit and set ablaze, causing ammunition to explode in all directions. Ignoring the danger, Cross left the safety of his trench to rescue a severely-injured Grenadier warrant officer. He pulled the wounded man from the 3-tonner and carried him to the RAP (regimental aid post).[59]

Major Michael Gordon-Watson MC*, acting commanding officer at the time of the German attack, was with Dodds and Cross and organized the breakout from his headquarters, establishing a new one at a farmhouse behind No.2 Company. Having shot a number of Germans en route, he arrived at the new location with a dozen prisoners. He was awarded a second Bar to the MC he had earned in Palestine in 1938; his first Bar had been for Norway in 1940. The citation noted that he had 'shown the greatest personal bravery all through that night and undoubtedly his own efforts in shooting his way back made others realize that it was possible. His coolness and brave example [were] remarked on by all … .'[60]

Major George Fitzgerald, commanding No.2 Company, was another to earn the MC. In his case, the citation covered the night action at the end of January and another on 21/22 February when No.2 Company was relieving II/6th US Armored Battalion. En route to take over, No.2 Company suffered several casualties from heavy shelling. Leaving his second-in-command to lead the company to the American positions, Fitzgerald organized the safe evacuation of the injured under heavy fire before rejoining his company. Over the next four days, No.2 Company was assailed persistently by fire from artillery, mortars and snipers but, by constantly changing positions and sending out raiding parties, Major Fitzgerald maintained the initiative. His guardsmen, although tired, took many prisoners and the Germans were unable to penetrate the company positions.[61]

The German attack on the night of 3/4 February has already been referred to. Several others earned gallantry awards that night, including Captain Simon McCombe, acting adjutant, who was one of about thirty Micks captured. However, McCombe seized a rifle, shot the nearest German and then, with a Thompson, shot several others, eventually turning captors into prisoners. He led the party back to British lines, engaging and overcoming German posts on the way. Lieutenant Timothy Keigwin was commanding No.4 Company, which was surrounded and subjected to heavy fire. Nevertheless, Keigwin kept control of the situation, fought off all attacks and, when daylight came, called a bombardment down on the enemy. He then rescued a platoon which had been cut off before counter-attacking the Germans and fighting through to battalion HQ. Both McCombe and Keigwin were awarded the MC.[62]

As already noted, 1st Irish Guards suffered heavily at Anzio with the total of dead, wounded and missing equating to the strength of a battalion. The suffering in the purgatory that was the beachhead continued until the day the Micks were relieved by 1st Duke of Wellington's Regiment on 24 February. Even on that day there were losses. As the hand-over was being conducted, with both Micks and Dukes in the open, German shells and mortar bombs crashed into the 'Boot', the location the Micks had been holding.

> The last-minute losses were heart-breaking for the Irish Guards. Sergeant Wylie DCM was killed – solid Jimmy Wylie, as brave as a lion and as patient and gentle as an ox, who had survived the worst of three campaigns and was looking forward to a fourth.[63]

From Aughnacloy in County Tyrone, 37-year-old Jimmy Wylie had earned the DCM in 1940 during the Norwegian campaign.[64] Andrew Scott, the Micks' commanding officer, had asked his Dukes' counterpart, Brian Webb-Carter, 'to keep a particular eye on a Corporal Moriarty, who had not yet left the Boot, and who – Andrew said – had done particularly good work'. However, as Webb-Carter noted,

> At that moment, almost, the lifeless body of that gallant NCO was toppling into an empty slit trench as, looking for a wounded man in the darkness, he was hit by a fragment of mortar shell.[65]

According to Verney, 'the redoubtable' Moriarty had been going to the aid of his old friend, Jimmy Wylie.[66] Maurice Moriarty, from Dingle in County Kerry, and Jimmy Wylie lie with so many of their comrades in Beachhead Cemetery at Anzio. On 7 March their Battalion sailed from Anzio with 267 officers and men, landing at Santa Agatha, south of Sorrento.

In spite of the travails of life under siege in wet slit trenches and ruined buildings, the battalion maintained its morale. The efficiency of officers, WOs and NCOs had much to do with that by ensuring that everything possible was done to ensure the guardsmen were fed, supplied with ammunition and other necessities, and that anything that could help sustain morale was done. One significant morale builder was the battalion's chaplain, Father Rudesind John

'Dolly' Brookes (since his mother was Irish/Swedish, he regarded himself as half-Russian, quarter-Swedish and quarter-Irish; his maternal grandmother, Elizabeth Hannaway, was Irish) who had been a Micks officer during the First World War and until taking Holy Orders in the 1920s. Father Brookes had served with the Micks in Tunisia in 1943 and was extremely popular. On 26 January, the day of the first German onslaught, when the early mist cleared, allowing the Germans a perfect view of the ground, the Padre took the opportunity to read his Office, pacing 'delicately up and down the track behind the embankment, a steel helmet perched on top of his cap, and his nose buried in his breviary. It was a very comforting sight'.[67]

Providing comfort to the Guardsmen may have been his intent although he later wrote that he could claim that not to have been the case: 'Every priest has the obligation of reading the Divine Office every day, though we were excused this duty under active service conditions.'[68] Of that day, Brookes later wrote that 'it was the worst I ever spent in either of the two World Wars'.[69]

Father Brookes was subsequently awarded the MC. The citation noted that he had shown 'almost unbelievable devotion to duty and bravery' in both Tunisia and Italy and that:

> No wounded or dying man wherever he may be, has gone without Father Brookes' attention. He has been in places where the fire was impossibly heavy and yet he has given comfort to the dying without any thought for his own safety. During the last few weeks, in probably the fiercest fighting the British Army has yet seen, this Priest moved through shot and shell never appearing too tired to go to the furthest points to help a wounded man. ... The sight of Father Brookes pacing up and down reading his breviary under heavy fire has restored the confidence of many a shaken man.[70]

* * *

Lucas's failure to seize the initiative at Anzio had allowed the Germans to besiege VI Corps. Such was the pressure they exerted that 168 Brigade, 56th (London) Division was placed under command of Penney's 1st Division from 4 February. Having sailed from Pozzuoli, near Naples, 1st London Irish reached Anzio on 3 February to dig in along VI Corps' stop line. Scarcely had they begun than a change of plan sent the Rifles to Aprilia to relieve 1st Reconnaissance Regiment, commanded by Lieutenant Colonel E.A.S. 'Paddy' Brett, a Royal Ulster Rifles' officer who had commanded 1 Recce since the previous CO had been wounded in Tunisia in April 1943.

With considerable mobility and much greater firepower than an infantry battalion, a recce regiment was an invaluable asset for a divisional commander and thus Brett's unit had been deployed to work with 24 Guards Brigade, protecting its left flank. This it did in the face of determined attacks, a stand that put the regiment on the front pages of UK newspapers. *The Times* used the description 'thin red line' to convey a sense of what Brett's soldiers achieved. Its correspondent wrote:

> a 'British thin red line' was strung out along two miles of the perimeter defences. The 172 men who manned this line held off at least two enemy battalions and by aggressive night patrolling caused chaos and confusion in the enemy camp. These were the men of the 1st British Reconnaissance Regiment .... Their spirited interpretation of their defensive role proved a decisive factor in countering the enemy's first testing thrust against the beachhead.[71]

The regiment's training and experience, coupled with its CO's leadership, foiled German efforts to dislodge the defenders.

Relieving A Squadron 1 Recce was the reason Ian Good was ordered to deploy his battalion into the line. The regimental history describes the laydown:

> D Company dug in near a road junction about half a mile to the north of Aprilia and along a spur, to link with a Guards battalion on the left flank. Deep wadis or [irrigation] ditches ran almost parallel on either side and these had constantly to be patrolled day and night. B Company was on the right of Aprilia, from a road bridge across the Fosso Della Ficoccia to a road junction on the fringe of the 'garden city'. C Company was directly south, between D and B Companies, also at a road junction, and had to be prepared to support either or both of the other companies. A Company was placed to guard the left flank and to link up by strong patrols along the west side of the 'Factory' area. Four anti-tank guns were used to cover the approaches to D and B Companies from the north. There were also Vickers guns from the Carrier Platoon and mortars in support.[72]

Battalion HQ was in a house behind C Company's locations, where the carriers were held in reserve. Captain Mace's Intelligence section established an OP on the upper floor, hidden from enemy view. With B Echelon closer to Anzio, re-supply was under cover of darkness. The Flyover bridge, remaining intact, was a constant target for German gunners.

The first night and day in Aprilia were quiet, apart from some brief skirmishes between patrols on the nights of 5/6 and 6/7 February. Then, at 0200 on the 7th, came signs of a German attack. Initially, strong enemy patrols tried infiltrating between the companies and the Berkshires to their right but were driven off. Subsequently, the German bombardment increased while reports were received of tanks and infantry concentrating to the north. Heavy firing, including smoke shells, began after 0500, providing cover for an infantry attack on the Rifles' and Berkshires' positions. That attack was fought off with 'rifles, bayonets, grenades and automatics'.[73] Similar attacks persisted throughout the day with a few tanks appearing. By evening, with D Company in danger of being cut off, Good sought permission to adjust its position, the better to conform with A and B. Permission was refused since that would have meant giving up ground. The decision would have dire consequences for D Company.

There had been little opportunity for sleep since the battalion's arrival, a situation exacerbated by the attacks. Casualties mounted as the enemy maintained pressure on 1st Division's positions. Positions held by 2nd North Staffords were surrounded as Germans encroached on Point 80 on Buonriposa Ridge, west of Aprilia, on the night of 7/8 February. Some enemy who penetrated the Rifles' area were seen off. One party reached the battalion mortars to be repelled by rifles, grenades and Corporal Allen who propped his mortar 'almost vertically on ammunition boxes and fired bombs with considerable accuracy, using the primary charges only'.[74]

In spite of heavy shelling, small-scale infantry attacks with some armour support, the Germans made little headway on 8 February. The Rifles continued controlling the approaches to Aprilia from the north and the Lateral Road to the east, with the Buonriposa Ridge situation unclear. HQ 1st Division had identified the opposition as I Fallschirmjäger Corps, including elements of four divisions and a total of six regiments. Attacks were in regimental-sized battlegroups with armour and artillery support, the latter being much heavier than previously experienced.[75]

The Germans made no significant gains but maintained pressure on the defenders. Soldiers already tired became yet more weary. On the evening of the 8th, Good visited his companies, all reduced by casualties and very tired. Shortly afterwards, D Company reported that its forward platoon locality was empty. Since no firing had been heard, the company commander believed that the riflemen 'had collapsed through utter exhaustion' before being surrounded and taken prisoner. Another request to move D Company was rejected. Attempts by patrols to reach the company were rebuffed by German patrols that had infiltrated the area. B Company was also suffering from small-scale attacks that prevented contact with the Berkshires. Moreover, the Rifles had been unable to mine the Fosso Della Ficoccia, and the enemy were using both branches.

At 0130 on the 9th, D Company's two surviving platoons came under heavy attack. Battalion HQ received a brief message of an attack before radio and telephone connections were lost.

> The Germans came in at close quarters from all sides, and the platoons were cut off from the rest of the battalion. That possibility had all along been feared, but permission to withdraw the company to sounder positions had been refused. Attempts to make contact with them made no headway, even a troop of Shermans could not face the short-range fire of enemy anti-tank guns. German machine-gun fire covered all the approaches.
>
> Attacks developed to the right and left of the London Irish front, and it was impossible to find any troops to launch an attack strong enough to break through to D Company. At daylight, still with no message from them, it was concluded that they had been completely overrun and that those who had survived the frenzied onslaughts of the enemy had been taken prisoners.[76]

The defenders had fought strenuously against a much stronger force, led to the end of the battle by their company commander, and sole remaining officer, Major McMahon Mahon. As a prisoner, Mahon received severe injuries from Allied gunfire.[77]

The Germans continued taking advantage of the gap created by the seizure of D Company's localities to support attacks via Aprilia on B Company and the Berkshires, whose left forward company had also been eliminated. B Company was forced back and Good decided to risk moving A Company from the left flank to mount a counter-attack, for which artillery support was arranged. Although the Germans had anticipated such a move, and were ready, such was A Company's determination that it reached a line along a ditch just south of B Company's lost positions.

Desperate fighting with many acts of gallantry ensued. When Germans broke into one house, Lieutenant Richard Haigh used a PIAT to evict them. Although wounded, Haigh, later awarded the MC, continued directing the defence. Elsewhere, Fallschirmjäger closed to within fifty yards of the defences and gained a foothold, allowing them cover in a gully, from which they engaged the defences with a machine gun. But they were also seen off by a spirited defence which included Major Brooks firing a Bren from an upper window.[78]

Elsewhere on the Rifles' front, equally desperate fighting was underway. Germans pushed into A Company's positions but Captain Ray Mullins reorganized the survivors to repel them. Mullins then led an assault on the Germans threatening B Company's HQ, driving them off and taking almost three dozen prisoners. All the while, Ian Good maintained a close watch on the situation as the enemy switched from objective to objective in an effort to overwhelm all his companies' positions.

> Although they had achieved some success the enemy had been thwarted in their main design – to break through to the sea. The magnificent fight put up round the vital road leading to the south had completely foiled the plan, and there came a lull in the fighting while the enemy recovered from the severe mauling he had received.[79]

D Company had been lost while A and B had suffered losses such that neither could muster even a third of its normal strength. C Company, although also understrength, was not hit quite so badly. Three company commanders and many platoon officers were casualties and A and B Companies were combined under C Company command while 1st London Scottish lent the Rifles an understrength company.[80]

Although 168 Brigade had been hard pressed, the attacks, even with armour support, had not yielded success. The waterlogged ground in which 1st Division's soldiers had dug slit trenches had hampered tanks, the use of which was constrained further by the many waterways. The rebuff of the attacks allowed 1st Division to modify its organization, placing 168 Brigade south of the road running east from the 'Factory' while 24 Guards Brigade continued holding Carroceto and 3 Brigade was along a 'wadi' south of Buonriposa Ridge.

That re-organization was disrupted by an attack on Carroceto which, while the village was not taken, allowed the Germans to seize the railway station and consolidate their positions; they, too, had suffered heavy losses. On the night of 10/11 February, 168 Brigade was withdrawn for rest. The attrition the Rifles had undergone was underlined by the fact that the battalion was relieved by a single company with more personnel than Good's battalion.[81]

That rest period was used to absorb reinforcements, albeit no more than a company and a half, mostly raw, inexperienced men. Some 'veterans' who had recovered from wounds or illness, rejoined, including Captain John Strick who had been wounded at the Garigliano. 'Rest' was, of course, a comparative term: nowhere in the beachhead was outside German artillery range while the Luftwaffe, although much reduced, was still attacking VI Corps. A typical nocturnal raid would involve some high-explosive bombs being dropped on Allied positions as well as many butterfly anti-personnel bombs. The regimental history records that some Luftwaffe ordnance led to casualties from direct hits on slit trenches.[82] During February the German artillery was reinforced by the arrival of two Krupp K5 railway guns, dubbed 'Robert' and 'Leopold' by their German detachments, but known as 'Anzio Annie' and the 'Anzio Express' to those in the beachhead. The K5s, with a calibre of 283mm (11.1 inches), fired a 243-kilo (536lb) round forty miles (64km).

While 1st London Irish rested, General Sir Harold Alexander, commanding Allied Armies in Italy, visited the beachhead and the battalion, congratulating all ranks 'on their fine fight during a very critical period of the battle'. Both Alex's visit and the chance to rest boosted morale. At much the same time, the remainder of 56th (London) Division arrived and 168 Brigade reverted to 56th from 1st Division and became the Black Cats' reserve brigade.[83] Major General Templer and some of his HQ staff arrived on the 12th with 167 Brigade arriving next day and 169 Brigade on the 19th.

Meanwhile, Allied attacks had been launched on Carroceto, the Factory and Buonriposa Ridge but the Germans remained in possession, although the Factory changed ownership on two occasions. On the 15th, the day of Alex's visit, five days had passed since a German attack, thus allowing VI Corps to be reinforced and re-organize its dispositions. Alexander's visit confirmed his belief that Lucas should be relieved and Clark, claiming that he 'had for some time been considering a change' did so.[84] Truscott, commanding 3rd Division, would be the new corps commander with Lucas moving to Fifth Army HQ. The handover was to take place on the 16th, but events delayed it until the 22nd.

Of course, the lull had also allowed the Germans to re-organize, as confirmed by aerial reconnaissance and reports from various sources, including German prisoners who assured their captors that a major attack was planned: Operation FISCHFANG (Catch Fish).

H Hour for FISCHFANG was 0630 on the 16th. Lucas remained at the helm of VI Corps as the Germans attacked, their first phase a three-divisional thrust with strong armour support. Objectives were the Fosso di Carrocetello, along which the corps defence line was established, and Padiglione woods, east of the main road. A successful attack would take the assaulting forces to Nettuno, cutting Allied forces in two.[85]

Although the attackers made some progress, reaction was strong and led to 168 Brigade returning to the fray, still under 1st Division operational command. The first deployment was changed rapidly to one of relieving 7th Oxfordshire and Buckinghamshire LI who were hard-pressed in the Buonriposa Ridge area but as the Rifles emerged from the cover of the 'wadis' they came under 'savage artillery, mortar, and small-arms' fire that caused many casualties and stopped their advance. Nonetheless, the battalion was ordered to continue and find the Oxford and Bucks. All efforts failed and, on the 18th, an exhausted Ian Good was ordered to rest by his brigade commander. Major Monty Stopford, the second-in-command, stepped up as acting CO. The search for the Oxford and Bucks continued but at heavy cost to the Rifles, with Captain John Strick and CSM Flavell among those killed. The remnants of the Oxford and Bucks HQ and of one company were located eventually. However, as the Rifles tried to extricate them, the Germans renewed their attack; two Tiger tanks penetrated to a point some 800 yards behind them but, fortunately, with ground impassable for tanks between Tigers and Rifles.

Such was the general situation that 'fitters, mechanics, electricians, drivers and transport maintenance men were thus called into the line. They dropped their spanners and seized their rifles. Even the staff of a mobile laundry had to prepare for action.'[86]

Penney, GOC 1st Division, was wounded and Templer took command of the entire British sector. The battle continued with the Germans pushing hard against the defences. It descended in some instances to hand-to-hand fighting as both sides fought for the Flyover and the road. By the 20th it seemed that the attackers had exhausted their energy, but fighting continued although the offensive was at a standstill.

Small raids, constant shelling, mortar and machine-gun fire continued harassing the Rifles, inflicting a seemingly-endless stream of casualties. Re-organization was needed and a reinforcement company, Y Company, under Major Corbally, arrived, its personnel from a variety of regiments. An attempt by Captain Ivor Crozier and men of C Company to clear Germans from the wadi ended in failure; none of the attackers was seen again. Still the Rifles persisted in efforts to relieve the Oxford and Bucks. Finally, an attack succeeded in doing just that. It required almost the entire battalion strength, then no greater than two companies, one being the combined survivors of the rifle companies and the other the HQ staff and drivers.[87]

Those who survived Anzio recalled the exhaustion they endured in the beachhead. The experience of Rifleman Eddie Cassidy, who had enlisted in the Royal Inniskilling Fusiliers in his native Londonderry early in the war, provides some idea of what riflemen endured. One evening, Eddie and another rifleman were posted in a slit trench on his company's perimeter. They were to look out for any enemy and raise the alarm if they sighted Germans. Both were so exhausted that they fell asleep in the trench. Rifleman Cassidy remembered feeling something prodding his shoulder and opened his eyes. He could scarcely believe what he saw: a German soldier was looking down into the trench and the muzzle of his rifle was doing the prodding. Seeing Eddie open his eyes, the German signalled to him that he should awaken the other soldier and that both should climb out. Groggily, both men did so, to be marched off by a German patrol. En route, Eddie noticed how clean the Germans' boots and trousers were and wondered at their turnout; he later discovered that they were from a unit that had arrived the previous day. Both riflemen spent the remainder of the war in prison camps.[88]

At the beginning of March, the battalion was engaged in two company attacks, both of which were stopped by heavy fire with D Company reduced to fifteen men. Next morning, with supporting fire from a commando troop, and about twenty fit men, Captain Mervyn Bonham-Carter led it in another attack. Bonham-Carter, although wounded in the thigh by machine-gun fire, rose to his feet and continued, silencing the first MG post with a Tommy gun. He then collapsed across the gun. His courage and self-sacrifice proved inspirational as his small party overcame the German resistance. Although taken back to the dressing station, Captain Bonham-Carter died from his wounds. The survivors of the company had taken their objective, killed some thirty Germans, captured a similar number and rescued fifteen Royal Fusiliers taken prisoner earlier. D Company, despite its reduced strength, had played a critical part in preventing a German breakthrough 'and thus had a great bearing in keeping the beachhead intact'.[89]

During the battle, Lieutenant Colonel Baucher had arrived to assume command, relieving Monty Stopford who 'despite ill-health and the terrific strain of the Anzio battles had done yeoman service' as Ian Good's second-in-command and then as CO. There was little doubt that the situation had been stabilized with the beachhead secure. For 1st London Irish, their time at Anzio was almost at an end. No further action occurred, although enemy shelling continued while two Sapper companies helped strengthen the ranks. With the arrival of 5th Division, including 2nd Royal Inniskilling Fusiliers, 56th Division was withdrawn. On 11 March 1st London Irish embarked for Pozzuoli after almost six weeks in Anzio. The Rifles had sustained 582 killed, wounded or missing. The battalion that embarked for Naples numbered only 312 all ranks, many recently returned from hospital.[90]

* * *

While 1st Irish Guards and 1st London Irish fought in the Anzio beachhead, John Logue's daily routine continued. High above the ground in his DUKW, he was exposed to everything the enemy could launch into 'Hell's Half Acre', as many called the beachhead. The DUKW offered no protection to its driver, or anyone aboard. Since even the field hospital suffered from enemy fire, casualties were evacuated to Naples as soon as practicable.

On 9 March, John Logue had finished his shift and parked his DUKW. Usually, another driver would take over but, on that day, the relief driver pointed out that one tyre was punctured. Driver Logue assisted in the repair but

> as I climbed up the ribs on the side of the DUKW a shell burst above me and something hit me in the leg. I just dropped down … an ambulance arrived and I was put on a stretcher and was slid into the ambulance, just like sliding a drawer into one of the old bread vans. … there I was lying with my head up towards the driver's cab when the ambulance was hit by a shell. It landed at the front and the next thing we knew the vehicle was on fire. I thought to myself, 'Paddy, this is it', for the driver was on his own and he was running round the back … screaming for help; but there were three of us inside who couldn't even help ourselves, let alone him.

Fortunately, others came to the driver's aid. With their help he rescued his patients. John Logue and the other wounded were taken to the field hospital before being evacuated to Naples. While in the hospital, it was hit by German shellfire, convincing John that Hitler was out to get him. Eventually he was placed on a hospital ship for Naples.

> On the way down … one of the nurses … turned me on my side and told me to look out of the porthole. There was Vesuvius blowing its top [and] all this smoke and flame and ash flying everywhere. I can tell you that I was certain that somebody was out to get me and if it wasn't Hitler, then it was a great big volcano.

The volcano had shown signs of activity before but, on 17 March, lava poured down its western slopes towards Naples. That suggests that John Logue's hospital ship reached Naples shortly afterwards. His journey was not to end there: he was flown to North Africa for treatment and convalescence and would return to Anzio in time for the breakout from the beachhead.[91]

* * *

On the day Vesuvius began spewing lava, Peter Vincent Donaghy from Moy, County Tyrone, a lance corporal in the Corps of Military Police, was with

5th Division Provost Company at Anzio; the handover from 56th (London) Division had been completed by the 15th. Formerly a Royal Inniskilling Fusilier, Lance Corporal Donaghy was resting on the early morning of Saint Patrick's Day when German bombers attacked. One bomb hit a carrier loaded with mortar rounds, quickly setting the vehicle alight and posing a major danger to personnel and vehicles nearby.

So fierce were the flames that they threatened to detonate the bombs. Donaghy dashed from the safety of his dugout to the carrier and began throwing its cargo clear. By then, the rounds were hot to the touch; some had begun to explode and Luftwaffe aircraft were still dropping bombs. Ignoring the immediate danger, Lance Corporal Donaghy continued, despite a leg wound from an exploding bomb. Only a serious back injury made him desist from his efforts. Other personnel brought the conflagration under control but Donaghy's immediate reaction and courage had saved many of his comrades from death or injury, as well as saving vehicles. He survived his injuries and was awarded the MM.[92]

* * *

With 56th (London) Division withdrawn from the beachhead, the Irish infantry banner passed to 2nd Royal Inniskilling Fusiliers who arrived with the relief formation, 5th Division. The Inniskillings' historian noted the battalion arrived 'at a period of trench warfare' with the situation in March being one

> of two entrenched armies facing one another, with a no man's land, narrow and occasionally fluctuating, between. Hostilities ranged from patrol work to full-stage attacks on both sides. Perhaps because of the repute the Inniskillings had won in patrols and assaults, they had been directed to this quarter.[93]

On 12 March the convoy carrying 2nd Inniskillings arrived off Anzio and began disembarking. The war diary noted that it rained heavily for most of the day, a foretaste of conditions to come.

That the Luftwaffe could still pose a threat was shown on the 14th when nine fighters attacked La Cogna to be dispersed speedily by anti-aircraft fire. Further air attacks included strafing the Lateral Road on 7 April, which was met by fire from D Company's Brens; it was claimed that one intruder had been hit on the tail. In another attack, on 21 April, seven aircraft were claimed as shot down.

Greater threats were posed by artillery, mortar and machine-gun fire, B Company suffering seven casualties from shellfire on 16 March. Six days later, A Company's area was shelled heavily, killing two and wounding four. That day also saw the company capture two Germans from a group laying mines in front of their forward positions. On 7 April, at La Cogna, A Company suffered one death and five injuries from mortar fire. However, the Lumps, as with all of 5th Division, had excellent artillery support which could put down retaliatory fire on enemy guns and mortars. An example of that came on the 7th when an AOP (Air Observation Post) directed 155mm fire on enemy positions, scattering the Germans. A USAAF officer, Lieutenant Rogers, a B-26 Marauder pilot, was attached to the battalion on liaison duties for twenty-four hours that day.[94]

On 21 March the battalion moved to the Fortress area, relieving 1st Cameronians, also of 13 Brigade. The 'Fortress' was described as 'the most famous of all the areas to be held and one that epitomized the performance of the Division'.[95] With mud and rain prevailing, it resembled what an earlier generation had experienced in Flanders. Bobby Scott wrote of the 'cynically named' sector:

> our forward trenches were positively within talking distance of the enemy, cold comfort when the other side had better observation and tactical freedom ... the occupants of our positions asked that they should not be visited as it was impossible for a newcomer to avoid tripping over empty tins and the clatter inevitably brought mortar fire.[96]

Fox suggests that 'Fortress' was intended facetiously, since the area was largely underground with shelters from shells, mortars and aerial bombs. However, the forward trenches were mud-filled, those manning them sheltering in 'fox holes' during the day. Facing the battalion were paratroopers of 4th Fallschirmjäger Division – hardened in combat and, therefore, tough opponents, 'but not quite tough enough and soon outclassed in patrol exploits'. The area was 'the grimmest sector of them all', consisting of 'a winding wadi full of shell holes, mines, splintered tree trunks and wired bushes, surrounded by banks'.[97] It also included a feature known as the 'Cutting'.

On 26 March, in daylight, Fallschirmjäger attempted to evict C Company but met a response much doughtier than anticipated from Captain John Duane MC's men. The German tactic was a three-wave attack, the first by grenadiers, whose grenades were intended to force the defenders to ground, the second using automatic weapons to pin down the Lumps while the third was to mop up any survivors. However, Duane was aware of the procedure and so met the first wave, the grenadiers, with grenades, Bren and rifle fire, stopping them completely. C Company did not go to ground 'but open[ed] fire and thr[e]w grenades back, thus making it impossible' for the second and third attacks to develop.[98] The onslaught was broken up – surely a case of the engineer hoist with his own petard?

The Inniskillings would also serve in the Coastal Sector and the 'Lobster Claw'. Each had its own particular problems although the former was more comfortable with better trenches and offered better opportunities for snipers to harass enemy positions; the rifle companies vied with each other to the extent that scoreboards were set up to record their competition. The sector was 'a tongue of dune where the Moletta river swung into the sea' and was flat with no cover 'right across to the lines of poplars indicating the coastal road that ran back from S. Lorenzo to Anzio'.[99] No man's land came under the Lumps' oversight. The main danger came from three minefields – one each laid by British, American and German personnel – which patrols had to negotiate carefully as they sought to attack German posts.[100]

In one period of twenty-four nights, B Company sent out twenty-one patrols, an average that set the standard for the battalion.

> The reputation, from the Higher Command, for patrolling had to be kept up. It was, however, the fortune of war that, whenever a really special effort was organized, the results were disappointing: best bags came from the routine affairs when a patrol went out determined on bringing in some birds. C Company arranged one big affair with artillery support, reached the German advanced trench, but the enemy scurried back so quickly that not a prisoner was taken, only a considerable amount of small arms.[101]

There were few reprisal raids; the Germans were never especially keen on nocturnal operations. However, there were some exceptions, as on the night a strong German patrol attacked C Company. A Company went to C's aid and, after a severe mauling, the attackers withdrew. Fox noted that the battalion suffered but fifty-seven casualties during its spell in the Coastal Sector.[102]

The Lobster Claw, so called from its shape on the map, was the third sector in which the battalion did duty. A 'form of wadi' immediately south-east of the Fortress, tapering off to the Lateral Road before that artery entered 1st Division's front close to the Flyover, the trench system, resembling First World War defences, outshone that in the Fortress.

> Conditions were much the same, with even more evidence of death, buried and unburied. There was a gap of about 200 yards between the two areas covering a convex slope ... swept by [machine-gun] fire of deadly accuracy. This area had to be covered nightly by the porters who brought up ammunition, food and water .... [103]

Supporting that comment, Fox identified supply as the chief difficulty in the Lobster Claw, numbering the porters at about sixty. Although the entrenchments were reasonable, constant artillery fire and continued Luftwaffe bombing caused casualties.[104]

Casualties also resulted from patrol clashes. On one such Captain Jock Crawford MC GM lost his life just forward of C Company's positions.[105] He was killed on 18 May at the age of 22 by stepping on an unexploded mortar round.[106]

> He was gallant, unfearing and full of the spirit of the old 'buccaneers'. In the words of a contemporary officer in the Battalion, 'He was the nearest living person to Leslie Charteris's "Saint" we had ever met'. His grandfather and father had commanded battalions in the Regiment, his father being in command of the 1st Battalion at the action [at] Fontaine-les-Clercs, St Quentin, in March 1918.[107]

Bobby Scott felt that Jock Crawford's death 'filled the whole battalion with sorrow and a sense of loss'. He described the background to the loss: Brigade HQ had asked the battalion to ascertain whether a small salient facing 2nd Inniskillings was still in German hands.

> Jock Crawford was chosen for this task and I briefed him myself. I told him the terms of reference, a simple yes or no, and ordered him in no circumstances to get involved in a scrap – just get the information and come straight back. He led his patrol out on a well-beaten track used continuously by patrols but before he had left the vicinity of our lines he trod on an unexploded mortar shell which exploded and killed him. ... He was a most upright and gallant officer and a lovable friend to all who knew him.[108]

Before the deployment to Anzio, the Lumps' commanding officer, Pat O'Brien-Twohig, had been hospitalized. His intended successor was Lieutenant Colonel R.W.H. 'Bobby' Scott who joined the battalion in the beachhead 'after a frustrating period of disablement over more than a year'. He wrote that his posting was as second-in-command to Pat O'Brien-Twohig and that his arrival at Anzio was a 'bit of an embarrassment' since Peter Slane, a pupil of Bobby Scott at Sandhurst in 1939, had assumed command.

> Luckily, 5th Divisional Commander [Major General Philip Gregson-Ellis] and I were old friends and I had no difficulty in assuring him that I was perfectly happy to be 2 i/c to Peter and get a chance of learning what was going on. This was indeed necessary as the German stranglehold on the beachhead had imposed upon us a form of trench warfare long ago forgotten in infantry training.[109]

The 'Cutting', already referred to, was between the Fortress and the Coastal sectors in country more open than the inland wadis with the command post (CP) in the embankment of the circular road marking the forward limit for wheeled vehicles. The Inniskillings were to relieve 1st King's Own Yorkshire LI of 15 Brigade, commanded by Lieutenant Colonel Charlie St Clair-Forde. Scott, who was to lead the advance party to conduct the handover, was unimpressed by the 'new quarters'.

> The dry weather had arrived and there was dust everywhere, the dugouts were cramped and, being on the road, there was little privacy. I unburdened my thoughts to Charlie but got the answer I might have expected from one whose thoughts were rivetted on a hot bath and a jar of Egyptian rum: 'It's not too bad when you get used to it – and anyway it's SAFE.' Twenty minutes after he had left, a mortar shell landed exactly on top of the Cutting, killing a sentry, wrecking the Command Post, and reducing the evening meal to muddy refuse.[110]

The problem of malaria, encountered in Sicily, manifested itself again as the weather improved. Among the boasts of Mussolini's government was that it had cleared the Pontine marshes with a well-planned drainage system that allowed the area to be settled. However, the Germans had flooded that reclaimed ground, thus reviving the menace of the Anopheles Mosquito, a principal vector of the malaria-causing Plasmodium parasite. This led to anti-malaria precautions being taken by the Allies and a peculiar role for Bobby Scott, 'that of puddle inspector'. Because of the outbreak of malaria,

> foul-tasting tablets had to be taken twice a day by order as a preventative and neglect to do so was punishable as a crime. Furthermore, as the mosquito can breed only in stagnant water, all puddles left over from

> the rainy season had to be covered with oil. Companies were responsible for the anointment of their areas and it fell to me to see that they did it properly.[111]

The battalion's time in the beachhead ended with the Allied breakout which involved the Inniskillings, to which we shall return. Before that, a three-day training programme began on 23 May, including route marches, assault course and mining and wiring; personnel also had the opportunity to bathe. Next day, A Company was disbanded and, on the 25th, the battalion moved to the Fortress.[112] Meanwhile, 38 (Irish) Brigade had taken part in the final battle of Monte Cassino.

Chapter 5

The Road to Cassino

We left 38 (Irish) Brigade with 78th Division being relieved by 1st Canadian Division on 7 December 1943. Cyril Ray, the division's historian, recorded that 'Morale was still good, but the Division was thoroughly tired, and the intention now was that it should have a month of rest, re-organization, and training'. That month was to be spent at Campobasso, a rest-and-training centre in southern Italy's central mountainous area, well removed from the front. A peacetime holiday resort, its amenities included cinemas, an ENSA* theatre and officers' and NCOs' clubs.[1] For the Battleaxe Division, leaving the front also meant saying farewell to Major General Vyvyan Evelegh, whose departure was a sad blow: he was regarded highly, especially for his tactical flair and 'uncanny knack of seeing the weakest point in the enemy defence and going for it'. Fortunately, his successor was of the same calibre: Major General Charles Keightley, commissioned in 5th Dragoon Guards, later 5th Royal Inniskilling Dragoon Guards, had commanded 6th Armoured Division in Tunisia.[2]

The Battleaxe Division's soldiers would have been surprised had the 'promise' of a month's rest worked out for everyone. Before long 11 Brigade and 132nd Field Regiment were deployed to the Sangro area while, on the 22nd, 6th Inniskillings were sent to Capracotta. Overall, however, most enjoyed Christmas, even if Christmas dinner was a day late for some. Nelson Russell visited both Faughs' and Rifles' messes and company dining rooms, speaking with many soldiers before returning to Brigade HQ for his own meal. Jimmy Stewart, his brigade major and an Argyll, who accompanied Russell on his visits, later spoke eloquently about the 'large and happy family' of the Irish Brigade, an impression possibly enhanced by the generous liquid hospitality received during the day. Nelson Russell had chosen to avoid the danger such hospitality might pose to the dignity and sobriety of a brigade commander by ensuring that he limited his visit to the Faughs to one company dining room

* Entertainments National Service Association.

and the Sergeants' Mess.[3] Nonetheless, he enjoyed his visits, writing that he felt at home with each battalion.

> But there is a special well-known room in this good home – which is owned by the Faughs. It is furnished with old familiar things – all tried, tested, reliable and comfy. It is in this room I really sit back and loosen the waistcoat button. I am not particularly ashamed about this – my feet have helped to wear its carpet for nearly thirty years.[4]

For 6th Inniskillings, the day was spent at Capracotta, overlooking the Sangro's upper reaches, in company with Chavasse's Light Horse, 56 Recce. Other neighbours included a French colonial regiment and a Polish Carpathian unit. Not until mid-January would the Inniskillings return to the Irish Brigade fold.

On 27 December most of the brigade began the journey back to the line, not to the coastal sector where it had fought previously, but to the spine of Italy: it would take over a twelve-mile front from Castel di Sangro to San Vincenzo. The loosely-defined front was much too long for two battalions. Following a reconnaissance, Russell made some adjustments but had to accept that the positions were planned jumping-off points for a renewed advance; since matters were not promising on either army front, an early advance was unlikely. They were also under close observation from German positions some 1,500 feet higher.

The Germans were not the only foe. During the handover snow began falling. By the evening of New Year's Eve a blizzard was raging, reputedly the worst for thirty years. Caught in it were three companies of Faughs who stoically marched on to their new positions where the resident companies chose to remain rather than brave the blizzard. On the afternoon of 1 January, the blizzard began easing but the next few days were spent clearing snow to allow re-supply by mule train; the stranded companies made their way out to rejoin their own battalion.[5]

In spite of the conditions, there was still action, albeit on a reduced scale and, as the weather improved, active offensive patrolling resumed. The Rifles were especially busy and Major Desmond Woods of H Company provided his soldiers with suitable camouflage before deploying. White sheets were commandeered, riflemen became tailors, snow smocks were fashioned and weapons bound with white cloth. The Germans were also active. E Company suffered a surprise attack on 19 January, during which five soldiers were killed, fifteen wounded and most of 7 Platoon captured. However, a brisk counter-attack, organized and led by Major Mervyn Davies, saw off the Germans. Five of 7 Platoon, including its commander, were rescued.[6]

That incident sparked off a period of considerable activity as both Faughs and Rifles took the battle to the Germans around Castel di Sangro, the road junction known as the Bifurcation and the hills above Montenero. Sixth Inniskillings had returned to the fold but were placed in reserve. The battalion had suffered during its isolation alongside 56 Recce at Capracotta, although food had not been in short supply, some being air-dropped and some being found in deserted houses. A patrol that left on 31 December was lost in the blizzard and rescue parties on skis searched for them. Among five men found alive were Fusilier Henry 'Darkey' Elwood from Belfast and Fusilier Hanlon from Dublin although Hanlon had to have his legs amputated. The body of Sergeant Thomas 'Paddy' Sullivan from Glengariff, County Cork was later discovered by a civilian. Originally a Faugh, Paddy Sullivan, the patrol commander, had crawled nearly two miles before succumbing.[7]

Kendal Chavasse visited his squadrons of 56th Reconnaissance Regiment on skis after some instruction from Tony Michell MC, an expert skier. 'We acquired skis from the local inhabitants. We had only one officer who had even skied before – Tony Michell – and he trained a number of men.' Patrolling continued and over greater distances. On his visits he noted that 'I usually ended on my bottom when skiing downhill!'[8]

Reports were received of 'ghostly hooded figures' in a village priest's home; an American unit 'reported the loss of a perfectly good sentry not far away' and 'strangely coloured parachutes' were 'seen' near the Sangro. Those 'occurrences' were noted in an intelligence summary from 38 Brigade HQ on 8 January.[9] While there was intended humour in that summary, there had been none in an incident on the 4th with a patrol of strange soldiers 'acting suspiciously' in the Faughs' area. They were engaged, with one killed and another wounded, before it was discovered they were Belgians from the Belgian Troop of 10 Commando.[10] Other instances of 'friendly fire' beset 6th Inniskillings whose B Echelon was attacked twice by Allied aircraft, first by RAF Curtiss Kittyhawks and, two hours later, by USAAF Lockheed P-38 Lightnings.

What appeared to higher command to be a quiet time was described by Brigadier Russell as anything but: he believed he had had more leisure time on the Sangro.[11] However, Keightley was aware of the problems his new command faced and had 78th Division relieved to undertake training before any further offensive. At the beginning of February, it was relieved by 3rd Carpathian Division.

The division's new 'home' was near Capua, in Fifth Army reserve, with the Irish Brigade near Caserta in villages scarred by war with 'little comfort in the wet, muddy and miserable conditions'.[12] There Nelson Russell took ill and was sent to hospital. His active war was over. Although he considered his collapse inexplicable, it was anything but. The 46-year-old

> had led his Brigade from its arrival in North Africa through the mountains of Tunisia, across the sea to Sicily and the brisk but bitter campaign there, and then on to Italy with a series of actions in a very short period before the move into the 'quiet sector' in the high Apennines. He had always shared the risks with his men; he had done his utmost to ensure that they had the maximum support available ... to minimize casualties; he had come close to death himself more than once and, of course, he had borne the burden of command. Small wonder that he had burned himself out for he had never spared himself.[13]

On 18 February the Lisburn man took leave of his beloved Brigade with a special order of the day:

> The time has come when I say farewell to the Brigade.
>
> We have fought many battles together during three campaigns and it will always be my proud memory to have had the honour and the privilege of Commanding this fine Brigade – to my mind the best Brigade in the Army.
>
> My successor is well known to you all. In his sure hands you will certainly maintain your great reputation.
>
> I wish all ranks 'good luck' and 'good fortune' in the battles still to come.
>
> I also thank you for everything you have done in fifteen months' hard fighting.
>
> 'Everything' means a great deal.[14]

Pat Scott was Nelson Russell's successor as chieftain of the Irish Brigade and was well known to its officers and men, having commanded both 1st Royal Irish Fusiliers and 2nd London Irish Rifles. He had even commanded the brigade before – in Tunisia when Nelson Russell was appointed GOC of the ad hoc Y Division. Himself an Irish Fusilier, he was steeped in the Faughs' ethos and his father had been Colonel of the Regiment. An outstanding soldier, he was a formidable individual who commanded respect and admiration and never suffered fools gladly, irrespective of whether the perceived 'fool' was a subaltern or a general. He immediately set about a dedicated training regime, determined to create a very high overall standard of individual training in weapon handling and increase standards of platoon and section leading, which he considered 'likely to prove the decisive factor in battles in this sector'. COs were to organize training to improve, by day or night, individual weapon handling, individual use of ground, and platoon and section leading. The subsequent weeks were packed with a training programme that included co-operation with tanks and river-crossing in assault boats.[15]

In the best traditions of the regiments of the Irish Brigade, there was also time for celebration. With the training taking place in March, there had to be a celebration of Saint Patrick's Day on the 17th, as well as, in the case of the Faughs, Barrosa Day on the 5th. Barrosa Day was marked in the traditional way as the Faughs remembered the battle in 1811 when their predecessors of the 2nd/87th (Prince of Wales's) Irish Regiment of Foot captured the first of Napoleon's prized Eagle standards to be taken in battle by a British regiment. The ancient Gaelic battle cry of 'Fag an bealach', shouted by the soldiers as they charged the French positions was later adopted as the regimental motto, partially anglicized, or 'phoneticized', as 'Faugh a Ballagh'.

The Saint Patrick's Day celebrations deserve extended mention. Keightley's division was about to move but Pat Scott had extracted an agreement that, barring dire calamity, 38 (Irish) Brigade would not be ordered to move until late on the 18th. That agreement was not disclosed to the soldiery lest they decided to extend their orgy of drinking. The Inniskillings began celebrating on the eve of the saint's day with parties in officers' and sergeants' messes. When twenty-eight RASC personnel arrived with vehicles for the battalion's planned move they were invited to join the fun and celebrated enthusiastically. The war diary records that Saint Patrick's Day greetings were sent to HM King George VI; HRH the Duke of Gloucester, Colonel-in-Chief of the Inniskillings; both primates of all-Ireland; the Irish taoiseach (prime minister), Eamon de Valera; several generals, including Sir Claude Auchinleck, Colonel of the Regiment; and the other Inniskilling battalions. A later note indicated that the King had expressed appreciation for the greetings but de Valera's reaction is not recorded. According to the war diary, the day was 'celebrated in something more than the traditional style', with everyone quite certain that they had 'never enjoyed themselves so much for such a long time'. Traditional religious observances, parades and sports activities occupied the 17th for the brigade group.[16]

No calamity required a short-notice move and so, on the 22nd, the Irish Brigade set off to join the New Zealand Corps in Fifth Army. Before long the brigade was in the shadow of Monte Cassino.

As already noted, Fifth Army had attacked the Gustav Line, anchored on Monte Cassino, in January with 2nd Inniskillings and 1st London Irish Rifles involved. The former made the first break in that line. However, the overall attack had failed and the co-ordinated Allied landing at Anzio had resolved into stalemate. With the extemporized New Zealand Corps, of 2nd New Zealand and 4th Indian Divisions, under Lieutenant General Sir Bernard Freyberg VC, Mark Clark renewed the attack following the bombing of the ancient Benedictine monastery atop the mountain. That attack, with Indian units on the mountain and New Zealanders in the town below, also ended in stalemate. It was then that 78th Division was placed under Freyberg's command. A further attack by the New Zealand Corps was planned for mid-March, preceded by aerial bombing of Cassino town. Although 11 Brigade joined the New Zealand Corps, 78th Division had not deployed in full since no breakthrough had occurred. It returned to XIII Corps to occupy a sector from Cassino railway station to Monte Cairo in the heights overlooking the monastery. Before that, however, the Irish Brigade relieved 11 Brigade near Sant'Angelo in Theodice for five unpleasant days during which German mortars bombarded their positions. However, those bombs were reciprocated with a counter-mortar programme that returned about fifty rounds for every one the Germans unleashed. Patrolling was also difficult due to unmarked minefields. Even 6th Inniskillings' reserve positions were not safe. On 24 March at 1515 a German shell landed on D Company's latrine. The war diary notes wryly that 'luckily nobody was there at the time'.[17]

Following those five days, the brigade prepared to relieve French troops in the mountains. The reconnaissance for the handover involved two officers meeting a French officer at an arranged rendezvous 'before driving like madmen … along a road that was being shelled …'. When Pat Scott went to meet General Monsabert, commanding the sector, he enjoyed an excellent meal before moving to the general's observation post. From the OP,

> the whole war lay beneath us with the exception of Mount Cairo, which towered above from the other side of the Rapido Valley. There was the Monastery some hundreds of feet below. This was the only chance I had of looking down at it, except a long time afterwards from an aeroplane. In that clear, concise, logical way the French have, General Monsabert explained the ground, the positions of his own troops and the Germans. We were some distance away but it was the most comprehensive view I have ever had of that battlefield. … It had been a most interesting and amusing day, but the prospect of sitting on those hills didn't appeal to me at all.[18]

The handover took four days to complete since only one battalion could move each day with part of the journey under cover of darkness. Brigade HQ occupied a house, previously used by the French, on the edge of Caira. With space limited – the upper storey had been destroyed – staff numbers were kept to a minimum. The Inniskillings, commanded by Lieutenant Colonel H.E.N. 'Bala' Bredin, from a Longford family, were closest to the Germans and the Monastery. Their positions overlooked one of the German re-supply lines from Villa Santa Lucia. Bredin considered it an 'extraordinary position'. The Rifles, ensconced on Monte Castellone and the ridge dubbed 'Phantom Ridge', also enjoyed excellent observation of enemy lines while the Faughs held the valley from Caira up towards Monte Cairo with their battalion HQ the most shelled part of the sector after Brigade HQ. Caira village had an unwanted reputation as 'the most heavily shelled pinpoint in Italy'.[19]

Monte Cairo, from which German observers could direct artillery and mortar fire, loomed over the brigade positions. Movement in daylight invited a hail of mortar bombs or a salvo of artillery, thus restricting movement to the hours of darkness. It was impossible to dig in on the high ground which was 'like the mountains of the moon'. Instead, sangars were built from the rock that was plentiful and, since observers on Cairo could see those sangars, the occupants moved frequently so that the Germans were uncertain which were occupied. Re-supply took place at night when 'convoys which set out at dusk … really had a nightmare journey'. The transport assembled in an amphitheatre out of sight of German observers until dusk, then an MP would issue the order to 'move' and the drivers rushed off. On one section of road, 'everyone drove like people possessed in spite of the state of its surface; it very quickly received the soubriquet of "The Mad Mile"'. For those on the high ground the final stage of re-supply was by mule, the sturdy beasts making the final trek up to units such as 6th Inniskillings and Rifles. Mules were killed by mortar fire, machine-gun fire or falls from the narrow tracks. The terrain precluded burying them, adding the stench of decomposing flesh to the horrors of Cassino.[20]

Bala Bredin was aware that the French North African soldiers his battalion had relieved had carried out little patrolling but had suffered from active German patrolling. He decided that his battalion would take no nonsense and Inniskilling patrols were soon ambushing German patrols. Not only did they dominate the area below the ridge, they also made it impossible for the Germans to use one re-supply route from Villa Santa Lucia.[21]

Those weeks spent in the mountains were very trying for all concerned. One Kensingtons' officer wrote of the strain of 'sangar life' where the enemy dealt 'in generalized and wholesale death' and 'where throwing the contents of his lavatory tin out of the back of his sangar earned for many a man a hail of mortar bombs'.

> Just try sharing a rock hole about the size of two coffins with three others, then, in a prone position, lower your costume and fill a small tin held in the hand. The stink of excrement competed with the death smell on every position. Bowels will not wait for nightfall.[22]

Stoicism was evident throughout the brigade. When mortars, shells or rockets from the multi-barrelled Nebelwerfers showered down, stoicism met heroism, as on 6 April when Caira village was bombarded and 'every living soul in that heaving rubble lay flat and prayed' while one man 'walked calmly among the shell bursts carrying a dying man in his arms to shelter'. That man was the Faughs' chaplain, Father Dan Kelleher, who earned the MC that day. The Kerry man, the Irish Brigade's Catholic padre, had been in the Faughs' HQ when the shelling began and

> raced to the village which was under very heavy shelling. He found the wounded men and assisted the stretcher bearers in their work, carrying wounded in his arms, at great personal risk, to the shelter of a ruined building.
>
> He comforted the badly wounded man and assisted the overworked stretcher bearers in applying bandages to their wounds.
>
> His cheerfulness and practical assistance undoubtedly saved the lives of two men and gave fresh proof of his unfailing devotion to duty.[23]

One officer later wrote that

> no one begrudged Father Dan Kelleher, The Kerryman, that MC and he probably got a ghostly pat on the shoulder from Old St Benedict himself, peering from Heaven to see what we were making of all his architecture.[24]

Jim Trousdell, who had recently joined the Faughs (his father had served in the regiment in the First World War and two brothers would also serve with Jim), wrote that

> Dan seemed to be quite fearless and once told me that dying did not worry him as it would indicate that he had done what was required of him on earth and therefore the Almighty had a use for him elsewhere.[25]

Those three weeks were long ones and worrying for all concerned. Pat Scott, whose HQ was possibly in greater danger than almost anywhere else in the brigade sector, was concerned about the safety of his soldiers but considered

Brigade HQ 'a good place to be away from'. While HQ staff were expected to visit battalion locations, Scott was still recovering from a broken ankle which had not mended fully. He could, however, reach the Inniskillings' HQ by jeep, even during the day, although it was an uncomfortable journey on a route overlooked by Germans on Monte Cifalco. Later he could walk to visit the Faughs. Visiting the Rifles proved impossible.[26]

When the Irish Brigade's time in the sector came to an end, it was relieved by the Polish 6 Lwowska Brigade. The three-day handover was difficult: getting the Poles to the correct places at the right times was far from easy, there being no common language. However, Captain Brian Clark, the Faughs' adjutant, could converse with his Polish counterpart in German.[27] All the while, the positions continued to be bombarded although a heavy smokescreen was laid down. Scott was last to leave. Racing down the valley in a jeep towing a trailer, he was amazed that no German shells hindered his progress.

The Irish Brigade would return to Cassino but, meanwhile, its units were bound for Formicola, about ten miles north of Caserta, moving 'from winter into instant spring; it was like waking from the dead'. Formicola lay in an attractive, almost idyllic, valley, 'surrounded by a maze of wild flowers and the spring blossom of unspoiled country'. The contrast with the Brigade's previous positions could not have been starker. For four days, the soldiers could recuperate before training for their next operation.[28]

That operation was DIADEM, the final battle of Cassino. An intensive programme, including river-crossing exercises, had been drawn up by Keightley's headquarters. Battalions exercised with armoured regiments: 26 Armoured Brigade of 6th Armoured Division, whose GOC was Evelegh, formerly of the Battleaxe Division. Two of 26 Armoured's regiments, 17th/21st Lancers and 2nd Lothians and Border Horse, were assigned to work with 4th Division, which would execute the assault crossing of the Gari river while the third regiment, 16th/5th Lancers, would work with 78th Division, each brigade having a Lancers' squadron assigned. It was a happy coincidence to have 16th/5th Lancers assigned to the division and to the Irish Brigade; they also provided a Sherman command tank for Brigadier Scott.[29] The regiment, created in 1922 by amalgamating 16th Lancers and 5th Royal Irish Lancers, retained some Irish distinctions: NCOs' chevrons bore an Irish harp. The Lancers included at least one Irish-born officer in their ranks, Major Robert Gill, squadron leader of B Squadron, who hailed from Naas in County Kildare, while Captain John de Burgh MC, also from Kildare, was attached to 16th/5th as an artillery FOO.

Training and exercises with 16th/5th Lancers were as intensive as anything in the Irish Brigade's experience. Already, the armoured units had trained with

4th Division which, with 8th Indian Division, was to lead XIII Corps' attack, including the assault crossing of the Gari.

> A series of set-piece attacks with the infantry were simulated so that the armour could work with all the battalions of the division. They practised attacking fixed enemy fortifications and close-fire support on specified targets. By the end of the period the two arms had an appreciation of each other's needs.[30]

From 4th Division, 16th/5th Lancers moved to train with 78th. Since the Battleaxe Division would be breaking out from the bridgehead created by the assault divisions, similar training was carried out with the infantry battalions to build co-operation and trust between armour and infantry, dismantling the distrust infantry had hitherto harboured for their armoured comrades. Although it is commonly believed that the battlegroup system was born during the Normandy campaign, this was its true origin in the British Army. Not only did Lancers and infantry work hard together, but they also relaxed and partied together, adding further to the dynamic of trust. In the words of one Faughs' officer, 'the bigger the party, the better the blind'.[31]

Keyed in with XIII Corps' assault was a second 'prong', provided by II Polish Corps, into the mountains from the jumping-off points the Polish brigades had taken over from 78th Division. However, the main thrust was that of XIII Corps. The Polish attack was a holding one, 'although not often mentioned as such'.[32]

The opportunity to relax was also available through leave camps; six days' leave was granted to each soldier at camps near Amalfi, Ravello and Maiori, although some Irish Brigade personnel went to a camp near Bari on the Adriatic. While Irish Brigade soldiers relaxed, final touches were being made to the plan for DIADEM with Eighth Army's part codenamed Operation HONKER. Eighth and Fifth Armies would be involved along a nineteen-mile front from Cassino to the Tyrrhenian Sea, the remainder of the front being held by light forces. A successful deception plan persuaded the Germans that I Canadian Corps planned a seaborne landing at Civitavecchia, close to Rome. German forces deployed to deal with such an eventuality, and possible airborne landings behind the Gustav Line. With German commanders also believing that the Allied attack would come later in the month, a number of senior officers were on leave when, on the night of 11 May, over 1,000 guns opened fire across the Allied front.[33]

Both 4th and 8th Divisions crossed against strong opposition, creating and expanding bridgeheads, although not as quickly as had been hoped. On the morning of Sunday 14 May, the Irish Brigade began moving into the lee of Monte Trocchio which for some hours that afternoon 'was a screaming madhouse' as German and Allied artillery duelled.[34] Bailey bridges had been erected over the Gari, several involving the efforts of Irish sappers of the Royal Engineers and their support units. Sergeant Grenville William Ford, of 1801 (Bailey) Platoon, RASC, from Limavady, County Londonderry, was responsible for vehicles carrying bridging equipment on the first two nights of HONKER. His role was to ensure equipment was delivered when and where the sappers needed it; thus, he needed to maintain close contact with the sapper officer responsible at the site of Amazon bridge. The area where the vehicles were concentrated was being shelled and mortared but Ford ignored the dangers and, on the night of 12/13 May, not only showed personal coolness but inspired his drivers and earned an immediate MM.

> His outstanding conduct under very difficult conditions and coolness during the operations undoubtedly contributed substantially to the successful completion of the Bridge, as failure to deliver the equipment would have prejudiced the whole operation.[35]

A further Irish connection with Amazon Bridge occurred when 586 Field Company was deployed to assist in its construction. The company commander, Major Colin Clark, later Sir Colin, 4th Viscount Dunlambert, was recommended for appointment as MBE for 'his great energy combined with the soundest Engineering knowledge and organizing ability, but that service award was amended to a gallantry award, the MC. Clark had been Mentioned in Despatches with 78th Division in April.[36]

With all the sappers' bulldozers knocked out, Amazon bridge was pushed into place by a Sherman of 17th/21st Lancers, C Squadron of which was the first armour to cross. A Squadron, under Major George Thomas Ponsonby MC from Kilkenny, then crossed to support 2/4th Hampshires attacking south along the Gari. The obstacle of the Piopetto stream threatened the tanks' progress, especially as two bridge-laying tanks had been disabled. But Ponsonby, with 'great initiative and dash' got A Squadron forward over an improvised ford 'and so continued to give the infantry battalion much needed support'. Subsequently, Major Ponsonby organized the salvage of a scissors bridge from a wrecked bridge-layer, the laying of which he oversaw in spite of shell and mortar fire.[37]

Probably the most senior Irish officer to die in the Cassino battles was Lieutenant Colonel Patrick Kirwan OBE, Royal Engineers, who lost his life on 9 May. From Ballycastle, County Antrim, he was serving with 8th Indian Division.[38]

* * *

The Irish Brigade was led across the Gari by 6th Inniskillings. Bala Bredin reported to Pat Scott that they had crossed without hindrance to join 16th/5th's Shermans but were only a few hundred yards from the river since the locality was under heavy fire. Meeting the bridgehead commander, Bredin asked where the forward posts might be, to be told by Brigadier Stephen Shoosmith, of 10 Brigade, that he, too, would like to know that. Shoosmith 'waving a hand airily in the direction of the firing said, "Your guess is as good as mine, old boy".'[39]

Because of the confused state of the bridgehead, it was decided the Inniskillings would attack in daylight on the 15th. The battalion had first to cross the Piopetto, which had to be bridged to allow the Shermans forward. That was done, but the first tank to attempt crossing bogged in mud on the near side, blocking the approach and requiring the sappers to build another. By 0400 both leading companies were on Massa de Vendittis but the two companies that passed through towards Massa Tamburrini were brought to a standstill by machine-gun fire. German tanks appeared but their crews were blinded by heavy fog; one Inniskilling platoon commander narrowly escaped being crushed by a panzer. At 0800 the sappers had the Piopetto bridged anew, allowing tanks to join the infantry. Tamburrini fell within thirty minutes to Inniskillings supported by Lancers' tanks. Plans were laid for the battalion's final objective, Point 86, which would secure the *Grafton* reporting line. Artillery support was provided at 1000 and Point 86 was in Inniskilling hands within minutes, although several Shermans were immobilized by mines. Positions were consolidated with B Company moving on to *Grafton*. In spite of a counter-attack, supported by artillery, the Inniskillings held firm.[40]

The Irish Rifles were to make the next bound, to the ridge between Casa Sinagoga and Colle Monache. In their concentration area, they suffered from enemy artillery fire, especially when the mist lifted. One shell exploded in the commanding officer's O Group, fatally injuring Ion Goff and John Loveday, Rifles' and Lancers' COs respectively. Others injured seriously included G Company's Major Geoffrey Phillips and Lieutenant Ken Lovatt, the signals officer; most of Lovatt's team became casualties. Bredin had been ordered to go back to the O Group and, having crawled a quarter mile, arrived at 'a very shaken O Group'. He was joined by Major John Horsfall, the Rifles' second in command, who assumed command. Shortly after, Pat Scott arrived.[41]

The Rifles' H Hour had been 1500 but was delayed to 1930 due to the shelling which had so brutally disrupted the O Group. In the interim, Keightley decided to move 2nd Lancashire Fusiliers of 11 Brigade up to the Rifles' flank, postponing H Hour to dawn next morning. It was further delayed to 0900 on the 16th since the Lancashires, arriving only at nightfall, required time to plan and reconnoitre.[42]

John Horsfall held an O Group at first light in a former German gun emplacement. He planned to advance with E Company on the left, H in the centre and G on the right with divisional artillery and corps medium guns in support. The objective, Casa Sinagoga, a cluster of farm buildings, was described by Horsfall as a 'hamlet'. Major Desmond Woods MC, commanding H Company, observed that the bombardment timing was so perfect that 'the reports of individual guns were lost in the avalanche of projectiles screaming over our positions'. The guns would 'step forward' at intervals during the advance, dwelling – pausing – for about ten minutes midway and the infantry were to 'lean into' the bombardment, ignoring the danger from rounds falling short.[43]

Nonetheless, German fire took a toll of the Rifles in the advance. In H Company, Lieutenant Michael Clark MC, commanding the right-hand platoon, was killed while Geoffrey Searles, commanding the left-hand platoon was injured and out of action.

> I will never forget the noise. ... I remember diving into a shell-hole and a chap ... landing on top of me and I said, 'Get up, we must go on.' There was no movement; he was dead – he had a bit of shrapnel through his neck. ... the barrage dwelt for ten minutes and we were able to get down to ground. One wondered would anybody be able to live under this barrage as far as the Germans were concerned but, by God, they could.[44]

Woods called forward his centre platoon to maintain the impetus but there were times when shelling was so intense that they had to lie down. By then they had some German prisoners and the supporting Shermans were nearby. Shells were landing in H Company and among the Shermans while mortars, Nebelwerfers and machine guns were also flaying the attackers. As the riflemen closed on Casa Sinagoga, German anti-tank guns engaged the Shermans, disabling some. As the infantry pushed towards Casa Sinagoga, the tanks had been crippled but a young NCO from County Monaghan, Corporal Jimmy Barnes, made an unforgettable intervention, leading his section in an attack on the gun that had been causing such havoc.

> One by one the men were cut down by machine-gun fire on their left flank until Corporal Barnes remained alone. He went on by himself and then he fell dead ... but by then the crew of the 88mm* had baled out and the tanks were able to get forward once more.[45]

Jimmy Barnes had lobbed a grenade at the gun, killing at least one of its detachment and prompting the remainder to flee. Desmond Woods wrote a recommendation for a posthumous Victoria Cross, but without success. Major Woods was awarded a Bar to the MC he had earned in Palestine in 1938 but always regretted that Jimmy Barnes never received a posthumous VC.[46]

Elsewhere, Major Mervyn Davies' E Company took Sinagoga wood, also suffering losses but nowhere near as severe as those of H. Among Davies's dead was 24-year-old Corporal Edward O'Reilly of Arva, County Cavan. Alongside Sergeant Eddie Mayo MM, a Londoner, Davies considered him one of the best men in the company. Tragically, both were killed not in the attack but in a subsequent Nebelwerfer stonk. E Company had also lost both forward platoon commanders. One of Davies' platoon commanders, Dubliner Desmond Fay, received the MC for his 'skilful leadership and personal conduct'. Not only did he take his objectives but, in the latter part of the attack, conducted a move that wiped out an anti-tank gun position and prompted other defenders to surrender.[47]

Twenty of the Rifles had been killed, eleven in the concentration area and nine in the attack while eighty had been wounded. In the battle's aftermath over 100 Germans were buried while 120 had been taken prisoner; nine tanks had been captured. Medical attention was given to the wounded and a German medical officer arrived to assist his Rifles' counterpart, as did some German stretcher-bearers. (It is worth noting that no Fallschirmjäger were among the dead or wounded, although a story, from a former German officer, has gained some credence in recent years that a small group of Fallschirmjäger were responsible for imposing significant delay on the Irish Brigade advance.)[48]

Some enemy attempts to counter-attack were repelled, including one by tanks penetrating between 2nd Lancashire Fusiliers and the Rifles towards G Company. That was rebuffed by a troop of 16th/5th Lancers, with one panzer destroyed and the others withdrawing. E and H Companies advanced for another half mile so that the entire Colle Monache ridge was in Rifles' hands. Reporting line *Pytchley* was secure.

Fernie was the next reporting line, the advance to which was to be made by 1st Royal Irish Fusiliers. The Faughs moved to their concentration area that

* The gun was probably a 75mm, rather than an 88.

night. Having had a relatively quiet time thus far, with very little shelling and former German dug-outs as accommodation, the move actually took them out of the target area for a Luftwaffe raid on Brigade HQ, near which they had been located. There were only a few minor injuries from anti-personnel bombs.

On the morning of the 17th the Faughs attacked, supported by B Squadron 16th/5th Lancers. At much the same time, 2nd Lothians and Border Horse set off on the Irish Brigade's left front to strike through and beyond Piumarola. C and D Companies, commanded by Laurie Franklyn-Vaile and Jimmy Clarke MC respectively, led the Faughs' advance with Jack Phelan's A and Dickie Richards' B Companies ready for the next phase. Only in that phase were Fallschirmjäger encountered; the Faughs were showered by mortars and shells while machine guns lashed at them. Rounds were falling with deadly accuracy as far back as the start line. Less than fifteen minutes into the advance, Franklyn-Vaile was killed but C Company carried on.[49] Also dead was B Squadron's Major Robert Gill from Naas, County Kildare; the 27-year-old was killed by a mortar blast while climbing onto his Sherman.[50] Lieutenant Jim Trousdell, who had recently joined the battalion, noted that the only fatalities he could recall were the company commander and his runner. His memory of the advance was vivid.

> The noise was terrific. ... I found it difficult to keep up with the [artillery] due to various interruptions such as keeping in line with the troops on either side of us. The only Germans that I saw were two dead, killed by our shellfire on the objective. I recall coming up to a farmhouse and throwing a 36 grenade inside in case it was still occupied but the late inhabitants had left – in a hurry it appeared as a half-eaten breakfast was on the table.[51]

C and D Companies secured and consolidated their objectives within two hours and supporting arms had joined them. The adjutant, Captain Brian Clark, brought Tactical HQ forward and, later, the other two companies passed through to engage in a battle that lasted into the afternoon, although Clark was able to report to Brigade HQ that *Fernie* was secure. He was ordered to exploit the situation and D Company moved forward to do just that by consolidating a group of buildings close to Highway 6, Via Casalina. After dark, a patrol under Lieutenant Jimmy Baker harassed traffic on that road by calling down mortar fire.[52]

Meanwhile, A Squadron 17th/21st Lancers had continued supporting infantry but had switched to 78th Division's 5th Northamptons of 11 Brigade.

Throughout the period from the 14th to the 17th, Major Ponsonby had led the squadron 'with equal determination, skill and gallantry' in no fewer than three significant engagements. Then, on the 19th, his 'coolness and skill' ensured that contact was regained with 8th Argyll and Sutherland Highlanders of 36 Brigade in an attack at Aquino where confusion was caused by mist and 'very close and difficult country, infested by enemy infantry'. George Thomas Ponsonby was awarded a Bar to the MC he had earned at Kasserine Pass in Tunisia more than a year earlier. (One of his ancestors, General William Ponsonby, had served with Wellington at Waterloo and had been MP for Londonderry; another family member, the Right Reverend Richard, became Anglican bishop of Derry in 1831.)[53]

* * *

Irish Brigade HQ had been seeking accurate information on the whereabouts of 2nd Lothians. Pat Scott was told by their brigade commander that they were well beyond Piumarola. If so, their gains would have to be consolidated, and exploited by infantry. Keightley ordered the Irish Brigade to seize the ground overlooking Piumarola. Scott gave the task to 6th Inniskillings.

At much the same time as the Inniskillings received Scott's orders to seize three groups of buildings around Piumarola, Bredin's HQ became the focal point of a Nebelwerfer bombardment. His O Group proved an unforgettable experience, each paragraph of the plan punctuated by a salvo of rockets. The tactical situation was uncertain since the occupancy of Piumarola was unknown; there was only a *belief* that the Lothians were 'thereabouts' and that 6th Armoured Division's reconnaissance regiment, 1st Derbyshire Yeomanry, was en route to Aquino.[54]

In preparation for his attack, Bredin and the 16th/5th squadron leader moved to Masso Cerro to reconnoitre from the Faughs' position; he then ordered his battalion there. An armour/infantry patrol reported Piumarola in enemy hands with the Lothians some 600 yards away. From the Lothians it was learned that the village was held by a garrison with anti-tank guns, SP artillery and a Mark VI tank (actually a Mark IV). Before making his plan, Bredin moved to the Lothians' positions for a further recce. A and C Companies, supported by a tank squadron and a heavy artillery concentration, would make the main attack while D Company, supported by Lothians, struck northwards to seize buildings around Campolargo Lupitti.

The subsequent operation was 'a textbook example of tank/infantry attack' with A Squadron Lothians forcing the Panzer IV to take refuge in a wood where it was 'sealed off' while two troops supported an Inniskilling company to the village's northern end. There the tanks moved to the far side of Piumarola while the battalion and A Squadron 16th/5th provided supporting fire and a 200-gun artillery concentration was called down.

The Inniskillings endured thirty minutes of shelling and mortaring in their forming-up positions but at H Hour, 0545, 'the attack went in with an almost indecent haste'. Wounded in both legs on the start line, Bredin refused to be evacuated and insisted on advancing strapped to the bonnet of a jeep. Only when he passed out from loss of blood were his men able to evacuate him. His inspiring leadership was rewarded with the DSO to add to the MC and Bar he already held. Major John Kerr, a battalion signals' warrant officer only twenty months earlier, took command. Despite some delays, the attack succeeded and a steady stream of prisoners was soon coming back, mostly from 1st Fallschirmjäger Division: 'their appearance with hands up was unusual and heartening'. After a day of house-to-house fighting, the Inniskillings were consolidating on all their objectives. Preparations to repel a counter-attack were redundant: none materialized, the paratroopers having been caught unprepared.[55]

Having gone farther than intended, 6th Inniskillings had taken over 100 prisoners, three StuGs, several anti-tank guns and many small arms. They had suffered only four dead and thirty-one wounded, mostly en route to their start line. With the Inniskillings in full flow, Pat Scott ordered the Rifles to move forward, echeloned back on the Skins' left flank. E and H Companies did so without challenge, other than the shelling, but G was stalled by paras supported by some concealed tanks. The latter were dealt with by 16th/5th Lancers and 17th Field Regiment, allowing G Company to reach its destination with fifteen prisoners in their custody. In their advance the Rifles had lost twenty-five men, mostly from G Company.[56]

The Fallschirmjäger encountered at Piumarola had been withdrawn from the heights around Cassino. Those bounced by Bredin's Inniskillings were establishing defensive positions while those met by the Rifles were also getting away from Cassino. The mortaring on Highway 6 called down by Jimmy Baker's Faughs had hastened the German withdrawal to the Senger Barrier, the former Hitler Line. Monte Cassino had fallen and the Gustav Line smashed. Both Alexander and Leese, Eighth Army's commander, sent messages of congratulation to 78th Division which Keightley passed to the Irish Brigade with his own praise:

> As the leading Bde of the Division over the R [Gari] you set the pace of the advance of the Division, and from the high standard you set we never looked back.

> Each of your Bns has had its battle, and in each case the Bn objectives were gained and passed. This is a fine record and reflects the greatest possible credit on every officer and man who went through the battle.[57]

Passing Keightley's message to his brigade, Pat Scott commented that 'I cannot speak too highly of the magnificent spirit and fighting qualities shown by all of you during the first very difficult days of the advance that brought us here'. He added that Rome was the main objective and 'the Army knows that the Irish Brigade and all the magnificent fighters in its three famous battalions are certain to rise to any occasion'.[58]

The Irish Brigade had some action in the following days as the Poles fought for Piedimonte and 78th Division thrust towards Aquino. Casualties resulted from artillery rounds falling short and an almost farcical episode when 6th Black Watch attacked 6th Inniskillings, prompting a message from the latter's HQ to Pat Scott that they were 'being attacked by some "bare-arsed barbarians"'. The problem was resolved when Pat Scott's HQ redirected the Highlanders 'in the general direction in which they might expect to find Germans'. Scott commented that 'We have often fought the English, but seldom the Scottish, and I was glad not to have broken a good record in that respect'.[59] An attack on Aquino was planned but the Germans abandoned the town, as they did Piedimonte, while withdrawing to the Hitler Line.

General (later Field Marshal) Sir Harold Alexander (centre in peaked cap), commanding the Allied Armies in Italy, in Anzio, conferring with the newly appointed commander of VI US Corps, Major General Lucian K. Truscott. Although born in London, Alexander was Irish with family roots in the north-western counties of Donegal, Tyrone and Londonderry. (*IWM, NA14593*)

Lieutenant General Sir Richard McCreery (left), final commander of Eighth Army, with Brigadier Adrian Gore of 61 Brigade in Klagenfurt, Austria on 15 May 1945. McCreery's family roots were in County Tyrone while Gore had been born in Ireland to a Donegal family; much of his childhood was spent in Kildare. (*IWM, NA25148*)

Major General (later Field Marshal) Gerald Templer, GOC 56th (London) Division, with Lieutenant General Mark Clark, Fifth Army commander. Templer, with roots in County Armagh and the west of Ireland (a great-grandfather had commanded a Connaught Rangers battalion), seems to be looking sceptically at Clark; the American had very little experience compared to Templer. (*Royal Irish Fusiliers' Museum*)

Brigadier Pat Scott, commander of 38 (Irish) Brigade, leading belated St Patrick's Day celebrations in Forli on 29 March 1945. Having commanded both 1st Royal Irish Fusiliers and 2nd London Irish Rifles, he later succeeded Nelson Russell as commander of the Irish Brigade. Born in India, Scott's family roots were in County Fermanagh where he was buried in 1977. (*Royal Irish Fusiliers' Museum*)

Captain Billy Hanna, from Portadown, was killed in Sicily serving with 1st Royal Irish Fusiliers. Commissioned in the Royal Ulster Rifles, he fell during the battle for Centuripe while leading the advance of the Faughs' D Company. (*Author's photograph*)

Colonel Kendal Chavasse DSO* MiD was commissioned in the Royal Irish Fusiliers alongside Pat Scott in August 1924. From County Waterford, he commanded 56th Reconnaissance Regiment in Tunisia, Sicily and Italy. The only Recce officer awarded a Bar to the DSO, in the final months of the war, as a colonel on the staff of the British element of Fifth US Army, he was decorated by the US government. (*Royal Irish Fusiliers' Museum*)

Lieutenant Colonel Chavasse, fourth from left, with other officers and men of 56 Recce in Sicily in August 1943. (*56 Recce OCA*)

Operation HUSKY on 10 July 1943, saw the first use in Europe of the amphibious lorry known as the DUKW which made re-supply across beaches much more efficient. John Logue of the RASC, formerly a Royal Inniskilling Fusilier, drove DUKWs in Sicily, Salerno and Anzio and was twice wounded. (*Author's collection*)

At Termoli in October 1943, during Operation DEVON, the battle's outcome was decided by 38 (Irish) Brigade supported by tanks of 12th Canadian Armoured Regiment (Three Rivers Regiment). To show appreciation, Irish Brigade HQ presented a brigade pennant to their Canadian comrades. (*Libraries and Archives Canada*)

Having deployed as infantry in the Salerno beachhead, 9th (Londonderry) HAA Regiment moved to Torre Annunziata en route to Naples on 1 October 1943. A Matador gun tractor tows a 3.7-inch HAA gun. (*9th HAA Regiment Archive*)

Lieutenant Eveline McGrath, Queen Alexandra's Imperial Military Nursing Service, the QAs, was the first to recognize that casualties from the Luftwaffe bombing of Bari harbour on 3 December 1943 had suffered mustard-gas burns. The gas shells had been on the US Liberty ship SS *John Harvey*, but the US government had not informed the UK authorities of the cargo. (*Dr Paul Stewart*)

Two close friends from Naas, County Kildare, Michael 'Mickser' Mahon (left) and Jackie Sheridan, joined the Royal Sussex Regiment in 1941 and served in Italy during the Monte Cassino battles in 1944. Jackie Sheridan was killed on 20 March and is buried in Cassino War Cemetery. The inscription on his headstone reads: 'In loving memory of our dear son who died so gallantly. May he rest in peace.' (*James Durney*)

Overlooking the bombed ruins of Monte Cassino's monastery, Lieutenant Colonel Bala Bredin's 6th Royal Inniskilling Fusiliers spent most of April on 'Phantom' ridge. Although overlooked in turn by Germans on Monte Cairo, the Inniskillings' aggressive patrolling cut one of the German supply routes from Villa Santa Lucia. (*Author's collection*)

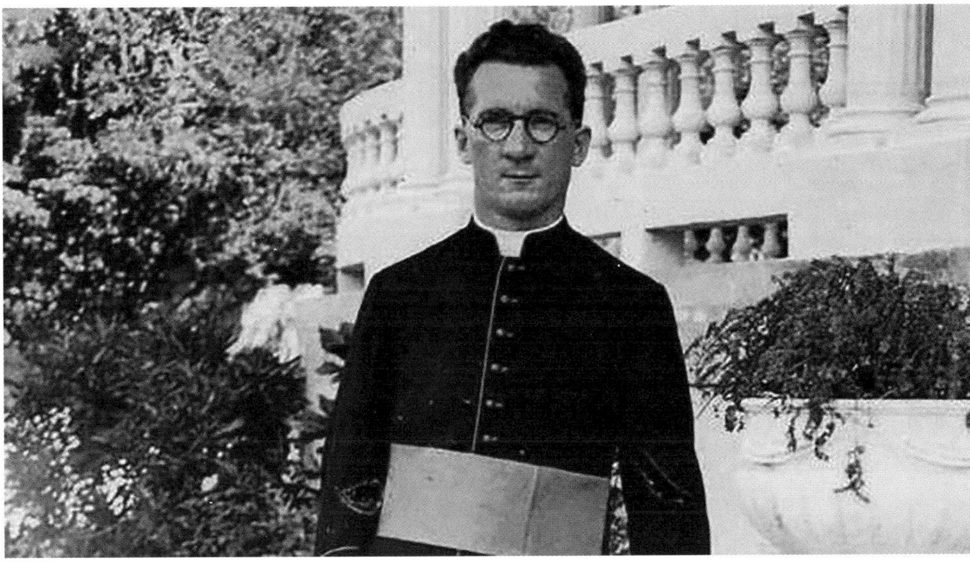

'The Scarlet Pimpernel of the Vatican', Monsignor Hugh O'Flaherty, played a major role in protecting Jews from the Germans and helping escaped Allied prisoners of war. The Kerry man was at the heart of an effective escape organization. (*Hugh O'Flaherty Memorial Society*)

Delia Murphy, the well-known singer and wife of the Irish minister to the Holy See, Dr Thomas Kiernan, was an invaluable ally to Monsignor O'Flaherty, as was her daughter Blanaid (Blon). (*Hugh O'Flaherty Memorial Society*)

Lieutenant Colonel Eugene 'Strick' Strickland, born in India of an Irish family, took command of the North Irish Horse on 3 May 1944. He was CO when the Horse supported the Canadian assault on the Hitler Line on 23 May and the regiment suffered its heaviest single-day casualties in two world wars. The Hitler Line was broken, and 'Strick' was appointed DSO for his skill, courage and leadership. (*Tim Strickland*)

On 12 June 1944, a Papal audience was held for Irish personnel. Watching in St Peter's Square are Brigadier Pat Scott DSO (left), Lieutenant Colonel 'Monty' Stopford who had commanded 1st London Irish at Anzio and Captain Brian Clark, adjutant of 1st Royal Irish Fusiliers. (*Royal Irish Fusiliers' Museum*)

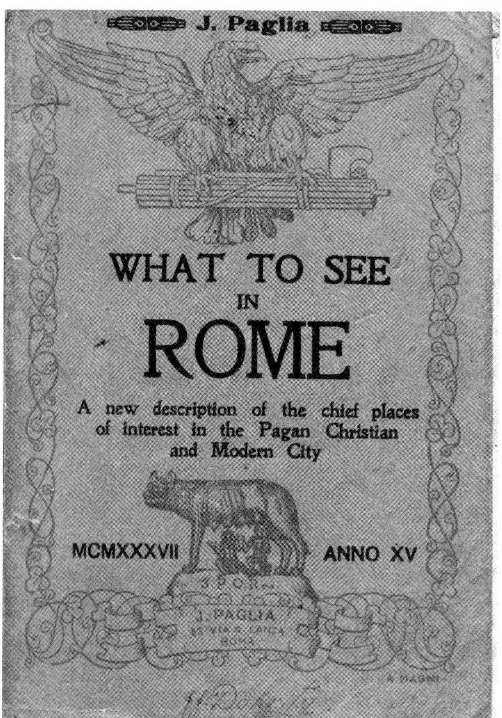

Many personnel were keen to see the historic sites of Rome and even in wartime English-language guidebooks were available. (*Author's collection*)

On 12 June 1944, Pope Pius XII addressed an audience of Irish soldiers, reminding them that the Irish had taken the Christian faith to many lands before giving them a Blessing. Brigadier Scott presented the Pope with a commemorative scroll and asked him if he would like to hear the pipes. (*Author's collection*)

Pipers from the Inniskillings and London Irish talk with two members of the Pope's Noble Guard. (*Author's collection*)

A painting of a piper of the Royal Irish Fusiliers, based on a photograph of a London Irish piper. (*Author's collection*)

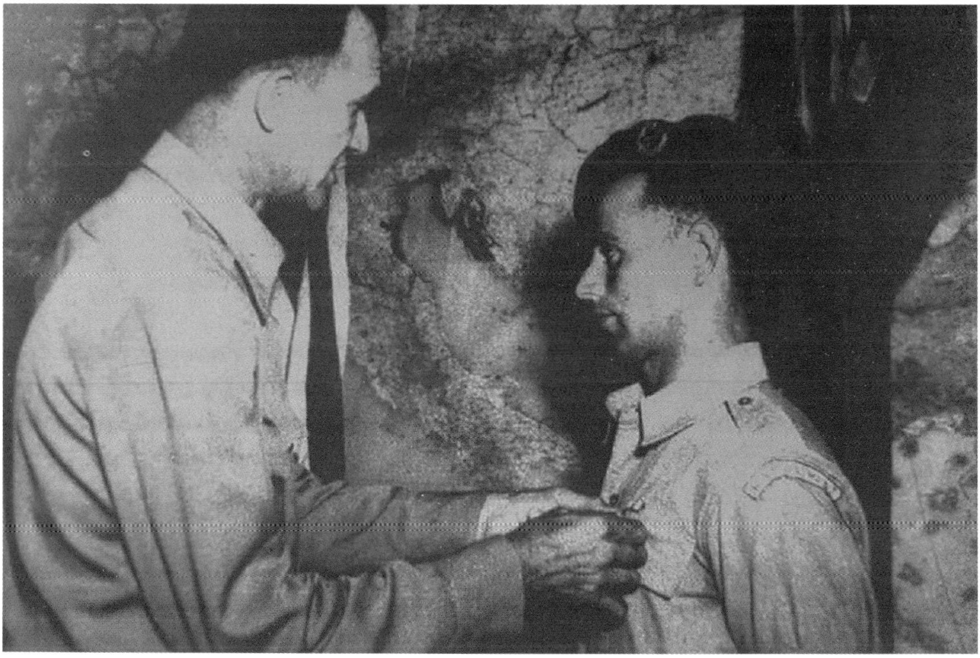

Sergeant George Overend, RAF Regiment, receives the US Soldier's Medal from Brigadier General Edward M. Morris for his work in rescuing US personnel from an LST that had run aground in the Pontine Islands in February 1944. (*NARA*)

In happier times. Squadron Leader Ernest Kee DFC of No.241 Squadron with family members at a family gathering. Ernest Kee was killed on 20 April 1944 off the Yugoslav coast. A brother also served in the RAF and survived the war. (*Richard Kee*)

From left to right: Sergeant Jimmy Soutar, Sergeant Jim Canning and Battery Sergeant Major Walter Wray of 25 Battery 9th (Londonderry) HAA Regiment in summer 1944. Both Jimmy Soutar and Walter Wray wear the ribbon of the Africa Star with Eighth Army clasp. (*9th HAA Regiment Archive*)

As autumn moved into winter in 1944 conditions in the Apennines became more difficult. These vehicles are struggling with a rain-soaked mountain road. (*Author's collection*)

When snow fell, conditions worsened and mules were needed to take supplies to units in the mountains. This mule train is re-supplying 1st Royal Irish Fusiliers. (*Royal Irish Fusiliers' Museum*)

The redoubtable Father Dan. A Kerry man, Fr Dan Kelleher had earned the MC at Caira for rescuing wounded under fire. In this 1945 photograph he wears the ribbon of the MC and those of the 1939-43 and Africa Stars. The Battleaxe emblem of 78th Division is visible on his sleeve above the Irish Brigade shamrock. (*Author's collection*)

Gunner J.J. Doherty, senior despatch rider of 9th (Londonderry) HAA Regiment wearing jodhpurs with despatch rider's high boots. A despatch rider's helmet is also visible. Other than the Royal Artillery arm-of-service strip on his shoulders, the sole distinctive marks are the four chevrons, good conduct badges, on his left forearm, representing sixteen years' unblemished service. (*Author's collection*)

Squadron Leader Brian Considine from Dublin flew with No.111 Squadron from Malta, supporting Operation HUSKY. Later, the squadron flew close-support missions from Sicily and Italy. A veteran of the Battle of Britain, Brian Considine had shot down a Bf.110 and shared the destruction of a Do.17P bomber. After the war he married Nuala Kiernan, daughter of Dr Thomas Kiernan and Delia Murphy. (*Public domain*)

Rifleman Joe Robinson, Royal Ulster Rifles (L) and Sergeant Joe Robinson, 2nd London Irish Rifles. The first photograph was taken in January 1942 but the toll of active service, and being wounded, is obvious in the second image, taken in Rome in October 1944. (*Robinson family*)

Signalman Joe Radcliffe in Rome in late 1944/ early 1945. Joe Radcliffe's father, John, had served in the Royal Inniskilling Fusiliers in the Great War and re-enlisted in September 1939. John's brother Joseph, also an Inniskilling, had earned the Military Medal in November 1917 but had later been killed. Signalman Radcliffe joined the Territorial Army in Watford before war broke out while training as a teacher. He saw service in North Africa and Italy. (*Marina Radcliffe Petri*)

Third Officer Elizabeth Beresford-Ellis (née Chamberlain) had served in the WRNS in the UK. Transferred to Italy, she was surprised to see three people whom she knew on Naples' Via Roma on her first day in the city. (*Author's collection*)

Squadron Leader Robert Turkington DSO DFC* from Portadown served in the UK before being posted to the Mediterranean. From Algeria, his squadron moved to Malta and then Sicily and Italy where he displayed outstanding leadership and personal courage, earning the DFC and Bar and being appointed DSO. He survived the war to be killed in a flying accident in July 1945. (*Public domain*)

WOII (Company Sergeant Major) Robbie Robinson DCM, 1st Royal Irish Fusiliers, in early 1945. Although Robbie had earned the DCM some months earlier, he is wearing only the ribbon of the Africa Star with First Army clasp. He wears a khaki caubeen with the Faughs' distinctive cap badge, set on a green shamrock, and green hackle. The inverted white triangle set on the Irish Brigade shamrock on his sleeve also indicates the Royal Irish Fusiliers. (*Author's collection*)

Lieutenant Colonel Bala Bredin DSO MC*, CO of 2nd London Irish, discusses a forthcoming operation with Major General Arbuthnott, GOC 78th Division and Captain H.N.D, Seymour, Arbuthnott's ADC. (*IWM, NA23180*)

The character and ethos of the Irish Brigade were enhanced by the production of the Irish Brigade song book in the winter of 1944-45. It included a selection of traditional Irish songs, as well as some that might have led to fisticuffs in certain areas. (*Author's collection*)

Lance Sergeant Patrick Joseph 'Rex' Doherty, 2nd Inniskillings, had been Mentioned in Despatches at Anzio. He earned the Military Medal on the Senio Line in March 1945. (*Mrs Barbara Downey*)

A Churchill of C Squadron North Irish Horse advances with an infantry section from 21st Regiment of Gruppo Cremona riding into action. The photo was probably taken during Cremona's Operation SONIA. (*Author's collection*)

Fusilier Alexander 'Alex' Carlin of 2nd Royal Inniskilling Fusiliers, from Redcastle near Moville in County Donegal, was killed in action on 17 April 1945 during Operation BUCKLAND. Since he is wearing a beret with the grenade cap badge, the photo was taken in Egypt before he joined the 2nd Battalion which wore the caubeen with the Castle of Inniskilling badge. (*Alwyn Buchanan*)

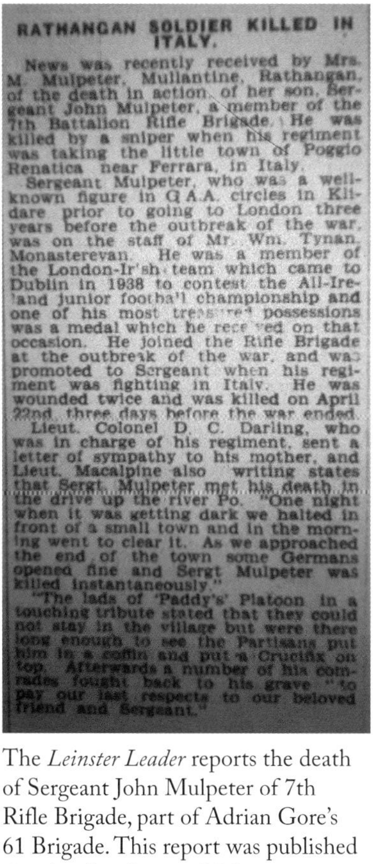

RATHANGAN SOLDIER KILLED IN ITALY.

News was recently received by Mrs. M. Mulpeter, Mullantine, Rathangan, of the death in action of her son, Sergeant John Mulpeter, a member of the 7th Battalion Rifle Brigade. He was killed by a sniper when his regiment was taking the little town of Poggio Renatica near Ferrara, in Italy.

Sergeant Mulpeter, who was a well-known figure in G.A.A. circles in Kildare prior to going to London three years before the outbreak of the war, was on the staff of Mr. Wm. Tynan, Monasterevan. He was a member of the London-Irish team which came to Dublin in 1938 to contest the All-Ireland junior football championship and one of his most treasured possessions was a medal which he received on that occasion. He joined the Rifle Brigade at the outbreak of the war, and was promoted to Sergeant when his regiment was fighting in Italy. He was wounded twice and was killed on April 22nd, three days before the war ended.

Lieut. Colonel D. C. Darling, who was in charge of his regiment, sent a letter of sympathy to his mother, and Lieut. Macalpine also writing states that Sergt. Mulpeter met his death in the drive up the river Po. "One night when it was getting dark we halted in front of a small town and in the morning went to clear it. As we approached the end of the town some Germans opened fire and Sergt. Mulpeter was killed instantaneously."

"The lads of 'Paddy's' Platoon in a touching tribute stated that they could not stay in the village but were there long enough to see the Partisans put him in a coffin and put a Crucifix on top. Afterwards a number of his comrades fought back to his grave "to pay our last respects to our beloved friend and Sergeant."

The *Leinster Leader* reports the death of Sergeant John Mulpeter of 7th Rifle Brigade, part of Adrian Gore's 61 Brigade. This report was published shortly after the war. Irish government censorship regulations would have prohibited earlier publication. (*James Durney*)

Brenda Graham was one of several VADs from Ireland who served in Italy, having been trained in Dublin by St John Ambulance Brigade and in hospitals in England before her posting to the Mediterranean. (*Clark family*)

Captain Brian Clark MC, adjutant of 1st Royal Irish Fusiliers for most of the Sicilian and Italian campaigns. He was awarded the MC in January 1945 for his consistent gallantry over 18 months. He met Brenda Graham in Austria after the war and married, eventually settling in County Wicklow. (*Clark family*)

Another wedding. Joe Radcliffe of the Royal Signals and Lucia Bedeschi married, appropriately, in St Patrick's Church in Via Boncompagni in Rome on 6 October 1946. Their first child, Marina, was born in Rome before the family moved to live in Northern Ireland. On Joe's retirement from the Ministry of Defence, he and Lucia returned to Rome. Joe died in 2005 and Lucia in 2018. (*Marina Radcliffe Petri*)

PEACE WITH JUSTICE (Pius XII)

I.N.R.I.

NAME
RANK No.
UNIT

I am a Catholic

PLEASE INFORM THE CATHOLIC CHAPLAIN

God bless the Pope : God save the King

World War, 3rd Sept. 1939 — VICTORY

A prayer card issued to Catholic soldiers by their chaplains. Note the date range for the 'World War'. (*Author's collection*)

Chapter 6

Breaking the Hitler Line

I Canadian Corps (1st Infantry and 5th Armoured Divisions) had moved into position behind XIII Corps ready for the irruption into the Liri valley. The first obstacle, the Hitler Line, a switch-line of the Gustav had been renamed the Senger Barrier, when common sense had overtaken German commanders, after the corps commander in the sector, Lieutenant General Fridolin von Senger und Etterlin (named for a German saint, believed to have been an Irish missionary). The Canadian plan to crack open the line was Operation CHESTERFIELD.[1] Supporting Canadian infantry in their attack were two units of the British 25 Tank Brigade, the North Irish Horse and 51st (Leeds Rifles) Royal Tanks. As tank units, both were equipped with Churchill I (Infantry) tanks, heavily armoured machines that had demonstrated remarkable agility over difficult terrain in Tunisia.

That 25 Tank Brigade* was not deployed earlier to Sicily or Italy may have been due to Montgomery not considering the Churchill a practical AFV for Italy. However, Monty had been recalled to the UK to plan and command the Normandy landings. Whatever the reason for being retained in Africa, the North Irish Horse embarked for Naples on 16 April. Whilst entering Naples harbour two days later, the ship came under air attack. Fire and smoke were seen coming from Vesuvius.

The regiment received eighteen Shermans in addition to its complement of Churchills with squadrons re-arranged from five troops of Churchills to three of Churchills and two of Shermans. All tanks were loaded on trains for Foggia and a brigade location near Lucera.

Following a move to Mignano, the regiment joined I Canadian Corps for CHESTERFIELD, D Day for which was 23 May. Since Lord O'Neill, CO of the Horse, was in hospital, command had transferred to Lieutenant Colonel Eugene Strickland MM, CO of 145th Regiment RAC who had served with

* A tank brigade differed in role and equipment from an armoured brigade with its three regiments equipped with slow-moving infantry tanks, or I-tanks. Since its task was to support infantry, it had no infantry battalion.

distinction in the Horse in Tunisia.* 'Strick', born in India, but with family roots in Kerry, would lead the regiment through the most difficult days of its history. The North Irish Horse was partnered with 2 Canadian Brigade. Some late amendments to the plan delayed H Hour to 0600 on the 23rd: A Squadron supported Princess Patricia's Canadian Light Infantry (PPCLI) on the right and B Squadron the Seaforth Highlanders of Canada on the left. Two brigades were to break through the Hitler Line on a 3,000-yard front to allow 5th Armoured Division through to force a crossing of the Melfa river.[2] Still holding Monte Cairo, the Germans felt confident that their line was tenable.

For fifteen minutes before H Hour, 600 guns bombarded German positions. Although the day dawned bright and sunny, a smokescreen and dust from the baked ground reduced visibility, making it impossible to maintain formation. The very strong defences included Panther tank turrets, their 75mm guns mounted in reinforced concrete emplacements, and machine guns similarly mounted. Lush spring growth helped camouflage those strongpoints, which took a heavy toll of infantry and tanks. So great was the intensity of machine-gun fire, small-arms fire and shrapnel that tank commanders found it virtually impossible to have their heads out of their turrets.[3]

Early in the battle, B Squadron under Major Russell was closing on its objective when anti-tank guns opened fire from about 100 yards, crippling five tanks, including Russell's and that of Captain Pope. Both were wounded, Russell so seriously that his gunner, Lance Corporal Hughes, thought the top of his head had been blown off. 'It appeared [that] an AP round had ricocheted off the turret and glanced off his head.' Hughes and the wireless operator, Gerry Chester, got Russell into the relative safety of a ditch. The driver, Lance Corporal Harry Jenkins from Glenageary, County Wicklow, was entangled in metal from the track-guards but his co-driver, Bill Wheatley, freed him and took him to the ditch. While Harry Jenkins did not survive, Pope's injuries were less severe.[4]

Trooper Dawson, in one of the tanks to reach the objective, recalled that his Churchill was hit as it returned. Sergeant Tommy McAughtry, from Belfast, later told Dawson that the turret had been blown twenty feet into the air. Three crewmen were killed: Sergeant Leslie Reeve, a Londoner, Lance Corporal James Pryde from County Antrim and Trooper Reginald Ellis from Hertfordshire.[5]

---

* Commissioned in the early 1930s, Strickland had resigned but enlisted as a trooper in the Royal Tank Corps in 1935. By 1940 he was a sergeant. Earning the MM in the Arras counter-attack in May 1940, he was re-commissioned in the Royal Armoured Corps in December.

That day the North Irish Horse lost thirty-six dead or dying with as many wounded. Of the twenty-eight who died on the 23rd, twelve were from Ireland; other Irish soldiers succumbed to their wounds later.[6] (That almost half the dead were Irish indicates how strong remained the Irish presence in the regiment at a time when the traditional reinforcement system had ceased to exist, the General Service Corps had been created and the last reinforcements from the UK had arrived.) Thirty-two tanks, 60 per cent of the regiment's complement, were lost. Among those decorated, Sergeant William Maxwell was supporting a Seaforth platoon when his tank was knocked out by an anti-tank gun. With the immediate area being bombarded heavily by shells and mortar bombs, Maxwell ordered his crew to remove the tank's Besa machine gun and set it up in a firing position on the ground. He then told his crew to take cover in the tank while he fired the Besa.

> His action was instrumental in pinning down a complete enemy strong point. This so angered them that a heavy concentration was put down on his position as a result of which his Besa was put out of action and he himself severely wounded. His devotion to duty had been an inspiration to the Regiment … .[7]

Strickland recommended Maxwell for an immediate DCM but he received the MM.

A Squadron's leader, Major Robin Griffith, who would earn a Bar to his MC from Tunisia, was on the right flank and reported several tanks and anti-tank guns forming up close to the road along the bank of the Forme d'Aquino, a deep watercourse. He decided to reconnoitre the situation and, having done so, chose not to request artillery support since Canadian infantry were too close. Instead, he had sappers gap the minefield, following which two Churchills passed through, only to be knocked out by concealed anti-tank guns. Sergeant Walter Best from Belfast, commanding the tanks, was killed. Griffith had left his tank and spent many hours on foot under heavy fire controlling his tanks, which claimed two Panthers knocked out; Griffith himself accounted for several snipers and only left the battlefield when ordered to do so next morning. In writing his citation, Strickland recommended Griffith for the DSO but this was changed at higher level.[8]

In the poor visibility, one A Squadron Churchill slid into a very steep ravine to land 'with an almighty thump on the turret, the force being so great we rolled over onto the tracks!' The tank was on a plateau about fifty feet down the ravine which was at least 300-feet deep. Davy Graham then demonstrated his driving skills and the Churchill's agility. He

> set off at a very, very steep angle to get to the bottom before climbing up the other side. … a superb piece of driving requiring the greatest skill. At last we got to the top on the other side only to be met by a sheer ten-foot climb to get out. We required three attempts to master it. It was the finest piece of driving I had ever seen, no words can describe his skill, at any moment it seemed the tank might run head over heels, the angle was so steep.[9]

With his tank disabled by anti-tank guns, Trooper John Neilson MM earned a Bar to the MM gained at Longstop Hill in Tunisia. Refusing to quit the battlefield, Neilson set about collecting wounded.

> Under heavy fire and in full view of the enemy, Tpr Neilson organized and directed the evacuation of many wounded. Three times he carried wounded men back to safety and each time he returned to the battlefield for more. He seemed to bear a charmed life and for more than 20 hours remained under fire collecting the wounded. It was not his duty, and on two occasions he went to help wounded men when stretcher-bearers were unable to do so owing to the heavy enemy fire.
>
> His unfailing calmness and cheerfulness under these conditions were an inspiration to all troops in the area.

As with Sergeant Maxwell, Lieutenant Colonel Strickland recommended Trooper Neilson for the DCM; it was amended to a Bar to the MM.[10]

Strickland himself was appointed DSO for his courage and leadership. The citation, written by Brigadier Gibson of 2 Canadian Brigade, stated that the regimental commander

> was almost continuously in the forward area organizing and inspiring the repeated tank attacks in support of the infantry. When the situation was critical … Lieutenant Colonel Strickland personally organized a tank force in the forward area to assist the elements of two companies of the Seaforth Highlanders of Canada isolated on their objective.

The citation includes a handwritten note by Armagh-born Major General Chris Vokes, commanding 1st Canadian Division: 'This offr's conduct during the battle was an outstanding example of personal bravery and determination to win, in the highest traditions of the service.'[11]

Both the Horse and 51st Royal Tanks were granted the privilege of wearing the Canadian Maple Leaf symbol on their uniform tunics in appreciation of their support for 1st Canadian Division in the battle. This was formalized by the War Office in 1947 when the Horse was re-formed as a Territorial Army unit.[12]

Eugene Strickland later recalled that, in the 1950s, Field Marshal Alexander, then Minister of Defence in Churchill's government, had told him that 'the breaking of the Hitler Line was due to those two Churchill Tank Regiments and gave him his most satisfactory day of a long and very distinguished military life'.[13]

On the night of 23/24 May the Germans abandoned the Hitler Line. On the 29th the Horse rejoined 2 Canadian Brigade to work with the Canadians over several days advancing against enemy rearguard actions. Strickland handed command back to Lord O'Neill on 4 June, the day Rome was liberated, and returned to command 145 RAC. There was little respite for the regiment with 25 Tank Brigade ordered to support 28 Brigade of 4th Division that day. However, it remained in reserve before being transferred to 17 Indian Brigade of 8th Indian Division.

* * *

Rome's Liberation Day was also significant for 2nd Royal Inniskilling Fusiliers whom we left in the Anzio beachhead as US VI Corps prepared for the breakout. That began on 23 May with both 1st and 5th British Divisions involved. In the former, Lieutenant Colonel 'Paddy' Brett's 1 Recce formed the core of Brettforce, a battlegroup including armour, artillery and sappers spearheading the advance.[14] Both British divisions were to advance along the coastal sector; the main element of the advance was American.

On the 25th the Inniskillings moved to the Fortress. Two days later the war diary recorded a patrol under Lieutenant Brackenridge being ambushed in Commando Wadi, described by Fox as a 'German trench'. They shot their way out with four men wounded. Next day four deserters from 4th Fallschirmjäger Division surrendered to D Company while a D Company platoon occupied Commando Wadi.[15]

Bobby Scott recalled that two other deserters claimed their infantry were withdrawing. As MPs were about to march the prisoners to Brigade HQ,

> a thought crossed my mind. 'Don't you think,' I said to our IO and interpreter Jack Scarratt, 'that these poor fellows should be allowed to collect their belongings before being locked up for the duration?' Jack looked at me with some concern before he saw the light. He then conveyed this generous offer to the prisoners who actually showed little gratitude and no enthusiasm. But beggars can't be choosers and at first light the

> 2nd Inniskillings left the Fortress in single file, crossed no man's land led by two prisoners and two mine detectors and occupied the enemy's forward defensive localities without losing a man.[16]

That 'truly daunting experience' was the first daylight movement through no man's land since Allied withdrawal to the Fortress in February.

> The smell of death hung like a cloud over an area of sheer desolation, pockmarked with shell holes, scoured with tangled wire and broken metal, and, worst of all, a greater number of dead soldiers than one would ever have expected. One assumed that most … were victims of the minefields, casualties who had to be left where they died, when attempts to bring them in would be virtual suicide. Whatever it was, anyone who passed safely through the mines, as we did, must have felt a great surge of pity for all who ended their war in that way.[17]

The Inniskillings, advancing more quickly than the Cameronians or Wiltshires (both delayed by minefields) and with no sign of 1st Division to their right, found themselves in a salient with high ground to their right. There, on 31 May, they came under heavy shelling and mortaring, resulting in casualties. Among those who lost their lives in the breakout were Fusiliers William McCormick from Moneymore, County Londonderry, William Patrick from Newtownstewart, County Tyrone and Patrick Stapleton, from Éire. Bobby Scott recorded that one fusilier was killed by a booby-trap before the Moletta was crossed.[18]

Another enemy emerged during the advance with an outbreak of malaria, in spite of those daily doses of mepacrine. The doctors concluded that it was due to extreme exhaustion suffered by men who had earlier served in Madagascar and in whom their tiredness 'had awoken the lurking fever'. Further investigation confirmed that theory.[19]

Lieutenant Colonel Scott had 'an unusual experience' while answering a call of nature. Retreating behind a nearby rocky outcrop, a deserter from 4th Fallschirmjäger invaded his privacy 'to the acute embarrassment of both of us!' The CO returned with a prisoner but later wrote that he 'was prompted to compose a new paragraph for King's Regulations: "Officers will adjust their dress before accepting the surrender of an enemy"'.[20]

German troops continued rearguard actions, one tactic being to 'establish a strong machine-gun post in the basement of a house, then demolish the house', thus providing both cover and protection.[21] However, Allied pressure on the Germans was inexorable. As the forces from Cassino advanced through the Liri valley, elements of Juin's FEC had moved rapidly through the Aurunci mountains, considered impassable by German commanders, and VI Corps added its heft.

The Lumps earned the battle honour 'Advance to the Tiber' for their role in the breakout while Captain Paddy Long earned the MC, as did CSM John Nolan. Corporal Albert Godber was awarded the MM and Corporal Jack Hassard received a Mention in Despatches.[22] Sergeant Stephen Hughes DCM MM, from Belfast, commanded the battle patrol and, although unable to read or write, he could 'read an air photograph with an exactitude that none of us could hope to equal'. As the advance continued, Hughes found an OP affording observation of a reverse slope in German-held ground north of Banditella and which allowed the FOO to bring down a bombardment on a German rest area. Such were Hughes' qualities that the CO considered recommending him for another decoration but the sergeant had other ideas and recommended one of 'them corporals of mine … it's time one of them got something'. As a result, Godber received the MM.[23]

On 4 June Rome was liberated, giving Mark Clark his moment of glory. His desire to be seen as the 'conqueror' of Rome had blinded him to the imperative of destroying one of the German armies, an opportunity he threw away in his lust for glory. Clark never admitted to his error. Moreover, determined that only American troops of Fifth Army should enter Rome, he ordered that no Eighth Army personnel should do so. Oblivious to Clark's orders, of which they were undoubtedly unaware, Major Peter Slane and Lieutenant Jack Scarratt of the Lumps left the battalion by jeep to recce Ostia Lido. En route, a recce car in front (possibly a vehicle of 5th Reconnaissance Regiment) drove over and exploded a mine, prompting Slane and Scarratt to turn about and make for Rome. They entered the city at 1027 on the 5th, ahead of US infantry who 'are marching in to occupy [*sic*] the city' to a warm welcome.[24]

* * *

Following the breaching of the Hitler Line, 38 (Irish) Brigade had a series of tasks. On 27 May, the Faughs deployed near Ceprano to relieve the Irish Regiment of Canada around a road junction. At some point, a Canadian soldier, possibly a military policeman, was heard instructing 'Canadian Irish this way; English Irish that way!' No retaliatory action was taken.[25] That evening the area around battalion HQ was shelled heavily for about ten minutes, with seven killed and fifteen injured. Pat Scott's account notes twenty-nine casualties while *Soldiers Died* records nine dead, only one of whom, Michael O'Donnell from Aughnacloy, was Irish-born. Their service numbers show that two had joined after the creation of the General Service Corps in September 1943, while others had earlier served in other regiments. Next day brought more casualties, one of the wounded being Captain Norman Bass, from Belfast, the transport officer.[26]

As the advance continued, so did casualties while 3rd King's Own Hussars, providing armoured support, found the going very difficult in what was described as the worst tank country the Irish Brigade had encountered in Italy, other than Monte Cairo. The Rifles were deployed to the Faughs' right with E Company under Mervyn Davies attacking Point 255. Captain Alan Parsons of 17th Field accompanied E as the FOO. Davies wrote that:

> At about [1600] the leading men, still on the country road, came under machine-gun fire. Desmond Fay ... was magnificent and rapped out 'battle drill' orders for 'right flanking' as if we were on an exercise. I could not see where the fire was coming from but there seemed to be two machine guns on high ground to our immediate front and 200 yards or more away. Desmond with the attacking right flank got stopped and it was evident to me, about 200 yards away, that some of his men were hit. Parsons told me that his wireless set was out of touch with his guns (or they were on the move, I do not remember) so that one was faced without support.[27]

However, John Horsfall decided to attack at night with artillery support. Platoon commanders were ordered to 'Charge for the place where you see the shells landing now'. The objective was taken and the advance continued towards Ripi, liberating the straggling village of San Giovanni en route. With close support from 3rd Hussars and 17th Field, Ripi's defenders were overcome in a three-hour battle. Although the Rifles had suffered twenty casualties, German losses had been as many as 100 dead with fifteen captured. In the aftermath, villagers celebrated with the Rifles although many had lost homes and possessions. Irish Brigade doctors tended to civilian casualties as well as their own, saving several lives. Taking over from the Rifles, 6th Inniskillings made the next bound through the hills, hampered only by poor roads, mines and sporadic shelling.[28] On 1 June the Irish Brigade went into reserve. With 78th Division in reserve, 6th Armoured took the lead.

Returning to the pursuit on 8 June, the Irish battalions had some varied experiences. The Rifles guarding Kesselring's former headquarters at Monte Oreste, some thirty miles north of Rome, found panelled rooms for his staff and huge garages for his transport in the mountainside, impervious to bombing. During their spell as guardians, the Rifles liberated considerable quantities of wine, liqueurs and tableware. That 'booty' contributed to a sense throughout both Allied armies that an end to the Italian campaign was in sight. It seemed the only thing delaying the armies was congestion on the roads, much of it caused by wrecked German vehicles and equipment, mostly due to Allied air attacks. Pat Scott wrote:

> One gratifying sight on all the main roads … was mile after mile of burnt-out German vehicles, varying from Tigers and seventy-ton Ferdinands down to volkswagens. One seldom went more than a quarter of a mile without seeing one of these edifying spectacles. … most of it had been done by the Air Force[s]. It was a most impressive, visible tribute to their excellent work. The Boche slit trenches, dug every four or five hundred yards along the road as funk holes from air strafing, were a tribute to the air activity that must have gone on for a longish period along these roads to Rome.[29]

At one point, A Company of the Faughs 'took over' a castle that, reputedly, had been home to a mistress of Mussolini. Fusilier Teahan, donning a mosquito net, even produced honey for tea by raiding the beehives. Rifles' companies deployed into San Oreste to deter enemy counter-attacks which never materialized, but the Rifles enjoyed a distant view of 6th Armoured Division's battle across the Tiber.[30]

* * *

The short period of reduced activity that followed was timed perfectly since the Irish Brigade was invited to attend an audience of Pope Pius XII in the Vatican on 12 June. That audience was not exclusive to the brigade but extended to Irish units in Italy. Thus 9th (Londonderry) HAA Regiment, then stationed in Anzio under Fifth Army command, and 2nd Inniskillings, who had beaten Fifth Army into Rome, as well as representatives of 1st London Irish (56th Division was in Egypt re-organizing) were also included. Among those who made the occasion possible were the Irish Brigade's Catholic chaplain, Father Dan Kelleher MC; 9th (Londonderry) Regiment's Anglican chaplain, the Reverend Louis Crookes; the rector of the Pontifical Irish College in Rome, Monsignor Denis McDaid, a native of Londonderry, and Major Sir Basil McFarland, commander of 25 HAA Battery, 9th (Londonderry)* as well as

* Msgr McDaid's brother had been involved in the IRA. When visiting his native city after the war, Denis McDaid stayed neither with his brother nor in the Bishop of Derry's 'palace' at St Eugene's Cathedral, but with his friend Sir Basil McFarland. In 1951 he was made a canon of Saint Peter's Basilica. He died in Rome in 1981 and is buried in the Irish College Plot at San Lorenzo.

Pat Scott who was most enthusiastic about the occasion. A few days earlier, McDaid had recognized the accent of one of two soldiers admiring Saint Peter's. Approaching the man, he tapped him on the elbow and commented, 'You're a Derry man, aren't you?' The 'Derry man' was Sergeant Willie Hunter of 24 Battery who hailed from the Fountain area of the city. After a long conversation about their native city, Willie Hunter returned to 24 Battery with a gift of wine and a rosary.[31]

At 0845 on the 12th the Pipes and Drums of the Irish Brigade, augmented by those of 2nd Inniskillings, led all attending the audience up the Vatican steps. Members of the Pope's Noble Guard (disbanded by Paul VI) headed the procession to the audience chamber. Some present noticed a warrant officer of the London Irish wearing an Orange sash. (The author first heard of that while still in primary school from his father, who was in the 9th Londonderry group. In 1968, a work colleague, Joe Robinson, who had served in 2nd London Irish, confirmed that he, too, had seen a CSM wearing a sash. While researching for a history of the Irish Brigade, the author interviewed Jim Hamilton, a former London Irish WO2 who had earned the MM in Tunisia, and, mentioning the comments, asked if he knew who the man was. With a smile, Jim replied simply, 'You're looking at him.')[32]

Pope Pius entered at 0900. Addressing the gathering in English, he drew attention to the role of the Irish in spreading the faith to many lands before blessing them. Pat Scott then presented the Pope with a commemorative scroll and asked if His Holiness would like to hear the pipes. When Pius said that he would, the pipers struck up 'The Wearing of the Green'. Officers and men were then presented to the Pope who had informed a cardinal that he was looking forward very much to the Irish visit. Before the Pope's departure the pipers played 'The Minstrel Boy' after which Pat Scott called for three cheers, followed by a 'Faugh a Ballagh one'. Pius left waving and smiling. Following Mass celebrated by Father Dan, the Pipes and Drums beat Retreat on the steps of Saint Peter's. That was enjoyed thoroughly by the many Irish priests present, some of whom had been virtual prisoners in the Vatican since they had been ordained after Italy's declaration of war in 1940.[33] Several were enrolled as 'curates' by Dan Kelleher, their roles being recognized officially by the Army. (At least one Irish priest had made a 'home run': Doctor Manus O'Doherty, ordained on 23 March 1940, who escaped via Spain and Portugal, was the author's first Latin teacher.)

The Irish envoy to the Vatican, Dr Thomas Kiernan, invited Irish officers to lunch and a reception which was attended by many, including Pat Scott. Kendal Chavasse recalled singing a duet with the minister's wife and complimenting her on her beautiful singing voice.[34] At the time he was unaware that Mrs

Kiernan was the acclaimed balladeer Delia Murphy. Nor was anyone then aware of the roles that Delia Murphy-Kiernan and her daughter Blánaid had played in helping Jews and escaped Allied prisoners in the escape organization run by Irish priest Monsignor Hugh O'Flaherty. (See pages 217–20)

Pat Scott paid tribute to the many volunteers from neutral Ireland.

> It is a matter of great concern to all of us who come from Ireland that when the war is over it will only be remembered against her that Éire was neutral. What we hope is that all the magnificent deeds wrought by the sons of Éire in this war against the barbarisms of Germany and her Allies, may be remembered to her credit. It is sometimes overlooked that the services of every Irishman from any part of Ireland are given of their own free will for the good of the cause, be they fighting men or those priests who helped the English prisoners in Rome.[35]

While 2nd Inniskillings left Rome after 12 June en route with 5th Division for Alexandria in Egypt to rest and re-organize, 38 (Irish) Brigade continued its advance. Arriving at Colleno, the brigade was ordered to move a further five miles and seize Civitella where elements of 56 Recce were engaged with the enemy. On his return from Rome, Kendal Chavasse took some of his armoured cars forward to Civitella which persuaded the Germans to leave. To discourage their return, the Rifles moved in and consolidated. The Germans, Fallschirmjäger yet again, were ready for battle which came next day with a Rifles' assault on Panicale overlooking Lake Trasimene and Point 208, supported by 17th Field Regiment, Priests of the Royal Horse Artillery and medium guns of 66th Medium Regiment. Even the Rifles' anti-tank platoon took part, their jeep-towed guns brought into action against machine-gun positions. As H Company infiltrated the village, 3rd Hussars' tanks lent support. In the second phase of the operation, G Company joined H and the German defence began splintering under the pressure with 3rd Hussars and 56 Recce armour surrounding the village. During the afternoon, the battle was all but over; about 120 Fallschirmjäger were made captive and many more killed; H Company suffered five dead.[36]

Keightley was pleased with the result. The Rifles' new second-in-command, Major Malcolm 'Murphy' Palmer, announced that 100 gallons of champagne had been captured 'and I have it all'. He also noted that the RSM was 'having apoplexy. That wretch Fitz [Captain Fitzgerald, anti-tank platoon commander] has fired off the whole of the anti-tank stocks and there's not a round left forward of division.' However, Fitzgerald had made very effective use of his guns.[37]

Murphy Palmer, a Faugh, when adjutant of 1st Royal Irish Fusiliers, had played a pivotal part in the Faughs' retreat to Dunkirk and successful evacuation in 1940. After a series of staff posts, he had inveigled a posting to the Irish Brigade, although his arrival had been delayed by a fall, breaking an ankle, disembarking from a troopship in Naples. The son of a Church of Ireland rector, he would command 1st Royal Irish Fusiliers in the final campaign in Italy.[38]

On the evening of the 13th the Faughs rejoined following two weeks detached on various operations. The Inniskillings, with John Kerr in command and a squadron of 3rd Hussars in support, advanced to Castiglione where Pat Scott established his tactical HQ. Early next morning, the Inniskillings, followed by the Rifles, left for Tordimonte, crossing the Paglia river before noon to create a bridgehead which the Rifles expanded. Brigade HQ then moved to Tordimonte castle.

The operation to expand the bridgehead was led by F Company with Desmond Fay's 7 Platoon of E attached. So quickly did the Rifles hit the enemy positions on the Morrano ridge that the Germans were still unorganized. Their hold on seemingly unassailable defences was broken. The attack was supported by Vickers machine guns and some 6-pounder anti-tank guns with Fay's men triumphant after an hour of fighting. Underlining enemy confusion, twelve hours *after* 7 Platoon had taken the ridge, the Germans were still trying to deploy men for its defence. The ridge gifted an excellent location for the gunners of 17th Field who made full use of it as the Rifles took further prisoners.[39]

Eighth Army's advance continued, the Inniskillings and Rifles having a brief opportunity to rest, but the Faughs were deployed, some as lorried infantry with 9 Armoured Brigade. One platoon, under Lieutenant Len Manson from County Down, captured Monteleone and then Citta della Pieve. The latter was defended by Fallschirmjäger whose resistance was broken by the excellent work of Corporal Samuel Patton and Fusilier Bell, for which the former was awarded the MM. Manson received the MC for 'his personal courage' and the 'high standard of his leadership [which] was responsible for the success'. Six Germans were killed and thirty captured. With a troop of Royal Wiltshire Yeomanry tanks, Manson's platoon consolidated in the town.[40] Unfortunately, they were ordered to withdraw by their own CO, James Dunnill. The Germans re-occupied Citta; evicting them again cost several days' hard fighting.

The bulk of the Faughs had been placed under 56 Recce command to advance from Orvieto to Lake Trasimene. 'Chavasseforce' included a Warwickshire Yeomanry squadron, a battery of 17th Field, two troops of 315 Anti-Tank Battery and a detachment of sappers from 237 Field Company. Since Kendal

Chavasse was himself a Faugh, it was a good combination. Indeed, Pat Scott was quite happy about the Faughs operating under Kendal Chavasse.

> His Regiment's performance is always of a very high order and, after all, he was a Faugh once himself [*sic*]. Maybe he still is. Anyway, he would never be able to live down losing the Faughs in Regimental circles.[41]

(Pat and Kendal were commissioned in the Faughs on the same day in August 1924.)

During its advance, Chavasseforce captured or destroyed twenty-six guns of over 26mm, fifty-five MGs and almost forty vehicles, took 121 prisoners and killed 145 Germans. One encounter between a Faugh company with mortar support and a German force left twenty-five enemy dead. Captured vehicles included a 'NAAFI' truck containing French brandy and sweets, a popular prize. D Company ended the advance by capturing Castello di Montalera on the 21st. Brigadier Scott was 'grateful to them for that excellent castle overlooking Lake Trasimene'.[42]

Many Irish officers and men were in other formations and units of Eighth Army. Captain Ian Blacker, from Kilcullen, County Kildare, was in 10th Rifle Brigade, one of the three battalions of Brigadier Adrian Gore's 61 Brigade, when he was killed near Rivotorto, where Saint Francis of Assisi had lived in a hovel early in his life of austerity.[43] At the time, 61 Brigade, the second infantry brigade of 6th Armoured Division, was supporting the armoured regiments of 26 Armoured Brigade fighting their way through difficult mountainous countryside.[44] Ian Blacker is buried in Assisi War Cemetery.

The Irish Brigade began concentrating for the next action on the shores of Lake Trasimene where, in 217 BC, Hannibal's Carthaginian army had destroyed Gaius Flaminius' Roman army during the Second Punic War. However, the Second World War battle of Lake Trasimene could have been avoided had not Citta della Pieve been abandoned. John Horsfall believed that '78th Division would have piled in to the enemy … three days earlier – before they were ready – and probably rolled the whole lot up in the process'.[45]

* * *

That delay allowed Kesselring time to consolidate defences along the Albert Line, from Orvieto via the Tiber and Lake Trasimene to Gubbio. Further lines behind were intended to fix the Allies in position before winter set in. The Germans were concerned that an Allied advance into Northern Italy would facilitate Alexander's armies striking into Austria or the Balkans. As a result, reinforcements, including four divisions from the Russian front, arrived in Italy as Allied formations were being withdrawn for landings in southern France. The Albert Line, intended to prevent an Allied breakthrough onto the Lombardy plain in 1944, proved effective.

On 20 June, 11 Brigade, with Warwickshire Yeomanry tanks, were repelled near San Fatucchio, as were 36 Brigade units between Strada and Vaiano, although Strada was taken. The Battleaxe Division was to be withdrawn to Egypt to rest and re-organize, but the move would be delayed until the Albert Line fell. The Irish Brigade entered battle on the 21st, led by the Rifles. At the Chiusi brickworks, John Horsfall contacted the COs of 2nd Lancashire Fusiliers, pinned down by the enemy, and 11th Canadian Armoured Regiment, the Ontarios, supporting the Rifles. Scott joined them as the final plan was agreed.[46]

No initial artillery concentration was possible: the Lancashires were too close to the foe but smoke was laid down to 'blind' the defenders. A frontal attack was ruled out in favour of swinging 'round the town through the folds to the west'. E and F Companies led, the former seizing buildings in the north-west corner of San Fatucchio while F made for higher ground beyond the town. The surviving Lancashire Fusiliers would lend support to the Rifles who also had Vickers guns from 1st Kensingtons and their own anti-tank platoon, its stocks well replenished. The 6-pounders had a dual role: defence against enemy armour and striking buildings in the village. German fire began once movement was spotted. Although smoke-laying was intensified, a German OP in a church tower still had a clear view of Irish Brigade positions. Skilful leadership from Major Ronnie Boyd of E Company and close support from the Ontario tanks allowed the attackers to penetrate the defences, but at heavy cost. Two hours after H Hour (0730), E Company blasted its way into the first buildings where the defenders were determined to fight or die. Many perished on both sides before the objective was taken. F Company had a fierce battle in the cornfields with close support from 17th Field and Canadian tanks. When 17th Field exhausted their smoke shells, the Ontarios' CO, Douglas McIndoe, brought down part of the church tower where German observers were posted.[47]

The battle was far from over since E and F Companies remained engaged in bloody struggle. Boyd's E Company fought from house to house against stubborn resistance while Captain Fitzgerald's anti-tank gunners prevented enemy troops in Pucciarelli from aiding their comrades in San Fatucchio. Firing over open sights in spite of enemy machine-gun fire, they also used armour-piercing rounds against the village, discharging over 400 AP and HE shells. At 1300 German resistance in San Fatucchio collapsed. Enemy soldiers were seen climbing out of the rubble to throw down their weapons. Horsfall then ordered both companies to organize the defence of the village as the Germans bombarded what was left. Kensington machine guns and Rifles' mortars were busily engaging enemy targets.[48]

Desmond Woods' H Company entered the conflict at 1430, attacking through the village towards the cemetery and crossroads on the rising ground some 800 yards beyond. Once again, the Canadian tanks were in support and 17th Field's 25-pounders hammered the ridge and crossroads. G Company was to follow H, sweeping the area around the village which 'was still crawling with German MGs'. A troop of M10 tank destroyers put down suppressive fire on the Germans on the flanks. During the attack, Major Woods was wounded.

> a message came from one of my platoon commanders in front to say that they were held up by German fire and I was bobbing up with my fieldglasses to try and find out where the fire was coming from when there was a loud explosion in my headquarters. This was actually a stick grenade … thrown by some Germans … near our position. I got hit in the leg, one of my platoon commanders was wounded and my company sergeant major was wounded and the second in command of the Company, Bill Craig, had to … take over command.[49]

Grenade lobbing by German soldiers hidden in the corn continued while an officer and some men held out under cover of the church which was shattered by the tanks. However, cleverly-sited German anti-tank guns picked off Shermans until only one remained. When the church fell, H Company moved on to the cemetery which became the scene of very close fighting. A counter-attack was launched almost immediately while over 100 mortar rounds fell in a few minutes. But the German grenades were hurled too far, landing well behind the attackers with little effect. The struggle at the cemetery wall ended when a German feldwebel glanced over the wall as the last grenades were thrown. His timing could not have been worse as Lieutenant Webb-Bowen of the Rifles did likewise. Webb-Bowen, with his revolver at the ready, shot the German from less than a foot away. The feldwebel's men then surrendered.[50]

And yet battle continued with another two hours of fighting in cornfields and orchards. E Company attempted to get onto Pucciarelli ridge and F to take the crossroads to the north. E, F and H Companies had each lost about a third of their strength while only seven tanks of the supporting squadron remained in action. Lieutenant George Dunseath, a Faugh commanding a Rifles' platoon, was killed attacking several machine guns 'in splendid impetuous valour'. Some 5.5-inch medium guns joined 17th Field in supporting fire as did a Sherman of the Ontario Regiment, as well as John Horsfall's command tank. The situation became even more difficult as, while the Rifles broke into the German line, they could not break through it. Horsfall contacted Pat Scott who arrived at the Rifles' HQ and brought forward John Kerr's 6th Inniskillings, already warned to be ready for a follow-up attack. An Ontario squadron would support the Inniskillings.[51]

Kerr's attack was delayed to 1645 by having to deal with a further German counter-attack but the Inniskillings and their Canadian cousins moved off just as German artillery bombarded their area – but too late. The Inniskillings, Ontarios and 17th Field worked well together and were on their objectives by 2000 but still facing determined opposition. As he rode in his tank, head out of the turret, John Kerr was targeted by a German with a submachine gun. Bullets sprayed around him, cutting the strap of his headphones but he was unscathed. Still the battle continued and did so through the night and into the following day. Many Germans were captured and many killed or wounded, but they fought on, even launching further counter-attacks. The Canadian Sherman squadron was reduced to three tanks while 17th Field answered every call for support, John Horsfall paying particular praise to Captain Alan Parsons, the FOO with F Company Irish Rifles, who was wounded in yet another German attack. Throughout the 23rd there was no respite for Inniskillings or Rifles, although their positions were secure. The Faughs were preparing to attack Pescia and Ranciano, south of the Pescia river.[52]

The Faughs' attack was by B and C Companies, the former directed on Ranciano, the latter on Pescia, both with Canadian tanks in support with D Company following up to clear the enemy from the ground between both towns. Major Dickie Richards' B Company reached Ranciano late in the morning and, after calling for an artillery bombardment, secured the town. By then, Neville Chance's C Company was in Pescia. During the advance, Lieutenant Jim Trousdell noticed Germans around a farmhouse which, it seemed, they were not determined to defend. He ordered his platoon

> to fix bayonets in preparation [for] rushing the farmhouse. They looked at me in amazement at such a warlike suggestion and when they eventually complied it was evident that their bayonets had not been out of their scabbards for some time.[53]

The threat succeeded, nonetheless.

Fusilier William Hobden, a Dubliner who had enlisted originally in the Royal Sussex, was a wireless operator with C Company. He played a major role in maintaining contact, especially when Neville Chance and his wireless operator were wounded by a mortar round. With little regard for his own safety, Hobden contacted the tanks and arranged with the reserve troop leader to take Major Chance to safety. With one platoon out of contact, Hobden dashed forward under fire to deliver a message before returning by a flank. En route, he passed some buildings, in one of which he found nine armed Germans with an officer pointing a pistol at him. 'With great initiative, [Hobden] immediately brought his 38 set and aerial to the "on guard" position and menaced the enemy' who surrendered. Hobden was awarded the MM.[54]

The Faughs suffered some forty casualties and took more than eighty prisoners. In addition, C Company found a 'truck laden with hams, butter, cheese etc., perhaps a German NAAFI wagon'. Included in the luxuries, a canvas-wrapped parcel was addressed to a Frau Schmidt of Berlin. One of Jim Trousdell's section commanders, Corporal Smith, took it and re-addressed it to his wife.

Positions were consolidated and the usual counter-attacks beaten off. The advance continued until the last Germans in the San Fatucchio/Pucciarelli area surrendered. Pockets of resistance were cleared up. The Faughs alone had over eighty prisoners, some of whom were unable to understand the phenomenon of Irishmen fighting for 'England', believing that both countries were permanently mutually hostile. That confusion was not helped when they were told that there were Irish regiments in the British Army and that 'we [Irish] took pity on them and, sure, we wouldn't want to see them beat, now'.

As evening fell, 38 (Irish) Brigade's situation was more secure although it remained a finger thrust into the Albert Line. German reinforcements continued arriving, as shown by the capture by the Rifles of men from 104th PanzerGrenadier Regiment.

That evening, at about 1800, 36 Brigade passed through to cross the Pescia, take the lead and create a bridgehead. In Pat Scott's words, the Irish Brigade

> had now shot its bolt. ... It had been a very hard battle these few days. ... as hard as the Gustav Line and, what was worse, we were not expecting it. ... I really think that in spite of all this the end of our 270 miles advance was marked by as fine a demonstration of leadership and guts as one may expect to see anywhere.[55]

With its armoured and gunner partners, the brigade had made a tremendous effort when many already knew it was about to be withdrawn. As its commander remarked, 'It requires quite an extra effort of guts to go in really hard when you know pulling out is in the offing. That extra effort was not lacking.'[56]

Scott went forward to visit his battalions on the 25th and learned that the Faughs' CO, James Dunnill, was missing, captured travelling to visit the forward companies when his driver made a wrong turn. Lost with him were the IO, Lieutenant Gamble, and Major Duffy Anderson, the battery commander attached to the Faughs. With no field officers available, Brian Clark, the adjutant, suggested that he take command. That was agreed and Clark, only weeks short of his 24th birthday, commanded his battalion for a few days.[57]

* * *

Since crossing the Gari on 14 May, 38 (Irish) Brigade had lost the equivalent of a battalion killed or wounded, the dead accounting for the strength of a rifle company. Almost half those casualties had been sustained by the Rifles.[58] It was fortunate that 78th Division was to be withdrawn to Egypt for rest, re-organization and training. The divisional history notes that an expected major German attack at Trasimene had never happened because the strength of the Trasimene position 'had rested, as in Hannibal's day, in the Fatucchio feature'. With that feature denied to them, the German line began crumbling.[59]

The withdrawal began on 1 July and the brigade concentrated near Rome with a 'Tactical HQ' established in the city's Eden Hotel from which HQ staff organized a ball, to be held in the Barberini Palace on the 8th. It was a memorable success with many local guests invited by the Irish Minister to the Holy See, Dr Thomas Kiernan, 'who had taken a proprietorial interest in the Irish Brigade'.[60] Bala Bredin, recovered from his wounds, returned while guests included Brigadier Alban Low, deputy commander Rome area, Kendal Chavasse and George French, a Wexford man who had commanded a battalion of the Manchester Regiment and whose brother, Maurice, had been killed in action on Leros in November 1943 while commanding 2nd Royal Irish Fusiliers. Both Low and French were Faughs.

Leave was granted that allowed visits to Rome and many took the opportunity to attend audiences in the Vatican, including numbers not of Pope Pius's flock. On 9 July came the news that 6th Inniskillings would be disbanded with the battalion's place in the Irish Brigade taken by the 2nd Battalion, which was being transferred from 5th Division. The brigade moved to Taranto to board troopships for Alexandria and Qassasin, a major tented complex some twenty miles from Ismailia and seventy from Cairo. Regular leave parties visited Cairo, Ismailia and Alexandria while a range of facilities was provided at Qassasin, including cinemas, recreational clubs and a well-stocked NAAFI. The Lumps were camped at Sidi Bishr, on the eastern outskirts of Alexandria, where they were visited by Pat Scott and John McClinton to discuss arrangements for the amalgamation, both Scott and McClinton having arrived earlier in Egypt for that purpose.[61]

The disbandment of 6th Inniskillings began on 6 August with the battalion ceasing to exist on the 10th. It was a sad occasion, especially as 6th Inniskillings had gained such battle honours as Bou Arada and Centuripe. One 2nd Battalion officer, Roy Hingston MC, who would return to his civilian banking career in Ireland, was moved to pen a ballad in tribute. It included these lines:

> We mourn our loss
> But through the sweet refrains,
> Of our sad Londonderry Air
> Come stealing all the skirling, savage strains
> Of Ireland's Battle Songs,
> The songs you played and sang.
> And where those Irish songs are ever heard
> No Inniskilling can forget
> The way you fought and how your voices rang
> And as our rolling drums play out your soul,
> Proudly we add your honours on our scroll.[62]

As the 6th Battalion faded away, seventeen officers and about 300 other ranks were absorbed by the Lumps, restoring the 2nd Battalion to full strength. The remaining soldiers were transferred to the Faughs and Rifles or held as future reinforcements for any of the battalions.

Plans to send 78th Division to Palestine were scrapped: its soldiers would remain in Egypt although the division was to return to Italy as soon as possible. 'As soon as possible' turned out to be early September.

Chapter 7

The Road to Florence and the Road to Rome

While the Irish Brigade was fighting at Lake Trasimene, the North Irish Horse, having enjoyed some rest at Valmontone, under twenty miles from Rome, were supporting 8th Indian Division's advance towards Perugia with a composite squadron of Shermans, including all the Sherman troops and Recce Troop. The squadron relieved 142 RAC's composite squadron at Bastia on 18 June. Two troops supported 17 Indian Brigade in actions along the Ripa ridge. Anti-tank guns immobilized two Shermans from Lieutenant Rogers' troop with one driver, Lance Corporal William Hill, a Tyrone man, killed. Trying to rescue the wounded Trooper Linton, Lance Corporal Archibald Jackson from Londonderry was wounded fatally by enemy fire. The composite squadron continued working with 6th Lancers, an Indian armoured unit, as 8th Indian Division advanced northwards from the ridge.[1]

On 21 June troops of the composite squadron supported mopping-up operations by their respective infantry companies in which Lieutenant Irwin's troop killed between thirty to forty Germans and captured six and Lieutenant Garstin's tanks knocked out two machine-gun positions. Both troops were later withdrawn to replenish, having been in action for twenty-six hours. Over the next two days the tanks provided harassing fire for the infantry before being relieved by 3rd Hussars. The Shermans were left at Bastia since the regiment was to be re-equipped. Churchill NA75s, fitted with Sherman 75mm guns and mantlets, were to become the main equipment of the regiment, the first to receive the modified version. (Initially, each troop received two NA75s, retaining one 6-pounder-equipped Churchill.) Some Shermans were retained for Recce Troop along with Honeys. A three-week period out of action allowed time for maintenance, training and shooting, as well as two-day leave passes to Rome.[2]

The regiment reverted to 4th Division on 17 July, joining 28 Brigade at Arezzo, roughly seventy-five miles to the north. Some of the impetus of the Allied advance had been lost but efforts were underway to restore it. Brigadier Montague Douglas-Scott, 28 Brigade's commander, explained that the division was to advance through Chianti country, via the Arno valley, to liberate

Florence. The route was difficult with a lack of roads restricting manoeuvre. When 1 and 2 Troops were moving to the start line for an attack on Meleto, a gully had to be crossed and Sergeant Terence McQueen from Bangor, County Down dismounted to guide the tanks across. He was killed by enemy fire.[3]

Fighting during the 22nd and 23rd involved close co-operation between A and C Squadrons and infantry, with the former supporting 2nd King's. When the attack on Meleto resumed at first light on the 23rd, A Squadron Churchills had great difficulty negotiating three river crossings, each having been damaged by C Squadron the previous day.

> This new problem was to be a constant menace thereafter; great driving skill was required as tanks skidded and slewed down the approach, followed by the scrabbled climb out on the far side; with the driver's view restricted greatly by the Churchill's tracks, good understanding between commander and driver was essential.[4]

Because of the delay, the CO asked that H Hour be put back. However, at 0530 Italian partisans reported that Meleto had been abandoned; two companies of the King's with A Squadron moved in, only to be shelled, mortared and machine-gunned while taking up positions. Some StuGs appeared, engaging the tanks from close range before moving off. Defensive positions were established but no counter-attack materialized.[5]

The advance continued over the following days with A Squadron working with the King's, B Squadron with 2nd Somerset LI and C Squadron with 2/4th Hampshires. On the 31st, San Martino was liberated and the squadrons moved on. By the morning of the 4th, leading elements of 4th Division were at La Croce overlooking Florence. Since an agreement had been reached to treat Florence as an open city, the advance was to stop at Vicchio, a mile and a half south of the Arno river. C Squadron and Recce Troop were instructed to rejoin the regiment near Le Carti but, as they moved back, came under heavy shellfire that killed two men and wounded seven. The dead were Sergeant James Clulow from Portadown, County Armagh and Trooper Bertie Coote from Luton, Bedfordshire.[6] Sergeant Clulow's father, Private Joseph Clulow, had been killed in action with the Royal Irish Fusiliers in Belgium in 1917.[7]

Subsequent days were spent working with infantry units on clearing-up operations, especially around Incontro where, once again, the regiment demonstrated the Churchill's remarkable mountain-climbing ability. D Company, 2nd Duke of Cornwall's was supported by B Squadron in its attack on the German-held monastery at Incontro with the tanks putting fire down on enemy positions only fifty yards ahead of the infantry. Eventually,

Major Mackean ordered 4 Troop to assist the infantry who had taken the monastery but were being counter-attacked and under heavy artillery bombardment. Since 4 Troop was on a nearby ridge, the move involved descending a precipitous slope, a short drive along the valley floor and 'a slow, agonizing climb'. Against very light opposition, the troop made the move and entered the monastery grounds by demolishing a wall. None of the Churchills had suffered any damage, nor had they fired any shots. No anti-tank guns opposed them because the Germans had not considered the terrain suitable for tanks.[8] As in Tunisia, 4 Troop B Squadron had shown how the Churchill and determined crews could support infantry regardless of the ground. The 25 Tank Brigade narrative of operations comments,

> The capture of Incontro by tanks of the North Irish Horse, up what appeared to be an almost unscaleable height for tracked vehicles, completely disorganized the enemy.... The capture of this position undoubtedly forced the enemy to abandon his positions south of the Arno.[9]

German losses were significant, as were those of the Dukes, while the Horse had suffered only five wounded in B Squadron.

By midnight on 10 August 1st Division had relieved 4th and, in pouring rain, the regiment was concentrating east of San Donato ready to move farther south ready for its part in Operation OLIVE.

* * *

The number of Irish units in Italy was reducing. Not only had 1st Irish Guards been withdrawn and 6th Inniskillings disbanded, 117th LAA Regiment had also been disbanded. Its personnel, including 8th Royal Ulster Rifles' originals, were dispersed amongst the three Green Jacket battalions of the newly-formed 61 Brigade, commanded by an Irishman, Brigadier Adrian Gore. Born into an old Donegal family, Gore grew up in Kildare and lost his father, CO of an Argylls' battalion, who was killed in action in April 1918. Commissioned in the Rifle Brigade, Adrian Gore had seen service in 6th Armoured Division in Tunisia, becoming CO of 10th Rifle Brigade. Promoted to brigadier in February 1944, he took command of 2 Brigade in 1st Division on 23 February in the Anzio beachhead. When 61 Brigade was formed as M Brigade, he was chosen to command. It was quickly renamed 61 Brigade; the unofficial style 61 (Rifle) Brigade was preferred.[10]

Other factors influenced units in Italy, most significantly the manpower shortage faced by the Army which was involved in campaigns across the globe and had undertaken yet another, the liberation of North-West Europe. In preparation for Operation OVERLORD, Alexander was informed that no further reinforcements would be sent to Italy after February 1944 when 13,250 infantry personnel left the UK for the Mediterranean. Not until September could further reinforcements from the UK be expected. Eighth Army, and the British elements of Fifth Army, would have to rely on local arrangements to reinforce front-line infantry units. With the Luftwaffe threat diminishing, personnel from redundant anti-aircraft regiments could be retrained as infantry, as happened with 117th. The manpower situation worsened when both II US and Juin's French Expeditionary Corps were withdrawn to prepare for the planned landings in southern France, Operation DRAGOON.[11]

The Black Cats of 56th Division returned to Italy, 1st London Irish travelling from Taranto to Tivoli and thence to Assisi, birthplace of Italy's patron saint, Francis. At Tivoli the battalion had been visited by King George VI who also ventured close to the Allied front line and walked some of the Cassino battleground.[12] However, it was at Assisi that the Rifles learned something of the planned Allied offensive against the German Gothic, or Green, Line, another formidable set of defences that had to be broken before Allied armies could debouch on the plain of Lombardy. V Corps, parent of 56th Division,

> with overwhelming forces of armour, guns and infantry, was to smash through on the Adriatic, while [Fifth] Army was to forge on to Bologna and beyond. 'First Stop Venice' was the theme and then Vienna. A formidable force was augmented by men of the Polish Army and by our redoubtable cousins from Canada.[13]

* * *

Preceding OLIVE, the attack on the Gothic Line, a deception plan, Operation ULSTER, was designed to confuse the Germans about Allied intentions. The initial plan for both armies to attack in the central region, through the Futa and Il Giogio passes, was revised when the FEC was assigned to DRAGOON and because of friction between Leese and Clark. While Eighth Army attacked on the Adriatic sector towards Pesaro and Rimini, forcing Kesselring to deploy reserves from the central area, Fifth Army would punch into the Apennines towards Bologna, with XIII British Corps on its right, swinging towards the Adriatic in a pincer. To execute the plan, most of Eighth Army had to sidestep right with Operation ULSTER's aims including concealing that move from the Germans. The deception was successful: General Heinrich von Vietinghoff, commanding Tenth Army, and Major General Richard Heydrich, commanding 1st Fallschirmjäger Division, were on leave when Eighth Army struck.[14]

Operation OLIVE would also include 38 (Irish) Brigade but, with 78th Division, in XIII Corps in Fifth Army. We shall return to OLIVE after considering the roles of other Irish units in the meantime, beginning with 9th (Londonderry) HAA Regiment, by then the longest-serving Irish unit in the Mediterranean, having arrived in Egypt in November 1939. When last we encountered the Derry Boys, they had moved from Naples to new positions in Torre Annunziata and Castellammare di Stabia, two small ports used to re-supply the Allies. New landing grounds at Vesuvius and Pompeii also became regimental responsibilities with Lieutenant Colonel Aitken as AADC for both ports and Majors Jimmy Henderson and Sir Basil McFarland, commanding 24 and 25 Batteries, AADCs of Vesuvius and Pompeii respectively. The gunners were also to defend ships engaged in beach-landing exercises, rehearsals for Operation SHINGLE, the Anzio landings.[15]

February was one of the quietest months 9th Regiment had experienced since June 1940 with few enemy aircraft appearing. That allowed time for training and recreation. Sir Basil McFarland had established a regimental rest camp at Ravello, close to the Italian royal family residence. At the end of February, 26 Battery said goodbye to its second commander in under a year when Jack McVeigh of Londonderry was transferred to a training role in the UK; his predecessor, Major Sam Haughton, from Cullybackey, had been invalided home early in 1943. March began quietly with training continuing and no alarms until the 15th. Saint Patrick's Day, a regimental holiday, was marked in the usual manner but no one expected the nearby volcano to join in the celebrations.[16]

For the first time in eighty years, Vesuvius erupted. Only days before, gunners from 9th Regiment, including the author's father, had been on top of the mountain looking into the crater. The eruption brought the regiment a new role: aid to the civilian population. For over a week, streams of lava poured from Vesuvius as clouds of ash and dust rose into the sky; a 25 Battery height-finder recorded clouds rising to 20,000 feet. Gunners were mobilized to evacuate civilians from homes threatened by lava, dust and ash. Radio signals were blacked out and visibility at times was under 100 feet. One veteran told the author that it was his most frightening experience of the war since he had been too busy to worry during air raids.[17]

Local roads were cleared by the end of the month when 9th Regiment moved again. Although 26 Battery remained near Castellammare, 24 moved to Salerno and 25 to Naples. Both 25 and 26 Batteries engaged intruders on 16 and 21 April while, on the 22nd, fourteen rounds were fired at a group of aircraft that quickly identified themselves as 'friendly', the first of three such incidents that month. There was a major Luftwaffe raid on Naples harbour on the 24th with about fifty bombers attacking from all directions with *Düppel* used. However, the guns had no problems tracking aircraft. Raids on Salerno followed, plus more on Naples, but Luftwaffe strength continued waning.[18]

Following some training as field artillery, a role the regiment had undertaken 'for real', 9th moved to Torre del Greco, home to Italy's first president, Enrico de Nicola, and chef Gino D'Acampo, prior to travelling north to Anzio. From Anzio the regiment sent its representative party to Pope Pius XII's Irish audience in the Vatican on 12 June (some had attended an audience on the 9th).[19] At least one 25 Battery member had foreseen the regiment travelling up the road to Rome as far back as July 1942. How so?

At Kasfareet in the Canal Zone on 12 July 1942 the Derry Boys celebrated the anniversary of the 1690 Battle of the Boyne. At home, the date was marked by parades of the Orange Order, a Protestant organization but, in Egypt, it was marked by all denominations, with a Catholic gunner even speaking from the platform at 'The Field'. To mark the occasion, an Orange arch was built from packing cases and other materials. It included a representation of King William on a white horse at the Boyne, created by Johnnie Kitson who declared that 'King Billy' should be retained: 'we can put him on the Number One lorry when we drive up to Rome.'[20]

True enough, 25 Battery's No.1 Matador, as well as its usual 'Aberfoyle' (Sir Basil McFarland's home) headboard, had the painted metal image of King William wired to its radiator. The effect was to prompt the senior US Army officer in charge of movements, to have the Matador stopped to interrogate the driver, Gunner Cameron 'Cam' Finlay, on the significance of the image. The reply that 'It's King Billy crossing the Boyne on his white horse, sir' meant nothing, and the American could elicit no further information. Exasperated, he noticed the jeep bearing the white saltire of a major and, probably, the battery commander which he then stopped; it was Major McFarland's jeep. When the American explained his frustration – who was King Billy? why was he on a white horse? where was the Boyne? – Sir Basil suggested that a Don R (despatch rider) close behind could help. Thus, the Don R was stopped and, to the American's delight, explained something of the Williamite/Jacobite war in Ireland and, particularly, the battle of the Boyne. Thanking the Don R and telling him to 'drive on', the colonel expressed his thanks to a smiling Sir Basil who commented that the American had missed the best element of the story. 'What was that, Major?' 'The man who couldn't tell you much is a member of the Orange Order, to whom King Billy is a bit like the Second Coming. The man who enlightened you is a Roman Catholic, to whose community King Billy is almost the devil incarnate.' Sir Basil then asked Tom Patton, a Strabane man, who was also in the Matador's cab, 'Did you not know, Gunner Patton?' 'Sure, I thought it was Patrick Sarsfield, sir.'

That evening the Don R was questioned by his comrades about his knowledge of the Williamite war. He explained that he had started his Army life in the Royal Inniskilling Fusiliers 'and it's part of our regimental history'. The Don R, Gunner J.J. Doherty, from Drumenny, County Tyrone, had enlisted in the Corps of Royal Inniskilling and Royal Irish Fusiliers in January 1927, serving most of his career with the Faughs.[21]

Ninth Regiment spent only a short time at Anzio, with 24 Battery detached defending bridges over the Garigliano (a radar unit had been detached to Ischia for weeks under RAF command). There were alerts on each of the first three nights at Anzio; the third was an attack by more than a score of enemy aircraft, again using *Düppel*. That lasted seventy-five minutes with one aircraft claimed as shot down; although fires were started in an ammunition dump, no ships were damaged. Weary gunners, dripping sweat, welcomed the 'all clear' when it sounded at dawn, completely unaware that they had fought their last anti-aircraft engagement in Italy. In their remaining time in Italy, they would serve as field gunners in Fifth Army.[22]

Chapter 8

The Gothic Line

Of the Irish infantry units, the first to return to Italy was 1st London Irish, with 56th Division arriving at Taranto in mid-July to entrain for Tivoli. Whilst there, Pope Pius granted an audience; only a small representation of the battalion had been present for the Pope's Irish audience in June.[1] King George VI was visiting Italy at the time and visited 56th Division at Tivoli. The king also knighted Lieutenant General Richard McCreery, X Corps' commander.[2]

However, the business of war had to be dealt with and Alexander's armies were preparing to attack the Gothic Line. With the term 'Gothic' harking back to the Goths, a Germanic people, its use for a defensive line had significance for the Germans not far removed from that of the Hitler Line. As with the Hitler Line, the name was changed to Green Line by Kesselring (on Hitler's orders) lest it be broken, a change ignored by the Allies and most subsequent writers.[3]

The Black Cats, as part of V Corps, would not be involved in the opening phase of OLIVE, the corps being disposed in the centre left of Eighth Army's line, from east of Fossombrone to the boundary with X Corps, roughly along Highway 73. Moreover, 56th Division was in reserve when OLIVE began, as were 1st Armoured Division and 25 Tank Brigade. The last formation included the North Irish Horse while 1st Armoured Division included Brigadier Richard Goodbody DSO's 2 Armoured Brigade. Goodbody had commanded 11th Royal Horse Artillery in HUSKY and had taken command of the brigade in February.

Leese's plan was in three phases, the first an assault on the defences before they were manned fully. Should that not achieve its aim, the line would be forced. That done, success would be exploited through 'a deep and rapid advance with the aim of encircling and destroying the whole left wing of the German Army'.[4] As with DIADEM in May, a deception scheme, ULSTER, had been developed which, again, proved successful.

In his order of the day to Eighth Army, Leese wrote:

> Now we begin the last lap. Swiftly and secretly, once again, we have moved right across Italy an Army of immense strength and striking power – to break the Gothic Line.
>
> Victory in the coming battles means the beginning of the end of the German Armies in Italy.
>
> Let every man do his utmost and again success will be ours.[5]

The impression was created that Eighth Army was about to enter its last major battle and there certainly was an air of optimism.

Set against that optimism was weakness in the command structure of HQ V Corps and three of its divisional HQs, including that of 1st Armoured Division. Jackson noted that none of them were 'run in', with V Corps not having undertaken a major operation since December 1943 after which it held the Adriatic sector. By August 1944, it was at its strongest and almost an army, deploying an armoured and four infantry divisions, plus the Italian Corps of Liberation. First Armoured Division had last deployed for action in Tunisia and, while its brigades and units had been assigned in July and August, the GOC, Major General Richard Hull, was not appointed until 14 August. Although Goodbody had been appointed to command 2 Armoured Brigade (The Bays, 10th Hussars and 9th Lancers with 1st King's Royal Rifle Corps the infantry component) in February, there had been little time for training as a formation and none to train with the two infantry brigades, 18 and 43 (Gurkha). The Gurkhas had joined on 2 August but 18 Brigade arrived only on the 18th.[6]

Shortly before midnight on 25/26 August, British, Canadian and Polish brigades crossed the Metauro river. Only then did Eighth Army's artillery begin bombarding the seven-mile front. By dawn the leading units had advanced two miles. From prisoners came confirmation that both von Vietinghoff and Heydrich were on leave; ULSTER had worked. Moreover, Kesselring saw the Allied offensive as a diversion, in an example of what has been described as his 'Anzio Syndrome' whereby any Allied ground offensive in Italy was seen as an attempt to cloak different intentions. As Eighth Army moved forward, Kesselring suspected Fifth Army would launch the main Allied attack. In Germany the head of OKW, Jodl, already believed the Allies might attempt to land at the head of the Adriatic.[7]

In the early stages good progress was made and it seemed the Germans were falling back, although a planned re-organization was underway. I Canadian Corps met some strong opposition, the British Columbia Dragoons losing thirty Shermans in half a mile. The CO, Lieutenant Colonel Frederick Vokes, younger brother of Armagh-born Major General Chris Vokes, was among those killed.[8] On the night of 30 August, 46th Division deployed Brigadier Kendrew's 128 (Hampshire) Brigade, supported by the North Irish Horse and 46th Reconnaissance Regiment in an attack on the German bastion of Montegridolfo.[9]

During the night of the 29th/30th tank and infantry personnel recce'ed approaches to the Foglia river, finding only a single crossing suitable for armour. Early on the morning of the 30th, Lord O'Neill and Brigadier Kendrew made a recce from Colbordolo, from where the Gothic Line looked truly formidable. One Horse officer described it as 'an elaborate killing ground', adding that 'All houses had been razed to the ground, trees and vines felled and avenues prepared between extensive minefields for a hail of machine-gun fire'.[10]

An initial plan to use Recce Squadron tanks to support 2nd Hampshires came to naught because of the terrain but, on the 31st, A and B Squadrons crossed the Foglia by a Sherman-dozer-made crossing. Thereafter, A Squadron supported 2nd Hampshires' attack on Monte Le Vecchie which commanded the lower ground south of Montegridolfo. Extensive mining, both off and on the road, meant that sappers had to be called upon while a concealed StuG opened fire. So jagged and steep was the hillside that not even Churchills could ascend. A Squadron was ordered to remain in place to provide fire. Also supporting the attack, intended to outflank Montegridolfo, were Recce Troop, 46th Reconnaissance Regiment and 5th Hampshires, all under Kendrew who had borrowed the North Irish Horse 'Gin Box', the CO's armoured command vehicle. At the same time, 2nd Hampshires had made steady progress. The lead was taken over by 1/4th Hampshires, supported by B Squadron, who captured Montegridolfo just before 1800. Kendrew's brigade with its Horse support had advanced almost two miles. In two days, a crack had been created in the Gothic Line but there remained much more fighting.[11]

Major General 'Ginger' Hawkesworth, GOC 46th Division, urged his troops forward to the Coriano ridge, about three-and-a-half miles inland, behind which lay open country. From the ridge, the final high feature before that open country, 1st Armoured Division could advance to the Po and the Lombardy plain. Hawkesworth's division attacked on 1 September with all three brigades up; 128 Brigade, the centre formation, was again supported by the Horse. Working with 5th Hampshires, A Squadron supported the infantry on the high ground west of Montegridolfo and then, before midday, co-operated with both 1/4th and 5th Hampshires in mopping up the area. Not long after, some StuGs were observed approaching from the east, heading south towards Meleto. When another group of five StuGs entered the Colle Longhi area, one was engaged by Major Robin Griffith's tank while another, spotted by 5th Hampshires in Meleto, drove off when engaged. It was late evening before another StuG was sighted – and knocked out by Lieutenant Hunt's No.3 Troop.[12]

At 0200 on 2 September a German counter-attack, including some tanks, was beaten off by 5th Hampshires and their supporting Churchills. A Squadron remained firm near Montegridolfo but was not committed to action. Later the squadron was recalled to the regiment.[13]

The Horse relieved 142nd Regiment RAC at Maria del Monte and, on 3 September, crossed the river Conca. An attack on Coriano followed to secure bridges over the river Marano. Five days after crossing the Conca, the regiment was withdrawn. The fighting had been difficult and it became clear that Coriano ridge was held in greater strength than had been believed. One Churchill was hit, killing four men, although Captain Hern, the commander, was uninjured. However, traffic chaos on the route forward delayed 1st Armoured Division whose attack was not launched until late afternoon. Although the Horse and 46 Recce had encountered stout opposition in the morning, the Germans subsequently evacuated Coriano ridge. When no major British attack occurred, German units returned.[14]

The war diary of Kendrew's brigade includes a tribute to the North Irish Horse.

> A special tribute must be paid to squadrons of the North Irish Horse. Day after day their Churchills forced positions and supported our infantry over appalling tank country. Undaunted, squadron leaders on foot led their tanks up seemingly impossible slopes. One tank actually slipped over and crashed 200 feet.[15]

* * *

Goodbody's 2 Armoured Brigade was to spearhead the armoured thrust off Coriano ridge on 5 September but it was 1545 before the armour advanced. By then the sun was low and Goodbody's units had it glaring into their eyes. On the other hand, the defenders enjoyed perfect visibility and the tanks, StuGs and anti-tank guns that had returned to the ridge during the day took a heavy toll of the British armour. Of 141 tanks, fifty-five were lost, although not all were knocked out by enemy action; the difficulties of the move forward meant that many had mechanical problems. The heaviest toll had been suffered by 9th Lancers. The absence of 1st Armoured Division's two infantry brigades had also contributed to the attack's failure. (Because of the mountainous terrain of Italy, the infantry component of armoured divisions had been increased to two brigades.)[16] In the aftermath of the battle, the division was withdrawn from the line; it was disbanded formally in January 1945. However, 2 Armoured Brigade survived and Richard Goodbody remained as commander.[17]

By the time 2 Armoured Brigade made its attack on Coriano, 1st Irish Rifles were back in action, their part in the battle beginning with the companies approaching the battle area being shelled in their troop-carrying vehicles. The 56th Division historian commented that, for the Black Cats,

> the battle for the Gothic Line started a little unsatisfactorily, for, unlike 4th Indian Division on its right and the 46th Division on the left, it was not launched on a set timing, but insinuated at short notice into a gap between the two formations.[18]

Unsatisfactory is an understatement where the Rifles were concerned. Arriving at Morciano, the battalion was directed to Croce but, moving there, came under heavy shelling and mortaring from both Croce and Gemmano, a nearby hill. Two companies with a tactical HQ moved onto a ridge leading to Croce, dug in and found a Royal Fusilier company nearby: it had been believed that the Fusiliers were in Croce. Battalion vehicles following up were machine-gunned, mortared and bombarded by 88s at a crossroads that became known as 'Stonk Corner'. To add to the confusion, orders were received from brigade HQ to attack San Savino cemetery and Point 168. Lieutenant Colonel Baucher had to reconnoitre in fading light before issuing his orders with the help of a map and a compass bearing on a burning haystack. As the regimental history comments, time for reconnaissance was rarely given by higher authority at that time, 'the mistaken impression still persisting that the Germans were on the run in spite of obvious evidence to the contrary'. It was 'a lamentable and noticeable feature of the conduct of the campaign at that period' was the regimental historian's acerbic view.[19]

D Company, led by 18 Platoon, set off across a valley to climb San Savino ridge. B Company followed. Both were suddenly assailed by machine-gun fire from concealed positions and went to ground, waiting for complete darkness before resuming their march, with artillery support. Then 18 Platoon came under fire from a house some fifty yards away. Lieutenant Spiller of 16 Platoon sent two sections to attack with grenades and Brens, taking the Germans by surprise and surrounding the house. Not far away, 17 Platoon was also battling with Germans holding out in houses on the edge of Croce. When the Germans counter-attacked, 17 Platoon was able to beat them off but further attacks were stronger and the Rifles fell back about 100 yards.[20] In that withdrawal, 18 Platoon, led by Sergeant Sam Henry and Corporal Laurence Martini, fought the enemy to a standstill. Both Sam Henry and Laurence Martini were awarded the MM. Henry showed 'the highest qualities of leadership and individual courage [and] controlled his platoon with magnificent combination of dash and coolness, encouraging his men, and himself going to meet the enemy attacks'.[21] Martini showed 'aggression, initiative and cool courage [and] kept his section together and beat off all attacks' during ninety minutes of brutal close-quarter fighting.[22]

The Germans made a further attack, their third, and in greater strength, on D Company. Although having had no rest, the riflemen held off the attack for fifteen minutes before, although much stronger, the attackers withdrew. A short spell of silence was broken when a German officer called out that he and his soldiers wished to surrender. D Company's OC, Major Terry Sweeney, approached to accept the surrender. The Germans challenged him and, without further warning, shot him dead. So enraged were the company's men that they charged from their defensive positions and set upon the attackers. Although short of ammunition, the charge caused the Germans to throw in reinforcements, prompting the company to quit Point 168. They left seventeen dead Germans there.[23]

Company Sergeant Major Patrick McDaid was awarded the DCM for his outstanding work in rallying his men and taking over command when Major Sweeney was killed. He 'conducted the fight with the greatest skill and determination, keeping a steady control of the situation, yet not sparing himself to move up immediately to deal with any enemy infiltration.' He then oversaw the evacuation of the wounded before volunteering to go forward with another company to retake Point 168.[24] During the evacuation, the stretcher-bearers were outstanding while Rifleman McDonald at the RAP earned the MM for his courage in attending the wounded during the action and for getting all but one – a rifleman who remained with his Bren – to safety. The citation noted that 'his selfless and courageous persistence in his duty without doubt saved the lives of several men'.[25]

Next morning a further attack on Point 168 was planned but, as Lieutenant Colonel Baucher and both surviving company commanders were holding their O Group, a passing British tank was targeted by German guns and a shell landed in the O Group, killing three soldiers and wounding the others present. Major Alec Smith of 445 Battery, 65th Field Regiment, who was among the wounded, refused evacuation until he had passed the CO's plan to Major Brett, the second-in-command, who arrived from B Echelon on a motorbike to take command. Smith was later awarded the MC.[26]

C Company, under Lieutenant John Prosser, attacked Point 168 with strong artillery support and secured the position. Sergeant Robert Gamble led his platoon across open ground and under heavy fire 'with a magnificent display of determination, courage and cheerfulness'. When one of the two surviving officers was wounded, it was 'largely due to [Gamble] that the morale of the Pl[atoon] was maintained under those very adverse conditions'. A former Royal Irish Fusilier, Robert Gamble organized attacks on each of six MG positions, eliminating three of them himself. His example inspired all of C Company 'and largely contributed to the successful capture of the objective'. Sergeant Gamble was awarded the MM.[27]

The divisional history notes that the 'Irish attacked during the relief of a German battalion, with the result that they had in fact two battalions with which to contend'. Company seconds-in-command took over A and C Companies, the regimental history noting that 'the battalion was prepared to stay in its positions indefinitely, and if necessary to advance'.[28]

No opportunity for rest was given. Having buried the dead, the battalion, less A Company, was ordered to Morciano; A Company was to protect the London Scottish right flank, the Scots being in Il Palazzo, the centre of a horseshoe-shaped ridge. Croce and San Savino were on either edge of the ridge. During the night, the Germans prepared an attack which was launched in the early morning, forcing the London Scottish to quit Il Palazzo although A Company held on to its pivotal position. Gemmano fell to 167 Brigade and 1st Welch of 168 Brigade remained in Croce. Following only sixteen hours' 'rest' 1st London Irish returned to the fray and positions they had left only the day before.[29]

San Savino ridge was the key to Croce, itself key to V Corps' line. For three days the battalion remained there, enduring heavy shelling and mortaring and attempts by enemy patrols to penetrate the line. There were many casualties but the greatest loss in those days was 39-year-old CSM Patrick Keenan from Belfast, who had enlisted in the Royal Inniskilling Fusiliers almost two decades earlier. Keenan, 'a magnificent soldier and man', died in his slit trench when a mortar bomb burst in trees above it. Lieutenant Alan Soutar, formerly of the Highland Light Infantry, was killed while on a patrol towards Il Palazzo. Soutar died during an exchange of fire with Germans, although he may have been killed by British artillery which put down a bombardment on the immediate area where he was. The NCO accompanying him, whom Soutar had ordered to remain in a ditch, found no trace of the subaltern but did find two dead Germans.[30]

During the battalion's days on the ridge, the mortar platoon was kept busy but received considerable return fire that injured men and damaged vehicles. A direct hit on a house wounded a sergeant. On the night of the 10th/11th, the battalion was relieved and set off for Morciano from where personnel were ferried to 'a delightful spot near the coast away from the shells and smells of battle'. An intelligence section sergeant was wounded by a stray shell during the move.[31]

A well-rested battalion went forward beyond San Savino on the 16th, crossing the Marano at Francescini and suffering casualties before fighting for the ridge overlooking the river, during which they endured Nebelwerfer bombardment. The ridge was taken, the London Scottish passed through and the Rifles set off next morning to seize Monte Olivo, an attack led by A and D Companies who secured the crossroads at Cortellini, which was critical to the plan. A Company accounted for two horse-drawn anti-tank guns while D Company, pushing on, crested Monte Olivo and was brought to a standstill. B and C Companies joined the battle and the mortars were emplaced nearby. Fighting continued throughout the day with no further progress being made. Although 1st Welch passed through at Cortellini, intending to outflank Monte Olivo, they were pinned down on the exposed ridge at Point 227. A Company deployed to assist them.[32]

Next day both the Welch and Rifles tried to advance but remained fixed by intense enemy fire. Although B Company tried to flank around 227, the platoons were caught in V Corps' bombardment and had to go to ground and dig in. Enemy fire intensified with many more casualties occurring: the medical team and 'the stretcher-bearers were beyond praise for their work in coping with the steady stream of wounded which they got back to the regimental aid post'.[33]

Late in the afternoon of 19 September, Brigadier F.R.G. Matthews, commanding 168 Brigade, announced that the London Scottish were on the banks of the Ausa and ordered 1st London Irish to disengage and join the London Scottish to help them cross the river. Not until darkness fell was it possible to disengage since the Germans were so close but, under cover of night, 1st Welch took over 'and the London Irish, tired almost to exhaustion, set off on a seven-mile march and to cross a river which no one had seen'.[34]

In concert with the London Scottish, the battalion made a plan for crossing the Ausa but, contrary to what had been believed, the river was held in strength and both battalions met severe opposition with B Company and a London Scottish company involved in attacks and counter-attacks in which both they and the opposition suffered many losses. However, B Company rallied and made it to the far side to be joined by C and D Companies; A had a difficult time, suffering several German assaults that threatened to force it back across the river. But the joint Irish-Scottish lodgement remained and other battalions crossed to both their left and right. When San Marino, the tiny landlocked republic to the west, was taken, it appeared as if the road to the Lombardy Plain was open. For the time being, the battalion remained in place before being withdrawn that afternoon. Such was the toll of the fighting thus far in OLIVE that 1st London Irish could muster only two understrength companies.[35]

Across 56th (London) Division, the manpower situation was equally dire, the Black Cats having suffered 6,000 casualties in September. At the beginning of October, a re-organization took place in which 168 Brigade ceased to exist, 1st Welch, 7th Ox and Bucks and 8th Royal Fusiliers were reduced to cadres, their personnel dispersed to reinforce other battalions. Many of 1st Welch joined the London Irish which moved to 167 Brigade with the London Scottish and 9th Royal Fusiliers.[36] At much the same time, 1st London Irish welcomed its new CO, Lieutenant Colonel John A. Sperling DSO, who had been CO of the disbanded 8th Royal Fusiliers with whom he had earned the DSO at Croce earlier in the month.[37]

On 26 September the battalion was on the move again, but the operation in which it was intended to participate was postponed. The Rifles returned to Morciano on 2 October and thence to Fermo, close to Ancona. In the September battles along the Gothic Line, eighty-five officers and men had perished and a further 245 were wounded. The price had been high and the battalion needed to be rebuilt. Until that could be done, A Company was disbanded.[38]

Mention has already been made of the ending of reinforcements from the UK in February which meant that British formations in Italy had to find reinforcements from within the Mediterranean region. In Egypt after the Anzio campaign, Baucher had tried to find as many Irish soldiers as possible but was unable to find enough to restore his battalion to its normal strength. Included in the personnel posted in were gunners from disbanded AA units, among whom were some Irish; there was a higher proportion of Irish among the officers of those units. Thus, when the battalion returned to Italy with almost 1,000 personnel, only about 250 were Irish.[39] However, the Irish ethos remained strong. The same problem would affect the infantry of 38 (Irish) Brigade.

* * *

The North Irish Horse had fought in shaping actions leading up to Operation OLIVE as well as the opening days of the offensive and at Coriano. On 8 September the regiment moved to Tomba di Pesaro with 51st Royal Tanks, leaving 142 RAC with 46th Division, to come under I Canadian Corps and supporting 4th Division. Once again, the Horse would support 28 Brigade with squadrons resuming previous battalion affiliations.[40]

Three days earlier, Alexander had launched Fifth Army (II and IV US Corps, plus XIII British Corps) on its offensive. Since Eighth Army's offensive was 'sticking' on the left flank, Leese chose to shift its weight to the right and transferred the role of 'pursuit corps' to the Canadians, reinforced by 4th Division and 2nd New Zealand Division; HQ 25 Tank Brigade, the Horse and 51st Royal Tanks, were assigned to 4th Division. His plan to destroy von Vietinghoff's Adriatic defences involved I Canadian Corps deploying both 5th Canadian and 1st British Armoured Divisions on the right flank and 46th British and 4th Indian Divisions on the left. In the second phase, 4th Division was to pass through 5th Canadian Armoured and, with 1st Armoured, seize and secure Ripabianca ridge which overlooked the Marano river. Between those two formations, 56th Division was to take 'any features vital to defence'. Bridgeheads over the Marano would then be created by 1st Canadian and 4th Divisions with artillery support from I Canadian Corps artillery. In Phase III, 1st Canadian and 4th Divisions would break through the Rimini Line by destroying LXXVI Panzerkorps' defences on San Fortunato ridge, following which 5th Canadian Armoured Division was to be prepared to pass through and exploit to the Marecchia river and the Po valley.[41]

With bad weather delaying the regrouping process and thus the launch of Eighth Army's renewed offensive, it was 0100 on 15 September before A and C Squadrons moved off to marry with their infantry, 2nd King's and 2/4th Hampshires. Having crossed the river, both took their objectives: C Squadron and the Hampshires were on the Bagli ridge by 1200 and A and the Kings were farther along the ridge by noon, looking down on the Ausa. Both squadrons remained with the infantry through the day, enduring shelling that confined them to their tanks. Commanders became adept at gauging when enemy artillery was about to strike a tank and choosing the moment to move 100 yards or so to right or left. The call of nature was dealt with by using an 75mm round which, when full, was emptied by the commander, who 'had to stick his head out to make sure there were no friends in the vicinity'.[42]

That night an infantry handover was accompanied by the arrival of a troop of B Squadron under Lieutenant Basil King. Covered by another troop, King, moving on foot to recce the ground and contact the infantry, spotted a Panzer IV. As he manoeuvred his troop to engage it, the Panzer IV almost simultaneously knocked out two of his tanks before being knocked out by another troop of Churchills. After evacuating the wounded crewmen, King made another recce and discovered a Panther on which he directed sustained and accurate fire that prompted the crew to bale out and surrender. Although wounded, King continued such work until he was evacuated. He was awarded the MC.[43]

While there were small successes, the impetus of 4th Division's advance remained slow and the tanks were kept busy in their infantry-support role although, on occasion, communications were almost non-existent. The Marecchia, about five miles north of the Ausa, had to be crossed before the autumn rains began. The Horse became involved on the night of 21/22 September, but rain had already begun and continued falling heavily on the 21st, forcing cancellation of tank operations. That was the day the Canadians liberated Rimini and Fifth Army broke through the Futa Pass. During the afternoon of the 22nd the tanks were back in action with Sergeant Tommy McAughtry, temporarily commanding a troop, leading the first tanks to reach Highway 9, having led a last-light attack on a German strongpoint in San Giustina. During the night the Churchills remained with 2nd Somersets and McAughtry's tanks helped them fight off a series of counter-attacks. On the 10th the tanks 'drew exceptionally heavy shelling but McAughtry spent the day in and out of his tank liaising with the Inf Comd and fighting his troop in an exemplary manner until relieved at last light'. That was the first in a series of actions that earned Tommy McAughtry the DCM.[44]

By last light on the 25th the North Irish Horse had handed over to Canadians at the end of thirty-two days of almost constant fighting. The weather had become a major factor with the Marecchia, ankle-deep on 21 September, twelve-feet deep and a seething brown torrent only a week later. From the 29th it rained without cease until 2 October. Every ford was impassable. The advance literally bogged down.[45]

* * *

When Operation OLIVE began on 25 August, 9th (Londonderry) HAA Regiment was preparing to withdraw from operations along the Arno and return to the UK for the first time since November 1939. In its final months in Italy the regiment served as part of British Increment, Fifth Army.

Having left Anzio at the end of June, the Derry Boys moved to Civitavecchia to relieve US anti-aircraft units. There they had alerts each night but only two engagements before handing over to batteries from two regiments and moving to Campiglia to await an order to move to Leghorn (Livorno) once that port was liberated. However, 26 Battery was sent to San Stefano under operational command of 12th (Finsbury Rifles) LAA Regiment.[46]

On 12 July, B Troop 24 Battery and C Troop 25 Battery moved to Rosignano Solvay to serve as field artillery alongside two troops of 55th (Kent) HAA

Regiment, making a total of sixteen guns. The move forward over bad roads was difficult and had to be carried out at night due to German artillery with, at one point, the guns being winched. Nonetheless, both troops were in position by 1030 on the 14th. The guns were 'shot in' on five targets in the Montenero area so that the locations could be 'registered' for fire support for attacking infantry. Later a concentrated shoot on enemy artillery positions on Montenero was called for; B and C Troops each fired thirty-eight rounds of high-explosive ammunition using Fuze 208, creating airbursts with each shell spraying over 300 'bullets' on the target. Fired in five salvoes, the shoot silenced the German field guns.[47]

The field deployment was to support the American 34th (Red Bull) Division, which had trained in Northern Ireland in 1942, and, especially, its 804th Tank Destroyer Battalion. (Tank destroyers were highly mobile anti-tank guns mounted on M4 tank hulls; the guns were 3-inch calibre.) Accordingly, close liaison was established with 34th Division's artillery and with 804th TD Battalion. OPs from both 24 and 25 Batteries, a recce troop from 34th Division HQ and 804th TD Battalion moved forward on the morning of 15 July. At the same time, the other troops of 24 and 25 Batteries were ordered to join their comrades; 25 Battery's guns remained at the existing position while 24's occupied a new position. Likewise, the remaining guns of 55th Regiment moved forward into the field role.[48]

As 804th TD Battalion moved forward, requests were relayed to the Derry Boys to engage a series of targets, among them a tower at Montenero that housed German OPs. Airbursts in the area and several hits on the tower led to a rapid German evacuation. That afternoon, 804th entered Quercianella, almost seven miles north of 9th Regiment's guns, but with effective fire support from 24 and 25's guns at Castiglione. Later in the day both batteries' OPs moved forward, 25's coming under heavy shelling at Quercianella. That shelling, by 88 and 105mm guns, drew a fast response: 330 airburst rounds were fired over the offending German guns, which ceased firing. The advancing tank destroyers and other elements of 34th Division also had the services of air OPs (AOPs).[49]

The German shelling of 25's OP was a response to a bombardment on their positions on Point 210. One German shell fell close to 25's wireless vehicle, wounding Battery Sergeant Major Walter Wray, an original member of the battery from its home city, who was evacuated to a US field hospital for surgery. Although the wireless lorry was damaged, the wireless operator continued transmitting. Throughout that night, eight guns from 24 and 25 Batteries fired over 500 rounds in harassing fire at irregular intervals on enemy positions.[50]

Walter Wray's wounding illustrated the dangers faced by OPs, as had the knocking out of the German OP at Montenero. Since the OP's role was to observe enemy activity, locate enemy units and call down fire, forward observers, who could move with infantry or armour, or independently, were prime targets. Those on the ground needed good vantage points which, whether hills or tall buildings, were more easily identifiable and presented valuable targets.

As the Red Bulls pressed on to Livorno on the morning of 16 July, concentrated supporting fire was laid down for them. At 1318 all guns fired on a 'suspicious target' from which so much smoke and dust rose that it was believed to be an ammunition or fuel dump. With air observation via 125th (US) Gun Battalion, both 24 Battery troops engaged several targets that evening and night, firing 482 rounds, while 25 Battery fired on anti-tank guns, infantry concentrations and road intersections at the request of 804th TD Battalion. Not only did the AOP pilot comment especially on the speed and accuracy with which both batteries reacted to requests to engage targets, but US field artillery units reported to HQ Fifth Army on the effectiveness of the British AA gunners in their adopted role. C Troop 25 Battery continued supporting the tank destroyers with harassing fire during the night as patrols encountered resistance; the four guns discharged 192 rounds. The Derry Boys continued to be called upon for support by 34th Division's artillery and throughout the morning of the 16th fired several concentrations, one of which, at 1115, broke up a formation of tanks and infantry; all sixteen guns had engaged. In the afternoon, stocks of Fuze 208 ammunition ran low and restrictions were placed on its use: it was only to meet 'determined counter-attack'. Even Fuze 199 shells were running short and were rationed to a daily fifty rounds per troop until stocks were replenished. That happened quite quickly as lorries from 45th LAA Regiment arrived that evening with further stocks, although not in such quantities that would allow a harassing fire programme throughout the night. Next morning German mortars were silenced by 25 Battery, a feat repeated that afternoon by 24; a total of three dozen rounds was used.[51]

At 0800 on the 19th came the news that Livorno had been liberated and both batteries were told to deploy in the AA role for the city. When officers of 24 recce'ed the city local people told them of the effects of their gunfire: it had been 'terrifying' and the *Tedeschi* felt likewise, ten having been killed by one airburst. The airbursts had even affected the morale of Kesselring's *Alter Hase*, or 'old hares'.[52]

C Troop 25 Battery returned to the field role on the 26th taking up positions between Livorno and the Arno, their shooting the next evening being supplemented by D Troop firing from its AA position in Livorno. Targets included StuGs, infantry concentrations and moving vehicles. On the evening of 30 July, D Troop 25 Battery fired fifty-four rounds at ten targets between 15,200 and 17,600 yards from the guns. When the final round fired at the fifth target exploded, it started a fierce fire, punctuated by explosions, suggesting that an ammunition dump had been hit.[53]

There was no shortage of targets for the 3.7s over the following days and weeks. In the build-up to D Day for OLIVE, calls for fire remained at a high level with C Troop, which had moved close to the Arno carrying out most of the shooting although D Troop, still in Livorno, also contributed. C Troop fired every day from the 1st to the 26th, supported by D Troop on numerous occasions. On virtually every occasion OPs reported that the shelling had been successful. On the 4th, C Troop knocked out three German batteries in thirty minutes. Firing from Livorno, D Troop silenced another battery that day. The Germans were unable to target 25 Battery's guns effectively, although they came close to wiping out OPs.[54]

When Winston Churchill visited Livorno on 18 August gunners from 24 Battery were included in a guard of honour commanded by Major Jimmy Henderson, an original officer of the regiment. Four days later, B Troop 24 Battery deployed in the field role in a position 2,000 yards south of Pisa. The position was described as 'decidedly too close to the enemy FDLs to be a health resort' while moving there had to be done in darkness since German artillery had the road registered.[55]

B Troop's field of fire included the Leaning Tower of Pisa. The guns were ordered not to fire within an arc 5 degrees either side of the building; the same restriction applied to 25-pounders located closer to Pisa. Bombardier Robert Hamilton, an original member of 24 Battery, was not impressed by that order, especially when he saw German soldiers bathing in the Arno within the no-fire zone. 'To hell with the Leaning Tower of Pisa ... I couldn't care about it if it had [fallen] down on top of the Germans.'[56]

The Tower was an ideal position for an OP, as were the many church towers dotting the landscape. A 25 Battery OP party took over a church tower in Marina di Pisa. Sergeant Billy Smyth, from Strabane, County Tyrone, was in the party which approached the church along a deserted street. To avoid possible booby-traps of anti-personnel mines close to the buildings they walked in the middle of a road built by Roman engineers. The church door was open but there were no signs of people about. A curtain was fluttering, the sacristy was empty and the body of the church deserted. The OP party climbed into the tower on a steel ladder fixed to the wall and set up their equipment. It did not take long for the Germans to realize that the tower was occupied and it became the target for mortars. Some damage was caused to the church but the tower and the OP party survived. However, the church was not shelled, leading Sergeant Smyth and his team to conclude that it was out of range of any available German artillery.[57]

Robert Hamilton recalled that he first heard that the regiment was to be repatriated in a wireless message from Tommy McCready. B Troop 24 Battery returned to Livorno on 28 August and confirmation that they were leaving Italy.[58] Ninth Regiment had been in the Mediterranean since November 1939 and at war since June 1940, its overseas' deployment believed to have been the longest of any reserve forces' unit. In Livorno the regiment was visited by the Commander-in-Chief AA, Italy who complimented them on their service. He returned with none other than Field Marshal Alexander, for whom a parade that might even have pleased a Guards' drill sergeant was mounted. After all, 'Alex' was not just a fellow Irishman, but also had close family connections to the regiment's home city.[59]

En route to Naples they handed in their guns in Rome and, at Afragola, awaited transit to Naples docks for embarkation. On 4 September the Derry Boys embarked on the HMT *Orantes* and sailed for Liverpool and then home. The regiment would serve in AA Command in Great Britain in the final months of the war, but the Derry Boys had completed their duty in Italy, leaving only the North Irish Horse, 38 (Irish) Brigade and 1st London Irish in Italy, although many individual Irish personnel were to be found in other units.[60]

* * *

Returning to Italy on 15 September, the Irish Brigade moved to Fano and Eighth Army reserve. Pat Scott was sceptical about the 'idea that the war was ending; that the Hun was pulling out', noting that he had been told 'by a very highly placed officer that the Hun was merely waiting for the rain to pull out, blowing the roads behind him; with the country then too wet for us to get at him'. Indeed, he continued, 'The Americans still thought they were going to get Bologna at any moment.' Some brigade officers visiting San Marino saw just how stubborn German resistance was with Eighth Army still fighting to break through about San Archangelo and Savignano. News that battalions were to reduce to a three-company basis should manpower fall below thirty officers and 700 other ranks was dispiriting; the fourth rifle company had often made the difference between success and failure – or stalemate. But British manpower was reducing and Italy was taking a heavy toll due to its difficult terrain.[61]

With the other brigades and combat support elements of 78th Division, the Irish Brigade undertook training at Fano, learning of recent developments including using searchlights to support night attacks and new bridging equipment for sapper assault units. While 64th Anti-Tank Regiment was to lose its fourth battery, the support battalion, 1st Kensingtons, was to be restored to a complement of eight 4.2-inch mortars. Anticipating a move to V Corps, the division was surprised to learn on 2 October that it was to join XIII Corps under command of Fifth US Army.[62] Moreover, 38 Brigade was to take over the line from the right of 88th US Division, the 'Blue Devils', allowing Clark to concentrate his forces for an attack on Bologna while 78th Division made for Imola.

Pat Scott met with Paul Kendall, commanding 88th Division, to learn that his brigade would relieve 351st Infantry Regiment in the Monte Cappello-Castel del Rio sector, to the right of the road to Imola; road conditions were so bad that American four-wheel drive vehicles had to be borrowed. The plan for 78th Division's advance on Imola required constructing the highest Bailey bridge yet built in Italy, using the piers of a blown-up viaduct, the tops of which were levelled by 78th Division's anti-tank guns.[63]

The first encounter with the enemy involved an Inniskillings' patrol on 6 October and ended with a German withdrawal. Next evening a Faughs' patrol was fired on by what turned out to be an American patrol. Some minor injuries were sustained by both sides before the situation was resolved. The brigade had excellent observation over enemy positions along the Gaggio river towards Taverna and patrolling increased the levels of intelligence on the enemy. For the Faughs there was a deadly encounter when the battalion was ordered to clear the Codronco spur which was held by the Germans.[64]

The operation to clear the spur, assigned to Major Jimmy Clarke's D Company, took three nights to complete. Holding Point 382, the enemy had only 'to toss grenades out of the windows while they were having their evening meal'.[65] The Faughs' approach was via a knife-edged ridge, then a fortified church before a 45-degree slope to a summit on which stood several stout buildings while rain had made the approach muddy and slippery.

On the first night, D Company seized the church from determined Germans and from there called for a heavy bombardment of the summit. The Faughs reached the top on their third attempt to discover that all but two shell-shocked Germans had fled. Thirteen Germans from 756th Infantry Regiment had been killed and twelve wounded while the Faughs suffered seventeen casualties.[66] As D Company consolidated, Sergeant Robbie Robinson, from Enniskillen, led a fighting patrol forward and encountered another German post. Robinson tackled the defenders, two of whom were killed while he was wounded by a stick grenade. For his inspiring leadership and courage, Sergeant Robinson was awarded the DCM. The citation was written by John

Horsfall, who had succeeded to command of the Faughs. He noted that, having played a conspicuous part in capturing a feature at Fontanelice, the NCO had led a mopping-up patrol that 'bumped an enemy platoon around a house, subsequently found to be held by a company, some 500 yards away from our forward positions and came under fire from MGs and mortars'. Sergeant Robinson had closed with the defenders and, with four others, accounted for a section, as well as two Germans who tried to rush them from the flank.

Although wounded in the head and back by grenade fragments and with four of his men also wounded, he re-organized his patrol and continued the battle for over an hour, personally overseeing evacuation of the wounded. He then organized a withdrawal under heavy fire from machine guns and mortars, helping to carry other wounded and returning with valuable information. The citation for his DCM noted that 'His admirable leadership in this action is only equalled by similar conduct in the past'.[67] He was hospitalized but later returned to duty.

The patrolling routine continued with another tragic encounter with American troops for the Faughs when a US signals detachment encountered a Faughs' post in darkness. All the Americans were killed but when John Horsfall visited the commander of 351st Regiment to apologize he was told to 'Think nothing of it – it happens every night'.[68]

Planning continued for an attack towards Imola with information being accumulated on the formation facing 78th Division. However, those plans were abandoned as the Americans concentrated on reaching Bologna. The Battleaxe Division was to move and the Irish Brigade was relieved by Adrian Gore's 61 Brigade. A new objective had been set for 78th Division: Monte Spaduro. Before Spaduro could be assaulted, Monte Pieve had to be captured, a task assigned to 36 Brigade with the Faughs under command. The Faughs relocated to between Gesse and Pieve, near Apollinare, so that they could move against Spaduro once 36 Brigade had seized Pieve. Scott's HQ also moved to Apollinare although the Faughs remained under 36 Brigade command.[69]

Monte Spaduro was to the Gothic Line what Monte Cassino had been to the Gustav. Behind Pieve, the Gesso ridge ran across Spaduro's front while, on the eastern side, loomed the even higher Monte Acqua Salata. John Horsfall described the topography:

> At the point where the two ridges joined lay the narrow head of the Spaduro massif like that of a defunct dinosaur, and Spaduro was exactly like that, with its head towards us, the legs pointing westwards, and its bloated hindquarters rising substantially higher over three miles on from Gesso. It was bare of cover, repellent and sinister – black as the pit in the

> morning light, with dark grey caps on the high parts and fissures slashed across it where its ribs should have been. These served to complete the illusion of some long-dead monstrosity.[70]

The plan for 36 Brigade to seize Pieve became redundant when the Germans abandoned the feature, leading HQ 36 Brigade to order a speedy pursuit to prevent the enemy consolidating new positions: at 0200 the Faughs were ordered to take Spaduro immediately. It was not, as John Horsfall wrote, the kind of order Irish Brigade HQ would have issued.[71] Complying with the order, Horsfall sent C Company under Major Tony Morris OBE MC, from Galway, to create a firm base for the attack on Point 416. C Company reported success before the morning mist cleared while Horsfall learned that 36 Brigade had seized Acqua Salata ridge. At divisional HQ it was felt that the Spaduro operation needed only a single battalion. Pat Scott disagreed and ordered the Rifles to deploy a rifle company and Support Company as a firm base behind the Faughs. Meanwhile, following an early morning recce, Horsfall decided against a daylight operation.

During the day Point 416 suffered heavy bombardment. At dusk came a deserter who was taken to battalion HQ and provided details of positions at Spinello. The local defence was provided by an infantry regiment, the equivalent of a British brigade. Plans were laid for the attack on Spaduro but only A and B Companies were available since D was moving the battalion support weaponry up to 416. Major Maurice Crehan, an Irish Fusiliers of Canada officer attached to the Faughs, commanded A Company which was to take Point 387. Dick Jefferies's B Company would assault Spaduro itself, a mile on from 387. H Hour was 2100.[72]

A Company was secure on Point 387 by midnight, having used an unobserved flanking approach, their arrival prompting the defenders to take to their heels. B Company met with pockets of resistance. One platoon was surrounded with some men being captured. Dick Jefferies then had to deal with a well-defended high cliff. An outflanking move failed and not until 0330 was it cleared, allowing B Company to go for the final objective, overcoming several posts en route. By 0515, as dawn was breaking, the objective was secured. Both companies came under heavy machine-gun fire from flank and front. Artillery support proved ineffective and, at 0600, both companies were counter-attacked. The Faughs faced overwhelming odds and fought heroically with many resisting until their ammunition was finished. Maurice Crehan was among the dead, his body discovered with those of Sergeant Harry Elliott, from Londonderry, and eight other Faughs. All were close together and bullet-riddled, weapons in front of them and fifteen dead Germans around them.

The scene was silent testimony to their tenacious refusal to surrender. From the two companies, only about forty men returned, one officer having earlier been sent back with prisoners by Maurice Crehan. Lieutenant Wally Tyler, whose platoon had been surrounded, came back next night with nine men and several prisoners, having been under fire for thirty-six hours. Jerry Pierce from B Company returned with a feldwebel as a prisoner.[73]

C Company, which had moved forward of Point 416, and battalion HQ also came under small-arms and artillery fire. When heavy fire from Salata, supposedly secured by 36 Brigade, was added, John Horsfall felt that 'the crisis was complete'. He signalled his appreciation of the situation to Pat Scott who assumed control of the battle. Equilibrium was restored. Anti-tank guns were manhandled onto Monte Gesso and, with the setting sun behind them, the detachments engaged the enemy over open sights; even the cooks added their assistance.[74]

The battle continued with the Rifles attacking enemy positions on Spaduro's lower slopes the next night but with limited objectives, including Casa Salara, a house on the western side of the ridge from which it was intended to attack Spaduro. Since Monte Aqua Salata had been the fly in the ointment for the Faughs' earlier attack, it was decided that seizing that feature was a prerequisite for a renewed attack on Spaduro. The Argylls from 36 Brigade attacked Aqua Salata to find it all but deserted, the few Germans there being made prisoners.

The Rifles, commanded by Bala Bredin, crossed the start line at midnight 21/22 October to attack Point 387 and Casa Salara, but, despite artillery support, were rebuffed by Germans at Casa Spinello. Every attempt to advance was brought to a halt. F, G and H Companies consolidated what they had gained in six hours, lying low in gullies and behind reverse slopes as guns and mortars hammered German defensive positions while the Faugh 6-pounder anti-tank guns on Gesso joined in bombarding Casa Spinello. At 1700 on the 22nd, the Rifles attacked again. With E Company attacking from the flank, F struck at Spinello and H fought up the slippery slopes north of 387. Once again the attack failed with severe losses sustained, Major Craig being the sole surviving officer of H Company. F and H Companies were withdrawn behind 416, a move made without loss, thanks to G Company providing covering fire.[75]

Since the Germans were holding Spinello in strength, it would be almost impossible to take Spaduro. Taking Spinello was critical to the overall battle but the Rifles' companies were very tired, two having suffered heavy losses. Bredin saw Casa Spinello as 'a sentry holding the door. The Germans were very well dug in underneath and we couldn't get round as the Germans in Casa Spinello engaged us from behind.'[76] He chose to send a small patrol of

Lieutenant Desmond Fay MC, Sergeant Farthing and two riflemen to bring back a prisoner. Fay's patrol crawled most of the way to Casa Spinello and, reaching the ruins of the house unobserved, Fay rushed a German slit trench, shooting two men who challenged him and grabbing a third who had been dozing. Under fire, he rushed the third German, by then fully awake, back to the Rifles' positions.[77]

The German prisoner proved very talkative and supplied useful information on the dispositions at Spinello. That allowed development of a fresh plan for an attack by E Company with strong artillery support, including medium guns from corps which were directed on Spinello and other locations before the infantry moved off. The Faugh anti-tank guns continued harassing the position. As the infantry advanced, the divisional artillery's 25-pounders continued their concentrated fire while the mediums fell silent. Anti-tank guns also engaged what was left of the buildings with armour-piercing rounds.

E Company found the German defenders determined to contest every piece of ground. One rifleman commented that they 'had to be exterminated one by one'. So determined was one defender that he died firing up from a cellar through floorboards. And, of course, there was the usual German tactic of a counter-attack to disrupt consolidation. That was followed by two more counter-attacks. F Company, under Major Ronnie Boyd MC, moving up to help combat the counter-attacks, ran into a minefield in which four men were killed including Boyd, a 'neutral' from Éire, who was fatally injured. CSM Kelly DCM took command. When the fighting was over, nineteen of the Rifles had been killed and fifty wounded.[78]

At much the same time, 2nd Inniskillings attacked from the left flank while 11 Brigade tackled Spaduro itself. The Inniskillings moved up the Casa Salara ridge, advancing to Point 362 and thence to 387 before making their way down the Sassatello valley with an artillery bombardment for cover. There was a stiff fight for Casa Salara and another for 387 but the Lumps emerged with almost fifty prisoners and a relatively light casualty toll of three dead and eighteen wounded. Before long, D Company was sending patrols out to Casalina which was found to be clear. Spaduro had fallen to 11 Brigade. Over eighty Germans were captured and about a hundred killed or wounded by the Irish battalions.[79]

With US troops to their left, the Faughs became the envy of their GI neighbours. Surviving on ration packs in waxed boxes, the Americans could not comprehend how their neighbours enjoyed a hot meal each evening. The Faughs' Quartermaster, Bud Maginess, kept his cooks as close as possible to the front so that food would be warm when it was taken forward. Corporal Gerry Strainger from Fermanagh, C Company's cook, was busy preparing the evening meal on 21 October when his hut received a direct hit. His cooks were wounded but Strainger

> got going immediately, saved the meal and continued its preparation alone. … he got the food up to his men up a small track at dusk, which was fired on consistently by German MGs at 400 yards. He and the three who went with him were unhit and the arrival of the meal had an effect on the men which was only equalled by Cpl Strainger's amazing cheerfulness on his arrival. This one act did more for C Company that day than any other factor and made all the difference to their morale and will to fight.[80]

Strainger was awarded the MM, a rare award for a member of the Army Catering Corps* and an indication of the leadership qualities of his CO, John Horsfall.

In the aftermath of the fighting, the Faughs and Rifles were reduced to three companies. On 7 November the Lumps also reduced to three companies, plus the battle patrol. Most units in Italy would do likewise as reinforcements from the UK remained unavailable. Re-roled gunners, sailors and airmen were making up the deficit but had to be trained as infantrymen.

On the 24th the rain began with ten inches falling in twenty-four hours. Operations stalled as the battlefield became a morass. Supplies could only be brought forward by mules, some of which drowned in the mud. Fifth Army suspended operations on the 27th. By the beginning of November, Operation OLIVE had shuddered to a standstill.

* * *

The North Irish Horse relieved 6th Royal Tanks at Poggio Berni, with C Squadron first to arrive, on 3 October. By then the autumnal rains had arrived. The regiment was to support 10th Indian Division which was transferring from the Adriatic sector to the Arno-Tiber front. C Squadron was welcomed by shelling from 721st Jäger Regiment. On the 4th, the regiment was complete at Poggio Berni: C Squadron was to work with 25 Brigade, A with 20 Brigade and B with 10 Brigade, the last in the centre of the divisional line.

---

* Only one other of the same nature can be traced, also to an ACC NCO who was originally a Faugh.

There was no opportunity to get to know their affiliated units as 10th Division's attack began on the night of the 4th/5th with 20 Brigade and A Squadron on the right and 25 Brigade with C Squadron on the left. The weather was foul and earlier rainfall kept the tanks roadbound, although they provided support as best they could. At Sogliano 2nd/3rd Gurkhas met no resistance, the Germans having abandoned the village to the Punjabis who had diverted from their own objective. In 25 Brigade's area, artificial moonlight and tanks firing on fixed lines helped 1st King's Own take San Martino, not once but twice, the Germans having counter-attacked several times. In two days' tough fighting, 10th Division cleared the five-mile ridge from Strigara and reached the Fiumicino river.[81]

In its advance, 20 Brigade took Monte Farneto from the enemy in the early morning. Unusually, it was early afternoon before the expected counter-attack hit. By then the infantry were well dug-in, with B Squadron in support, the divisional machine-gun battalion on its way, the artillery ranged and the Desert Air Force on call. The first counter-attack, at battalion strength, was beaten off with Horse tanks and the artillery helping break it up. A follow-up attack was smashed with fighter-bombers playing their part and the final German effort was also smashed with the help of the Northumberlands' machine guns. In the early evening, B Squadron's leader, Major William Mackean from Dunadry, County Antrim, left his tank to travel in a jeep to attend evening orders. Struck by a shell splinter, he was rushed to the RAP but died shortly after arrival. Captain Sidebottom took command of B Squadron.[82]

B Squadron and the Indian infantry remained on alert throughout the night during which enemy patrols were active. Rain made re-supply difficult but, using jeeps and trailers, was completed under heavy fire. B Squadron remained on Monte Farneto for some days, during which the redoubtable Sergeant Thomas McAughtry, despite heavy shelling, spent much time out of his tank, liaising with the Gurkhas and controlling his troop's support of the infantry. The squadron, switched to support 43 Gurkha Brigade, remained with it for some days during which the brigade achieved its objectives. Returning to 10 Brigade, B Squadron was advancing towards Adrano when, on the 15th, McAughtry's tank, leading the move, broke a track while crossing a most difficult stream. 'Under fire and up to the waist in water and mud [he], assisted by his crew, repaired the track and got across'. That episode was also included in the citation for Tommy McAughtry's DCM.[83]

Meanwhile, C Squadron had crossed the Fiumicino in conditions so wet that the other squadrons renamed it 'Sea' Squadron. During the time spent 'de-bogging' tanks and repairing broken tracks in persistent rain and shellfire, Trooper George King from Donemana, County Tyrone, was killed while in the open repairing a tank. One of three brothers who joined the regiment, only George went overseas.[84]

No progress proved possible and it was the evening of 12 October before twelve tanks reached Roccofreddo; one had 'drowned' en route and two awaited recovery. A further week passed before the river crossing was made and those days at the Fiumicino were the regiment's worst experience of weather and ground during the war. As 10th Division maintained its advance, the Horse had to deal with narrow roads through mountainous terrain, craters in some of those roads and enemy shellfire but continued to support their infantry comrades. The Royal Engineers, as ever, were invaluable, allowing vehicles to move in adverse conditions. At one stage the CO, Lord O'Neill, his second-in-command and B and C Squadron leaders, with the battery commander of 383 Battery 142nd (Royal Devon Yeomanry) Field Regiment,* reconnoitred on foot to identify tracks and secondary roads forward from Roccofreddo and Monte Farneto that tanks and 383 Battery SPGs could use, allowing supply vehicles to travel on the better roads as preparations were being finalized for crossing the Savio.[85]

The struggle was as much against the terrain and the weather as it was against the Germans. Lieutenant Reid's troop's experience on 17 October illustrates the frustrating nature of autumn campaigning. When 4th/10th Baluch Regiment of 10 Indian Brigade was ordered to take Monte Reale, Reid's troop was sent to marry with the Baluchis before switching to 1st/2nd Punjab Regiment attacking Aquarola. Following a nightmare trek in the dark over tracks that even jeeps could barely use, Reid's tanks were brought to a standstill by a recently-blown crater, courtesy of the retreating enemy. The troop was a quarter-mile short of Monte Reale where it remained for thirty-six hours. During that time the Churchills were shelled constantly but no casualties occurred. And so it went on. No Arks (bridging tanks) were available for 10th Indian Division in the Cella area, those only being allotted to 4th Division.[86]

Various means of maintaining contact with the infantry were tried but none was more novel than that proposed by Lieutenant Milne, a farmer from Argentina, who 'fitted in very well' with the Horse. With the two possible routes ruled out (one, a road, was impassable due to cratering and blown bridges; the other was soft, boggy ground that rose quickly into trackless hills), Milne proposed driving the Churchills down the bed of the Savio river, which

* The Royal Devon Yeomanry also received the right to wear the Maple Leaf in recognition of its support of Canadian forces in Italy.

he was confident that the Germans had not mined. His squadron leader, Major Morton, recce'ed the ground and agreed. Milne had offered to lead the tanks downriver and did so, walking four and a half miles in ice-cold water that sometimes came up to his chest. He was Mentioned in Despatches.[87]

On the morning of the 24th, as 4 and 5 Troops of B Squadron supported 3rd/5th Mahratta Light Infantry in its advance on Teodorano, unexpectedly doughty resistance was met short of the village. Major Sidebottom and his infantry counterpart devised a plan whereby 4 Troop and a Mahratta platoon moved to Ardiano, about 700 yards from Teodorano where the tanks assumed hull-down positions and 383 Battery's Priests were called upon for fire support before the advance continued. Lord O'Neill arrived and, with Sidebottom, walked to a small building on a nearby hill to watch the attack. With the Priests bombarding the German positions and the Churchills moving down the slope, German artillery engaged the tanks. Sidebottom suggested that he and the CO should use the lee of the building for shelter. O'Neill declined to do so since he wanted a clear view of the attack. Both remained in the open, smoking cigarettes. Sergeant White, commander of the leading tank, had not moved far when he was aware of a heavy shell passing his Churchill and landing near the barn. The round killed Lord O'Neill and seriously wounded Major Sidebottom. O'Neill's death was a grievous blow for the regiment. He had joined as a captain in September 1939 and was admired by all. His father had been killed in the First World War.[88]

The battle continued with 10th Indian Division pushing hard against the enemy and the Horse continuing to lend support although ground conditions were worsening and re-supply, by mules, became all but impossible. Even so, the infantry persisted, the Nabha Akal Regiment* eventually driving the enemy off the heights between the Ronco and Rabbi rivers. The Horse remained in action until 2 November, after which it was withdrawn from the line, concentrating in Cesena. Following a memorial service for those lost in action, local leave was granted.

* * *

Cyril Ray, 78th Division's historian, described the three months following Fifth Army's suspension of operations on 27 October as 'probably the worst period of the war for the Division'. He went on to quote Lieutenant Colonel

* The Nabha Akal Infantry was a princely state unit and not a permanent element of the Indian Army.

Malcolm of the Argylls who wrote that 'the horrible winter ... rivalled that in Tunisia for continuous life in the open; it equalled it in the volume of rain and beat it in the amount of real cold weather'.[89]

Pat Scott wrote that the first week of bad weather created more hardship 'than in any other during the winter'. Although snow fell on 10 November, two weeks of dry sunny weather followed and created a feeling that the worst had passed. Then came more rain. Driven by strong cold winds it sleeted across the mountainside and, in the Irish vernacular, was a lazy wind that 'went through you, not round you'. Keeping warm and dry was difficult as little shelter was available. However, John Kerr, commanding 2nd Inniskillings since Bobby Scott was ill, made use of whatever cover he could find, adjusted his positions to suit and established a 'divisional low record of sickness ... during this period'. Jim Trousdell remembered the low temperatures and 'living in a dugout on a mountaintop (reverse slope) [with] groundsheets worn over the shoulders the only protection we had against rain'.[90]

Needless to say, morale suffered due to the weather, the failure of the offensive to debouch onto the plains of northern Italy, the realization that Italy was being neglected and problems with re-supply in the early days of winter. Battalions were almost all reduced to three companies, reinforcements were scarce and, by the end of 1944, artillery ammunition was rationed to five rounds each day for 25-pounders. One gunner officer recalled the 'dreadful conditions in the mountains E of Florence – Castel del Rio to San Clemente – 3–4 months of that in mountain gun positions with virtually no 25-pounder ammunition'. The machine-gun and mortar crews of 1st Kensingtons were also afflicted by shortages, limiting their machine guns to 100 rounds per day and their mortars to four rounds, the sole exceptions being defensive fire tasks. It was a depressing situation.[91]

Notwithstanding the problems, morale in the Irish Brigade was good. Although perched on mountaintops, the infantry battalions' spirits were high. The Faughs had recovered from the setback of Spaduro and, in John Horsfall's words, 'like the rest of the Irish Brigade their spirit was now immune to whatever the fates might do – like Wellington's men in the Peninsula, or Lee's or Napoleon's, or any others long together'.[92] Although circumstances meant that infantry units had to accept any 'suitable reinforcements' rather than men from their own regiments, Sassenachs posted to the brigade quickly became imbued with the essence of their new units. Remembering Gerry Strainger's role in the October fighting, the provision of hot meals was another morale booster. Jim Trousdell felt that the

> policy of keeping the company cooks as far forward as possible so that we were supplied with a hot meal each day [was] a great boost to morale, especially when we were wet and cold. … [The Americans] were very envious of our ration system of fresh food each day. They were fed on K rations, a package of dried food (biscuits, meat, cheese, etc.). Each man was issued with a package each day.[93]

Something else that helped morale and impressed the Americans was the British policy of shaving each day.

> Even if it were not possible to wash, a shave helped to freshen one up and keep alert. It could be a painful process when the only water available was in the nearest shellhole and very cold as I remember on one occasion when we were on the Spaduro ridge and unable to move about.[94]

The Irish Brigade remained alert, especially as 1st Fallschirmjäger Division moved into the line facing 78th Division, reinforcing the formation already there. No relaxing was possible: as John Horsfall commented, 'The Paras were deadly to the bitter end.'[95] Defensive positions were improved and had the advantage of allowing better observation of the Germans than they had of the Allied positions. There was patrolling and artillery duels, although on both sides the latter was usually harassing fire on forward troops or supply routes. The Faughs' anti-tank guns continued harassing the opposition, especially as their effectiveness was improved by sighting equipment from a wrecked tank that enabled accuracy to up to 6,000 yards. Scoring twelve direct hits from fifteen rounds, the guns knocked out a German OP some 4,000 yards away. German retaliation led to one of the two guns being knocked out on 14 November with the other eliminated a week later. Over thirty-one days the guns had harassed the enemy, causing them to use copious quantities of ammunition to silence them.[96]

The Lumps welcomed a new CO on 14 November. David Shaw arrived to relieve John Kerr who was hospitalized with a serious stomach condition while battalions were relieved for rest and also rotated with other units. With a change in the overall configuration of the line as the Americans tried to push on to Bologna, 78th Division sidestepped to the left and the Irish Brigade took over Monte Grande on 18 November; Pat Scott's HQ moved to Passatempi, west of San Clemente. Such changes allowed the Germans observation over Irish Brigade positions, to counter which a permanent smokescreen was laid. Both sides deployed patrols at night, leading to several clashes.[97] Platoon commanders, including Jim Trousdell, found the patrols 'our main warlike feature' with few nights passing without patrols being deployed.

> Standing patrols to cover likely approaches to our positions were long, cold and often tedious. The patrol commander would be given an issue of rum to be shared among his patrol. I carried my issue in my water bottle which would be passed round for each man to take a mouthful. Everyone got a taste and there was always some left when the water bottle was returned to me.[98]

Improved weather conditions led to re-opening of activity at the beginning of December, by which time Kendal Chavasse's 56 Recce, less a squadron, was under Irish Brigade command. Although there was offensive activity by 6th Armoured and 78th Divisions, the Irish Brigade was not involved in attacks, although its units carried out some large-scale raids. One such was on Casa Tamagnin on 18 December. The raid was made by the Faughs' D Company under Major Pat Howard and quickly took the first building in the German positions, but the attackers were pinned down about thirty yards from the second house. A renewed attack resulted in some Faughs reaching the second house only to discover that it was barricaded firmly. As usual the Germans counter-attacked to be met with D Company's weapons supported by mortars and machine guns directed by Lieutenant Bert Parish. With the German attack disrupted, D Company was ordered to withdraw. Parish continued to call down fire to cover the withdrawal. Walking back with John Horsfall, 'and quietly discussing our opponents, we never heard the damn things coming – only the hiss of that split second, as the night turned to searing flame all around us'. Parish was wounded mortally and Horsfall so badly that he had to crawl back to his HQ. Although he hobbled to brigade HQ on sticks, Pat Scott ordered him to hospital. Murphy Palmer, second-in-command of the London Irish, 'at once took over command of the Faughs'.[99]

On the positive side, the supply system was much better than it had been in the previous winter and mountain warfare clothing was issued. That included windproof smocks and trousers as well as thick sweaters, string vests, sleeping-bags covered in oiled silk, white snow overalls, skis, sleighs and snowshoes.[100] The approach of Christmas provided another morale booster. At least one German paratrooper, having decided to celebrate early, staggered into the Faughs' positions burdened down with alcohol to wish his friends a happy Christmas. He was quite annoyed when he sobered up and was told that he would be staying with his friends.[101]

On the 20th a young Luxembourger para also crossed the lines. A company runner from 2 Company 3rd Fallschirmjäger Regiment, he was more than happy to stay and provided the Rifles, to whom he had deserted, with sound information that assisted the planning of a 'considerable and extensive harassing fire plan'. In addition, he warned of a planned attack on Valley Farm that was confirmed by wireless interception, as was its cancellation. A wireless message bemoaning a shortage of ammunition in the Monte Grande area led to the Germans losing some temporary gains they had made there.[102]

Christmas itself was celebrated in peace with an unofficial truce observed by both sides. It was also a white Christmas following two days of snowfall. Both Inniskillings and Faughs were in the line but still had an enjoyable day while the chaplains visited and an Anglican service was conducted, surprising Jim Trousdell with 'the number of my platoon who attended who would normally never go near a church. "Slit-trench Christianity" I believe it was called.' Brian Clark sent Faugh pipers out to play on the hillsides, a gesture the opposition seemed to appreciate since they responded by singing 'Stille Nacht'. Later they provided a colourful fireworks display by firing machine guns skywards, criss-crossing the December sky with tracer. The Christmas spirit allowed war to melt away for one day on mountains as cold as charity.[103]

On the 26th the Inniskillings captured two men from a Fallschirmjäger patrol while wireless intercepts suggested that there might be an air raid on the 29th but none materialized; 78th Division's LAA unit, 49th LAA Regiment had been stood down before Christmas and disbanded officially on 1 January 1945. The Irish Brigade continued its patrolling activities, including a daylight raid by the London Irish battle patrol under Lieutenant Montgomerie on Casa Tamagnin on the 3rd. The raid was supported by machine guns of the Kensingtons whose war diary described it as 'extremely audacious'. It was also supported by the Rifles' 3-inch mortars and 25-pounders with medium guns on call. The German main line was codenamed *Antrim* and it was noted that the enemy 'ran hard for Antrim followed by a scorched cat'. Montgomerie was awarded a Bar to the MC he had earned at San Fatucchio; from Suffolk, he was a Royal Artillery officer attached to the Rifles.[104]

The patrolling routine and regular reliefs of units at the front continued through the month, a period in which Pat Scott decided to implement a reward scheme for 'men who were continually performing some gallant or outstanding act'. His scheme involved publishing the names of such soldiers in brigade orders and awarding each with a commemorative certificate. His rationale was that Mentions in Despatches were restricted and took some time before they were published in the *London Gazette*. Once the scheme was initiated, it took only two months for the GOC to introduce a similar divisional scheme, known as the Mark of Merit, which allowed recipients to wear a small twist of black-and-gold braid below the divisional signs on their sleeves. Since the GOC made his scheme retrospective to early October, Pat Scott did likewise with his, while also announcing that the Irish Brigade Certificate would automatically carry an award of the Mark of Merit.[105]

Having spent some time alongside 85th US Division, the Custer Division, in the mountains, the Irish Brigade was relieved by 36 Brigade and moved to a rest area north of Florence although the Rifles remained under 11 Brigade command for several more days before moving to re-join the brigade. On 9 February the brigade began a move to Forli where 78th Division came under V Corps' command and was back in Eighth Army.

* * *

While the Irish Brigade suffered in the mountains, the North Irish Horse had returned to 4th Division as it continued its advance from river to river. On 7 November, Lieutenant Colonel Anthony W.A. Llewellen-Palmer DSO MC, who had been second-in-command in Tunisia, arrived to take command. At much the same time, Brigadier J.N. Tetley, 25 Tank Brigade's commander, ordered the immediate formation of a composite squadron to support 12 Brigade from first light on the 8th. The squadron was created with some difficulty since many personnel were on leave but, under Major Griffith, it came into being as A Squadron, formed from four Churchill troops of A, B and C Squadrons, plus a three-tank Sherman troop from RHQ.[106]

A Squadron joined 12 Brigade which was relieving 10 Brigade and moved to the Forli area where it was split: Major Griffith, with two troops, would support 6th Black Watch with Captain Irwin and the remainder of the squadron supporting 1st Royal West Kents. Tetley told Llewellen-Palmer that 142 RAC was to place two troops of its B Squadron with the composite squadron for which the Horse would provide the commander, a role Llewellen-Palmer chose to perform himself. The task of the reinforced A Squadron and the infantry battalions was to clear the area between Highway 9 and the airfield close to Forli. However, the terrain was unlike anything the Horse had previously encountered, being flat reclaimed land with floodbanks, canals and drainage ditches cutting across it. Since the watercourses overflowed as a result of the rains, off-road movement was close to impossible for tanks because the rich farmland had been transformed into a deep, glutinous mud. Visibility was restricted by vines and poplars while every road or track was covered by anti-tank guns. The enemy, with more infantry on the ground than Eighth Army, was determined to fight for every yard. Artillery, tank gunfire and air support, which depended on weather, were deployed in combination with infantry. Rarely would a day's fighting result in anything more than a few hundred yards' advance. Sapper support was also provided with 1st RAC/RE Assault Regiment available to bridge water obstacles.[107]

The ensuing fighting was ferocious. Llewellen-Palmer described it as some of the fiercest he had seen 'with the battlefield so small as to be almost pocket handkerchief size'. The Black Watch considered the battle as the worst since fighting the Fallschirmjäger at Cassino. In taking Casa Fortis, 6th Black Watch suffered about forty casualties, with a company commander wounded fatally; one house was defended with machine guns at each of its ten windows. A German company was wiped out with only six surrendering. The Scots' success was aided by Sergeant James Barbour who earned the MM. With Germans holding two rows of fortified houses and a crossroads, the infantry could not advance until the tanks cleared the way. The Horse engaged the houses one by one until the crossroads was reached but it was blocked by fallen trees and wire. Barbour charged the obstacle, taking his tank over it and disregarding mines, one of which he drove over although it failed to detonate. He then engaged the last enemy-held house, enabling the Black Watch to get forward. His MM citation noted that 'his skill and daring were an inspiration to all who witnessed the battle', and that his tank had been in continuous action for two days.[108]

The West Kents also had a difficult time and worked in close co-operation with Captain Irwin's tanks. With the infantry reinforced, the advance continued and, once again, Horse tanks provided invaluable support. As the Black Watch advanced towards a group of houses south-west of Villa Minuzzi on 14 November, resistance became even tougher and included hand-to-hand fighting. However, co-operation between tanks and infantry was excellent while air and artillery support were also available. Nonetheless, a platoon of A Company was pinned down by machine-gun fire. It was then that Sergeant Thomas Donaghy, commanding 1 Troop, intervened. He had to approach on a straight road covered by an anti-tank gun. As soon as he moved, his tank came under fire from enemy tanks and that gun. Just before he reached the infantry, his tank was disabled by a mine before being hit by a round, wounding Donaghy in the face. He refused to be evacuated and, when darkness fell, risked machine guns firing on fixed lines to repair his tank so that it could be towed back to a defensive position. There he maintained command of the troop, only going for treatment when ordered to do so next day. He, too, received the MM for 'devotion to duty and personal courage which were quite beyond praise'. The citation was written by the CO of 6th Black Watch and supported by the commander of 12 Brigade and the GOC 4th Division, eloquent testimony to the trust between the Horse and the infantry.[109]

That trust continued in operations that followed until the end of the month. Introduced to the Horse's operational bag of tools midway through November was a fascine-carrying Churchill which enabled the tank to drop the fascine into a waterway to allow the vehicle to cross without the aid of an Ark. Before OLIVE had begun, a specialized unit, 1st Assault Regiment RAC/RE, with two Ark/AVRE squadrons and a Sherman-dozer squadron, had been formed to support Eighth Army: it proved invaluable, the Horse benefitting from its support on several occasions. However, the regiment's resources were limited and it was decided to create an engineer brigade with Churchills from 51st Royal Tanks and 142 RAC converted as fascine-carriers and Arks, to which were added Crocodiles, flame-thrower Churchills, from the UK, and locally-converted mine-clearing flail tanks. HQ 25 Tank Brigade was chosen to command the new assets with the Horse transferring to 21 Tank Brigade. For the time being, 25 Tank Brigade remained an infantry-support formation.[110]

In the advance towards the Montone, the West Kents had support from troops of the Horse, including the fascine-carrier. On the 13th a fascine allowed Lieutenant Milne's troop to cross a deep ditch near San Tome and reach Casa Goberti. Next day, two squadrons remained with the infantry to shell any likely enemy escape routes on the far bank of the Montone. A small bridgehead on Highway 9 over the Montone had been created by a skeleton brigade group from 56th Division. The group, including 1st London Irish and three Shermans of Recce Troop 51st Royal Tanks, was to make the enemy believe that a fresh division was attacking along Highway 9. To aid the deception, the radio rear links in 25 Tank Brigade that were on 4th Division's radio net closed down and re-opened on 56th's net.[111]

After some days spent on maintenance, the Horse returned to 10th Indian Division, and 10 Brigade, for the next phase: forcing a crossing of the Montone north of Villafranca di Forli prior to advancing towards the Lamone. That was intended to give I Canadian Corps elbow room for an attack on Ravenna and advance to the Lamone. A Squadron was married with 2nd/4th Gurkhas and C with 2nd/10th Baluch; B Squadron was in reserve with 1st Durham LI. The ground over which the tanks were to operate was unpromising although a possible canal crossing place was identified. Nonetheless, the advance had support from the Churchills, although a fascine carrier bogged and had to drop its cargo which was then broken up so that individual logs could be dropped into a canal. That was done under heavy fire, allowing a Churchill troop to cross and shoot a Baluch platoon into the buildings that formed their objective. The advance continued next day with air support promised, as well as two Crocodiles. But heavy rain reduced the effectiveness of the air support while both Crocodiles bogged before reaching the fascine crossing. A frustrating day ended with the tanks unable to silence enemy machine guns, although both Gurkhas and Durhams had made lodgements in their sectors.[112]

Another day's nibbling advance followed during which the Royal Devon Yeomanry put paid to a German OP in a local church tower. Then followed a day during which occurred the first recorded deployment of a Churchill close-support (CS) tank armed with a 95mm howitzer. Although the howitzer proved very effective in demolishing buildings, the infantry were still unable to make progress and had to beat off counter-attacks over the following two days, C Squadron assisting them in breaking up the attacks.[113]

On 29 November A Squadron, under Captain Bowring – Major Griffith had departed for home leave in Ireland – crossed the Lamone to support 2nd/4th Gurkhas of 10 Brigade. Eighth Army was about to launch an offensive towards Faenza to assist the planned American attack on Bologna. D Day for 10th Indian Division was the 30th and 2 and 3 Troops A Squadron attacked towards Lamisoria with the Gurkhas. Good progress was made, the tanks destroying a StuG while the infantry captured another, the crew of which had baled out under heavy fire from the Churchills. With B Squadron in support, the Durhams pushed on to a road junction near Casa Bettini. Lieutenant Bullick of HQ Squadron deployed in a regimental Ark, the first such deployment, that allowed B Squadron to cross an otherwise impassable canal and continue supporting the infantry.[114]

The following day, the Gurkhas were relieved by the Baluchis who attacked with Lieutenant Mahony's 1 Troop in support. Lieutenant Maguire's 3 Troop had a successful advance with eighteen prisoners taken. Later in the day, the infantry dug in and, with the Churchills' support, smashed a counter-attack. With the advance resumed, steady progress was made until a blown bridge stopped the tanks. No.5 Troop attacked in support of the Canadian Royal 22nd Regiment, the *Van Doos*, but met doughty resistance. With a close-support Churchill, Lieutenant Mahon and Sergeant Burns attempted to engage houses sheltering German infantry. Sergeant Verso's Churchill also moved up. Both tanks were hit by an anti-tank gun. The turret crew of the CS tank perished: Sergeant Hugh Burns of Belfast and Troopers Robert Stafford and John Wood, from Liverpool and Lancashire respectively. Trooper Norman Corbin, co-driver of Sergeant Verso's tank, was also killed while Lance Corporal Wallace, the driver, and Trooper McClay were wounded.[115]

Verso, the troop leader, dismounted and, with his Tommy gun, laid down covering fire to allow the survivors to reach safety before returning to the burning tanks to assist the others, but they were already dead. He returned to his own tank in time to help repel a fierce counter-attack which by-passed the Churchill and reached HQ A Company Royal 22nd before being checked. Frederick Verso then remained with his tank, the fire having gone out, providing a communications link at great risk to himself since he had to move on foot to A Company HQ to pass on wireless messages. He was awarded the MM.[116]

At first light next day the squadron was relieved by A Squadron 12th Royal Tanks and returned to Forli. C Squadron was relieved by C Squadron 48th Royal Tanks at first light on 4 December and rejoined the regiment in Forli. That Saint Barbara's Day was also the date on which the Horse left 25 Tank Brigade with which it had served since September 1942. Its new home was 21 Tank Brigade, replacing 145 RAC which was disbanded. There was a happy coincidence for the regiment since the brigade commander was Brigadier David Dawnay, not only an Irishman, but a former CO of the Horse. Also in 21 Tank Brigade were 12th and 48th Royal Tanks.[117]

From Forli the regiment moved to Riccione which was close enough to Rome for leave parties to the Eternal City to be organized. At Riccione the regiment remained, performing the usual round of maintenance, duties and training, until moving to Ravenna on 12 January. Christmas and New Year had been celebrated in style, allowing the immediate horrors of war to be forgotten for a time. But all knew that there would be a return to the line.

Chapter 9

1945: The Last Battles

As 1945 dawned, the only Irish units remaining in Italy were the Horse, the battalions of 38 Brigade and 1st London Irish. Of course, there were other Irish personnel of all ranks throughout units of both Eighth and Fifth Armies. (Irish immigrants into the United States were conscripted and many served in Italy, as did descendants of earlier immigrants, including the US Army's most decorated soldier, Audie Murphy.) Lieutenant General Sir Richard McCreery, Eighth Army's commander since October 1944, was proud of his Irish roots in Killyclogher, County Tyrone while his Fifth Army counterpart, Lucian K. Truscott Jr also had Irish, and Cornish, ancestry. Mark Clark had been promoted to command 15th Army Group, following Field Marshal Alexander's elevation to theatre supreme command.

The Black Cats of 56th (London) Division welcomed the new year along the Senio in the plains of northern Italy. On the banks of that stream evolved a form of trench warfare recognizable to a Great War soldier. Since the Senio meanders across the flat landscape, the line did likewise. Since the Senio's level rises seasonally, the stream was flanked by high floodbanks, up to thirty-feet, with tops that large vehicles could drive along. Naturally, those floodbanks became defensive positions, although not simply a case of Germans occupying one floodbank and Allies the other, although that did happen on some stretches. On others, the Germans not only occupied the 'far' floodbank, but also the 'far' side of the 'near' bank. Warfare along the Senio was a close experience with deep defensive locations created, bridges spanning the Senio where the Germans occupied both sides, and tunnelling a part of daily life, together with raiding parties and, for Allied troops, an innovative use of the PIAT as a mortar rather than an anti-tank weapon.[1]

Some days before Christmas, 167 Brigade was relieving 43 (Gurkha) Brigade with the Rifles taking over from a Gurkha battalion. Visiting the Rifles was Colonel J.R.J. Macnamara, MP for Chelmsford, a former CO of the battalion, who had introduced the caubeen as standard headdress for the Rifles in 1937. Macnamara was with Lieutenant Colonel Sperling at battalion HQ and prevailed upon him to be allowed to visit forward companies. And so Macnamara left battalion HQ for the front line. He was talking by the roadside with C Company's commander, Major Boswell, when their group was targeted by a German mortar team and a shower of mortars rained down. Macnamara and Lieutenant Prosser MC were killed and Major Martin Boswell wounded. Part of Macnamara's mission in Italy was to bolster the integrity of the Irish battalions, an aim shared by Pat Scott and the officers of the Irish Brigade.[2]

Rotating in and out of positions along the Senio, 1st London Irish joined a battle in which 'both sides were able constantly to fling missiles at each other, in fighting that 'seemed unending and unfruitful'. On one occasion, the enemy sent over a barrel of explosive which failed to detonate. C Company were inspired to reciprocate with explosive-filled barrels which did explode. Both sides made small-scale raids, but the most memorable factor was the 'extraordinary amount of ammunition expended'. Gone were the supply problems of early winter. One day alone saw the Rifles receive 1,500 2-inch high-explosive mortar rounds, dozens of PIAT rounds, generous supplies of 36 grenades and 'endless boxes of .303-inch ammunition'. In contrast to a few months before, ammunition was unlimited.[3]

Corporal William Wardle, a section commander in 10 Platoon, may have been the first to use the PIAT as a mortar when his platoon was under fire from a German MG position which had killed one rifleman. At the time, the Rifles and Germans were on either side of the same floodbank, the latter also occupying houses in Cotignola from which they could overlook the former. Wardle volunteered to crawl to the top of the floodbank with a PIAT and engage the MG position. He did so not once, but three times, scoring two direct hits and silencing the machine gun. Subsequently, he volunteered to engage the occupied houses with phosphorous. That had to be done standing atop the floodbank. Again, he was successful. He received the MM.[4]

On the night of 23/24 February, B Company was ordered to seize positions on the far bank: 10 and 11 Platoons led with 12 Platoon, under Sergeant Joseph O'Connor, in reserve to give covering fire. However, 10 Platoon met strong resistance and was rebuffed three times. O'Connor, on his own initiative, went forward with another soldier to locate the MG positions hindering 10 Platoon. Although he found two posts, his attempt to overcome them by throwing grenades failed as he drew very heavy fire. Returning to his company HQ with the detailed information, he was ordered to carry out the mission the next night with 12 Platoon. He led three patrols that identified a mortar and four MG positions which, as a result, were overcome. Joseph O'Connor was awarded the MM, the citation noting that 'his offensive spirit and complete disregard for personal safety [had] been an inspiration to his whole Company'.[5]

* * *

The North Irish Horse had moved to Ravenna on 12 January to work with the Italian *Gruppo Cremona* on the right of I Canadian Corps.* C Squadron was to support one of Cremona's brigades between Highway 16 and the river Reno while A Squadron supported the other brigade from the Senio to the coast. RHQ, HQ Squadron and B Squadron remained at Ravenna. When a German attack dislodged the Italian defenders from Casa Giazol, Lieutenant William Reid supported Italian infantry in an effort to regain the position. Although infantry and tanks lost contact – it was the Italians' first experience of working with tanks – and the enemy staged a dogged resistance, Reid, although wounded slightly, showed such strong leadership, as well as courage and determination, during the sharp skirmish that he was awarded the MC.[6]

Although due to be withdrawn to join First Canadian Army in north-west Europe, the Canadians continued launching small attacks with the Horse involved in supporting some of those. A fourth, composite, squadron, dubbed Reconnaissance Squadron, was formed with Recce Troop, three 6-pounder Churchill command tanks, and a troop of close-support (CS) Churchills. Flexibility was being demonstrated on a regular basis. February passed with some alarms and incidents while C Squadron laid claim to eleven Shermans left by the Canadians but abandoned them after a few days. By the end of February, the Canadians had gone.[7]

March began with an Italian attack to clear the Spit, the base of a strip of land between the Adriatic and Lago Comácchio, with C Squadron supporting 9 Company 21st Regiment and C Squadron 11 Company 22nd Regiment. Air support and an artillery bombardment formed part of the plan, as did flame-throwers and CS Churchills. Resistance was stiff with the enemy counter-attacking along the beach; Allied aircraft strafed within 200 yards of the leading infantry. The attack was renewed next day with reduced air support but with the Churchills giving even closer support. The area around Casa Venti was cleared gradually of enemy infantry: some 200 prisoners, mostly Mongolian or Turcoman, were taken. By early evening, Italian infantrymen were consolidating their new positions.[8]

No serious counter-attack took place and the Churchills' supporting role continued. On the other side, the enemy seemed to have lost much of their fervour which allowed the Horse to celebrate Saint Patrick's Day with panache and enthusiasm. As those who had celebrated well woke on the 18th, it was

* Cremona Combat Group included two regiments, 21st and 22nd Infantry, as well as the partisan Garibaldi Brigade. Three such groups, effectively light divisions, served in Eighth Army with another three in Fifth Army. They formed the *Corpo Italiano di Liberazione*, Italian Liberation Corps.

to the news that the regiment would be supporting another attack on the 20th. However, it would be with a new partner, the Jewish Brigade, which had reached the sector earlier in March. In the attack, 4 Troop A Squadron supported soldiers of the brigade to capture two enemy-held houses and take eight prisoners. On the 21st, B Squadron was told that it would be working with 2 Commando Brigade to attack the Spit; training with 43 (RM) Commando began next day. A and C Squadrons were assigned to 8th Indian Division on the 25th and specifically to 19 Brigade, A Squadron marrying with 1st Argylls and C with 6th/13th Royal Frontier Force Rifles. Training with infantry partners began in preparation for the spring offensive. Officers made aerial reconnaissances from light observation aircraft to build a sharper picture of the ground over which they would fight. Training included cross-country night marching with the infantry, something that Royal Armoured Corps' experts considered impossible but which the Horse proved 'quite practical under certain conditions'. The regiment also asked for much specialized armour to be allocated to it and, after considerable discussion, received two Churchill bridge-layers, two Sherman-dozers, two Arks and two fascine carriers.[9]

Seizing the Spit was critical to the forthcoming operation since the German left flank lay on it. Separating Lago Comácchio from the sea, it is under a quarter-mile wide and was the objective of an amphibious operation supported by B Squadron. As well as taking the Spit, the commando operation aimed to draw in German reserves and distract German commanders from the main operation; should the opportunity arise, the operation could be continued around the north of the lake. As well as the amphibious assault from the lake, a crossing of the Reno was planned, for which tanks of two B Squadron troops were waterproofed while the other two troops would be rafted across before attacking, with two commando platoons, along a narrow track between floodbank and lake.

Despite difficulties, by 1600 on 2 April, Easter Monday, the Horse's tanks were engaging enemy positions at close range. Some forty prisoners were taken while the two troops along the Reno had knocked out enemy positions across the river mouth. Next day, B Squadron was rafted across and followed the commando advance to Porto Garibaldi where strong opposition was met with one tank struck by a shell but recovered immediately. Late in the day 10th Hussars relieved B Squadron.[10]

Those operations had prepared the way for Eighth Army's final assault, Operation BUCKLAND, the first element of 15th Army Group's Operation GRAPESHOT. Fifth Army would launch Operation CRAFTSMAN a few days after BUCKLAND. Irish personnel would serve in both armies. For the North Irish Horse, A and C Squadrons were under command of 19 Indian Brigade with B Squadron supporting Gruppo Cremona. D Day for BUCKLAND was 9 April.

* * *

Moving from the mountains, and Fifth Army, was a blessed relief for 38 (Irish) Brigade. From bleak, cold, wet mountainsides, fusiliers and riflemen moved to a fertile green land with many houses, and rivers and canals criss-crossing the countryside. Roads in excellent condition reduced transport problems and were 'a relief and a joy' after mountain tracks. As Brigadier Scott remarked, 'Traffic blocks were unheard of in this part of the world.' The brigade settled into accommodation outside Forli and into training alongside an excellent recreation programme.[11]

On 17 February the brigade's massed Pipes and Drums, with the Royal Ulster Rifles' band, beat Retreat in the Prefecture Square. More was to follow for the citizens of Forli when the Faughs celebrated Barrosa Day over two weeks later. A morning Irish dancing competition preceded a football match, played to a unique set of rules, that saw goalposts blown out of the ground, spectators covered in flour, Brian Clark, the adjutant, 'as usual torn to shreds' and 26 Battery of 17th Field Regiment Royal Hibernian Artillery discharging round after round. The game was nominally between officers and sergeants but no one ever knew the score or who had won. That night the Barrosa Cup was drunk after dinner in the officers' mess. The Faughs and their comrades let their hair down in the midst of war to enjoy a brief period free from war's immediate horrors as an Italian spring blossomed and the weather became warmer.[12] Of course, spring had always heralded the onset of the campaigning season: 1945 would be no different.

On 10 March the Irish Brigade began taking over part of the Senio Line from 169 (Queen's) Brigade. The brigade was strengthened by a squadron of the Bays, 56 Recce, a Kensingtons' support company, an anti-tank battery and a sapper field company with 17th Field on call. Rupert Lecky from County Carlow was CO of 17th Field while Marcus Hartland-Mahon, another Irishman, had succeeded Kendal Chavasse as CO of 56 Recce, which remained Chavasse's Light Horse. Both fusilier battalions and 56 Recce held the line, the Recce on the right, Faughs in the centre and the Lumps on the left. Less than an hour after taking over one position, 56 Recce was attacked, setting a pattern for the brigade's time in the line.[13]

Such was the intensity of life along the Senio that battalions deployed for no more than eight days with forward companies rotating on a forty-eight-hour basis. Platoon commanders became the most important leaders. Sergeant

Patrick Joseph 'Rex' Doherty of 2nd Inniskillings, had earned a Mention in Despatches at Anzio and was commanding the battle patrol. On the night of 12 March, he was ordered to deal with a machine-gun position that had been harassing a forward platoon, inflicting casualties. Rex Doherty led the patrol along the floodbank to within yards of the MG position where Schu-mines had to be lifted. The Germans, hearing the patrol, hurled grenades but the Inniskillings advanced and retaliated with their own grenades. The Germans then fired flares to illuminate the patrol and threw more grenades, wounding Rex Doherty and another soldier. At that stage, Sergeant Doherty withdrew his patrol, re-formed and charged the position. In spite of machine-gun fire and another shower of grenades, the attackers prevailed. Three men were wounded, one falling in front of the gun. Rex Doherty dashed to the wounded man, dragged him clear and took him to safety with the rest of the patrol. He was awarded the MM.[14]

Robbie Robinson DCM recalled that 'The real characteristic of this fighting was that the infantry were in very close contact – sometimes only about 8 to 10 yards apart – and that it was the infantryman's war almost entirely'. He also noted that:

> The main activity took place after dark when we kept up a continuous fusillade of small arms, grenades, 2-in mortars and a new use for the PIAT – fired as a mortar. The bomb made quite a noise falling and must have proved unnerving to the opposition. … PIAT bombs exploding on the roof of a dugout could cause damage and severe shock waves underneath and its blast effect was quite considerable.[15]

The Bays' Shermans would trundle up to fire at close range into identifiable enemy positions, occasionally ascending the bank to fire into the far bank. Although the Germans had good supplies of *Panzerfäuste* there were no tank casualties and no damaged Shermans. However, there were infantry casualties. With the Faughs due for relief by the Rifles on 16 March, an advance party arrived on the 15th, one of whom was 23-year-old Sergeant Norman Johnston from Belfast. Recce'ing the positions, Johnston crawled onto the bank from where he could observe enemy positions through a periscope. Wearing a caubeen and hackle, he must have drawn the attention of a sniper 'who simply waited' until Johnston moved away from the periscope and straightened up momentarily. Shot through the head, he died instantly.[16]

Taking over from the Faughs, the Rifles quickly found the rhythm of warfare on the Senio. Supported by a Bays' Sherman, they attacked a German outpost and, after a grenade duel, established a section post on the bank. After dark, Lieutenant John Gartside MC crossed to the enemy side, found the post unoccupied and lay low until he was able to take a prisoner and return with him to his own position. Possibly in retaliation, there was a small counter-attack in the early hours, but it was stopped. Another attack, on 22 March, was launched on 'Fritz's Bund', a floodbank marginally higher than the others. H Hour was 1500 and the raiders estimated that it would last only a minute. That was not believed. However, the assault party – a corporal, five riflemen and two pioneers – returned within a minute with five prisoners; three more Germans were wounded and one killed. The group had used a tunnel, completed the previous night, that broke into a German tunnel. They were covered by smoke, artillery fire and a diversionary attack on another German position. In addition, Lieutenant Eric Salter, who commanded the operation, gave covering fire from the top of the bank. Wounded by return fire, he was awarded the MC.[17]

On the 23rd, the Faughs, who had relieved 2nd Inniskillings, were attacked. The ensuing battle lasted almost a day, including three hours of vicious hand-to-hand fighting. Although a Bays' Sherman lent some support during that hardest spell of fighting, it was largely an infantry battle, 11 Platoon playing the leading role and inflicting severe casualties on the attackers.

Sightings of unusual numbers of German stretcher-bearers suggested heavy enemy casualties but also aroused suspicion that some were using the Red Cross to observe more closely the Faughs' positions. When one came too close, he was invited back to a company HQ and was followed with alacrity by a Polish deserter. A further two prisoners were also collected by D Company: described by Robbie Robinson as 'a very friendly pair', they revealed that their unit had suffered three dead and forty-seven wounded. Although the Germans demanded the stretcher-bearers be returned, those men were happy with their new surroundings.[18]

When, overnight, some 300 mortar rounds landed in the Faughs' area, it seemed that an attack was impending. However, intensive defensive fire prevented that. Some of that defensive fire came from the 'brigading' of D Company's PIATs and 2-inch mortars which were dug in near company HQ. Referred to as the 'Vino Victims' Battery' the group was commanded by 'a character called Muldoon who was very ably assisted by two other notables called McLean and Dornin'. The 'battery', with direct telephone communication with company HQ and platoons along the embankment, could respond very quickly to calls for fire with a 'quite staggering' number of mortar and PIAT bombs in a matter of minutes. Robbie Robinson was responsible for the company's ammunition supply but, most importantly, 'a ready supply of vino to fuel the main operators of this extraordinary battery'.[19]

Although the Vino Victims' Battery seemed to enjoy their role, no one was really sorry when 11 Brigade relieved the Irish on 26 March. It having been impossible to celebrate Saint Patrick's Day on the 17th, a proper celebration was organized for the 29th in Forli. That proved unforgettable for everyone present. In beautiful spring weather, the day began with religious services, Father Dan celebrating Mass in Forli Cathedral while Eighth Army's Assistant Chaplain General, Victor Pike, from Tipperary, who had been ordained in the Church of Ireland, led an Anglican service in the Asperia cinema, attended by Generals Keightley and Arbuthnott.

After the services, the brigade formed up in Saint Andrew's Square. Also present were men from the North Irish Horse, 1st London Irish, D Company, Kensingtons and 152nd Field Ambulance RAMC. From the balcony of the Prefecture, Pat Scott made a short speech and expressed delight that General Keightley was present to speak to them and present shamrock; he had commanded them in Tunisia and Italy, later becoming their corps commander and, of course, had been commissioned in the Inniskilling Dragoons. Some shamrock had been brought out from Ireland but, since there was insufficient, he hoped that 'its potency was sufficient to bless some of the local variety that I had to mix with it in order to make it go round'. After assuring the soldiers that their efforts were contributing to successes in north-west Europe, Keightley presented the shamrock. With the parade dismissed, the Irish Brigade Pipes and Drums, augmented by those of 1st London Irish, played in the Square.

At midday there was a cocktail party but the afternoon was given over to sport. It was not normal sport. Both Inniskillings and Rifles held Officers-versus-NCOs football matches, the latter degenerating into chaos, with a panzer being brought onto the field. The Faughs held a race meeting with mules rather than horses, some ridden by unsteady officers. At some stage, a pair of Faughs had 'borrowed' a water tanker, driven to a nearby distillery and filled the tank with gin, all of which was consumed during the day. That probably explained the reception that the CO, Murphy Palmer, received at the nearby hospital when he went to visit Faughs recuperating from injuries received along the Senio. When he and his driver entered the building he was met almost immediately by the matron who asked if he was the CO of the Irish Fusiliers. Expecting a compliment, Murphy replied that he did have that honour. He regretted doing so immediately when the matron lectured him about the number of drunken Faughs who had been admitted. Did he not know that the hospital was preparing to take in casualties from the front? With matron's comments that the Faughs were causing more casualties than the Germans, Murphy and his driver beat a tactical retreat. He told the author that facing a panzer division would have been less frightening than that QA matron.[20]

Despite sore heads, training resumed in earnest on the 30th. River-crossing exercises, infantry-armour tactics and wireless procedure were all practised and the Faughs and Rifles took part in Exercise HOSANNAH, which 2nd Inniskillings had undertaken on the 25th. Pat Scott also learned that infantry would be transported in heavy armoured vehicles known as Kangaroos, 'defrocked' Priests and de-turreted Shermans converted to carry an infantry section. The 'Kangaroo' was a Canadian innovation in north-west Europe. In the forthcoming offensive, 2nd London Irish would ride into battle in Kangaroos, earning the soubriquet 'Kangaroo Army'. Kangaroos were armoured personnel carriers (APCs) converted from Priest SP howitzers or Sherman tanks; REME workshops in Italy created 177 APCs from superannuated 75mm Shermans and from 'defrocked' Priests, 102 from the latter. First deployed in Normandy in August 1944, Kangaroos had already been used by the Canadians and 56th Division in Italy from January. However, the Kangaroo Army would provide the finest demonstration of the APCs in action.[21]

In 56th Division, 1st London Irish would go into action earlier in an operation involving crossing the Reno, part of 56th Division's Operation IMPACT to divert German attention and protect Eighth Army's right flank. There were two elements to the plan, IMPACT PLAIN and IMPACT ROYAL, with the Rifles in the former. The battalion was the tip of 167 Brigade's spear with the task of clearing enemy positions on the river's east bank, a task undertaken by B and C Companies who moved into their forming-up positions in the evening of 5 April, 'a lovely spring evening' with not a sound disturbing the stillness. At H Hour, 0115 on the 6th, a Bofors shell lighting the sky gave the signal for an artillery bombardment to cover the infantry advance. Six field regiments, two medium regiments, a heavy battery, 4.2- and 3-inch mortars as well as machine guns bombarded the foe as Captain Dorrity's B Company and Major Boswell's C stepped off from their start lines. Dorrity's company made good progress, although Lieutenant Hibbert's 11 Platoon was delayed by a strongly-defended enemy post. After fifteen men, including Hibbert, were wounded, the platoon attack was abandoned. The main body of B Company pushed on to the first major objective, a rice factory, taking twenty prisoners, before advancing about 1,000 yards to the main objective. Boswell's men had a more difficult time, losing two boats in the crossing and becoming pinned down on the north bank at Prato del Pozzo. The CO decided to deploy A Company under Captain Gallaher to cut off the Germans holding up C Company. Crossing the river by ferry at 0500, Gallaher and his men joined Dorrity after which two A

Company platoons went on, only to be delayed by enemy fire. Nos 7 and 9 Platoons reached cover and spent many hours in a 'keen and dangerous game of hide and seek'. However, by dawn, the battalion was firmly established in a mile-and-a-half-deep bridgehead which they held until tanks arrived. There was no counter-attack, possibly because German communications had been disrupted. Over 100 prisoners were taken and ferried back to battalion HQ for interrogation.[22]

For the next week the advance continued with several strong positions overcome and more enemy personnel taken prisoner. Sergeant John Graham was killed in a series of attacks on Pallazzo Tamba on 12 April, an objective eventually taken with assistance from dive-bombers. The operation to cross the Reno had been 'an unqualified success' in which the Rifles earned plaudits from the GOC, Major General John Whitfield, who had succeeded Gerald Templer in July 1944.[23]

Several gallantry awards were also earned: Boswell received the MC, as did Lieutenant Jack Cooke of 12 Platoon who, in spite of being wounded in the leg, continued leading his men until their final objective was taken. Lieutenant Satchell of 12 Platoon was also awarded the MC, while Corporal McClelland, who took command of 15 Platoon when both commander and platoon sergeant were wounded, received the DCM. In charge of the 2-inch mortar and PIAT group of the platoon, he led it to its objective and refused to be evacuated even though wounded in the leg. When an officer arrived, McClelland remained with the platoon and offered to act as a runner, in which role he performed sterling service. As 15 Platoon was finally relieved, he was injured by an anti-personnel mine but remained cheerful. The citation emphasized that the platoon's success was due to his 'courageous example and excellent leadership'. Seven others received the MM and three were Mentioned in Despatches.[24]

Lieutenant General Sir Richard McCreery laid plans for Operation BUCKLAND with confidence in Eighth Army's morale, which was higher than for some time with reported numbers of absent personnel at their lowest since the Italian campaign had begun. In his order of the day, McCreery stated that the enemy 'must not be allowed to use his Armies in Italy to form a garrison for a Southern German stronghold … . We will destroy or capture the enemy south of the Po'.[25] Eighth Army was to smash German defensive positions, seize crossings over the Senio and Santerno rivers, race for the Argenta Gap and onto the Lombardy plain where German forces south of the Po would be destroyed. We have already noted the role of the North Irish Horse in preliminary shaping of the battleground, and that of 1st London Irish, in the Commáchio area. In BUCKLAND, 38 (Irish) Brigade would play a major role in the advance to Argenta while 6th Armoured Division included 16th/5th Lancers and 17th/21st Lancers, the 'Death of Glory Boys' whose CO since 5 September had been Lieutenant Colonel Val ffrench-Blake, a Galway man who had succeeded Sir John Marling (posted to Fifth Army on 19 August). George Ponsonby MC* was acting CO in the interim. Sixth Armoured Division also included Adrian Gore's 61 Brigade with many Irish soldiers in its ranks.

D Day for BUCKLAND was 9 April. On that day, 825 heavy bombers of the Mediterranean Allied Strategic Air Forces (MASAF) dropped 1,511 tons of bombs, mostly 20lb fragmentation devices but including some 100lb general-purpose bombs, on German positions along the Irmgard Line, which followed the Senio. Accuracy was assisted by the 3.7-inch heavy AA guns of 12 AA Brigade firing smoke-shells to create an aerial demarcation line, a bomb line – the last use of 3.7s in Italy.[26]

That initial aerial assault on the Irmgard Line was intended to disrupt communications, the fragmentation bombs serving that purpose. Heavy bombers were followed by 234 medium bombers attacking along the fronts of II Polish Corps and British V Corps with another 24,000 fragmentation bombs. Meanwhile, fighter-bombers of the Desert Air Force and XXII (US) Tactical Air Command hit at communications to the rear before switching attention to command posts, strongpoints, guns and mortar positions. Some 720 tactical aircraft were involved. That was followed by the artillery, with 1,200 guns, ranging from 25-pounders to 240mm heavies, plus heavy mortars, hammering German forward lines and the ground beyond in Operation FESTA. It was the first bombardment of four, each between twenty and thirty minutes. Each time the guns fell silent, fighter-bombers returned. At 1910, as the guns fell silent yet again, the fighter-bombers swooped, but dropped no bombs, nor did they fire rockets, machine guns or cannon. That final swoop was a feint, covering the approach of Churchill Crocodile flame-throwers of 25 Armoured Engineer Brigade which belched flame on the enemy positions. And the artillery opened fire again, in a protective barrage on the far side of the Senio. The infantry, led by New Zealanders and Indians, began their assault and, with artillery support, relentlessly pressed on through the Irmgard Line to the Laura on the Santerno. Ahead lay the Paula Line on the Sillaro and the Genghis Khan on the Idice. Additional lines had been constructed even farther back.[27]

As 2nd New Zealand and 8th Indian Divisions consolidated their bridgeheads, V Corps' commander, Keightley, prepared to launch the Kangaroo Army, formed from the Irish Brigade and 2 Armoured Brigade, under command of 78th Division. The Battleaxe Division, extemporized into an all-arms force, included an armoured battlegroup, the Kangaroo Army, which, in turn, included two battlegroups, the Break-Out and Mobile Forces, under HQ 2 Armoured Brigade; there was also a Reserve Force.

Break-Out Force included both Fusilier battalions: 1st Royal Irish Fusiliers, supported by C Squadron Bays, an MMG platoon of D Support Group, a scissors bridge and recce party of Royal Engineers; 2nd Inniskillings were joined by B Squadron Bays, another MMG platoon of D Support Group, C Squadron 51st Royal Tanks with Crocodile flame-throwers and a Royal Engineers' recce party. Supporting Break-Out Force were two field artillery regiments, 17th Field, commanded by Rupert Lecky, and 11th (HAC) RHA, with which Richard Goodbody earned his DSO in Sicily. (Goodbody had commanded 2 Armoured Brigade until September 1944 when he was succeeded by John Combe.)

The Mobile Force, the Kangaroo Army, included HQ 2 Armoured Brigade, 9th Queen's Royal Lancers, 4th (Queen's Own) Hussars, who crewed the Kangaroos, Z Troop 209 Self-Propelled Anti-Tank Battery, a Royal Engineer assault detachment and 2nd London Irish 'empouched' in the Kangaroos.

D Support Group was D Company of 1st Kensingtons, 78th Division's support battalion. One Kensingtons' officer, Dubliner Brian Harpur, later wrote the first published account of the final campaign in Italy. (Major Harpur, son of a Church of Ireland rector, commanded C Support Group which worked with 36 Brigade.)[28] Cyril Ray, 78th Division's historian, described the Irish Brigade as 'swollen almost to the size of an armoured division'.[29] The Hussars had experience of working with the Irish Brigade operationally, knew its idiosyncrasies and had undertaken intensive training with its soldiers, including the Irish Rifles who would be carried in their Kangaroos. Each rifle company had eight Priest Kangaroos and Battalion HQ had a further eight. The Kangaroos could operate independently for forty-eight hours. The APC-borne infantry would advance close to the leading armour until opposition was met when the infantry would dismount to attack. At no time were Kangaroos intended to engage enemy tanks or anti-tank guns; they were to convey infantry across fire-zones at the speed of armour with a high level of protection against small-arms fire or grenades. While they had already proved the concept in north-west Europe and Italy, their role in 78th Division's break-out mission was almost certainly the most systematic application of that concept.[30]

The roles played by both the North Irish Horse and 1st London Irish in operations to 'shape' the battleground have already been covered, as have the earliest aspects of Operation BUCKLAND. Seventy-eighth Division entered the action on the evening of 9 April with 11 Brigade returning to the banks of the Senio which it crossed to link with the New Zealanders and, with 36 Brigade, create 'elbow room' for the Irish Brigade which, minus its armour, left Forli at 1300 on the 10th to concentrate south of Bagnacavallo where, next day, infantry and armour 'married' near Lugo. Before the brigade advanced, more elbow room was created by 36 Brigade. That task accomplished, it was time for Pat Scott's warriors to strike.[31]

Brian Harpur, commanding C Support Group with 36 Brigade, earned the MC for handling his command 'with such consummate skill that the infantry ... were saved many casualties and greatly assisted to their objectives by his tireless efforts and the sound tactical knowledge he has in the deployment of supporting arms'. Harpur, already Mentioned in Despatches at Cassino, was a constant inspiration to his men with his courage and cheerfulness.[32]

At 0630 on Friday the 13th, Inniskillings and Faughs moved off from their start line in 19 Indian Brigade's bridgehead and turned north. The Germans had been knocked off-balance by 36 Brigade. Both battalions advanced on a 1,000-yard-wide corridor between the Santerno and the Fossatone canal over flat ground with orchards, vineyards, farmhouses and, here and there, a hamlet.

Major John Duane's C Company of 2nd Inniskillings, in the vanguard, crossed a canal bridge and found cover from where Duane surveyed the area. He spotted two tanks and at least two anti-tank guns, one of which opened fire. Support from the Bays was called for but the three Shermans that responded were knocked out quickly. C Company was ordered to attack with artillery support, including smoke, provided. The smoke was an imperative since open space had to be traversed. Two platoons attacked at the double, overran the position, and captured an anti-tank gun and fourteen men but suffered six wounded. B Company joined C and the advance continued to the Fossatone canal. With engineer support, the canal was crossed and the infantry moved forward again. Major Duane recalled 'taking quite a number of prisoners for only one casualty'. Although the Germans were well dug-in with excellent camouflage, 'they surrendered quickly and appeared happy to do so'.[33]

And the advance moved on. The Inniskillings overcame strongpoints at San Bernadino where, supported by a tank, B Company fought from house to house until the Germans gave up. B Company lost one dead and four wounded while eight Germans were dead and fifty-six captured. By noon the advance had reached La Giovecca where determined opposition was encountered but a C Company assault prevailed after a bitter battle in which more than a hundred prisoners were taken. Eight Inniskillings perished and four were wounded.[34]

The Faughs had also made good progress, which earned the DSO for their CO, Lieutenant Colonel Murphy Palmer, a Kilkenny man. When enemy strongpoints were encountered along the Scolo Fossatone,

> [He] personally directed the attack on [them]. By his very quick appreciation of the situation, he was able to effect a considerable element of surprise … . In spite of the heavy shellfire, he continued to direct and encourage his men so that the strongpoints were taken and the momentum of the attack was delayed for the minimum amount of time.
>
> [His] courage and bearing throughout this day and during the advance from the Senio to the Po was of the highest order. His never failing cheerfulness under all conditions has been a great inspiration to all ranks privileged to serve with him.[35]

As the battle at La Giovecca ended, the Mobile Force arrived. The empouched Rifles, with 9th Lancer tanks, pressed on, taking the crossings at Conselice. Ahead lay the Reno where G Company led the attack against light resistance, much of it from Panzerfaust-armed infantry. Bala Bredin, the Rifles' CO, wrote that

> The Skins and the Faughs had given the enemy a good shaking and he was on the move back. Scattered enemy Bazooka men were met and one tank was lost through the fire of an anti-tank gun, but a number of prisoners were taken by G Company.[36]

As the ground between the waterways widened, H Company came up on G's left with C Squadron 9th Lancers. As the Lancers by-passed La Frascata en route to Cavamento, some two miles from Bastia, E Company cleared La Frascata and the Rifles had secured a bridgehead.

> The enemy had been surprised by the speed and weight of the attack. Few of them, not more than ten, had been killed, but all three forward companies had taken numbers of prisoners. By 1830 the total was eighty.
>
> The bridgehead was firmly established by 2200 hours and Companies were dug in for the night. Sappers were building a bridge over the canal, the armour was in leaguer and plans for the following day were being made. A large increase in the number of wrist watches possessed by H Company was noticed.[37]

Before dawn, Faughs' and Rifles' patrols were probing ahead. At first light, two armoured columns followed the Rifles, one making due north with the main road its axis, the second moving to the right to avoid minefields: the area was mined heavily. Houses were booby-trapped although the dangers were reduced by German failure to remove their warning signs. The Sherman Crabs of 51st

Royal Tanks set to flailing the minefields. As the Rifles advanced towards the Reno, eight Germans were captured while laying mines. They quickly became supervised mine-lifters. Road and rail bridges about six miles from Bastia had been demolished, but infantry could use the rubble to cross dry-shod.

After a reconnaissance, two E Company platoons crossed to establish a small bridgehead. That was achieved by 1130 under cover of smoke with no resistance. However, as the platoons advanced from the river, they were counter-attacked and overrun. The tanks could not help due to the high floodbanks and the lack of a bridge. As the platoons were advancing, Germans had appeared, apparently surrendering, but others rose up around the Rifles. The 'surrender' had been a ruse and both platoons were captured. Subsequently, it was decided that the battalion should hold its positions for two more days.[38]

Faugh patrols spent the 15th clearing marshland up to the Sillaro, the far bank of which was being held in several places by Germans in fortified house strongpoints. That evening 36 Brigade relieved the Faughs, allowing the battalion to concentrate and join the brigade group as the advance continued. At that stage, many partisans appeared, some of whom were 'fireside warriors' who had taken up arms only when the Germans departed; others had been fighters and gave excellent intelligence on enemy positions and minefields, information often supported with maps or sketches. Bala Bredin enlisted 'a platoon of these scoundrels from which he was expecting great things' but, commented Pat Scott, 'I never heard much more about them'.[39]

A re-organization of the Irish Brigade Group was effected on the 15th with Brigadier John Combe's 2 Armoured Brigade being placed under direct command of HQ 78th Division: 9th Lancers stayed with the Irish Brigade; the Bays moved to 11 Brigade. Assault sappers and 51 RTR's flame-throwers and Crabs passed to divisional command for the advance to the Argenta Gap.[40]

Eighth Army's operation was going to plan. Pressure on the Germans had increased on the 14th when Fifth Army launched Operation CRAFTSMAN. Following its re-organization, Scott's brigade was on the move again on the 16th as 11 Brigade moved towards Argenta. At 1700 the Irish Brigade was to pass through 11 when the latter established a bridgehead over the Fossa Marina. At the same time, the Kangaroo Army of 9th Lancers, 4th Hussars and 2nd Rifles would re-form under 2 Armoured Brigade with the Bays returning to Irish Brigade command. Congestion at the bridge over the Reno and on the approach roads slowed the Irish Brigade which made the crossing that evening and concentrated. The Rifles crossed early next morning to marry with 9th Lancers north of the Reno.[41]

The Lancashire Fusiliers had created a bridgehead across the Fossa Marina, through which both fusilier battalions would pass, and held it against determined counter-attacks. Strengthened by a company of East Surreys, and with 5th Northamptons on the edge of Argenta, they put the Germans under intense pressure; reinforcements had been rushed to the area, including what was left of 29th PanzerGrenadier, 42nd Jäger and 362nd Infantry Divisions. In the eyes of Eighth Army Intelligence, the appearance of the panzergrenadiers was a positive sign. Ray wrote that the Germans appeared to be preparing a 'last desperate stand' at Argenta,

> but the crust had already been cracked by the Lancashire Fusiliers, and the Divisional Commander [Major General Arbuthnott] was quick to realize that the strength of the whole Division would be needed to widen the crack decisively. On the morning of April 17th he ordered the Irish Brigade with the Irish Fusiliers on the right and the Inniskillings on the left to pass through the … tiny bridgehead … to widen the gap so as to allow the armour and the Kangaroos to pass through.[42]

Forming up was complicated by being done in a German minefield, albeit one with boundary markings still in place and maps available. The Faughs' C and D Companies crossed first, followed by the Lumps since the advance was to be on a two-battalion front. However, it was noon before the leading Inniskilling companies, C and D, crossed. Quickly, both battalions were engaged in bitter fighting and under fire from StuGs and tanks, some of which were claimed to be Tigers. Two Bays' Shermans with the Inniskilling C and D Companies were knocked out but A Company crossed to reinforce their comrades while a heavy artillery bombardment was called down. Breaking the German defences during the afternoon, the Inniskilling companies created a salient and prepared for the usual counter-attack, which never materialized; patrols captured some Germans trying to flee the Argenta area. Yet, in the midst of the clash, Corporal Harry Bell MM, a section commander in 17 Platoon D Company showed such leadership and cool courage that he was recommended for the Victoria Cross. Instead, he was awarded the DCM.[43]

As D Company formed up in the bridgehead perimeter, mortars and shells fell around them and Bell's section lay down. He continued strolling about, giving his final orders and smoking, in spite of twice being blown off his feet. He then led his section in an attack on two MG posts which were overcome by his actions although he had received an arm wound in the attack. On his own initiative, he led a further attack on another strongpoint which was taken with six prisoners. Bell refused to be evacuated, re-formed the section and advanced on a house that had been turned into a strongpoint, housing light MGs and a StuG or a Mark IV panzer. Bell, with three others, advanced across open ground under heavy fire, personally knocking out one MG before enemy mortars stopped the section. By then only Bell and one other man were standing. Corporal Bell was wounded badly, his right lower arm virtually severed. He ordered the section to be evacuated but refused to leave until all his wounded had been taken to safety. In his citation for the VC, David Shaw wrote:

> This NCO, throughout the day, more than fulfilled the task demanded of him. He continued to lead his section though wounded, he led an advance of nearly 800 yards and it is doubtful, but for his speed and determination, that the Battalion could have carried out their important work of cutting Route 16.[44]

Shaw added that Bell's actions and courage had made his name 'a byword in the Battalion'.

Shaw, too, was recognized for his role, being appointed DSO for his remarkable conduct of the battle on the 17th. Initially ordered to move north-westerly, he quickly realized that a flanking movement to the south-west would enable the battalion and its supporting tanks to cut off any Germans still in the Argenta area and cover 78th Division's north-westerly thrust. As Shaw executed the manoeuvre, a strong German counter-attack was being directed against a vulnerable part of 78th Division.

> With complete disregard of personal safety, ... Shaw personally established [2nd Inniskillings] on the bank NW of Argenta and [repelled] what was known to be a divisional effort by the Germans to restore their Argenta position.
>
> The magnificent fighting spirit which his battalion displayed on this occasion and again when he led them to the Condotto Motte was very largely due to the inspiring leadership and courage displayed by Lieutenant Colonel Shaw.[45]

Among Inniskilling dead on 17 April were 21-year-old Fusilier Alex Carlin, from Redcastle, County Donegal, and Lance Sergeant Hugh Dysart, aged 25, from nearby Londonderry.[46]

The Faughs had also encountered strong resistance, including mines, tanks, StuGs and MG posts, with Major Pat Howard of C Company and Lieutenant Tyler wounded. Some supporting tanks were knocked out. Over fifty prisoners were taken, all recent arrivals from a reserve formation. Pat Howard received the MC. Although supporting armour had been delayed by minefields and many obstacles, C Company pressed ahead, inspired by Major Howard's personal courage and leadership.

Throughout the day the company was engaged closely by enemy armour, StuGs and infantry with an assortment of weaponry. Each attack was dealt with by C Company under Howard's direction, although he was wounded in the arm and side during one of the first clashes. He did not report himself wounded until the threat to his positions had dissipated. The citation for his MC noted:

> The fierceness with which the enemy contested the battalion's advance NE of Argenta is proof of the importance which he attached to the holding of these positions and in no small way was the success of the operation due to Major Howard's courage and leadership.[47]

Booty taken from the enemy included two Mark IV tanks which amused the Faughs for a few days. Murphy Palmer's battalion was to move forward at first light next day to the Fossa Sabbiossola to ensure that the area was clear of Germans, a task carried out without opposition.

By evening on the 18th, the Irish Brigade advance was about 1,000 yards deep. All objectives were in sight with 2nd Inniskillings beyond Argenta and the Faughs almost up to the Scolo Cantenacci. German prisoners numbered 180, a score of them officers. Pat Scott commented that the advance

> did not look much on the map, but it was one of the toughest day's fighting we had had, and probably one of the most important. A gap had been opened to the right of Argenta, and 36 Brigade passed through [it] before it got dark, and I remember David Shaw calling me up on the blower and asking how anyone could expect him to fight his battle when all sorts of people were swarming past between him and his troops. I endeavoured to assure him that it was a 'good thing'. He said no doubt it was, but he would rather have his own battlefield to himself.
>
> It was a 'good thing' too. The Division was taking a big chance pushing its nose right out like that before the Argenta battle was settled. But more was to follow.
>
> At dawn the Kangaroo Army passed through.[48]

The Kangaroo Army advance was preceded by a nocturnal attack by 36 Brigade with 6th Royal West Kents and 8th Argylls striking at strongpoints where they met stout resistance, that encountered by the Argylls proving the toughest until then in BUCKLAND. Skirting 36 Brigade's action, the Kangaroo

Army made for country north of Argenta, in what Bala Bredin described as 'an unforgettable move'.

> Through the orchards north of Argenta, in the narrow gap between Lake and Canal, moved a mass of armour, all passing over one bridge that had been constructed over the main water obstacle. Wrecked vehicles, equipment and enemy dead strewed the route, whilst machine-gun fire, from an Argenta already surrounded, crackled away on the left flank.[49]

Out in open terrain, the Kangaroo Army engaged German tanks and StuGs to the right of the Argylls and beyond the Faughs. Strongly-held villages proved no match for the weight of armour and mobile infantry and, as darkness fell, the Kangaroo Army had taken three bridges intact and reached the area of Palazzo and Coltra. Late in the day, they fell on an enemy force that yielded some 200 prisoners, an officers' mess, a battery of 155mm guns and another of 88s, plus numerous pieces of lighter artillery. The group had tried to beat off the attackers, but, in spite of a spirited resistance including artillery firing over open sights, failed.[50]

By 1700 the Inniskillings had cleared up to the floodbank but were then counter-attacked by two German forces which, it was learned later, were part of a determined effort to re-close the Argenta Gap. The attack was beaten off and a heavy artillery bombardment forced a German withdrawal.

Highway 16 had been reached and Pat Scott decided to consolidate the gains while extending the positions. It was a wise decision since a strong German force lay not far beyond Highway 16 and two large floodbanks while, west of the Reno and advancing from the south-west, was 2 Commando Brigade which had suffered heavy casualties at the Germans' hands. It was believed that those Germans in the corner of the Reno were preparing a counter-attack, a move that could have had serious consequences since the bulk of 78th Division had moved north-west and the Germans could have created havoc in the gun lines and rear areas. Moreover, Nap Murray's 6th Armoured Division was due to traverse the area next morning.[51]

The German pocket had to be eliminated, a task Pat Scott felt had to be co-ordinated by the three British groups in the area: 2nd Inniskillings, 6th Royal West Kents and 2 Commando Brigade. Scott was given permission to execute his plan which involved the Commandos attacking at midnight under an artillery bombardment and the Inniskillings and West Kents launching a converging attack at 0130. Although the Inniskillings suffered some casualties from the artillery supporting the commandos, the Germans were forced to withdraw. The way had been cleared for 6th Armoured's advance.[52]

With 6th Armoured moving along Highway 16, Major General Arbuthnott decided to prevent the enemy creating a defensive line across the San Nicolo canal by bridging that waterway. The crossing operation was assigned to the Irish Brigade, supported by 10th Hussars and with flank protection from units of 11 and 36 Brigades. Although some distance behind, the brigade moved quickly and both battalions – Inniskillings on the right, Faughs on the left – executed a textbook crossing under a heavy bombardment that included medium guns. Although John Duane's C Company lost radio contact with battalion HQ, he took his company forward, despite the artillery support being late. As C Company advanced, the guns opened fire with rounds falling on the Inniskillings. Then the German artillery joined in and C Company suffered nineteen casualties, including John Duane and Michael Murray, the only surviving officers. Command was assumed by the CSM, but C Company's losses were such that, although it reached the objective, it was too weak to be effective in the next phase.[53]

Arbuthnott later told Pat Scott that the operation was 'about the highest test in the military art that he had yet asked us to undertake' while Ray wrote that 'The staging of this attack at short notice and in darkness was a particularly fine performance which could only have been achieved by very highly trained troops'.[54] With a bridgehead established and a tank crossing created, two 10th Hussar squadrons joined the Irish Brigade while 56 Recce eased the right flank by evicting Germans from their positions. It was time to send the Kangaroo Army forward again. So disorganized were the enemy at that stage that Pat Scott believed a deep penetration would be a greater threat to them than open flanks to 78th Division.[55]

To smooth the Kangaroo Army's advance, the Irish Brigade extended the bridgehead northwards over open country. The Inniskillings lost two supporting tanks but reached the objective, as did the Faughs. By noon Pat Scott gave the signal for the Kangaroo Army to make its fourth attack.

The attack was far from being a straightforward dash since the assembly area near Montesanto was shelled and mortared with the MO of the Rifles, Rhys Evans, wounded by a shellburst in a tree above his Kangaroo. As tanks and APCs advanced, concealed panzers and StuGs engaged them, as did MG posts and infantry with Panzerfauste. On occasion, infantry men debussed to engage MGs and infantry. Tanks and StuGs received attention from fighter-bombers of the Desert Air Force, operating a 'cab rank' above the battlefield and responding quickly to air support requests. Later in the day, as opposition increased, F Company dealt with groups of infantry, including some concealed in trees. Earlier, F Company had been struck by German artillery that caused four casualties, three of them prisoners. The leading companies were E and F, with B and C Squadrons, 9th Lancers but, at about 1800, G Company and A Squadron were called forward.[56]

The divisional artillery had been firing *Uncle* shoots* but, as twilight approached, the APCs and tanks were outdistancing the artillery, although 11th (HAC) RHA was moving with the armour in its SPGs, and two batteries of 17th Field were using supercharge to extend their effective range. With close air support ending for the day and no friendly forces to either flank, the decision was made to press on for the canal bridges at Cona and Quartesana, the final objectives.

At Quartesana, E Company met determined opposition, including Panzerfaust fire. F faced a similar reception at Cona, plus a 150mm gun about 100 yards from the bridge. At 2230, H Company arrived to support F and, by 0100, the latter was across the bridge, consolidating a bridgehead with tanks and infantry. Quartesana bridge was also seized intact although three panzers had knocked out two Lancer Shermans before withdrawing. Both bridges were taken in 'most unorthodox' battles during which the battlefield had been illuminated by moonlight as well as blazing tanks and farmhouses. Infantry and tankmen suffered casualties from machine-gun, rifle and mortar fire.

The front line had been moved forward by five miles in little more than twelve hours with almost sixty prisoners taken. Also captured was the 150mm gun, plus several lorries. At battalion HQ, prisoners included Poles, Czechs, Russians, Slovaks, a Frenchman and a Lithuanian, as well as Germans. Since the Kangaroo Army had been operational for seventy-two hours, the Rifles were relieved by 2nd Lancashire Fusiliers. In fact, the entire brigade was able to rest on the 22nd and into the 23rd before receiving orders for the final advance to the Po.[57]

South of Fossalta, 11 Brigade had crossed the Po di Volano, establishing a bridgehead through which the Irish Brigade would pass en route to the Po. Opposition was stiff and expected to become stiffer as the Germans defended successive water barriers to complete withdrawing their forces east of Ferrara. David Shaw's Inniskillings were to cross the Po di Volano near Saletta before advancing towards Zocca. Murphy Palmer's Faughs would follow but would turn left towards Ruina. Sappers and a 10th Hussars' squadron supported each battalion.

The Inniskillings' advance was speedy and, by 0245 on the 24th, the battalion had reached Saletta to engage its German garrison who fought until

* An 'Uncle' shoot involved all seventy-two guns of the divisional artillery engaging a specific target.

0500 before resistance ended with some twenty dead and four captured; the Inniskillings then pushed forward about 400 yards. The Faughs set out for Ruina at 0700. Both battalions were stopped along the Fossetta canal where LXXVI Panzerkorps (26th Panzer and 29th PanzerGrenadier Divisions) had established defences to cover the retreat. Having concentrated west of Fossetta, ready to operate on foot or in APCs, the Irish Rifles were again ordered to empouch and make for Ferrara to the west rather than the Po to the north. Supported by four armoured squadrons, one from 4th Hussars and three from 9th Lancers, Bredin's battalion formed two columns with reports from aircraft providing up-to-date information about which bridges remained intact.[58]

Opposition started up from about 1600 but prisoners were being taken in large numbers. Enemy tanks appeared and a tank battle ensued, the Kangaroos trying their best to keep out of the clash. It seemed that every farm in the area was burning. At 2200, as the Kangaroo Army closed on its objective, orders came for a 100-degree change of direction which was accomplished with little difficulty even while in contact with the enemy. By dawn the leading elements were on the banks of the Po 'in the midst of an extraordinary collection of abandoned and burning vehicles left behind by the enemy', including six Mark IV tanks and many lorries. 'Thus ended the fourth and longest advance made by the Kangaroo Army.'[59]

The switch in direction followed the interception of German radio traffic suggesting that the enemy had lost control of the situation and that their commanders had decided that it had become a case of *sauve qui peut*. With the greatest confusion around the river crossings north of Pescara and Francolini, Arbuthnott had turned the Kangaroo Army north over the Fossa Lavezzola and into the 'disorderly enemy'. Hence that final clash.[60]

Both Inniskillings and Faughs continued their advance to the Po and clearing the divisional area began early on the 25th. It was obvious that there had been a rout. In the Irish Brigade area, with C Squadron 56 Recce under command, over 300 Germans were rounded up. The amount of abandoned equipment amazed those who saw it.

> There was mile after mile of wreckage and rubbish intermingled with thousands of horses. It was an unbelievable sight! No wonder our last battle had been such a stiff one with all that stuff at stake. He had enough guns there to blow us off the earth, to say nothing of all the tanks and other things there were. …
>
> Whatever else had happened there seemed to be little room for doubt that the 76th Panzer Corps had been well and truly defeated.[61]

Disobeying Hitler's orders, Vietinghoff had ordered a retreat to the Po on 20 April but that was too late to save his forces. On the 21st, Bologna fell, liberated by Italian partisans before Polish and US troops arrived. Fifth Army then advanced to the Po, as did Eighth Army but without 78th Division and the Irish Brigade. Italian partisans struck again on the 25th with a major uprising on a signal from the Allied command. War in Italy was all but over and the Germans would surrender on 2 May. However, even as the Irish Brigade began to rest and re-organize, other Irish units and personnel remained in action.[62]

In 56th Division, 1st London Irish had a gruelling time in the advance to the Po, not so much from fighting as from the 'mass of plans and moves for attack' constantly being prepared and changed. For several days the battalion was at an hour's notice to move but it transpired that the last engagement with the enemy had been at Tamara, not far from Fossalta, where the Germans had 'put up a sharp and stubborn resistance before withdrawing during the night'.[63]

The North Irish Horse had also played a significant role in BUCKLAND, providing support to units of 8th Indian Division in the initial attack along the Senio with Lieutenant Michael Bexon earning the MC for knocking out a StuG, removing charges from the Arginello canal, and leading the advance to the Tratturo canal. B Squadron with Gruppo Cremona cut Highway 16 to allow Cremona soldiers to enter Alfonsine. Further gallantry awards came in the form of the MC for Lieutenant Albert Maguire MM and the MM for Sergeant Gerry Ballard. Maguire's troop was first across the Senio and he ensured the integrity of the bridgehead from which he led the breakout and then cleaned up along the Santerno, opening the ground for the advance of Gruppo Cremona. Londonderry's Sergeant Ballard, of Robin Griffith's A Squadron, led a dismounted patrol near La Pastorella, captured seven Germans, located enemy positions and searched buildings and abandoned dugouts, all while under machine-gun fire. Lieutenant Foott, also supporting Cremona, was another to earn the MC, the citation noting that he led Italian soldiers on foot to their objective.[64]

Subsequently, the Horse supported 8th Indian Division's advance to Ferrara, encountering opposition that became stiffer, including panzers in the city outskirts. The Germans withdrew overnight and, on the morning of the 23rd, Lieutenant David King's No.3 Troop C Squadron reached the Po at 1045, the first of Eighth Army to do so. King and his men captured a large haul of stores and guaranteed the isolation of the German garrison of Ferrera. King was awarded the MC for that and 'previous excellent work'. Major Bertie Sidebottom, commanding B Squadron, was another MC recipient for his part in overcoming the garrison in Ferrara, during which he displayed 'fine leadership, determination and courage' in a 'fierce and decisive action' when his squadron accounted for six StuGs, a Panther and seven Mark IVs, as well as over eighty prisoners. On foot with two men, Sidebottom captured forty of those prisoners.[65]

C Squadron fought the Horse's final action of the war when, on the 29th, it engaged a large column of tanks, artillery and soft- and hard-skinned vehicles trying to cross the Adige river. With the surrounding countryside littered with a defeated army's abandoned equipment and weaponry, more than had been seen along the Po, it was obvious that the Italian campaign was all but over.

On 30 April, the North Irish Horse was ordered to 'Stand Down' for the last time in the Second World War. The regiment had also achieved something no other armoured or tank unit matched: every tank in the regiment was still 'going' when the campaign ended.[66]

* * *

Those final weeks of war also involved Irish personnel in other units and formations, including 6th South African Armoured Division. The Reverend Fred Rea, a minister of the Methodist Church in Ireland, was a chaplain with the Engineer and Signals Corps. The division, which arrived in Italy in mid-1944, joined Eighth Army reserve and, following the liberation of Rome, took part in Eighth Army's advance and, later, in Operation OLIVE in the Gothic Line. Fred Rea was a constant presence for the sappers and signallers with his 'ready smile and reassuring manner'. He visited his parishioners in the most difficult of circumstances and locations and, if men were going out beyond the forward positions to repair demolitions after dark, 'his normal request was to be given a shovel and to be allowed to join the working party'. At the end of the campaign, he was appointed MBE for 'inspiring devotion to duty, outstanding courage beyond the call of duty, and for his consistently magnificent example in disregard for personal safety'.[67]

British 6th Armoured Division had been held as Eighth Army's reserve until Sir Richard McCreery determined on which axis it should advance. As noted, it moved north-westerly from Argenta towards Bondeno and the appropriately named Finale. Adrian Gore's 61 Brigade included 1st King's Royal Rifle Corps, also known as 60th Rifles, which joined the brigade in early March, and two battalions of the Rifle Brigade, 2nd and 7th, 10th having been disbanded. There were also changes in 1 Guards Brigade but 26 Armoured still included 16th/5th Lancers, 17th/21st Lancers and 2nd Lothians and Border Horse. The divisional advance was led by 16th/5th Lancers with the 60th Rifles. Lieutenant Michael McCorkell, from Londonderry, a troop leader, recalled the 'terrific speed'[68] of the advance, which was described by a regimental historian:

> we buffeted our way through the remaining enemy lines and lashed into his attempts to re-organize himself .... We had wonderful support from the 60th, from our guns and from the air ... to bounce our way over the various river and canal lines that the enemy might otherwise have made good ... [but] he was utterly beaten and disorganized south of the River Po and was forced to abandon practically all his equipment and vehicles.[69]

Val ffrench-Blake wrote of how the enemy rearguard had been broken and a breakthrough made at Segni after which 26 Armoured Brigade 'was thrust in like a sword nearly twenty miles deep, with the Regiment at the point'. It was the battlegroup of ffrench-Blake's 'Death or Glory Boys' and 7th Rifle Brigade that effected the breakthrough before leading the way to Poggio Renatico and cutting the only alternative road from Bologna to Ferrara. Fighting continued throughout the night with ffrench-Blake visiting all his fighting troops and encouraging them to give their all and thus overcome the strong enemy force opposing them. Five 17th/21st Lancers lost their lives, one of them Lance Corporal Fred Polley, a 'neutral' from Éire.[70] In the supporting 7th Rifle Brigade, Sergeant John Mulpeter from Rathangan, County Kildare, also perished. John Mulpeter had an Ulster Rifles' service number. He had moved to London in 1936 and enlisted in the London Irish. A keen sportsman, he played Gaelic games at home and in London. Discovering that he was a Catholic, Italian partisans erected a marble marker on his original resting place.[71]

For his leadership of the battlegroup, Val ffrench-Blake was appointed DSO. The citation is summarized in its final sentence: 'Lieutenant Colonel ffrench-Blake's punch with his force was a large factor in causing the German 278, 1 and 4 Parachute Divisions to withdraw so precipitately.'[72]

Major Desmond Woods MC*, who had been wounded at Pucciarelli in June 1944, had returned to duty, but not to 2nd London Irish. Instead, he had been posted to Gruppo Cremona, one of three *Regio Esercito* formations in Eighth Army in 1945. Commanded by Brigadier General Clemente Primieri, Cremona included two infantry regiments (brigades) with 28 Garibaldi Brigade of partisans. Major Woods' role was as an advisor and liaison officer as the Italian army became part of 15th Army Group. Gruppo Cremona acquitted itself well in April 1945: on the 10th it launched Operation SONIA in which, supported by its own artillery, it liberated Fusignano and then Alfonsine. At Fusignano the defence included 1 Company 504th Heavy Panzer Battalion with some Tiger tanks.[73]

Chapter 10

In the Air

Before the first landing craft grounded on a Sicilian beach, Irish RAF personnel had seen action over the island and mainland Italy. Bomber Command had made its first strikes against Italian targets on the night of 11/12 June 1940, the day after Mussolini declared war on France and the UK. Italy had endured many bombing raids but the pressure increased greatly as the Allies prepared for Operation HUSKY. As noted earlier, airfields on Sicily had been put out of action and, immediately before HUSKY, the island of Pantellaria had been bombarded from air and sea.

Since the Royal Air Force did not have 'tribal' units, there were no Irish groups, wings or squadrons. Irishmen served as individuals in bombers and fighters in the Mediterranean, many losing their lives on operations or in crashes. However, three distinguished Irish airmen served in the theatre: Wing Commander Anthony (Tony) Lovell DSO* DFC* DFC (US), Squadron Leader Robert W. Turkington DSO DFC* and Brian Bertram Considine.

Tony Lovell was born in 1919 in Ceylon where his father was a tea-planter, but the family returned to their home in Portrush, County Antrim when Lovell senior died in 1923. Educated at Ampleforth College, Tony joined the RAF in 1937, although his long-term aim was to take Holy Orders. After training, he joined No.41 Squadron and was rated an above-average pilot on Spitfires by September 1939. Gaining victories in the Battle of Britain in 1940, he was awarded the Distinguished Flying Cross (DFC) in November. Commanding No.145 Squadron from September 1941, he earned a Bar to the DFC. In early 1942, No.145 deployed to North Africa where he resigned his command and was posted to Malta, taking over No.1435 Squadron during a very difficult time for the island. His squadron helped defend the remnants of the Santa Marija convoy, Operation PEDESTAL; its arrival in Malta signalled the end of the siege of the island. As 1942 drew to a close, Lovell added another eight enemy aircraft to his tally and was appointed DSO. Shortly afterwards, he was promoted to be Wing Commander Lovell, continuing to fly in the defence of Malta and in offensive sweeps over Sicily which intensified as HUSKY drew closer.[1]

As Wing Commander (Flying), No.322 Wing, Desert Air Force, he transferred to Italy and further close air support (CAS) operations for Eighth and Fifth Armies. In many, if not most, of the ground operations described in earlier chapters, Lovell's airmen would have been in support. They operated the cab-rank system, known as Rover-David, in which an experienced RAF officer moved with forward troops and, in radio contact with aircraft in the cab-rank, directed fighter-bombers to deal with problems facing the soldiers. The system, born in the desert and developed in Tunisia, was refined in Sicily and Italy and adopted by the USAAF for its tactical air support squadrons. Tony Lovell later commanded No.244 Wing which protected US Army Air Forces' bombers operating from Corsica. Such was the wing's effectiveness in the role that Lovell was awarded the US Distinguished Flying Cross.[2]

Following the liberation of Rome, Tony Lovell had an audience of Pope Pius XII, after which he spent some leave on retreat in a Dominican monastery. His faith was such that he went to confession each time he shot down an enemy aircraft. The 'victory' was not a reason for rejoicing but one of concern for the soul of an opponent whom he may have despatched unprepared to meet his Maker.[3]

Wing Commander Lovell remained on active operations until the end of 1944, when he was posted to Ismailia in Egypt as chief instructor at the RAF Fighter Operational Training Unit (OTU). He was also awarded a Bar to the DSO for his 'courage, his flying ability and his tactical knowledge' which had been inspiring 'to all who have flown with him and of a quality seldom, if ever, equalled'.[4]

Tony Lovell was killed in a flying accident two days after VJ Day when he was an instructor at the School of Air Support at Old Sarum in Wiltshire. After a slow roll on take-off, his Spitfire failed to gain altitude and hit high ground. Since he died in the UK, Tony Lovell is buried in Portrush.[5]

Robert Wilkinson Turkington, from Lurgan in County Armagh, was born in India in 1920 where his father was a civil engineer with the railways. Enlisting in the RAF in September 1940, he was selected for pilot training. Awarded his 'wings' and commissioned in the RAF Volunteer Reserve (RAFVR), he was inevitably known as 'Paddy'.[6]

Having served in the UK, including Operation JUBILEE, the Dieppe Raid in August 1942, Turkington was posted to Algeria with No.43 Squadron, flying Hurricanes in support of First Army. The squadron converted to Spitfires in February 1943 before transferring to Malta in June to support the Sicily landings and Mediterranean convoys. From Sicily, No.43 moved to Italy to fly fighter patrols. Six weeks on support missions for Operation DRAGOON, the landings in southern France, followed before returning to Italy and the fighter-bomber role. Despite the squadron performing those duties, in November

Flight Lieutenant Turkington shot down five enemy aircraft and was awarded the DFC.[7]

He then moved to No.241 Squadron, another Spitfire unit, as a flight commander, increasing his 'score' in July 1944 when he shot down four Bf.109s, including two on the 21st. As a result, he was awarded a Bar to the DFC for outstanding work in both air-to-air and ground-attack operations. On 2 August he was appointed to command No.601 (County of London) Squadron which was engaged in the ground-attack role in Italy, proving an inspiring leader for the squadron. Appointed DSO in April 1945, just as the war in Italy was coming to an end, the citation noted that he

> has been inspiring and brilliant in his leadership .... As a fighter-bomber pilot he has, by personal example, taught his pilots with determination and accuracy from a low-level; the inevitable return fire he treated in characteristically light-hearted manner, although repeatedly hit himself. In this way he brought squadron morale, spirit and efficiency to the highest possible pitch, and commanded the absolute loyalty and devotion of those serving under him.
>
> Squadron Leader Turkington has a particularly inspiring record as a close support leader. Many times he has destroyed his target through sheer dogged persistence, strafing repeatedly until his ammunition was exhausted. Thus, on 26 December 1944, leading a formation of six aircraft against a strongpoint, four bombs were not seen to explode and the other two went wide; accordingly, he led his aircraft in to strafe no [fewer] than six times, despite return fire, and only left the target area when the strongpoint was reduced to burning wreckage. On 31 December 1944, under similar circumstances, and with a depleted formation, he strafed eight times to destroy the target completely.[8]

On 5 January 1945 his Spitfire was damaged severely by anti-aircraft fire during an attack but he brought it 'home' for a 'wheels-up' landing in spite of it stalling at 160mph. He was rested from flying duties during January.

Subsequently taking command of No.241 Squadron, he survived the war in Europe and expected to be demobbed in May 1945. Retained in Italy for a time, he anticipated returning home in August. It was not to be. Squadron Leader Robert Turkington DSO DFC* was killed in an accident after taking off for a cross-country flight to Naples on 29 July. The engine of his Spitfire was heard to cut out and, although he immediately turned to starboard to return to the airfield, the fighter lost height, crashed and burst into flames. He was 26 years old. Robert Turkington rests in Padua war cemetery.[9]

Brian Bertram Considine was born in Dublin in January 1920. Although his family was from Limerick, his doctor father was governor of the criminal lunatic asylum in Dundrum, County Dublin.[10]

Another Ampleforth College pupil, he joined the RAFVR in December 1938 as an 'Airman u/t (under training) Pilot' and did his early flying at No.20 Elementary & Reserve Flying Training School, Gravesend. Working for Lever Brothers, he was called up on 1 September 1939. From No.1 Initial Training Wing at Selwyn College, Cambridge, Considine went to No.3 Flying Training School, Grantham in November. Completing training in May 1940, he moved to 6 Operational Training Unit (OTU) to convert to Hurricanes and was posted to No.238 Squadron at Tangmere in June.[11]

On 21 July, Pilot Officer Brian Considine claimed the destruction of a Bf.110 while, on 27 August, he shared the shooting down of a Do17P bomber over Plymouth, the crew of which were captured unhurt. In November, he was shot down by Bf.109s over Bournemouth but baled out, wounded.[12]

When No.238 was posted to North Africa, the aircraft were embarked on the aircraft carrier HMS *Victorious* but some pilots, including Considine, travelled by troopship, disembarking at Takoradi and ferrying aircraft to Egypt. After a series of postings in Aden, Egypt and Palestine, Brian Considine joined No.74 Squadron as flight commander, later transferring to No.111 Squadron on Malta flying Spitfires on operations supporting Operation HUSKY. Moving to Sicily, the squadron occupied airfields there until it transferred to Italy after September. The squadron flew fighter-bomber missions until the end of the war, but Considine joined a communications squadron in Egypt from where he returned to the UK and became a Transport Command pilot. He survived the war and was later a pilot with Aer Lingus before moving into the advertising business.[13]

Sam McAughtry, from Tiger's Bay in Belfast, volunteered for the RAF and trained as aircrew. His brother Tommy served in the North Irish Horse and earned the DCM (pp.147 and 158) in Italy while another brother, Mart, was lost when his ship, the *Kenbane Head*, was sunk by the German battleship *Scharnhorst* in November 1940.[14] Mart's death inspired Sam to enlist and to later volunteer for aircrew. He spent much of his service in the Mediterranean as a gunner/observer in Bristol Beaufighters, twin-engine fighter-bombers that fulfilled a variety of roles, including anti-shipping strikes in the sea lanes across the Mediterranean. The 'Beau', as it was known, was robust and reliable and could absorb considerable damage. It was also manoeuvrable and well suited to the anti-shipping role which required low-level attacks almost down to wave height, often into heavy AA fire. McAughtry recalled that his first pilot on

Beaufighters was an unpleasant officer from northern England with whom he found it difficult to work. Sergeant McAughtry was particularly unimpressed by the way his pilot landed, which suggested he was not experienced. Since the Beaufighter was heavy on the controls, it was not the easiest aircraft to fly with landing a challenge for inexperienced pilots. Judging by McAughtry's comment that his pilot seemed to 'land' well above the runway before hitting the ground like a runaway lift, the man was indeed inexperienced. However, the situation was saved when he was taken ill and left the squadron, having completed twelve missions with Sergeant McAughtry in the rear fuselage. (McAughtry believed that the man had broken an aircraft in two in a hard landing.) In all Sam McAughtry, later promoted to flight sergeant and eventually commissioned, flew thirty-seven operational missions.[15]

* * *

Included in the RAF presence in Italy were squadrons of the RAF Regiment, a corps designed to defend airfields. Created in 1942 at the behest of Winston Churchill, it included field squadrons of light AA guns for the close defence of airfields against enemy intruders.

In February 1944, one such squadron, 2867 LAA Squadron, was based on Isola di Ponza (believed to be named after Pontius Pilate), one of the Pontine Islands in the Tyrrhenian Sea. During a gale on the 26th, a US Navy LST carrying 150 American soldiers and some German prisoners from Anzio to Naples struck rocks off Ponza. Sergeant George Overend and Leading Aircraftman (LAC) Frederick Canton were on guard duty at a gunsite on the coast when the incident occurred. Learning of the LST's plight from islanders, Overend, from Mullahead near Tandragee, County Armagh, organized a rescue party and led it to a steep 200-foot cliff.

Below, the ship was being pounded against the rocks. With no beach between cliff face and sea, Overend and Canton clambered downwards against an almost vertical cliff side. Wading chest-deep into the sea between jagged rocks, they reached the disabled vessel and began pulling survivors to the relative safety of the rocks, working for over five hours with LAC Canton washed into the waves at least twice. However, their endeavours saved many lives. As a result, Sergeant Overend was awarded the American Soldier's Medal, which equates to the George Medal, an award he later received from Brigadier General Edward M. Morris.[16]

* * *

I Know That I Shall Meet My Fate

Irish fatal casualties in the Royal Air Force in the Italian campaign were modest compared to those of the Army. A search of CWGC records indicates that nearly sixty Irish RAF personnel died. Many lie in Sicily and Italy with others as far afield as Enfidaville, Tunisia and Poznan, Poland; those whose bodies were never recovered are commemorated on the Malta Memorial, their squadrons having been based there. Nine ground personnel, including one member of the RAF Regiment, are on the Roll of Honour for Italy.

The RAF Regiment airman, Leading Aircraftman (LAC) Richard Hickey, aged 22, from New Ross, County Wexford, died on 10 August 1944. Buried in Bari cemetery, LAC Hickey served in No.2933 LAA Squadron which had been formed in Libya before moving to Italy where it was disbanded in Naples in November 1944.[17] LAC Robert Dowds, of No.221 Squadron, from Belfast, was also aged 22 when he died on 15 August 1943 when the squadron, equipped with Wellingtons, was based on Malta; it later moved to Italy but its maritime patrol and bombing missions were related to the Italian campaign.[18] AC1 George Nethery, from Drumquin, County Tyrone, was 23 when he died on 28 June 1944. He is buried in Rome.[19]

Sergeant James Macready, also of No.221 Squadron, is buried in Bari. He died on 2 February 1944 when his Malta-based squadron was flying bombing missions against ports in Italy, as well as anti-submarine patrols. Sergeant Macready, from Bushmills, County Antrim, was 21.[20]

LAC Michael Smyth, aged 29, was from Cork. He died on 16 September 1944 and is buried in Naples.[21] Another 29-year-old, LAC John Walsh, from Ballacolla, County Laois, died on 13 December 1933 and is buried in Ancona.[22] LAC Henry McCullough, a native of Lurgan, County Armagh, is buried in Coriano Ridge cemetery. He was 23 when he died on 30 May 1945.[23] Catania war cemetery in Sicily is the resting place of LAC Michael Murray who died on 19 March 1945. Hailing from Mostrim, County Longford, he was aged 27.[24] Also resting in Catania is LAC Charles Rutledge, a 24-year-old from Killen, County Tyrone, who died on 8 December 1945.[25] Belfast native LAC George Wilkinson was 25 when he died on 16 October 1945; he is buried in Naples war cemetery.[26] Corporal Edward Leckey, aged 26 from Belfast, is buried in Bari. Stationed at Foggia with No.272 Squadron, he died on 17 November 1944.[27] Lancelot Parke, an AC2 and native of Dublin, was only 20 when he died on 20 July 1945. AC2 Parke is buried in Phaleron war cemetery in Greece.[28]

Six Irish members of No.114 Squadron died between 20 December 1943 and 19 February 1945. The squadron had converted from Bristol Blenheim Vs to Douglas Bostons in Algeria in April 1943 before moving to Sicily in August. It later moved to Italy where its role was attacking enemy communications and airfields.[29] That role involved low-level strikes which were high-risk missions since the bombers had to face fire from ground defences ranging from light machine guns to medium and heavy anti-aircraft guns. The Germans had developed a range of multiple-barrelled AA weapons capable of creating intense screens of fire around and over a target.

The first Irishman of No.114 to die, Flight Sergeant Patrick Conway, lost his life on 20 December 1943. From Plumbridge, County Tyrone, the 30-year-old was one of the four members of the crew of a Boston IIIA that attacked a target at Miglianico but crashed near Apricena on its return flight, killing three of the crew, including the Royal Canadian Air Force pilot (who was from Washington State USA); the fourth man was injured.[30] Michael Conway is buried in Bari.

On 4 January 1944, Sergeant Edward Blair, aged 19, from Belfast died. No operational casualties are recorded for No.114 on that date. Edward Blair is buried in Moro River Canadian cemetery with the family inscription on his headstone including the phrase 'God is your co-pilot'.[31] Remembered on the Malta Memorial, 19-year-old Sergeant William Holland has no known grave. From Naas, County Kildare, he was the son of Major J.A. Holland, who served in the Royal Army Medical Corps. No operation is recorded for the squadron on that date.[32] Sergeant John Boyd from Londonderry is also commemorated on the Malta Memorial. The 24-year-old was married and his wife Catherine lived in Stirlingshire. On 25 August his Boston, flown by Warrant Officer Herbert Dowland of the RCAF, crashed into the sea off Piombino. No bodies were recovered.[33]

Sergeant William Bingham was a 20-year-old from Greencastle, County Antrim. On 1 October 1944, he was a crewman in a Boston that took off at 2202 on a mission along the Savio river. At 0020 on the 2nd what was believed to be his aircraft was seen in flames. The pilot, Sergeant Denis Hinchcliffe, also aged 20, William Bingham and 21-year-old Sergeant Edward Wright are buried in a collective grave in Argenta Gap war cemetery. A fourth crewman died but appears not to be buried in the same cemetery.[34]

On the night of 19/20 February 1945, Pilot Officer Samuel Taylor, aged 26 from Belfast, was a crewman in a Boston V flown by No.114 Squadron's CO, Wing Commander Ronald Thomson, on an armed recce over Padua-Mestre-Pordenone. Hit by AA fire over Nervesa della Battaglia, the Boston crashed near Susegana, killing all onboard.[35] All four crew members are buried in a collective grave in Udine war cemetery.

Six Irish members of No.104 Squadron lost their lives during the Italian campaign, two of whom shared the surname Scott. The first two to die were the pilot and a crewman of a Wellington on a bombing mission to Naples marshalling yards. V Victor took off from its Tunisian base at 2240 on 26 June 1943, piloted by Flying Officer John Thompson, a 21-year-old from Mountmellick, County Laois. It was shot down by Italian AA fire near Torre del Greco at 0200 on the 27th.[36] All six crewmen were killed, including Sergeant William Quaile from Lurgan, County Armagh. William Quaile, also aged 21, John Thompson and their comrades rest in a collective grave in Salerno war cemetery.

On the night of 7/8 August, Sergeant William Barriskill from Portadown, County Armagh was in the crew of a Wellington X on a mission to Cape Palmi, north-east of Reggio, from which three Wellingtons, two from No.104 Squadron and one from No.37 Squadron, failed to return. No trace was found of either Wellington from No.104. Sergeant Barriskill is commemorated on the Malta Memorial. No.104 Squadron was still operating from Tunisia.[37]

Also commemorated on the Malta Memorial, Sergeant Eric Jenkinson from Lurgan, County Armagh, was killed on 1 November 1943, aged 21. On the night of 1st/2nd, the squadron lost two Wellington Xs in a raid on an airfield at Perugia, one believed to have been shot down by AA fire; the other failed to return.[38]

From Derrylane, County Cavan, 22-year-old Sergeant Robert Scott died on 17 February 1944 when his Wellington crashed. By then No.104 Squadron was based at Foggia. Sergeant Scott was buried in a collective grave at Bari war cemetery. Flight Sergeant Andrew Scott is also buried in Bari. The 21-year-old Belfastman died on 4 February 1945.[39]

Three Irish personnel of No.18 Squadron, which re-equipped with Bostons in early 1943, died between January 1943, when the squadron was based in Tunisia, and August 1944 when it was in Italy. The first was Flight Sergeant Joseph Bartley DFM from Longford who died on 19 January 1943 although his death appears not to have been on operations.[40] Flight Sergeant Edward Coates from Cork was aged 32 when he died on 13 October 1943 when the squadron was operating from Brindisi. On that same day, Marshal Pietro Badoglio's new Italian government declared war on Germany and Italy became a co-belligerent partner of the Allies. At 1945 that day, Flight Sergeant Robert Pound of the Royal Australian Air Force took off from Brindisi in a Boston III to reconnoitre a road to Rome; Fifth Army had reached the Volturno river. Unfortunately, the aircraft flew into a mountain four miles north-east of Campo di Giovi near Sulmona, killing the pilot and two crewmen; another was taken prisoner. Edward Coates was buried in Moro river Canadian cemetery.[41]

Sergeant James O'Fee from Kilrea, County Londonderry died on 9 August 1944 and is buried in Cesena. Flying Officer Alfred Gaskell had taken off from Cecina at 2235 on an armed recce of roads along the Adriatic coast but crashed near Cesena. All four crew died and were buried in a collective grave in Cesena war cemetery. James O'Fee was 24.[42]

Two members of No.14 Squadron, equipped with Martin Marauders, died in 1944, Pilot Officer Maurice Reid on 1 February and Sergeant David Martin on 26 June. Maurice Reid, aged 25, was from Londonderry while David Martin, aged 21, was from Belfast. Pilot Officer Reid is commemorated on the Malta Memorial while Sergeant Martin was buried in Cagliari war cemetery. On a recce mission, Maurice Reid's aircraft, 'Dominion Upholder', failed to return; six men were lost.[43] David Martin's Marauder, piloted by Lieutenant M.J.W. Brummer, South African Air Force (SAAF), crashed off Sardinia while on patrol from Alghero with all six crew dying.[44]

Warrant Officer Scott and Flight Sergeant McDermott of No.19 Squadron SAAF crewed a Beaufighter VI shot down by AA fire during an attack on Banja Luka airfield in Yugoslavia on 18 August 1944. They are buried in a collective grave in Belgrade, Serbia with the crew of another Beaufighter shot down on the same mission. Scott, aged 23, was from Greystones, County Wicklow and McDermott, aged 24, from Londonderry.[45] In all, eight Irish airmen are buried in Belgrade. The others include Squadron Leader Ernest Kee DFC from Ballybofey, County Donegal, of No.241 Squadron; Sergeant James Magee, of No.40 Squadron, a 24-year-old Belfast man; Sergeant Sydney Wright, of No.31 Squadron SAAF, also 24 and from Belfast; Sergeant Matthew Lyttle, 19 and from Belfast, of No.70 Squadron; and 21-year-old Flight Lieutenant John Mulcahy-Morgan of 213 Squadron,[46] whose father had served in the Royal Irish Fusiliers and the Royal Flying Corps (another member of the family was commissioned in the Faughs in May 1944).[47]

Squadron Leader Kee's No.241 squadron had converted to Spitfires in December 1943 and flew from a series of Italian bases on a range of missions including tactical and shipping reconnaissance, escorts and close air support.[48] On 20 April 1944, Kee was strafing schooners off Petcane (Petrcane) when his Spitfire VIII was hit by AA fire. He crashed on Uljan (Ugljan, off Croatia) island.[49] James Magee's No.40 Squadron flew Wellington Xs from Foggia on missions over the Aegean and Yugoslavia. Sergeant Magee died on 17 July 1944.[50] Matthew Lyttle lost his life on 22 October 1944 when No.70 Squadron was operating Wellington Xs from Cerignola.[51] Sergeant Sydney Wright's No.31 SAAF Squadron had suffered serious losses supporting the Warsaw uprising, during which it was estimated that a bomber was lost for every ton of supplies dropped. The squadron's Liberators flew regularly over the Balkans where Sergeant Smyth lost his life on 22 September 1944.[52] Flight Lieutenant John Mulcahy-Morgan died on 4 January 1945 when his Mustang III was shot down by AA fire as he was strafing a train in the Brod-Doboj area of Yugoslavia.[53] Warrant Officer Ian Iago's Mustang IV was hit by AA fire over Cherso Bay at 1100 on 11 March. Although he baled out, his parachute failed to open and he was killed.[54]

One of the first Irish airmen to die after Operation HUSKY was Flying Officer Colin Buchanan, a 25-year-old from Sydenham, Belfast. One of the crew of a Martin Baltimore IIIA of No.55 Squadron, he was killed when Flying Officer John Wotherspoon's aircraft exploded when hit by AA fire during a raid on 25 July. All four crewmen were buried in a communal grave in Catania war cemetery.[55] Less than two weeks later, Sergeant David Lovesy, aged 20 from Belfast, died when his Tunisia-based Wellington X of No.150 Squadron was shot down, probably by a night-fighter, on 7 August when on a raid to Messina. Another Wellington X was shot down that night. Sergeant Lovesy, the pilot, and his crew are commemorated on the Malta Memorial, as are the crew of the second lost Wellington.[56]

Colin Buchanan was the first of three Irish members of No.55 Squadron to die. The others, Flight Sergeant William Dixon, aged 20, from Clontarf, County Dublin and 32-year-old Pilot Officer Robert Horne from Belfast, died on 13 October 1944 and 21 January 1945 respectively.[57] The squadron had relinquished its Baltimores for Bostons in October. William Dixon may not have died on operations,[58] but Robert Horne was killed on a mission from Ferrara to attack road traffic when Squadron Leader Ronald Stinger DFC's Boston was shot down. Stringer's crew were buried in a collective grave at Argenta Gap war cemetery.[59]

Sergeant John Robinson of No.178 Squadron was 21 and from Belfast. His squadron was equipped with Liberators and had moved to Italy in March 1944. It was engaged in bombing operations in Italy and the Balkans, plus supply-drops to partisans as far away as northern Italy and Poland. Sergeant Robinson lost his life on a supply flight and is buried in Budapest.[60] Sergeant David Nicholl from Newtownhamilton, County Down is commemorated on the Malta Memorial. A member of No.614 Squadron, he died on 2 March 1945. His squadron, based at Amendola in Italy, was engaged on missions to supply partisans as well as bombing raids on the Balkans.[61] Flight Sergeant Daniel O'Brien, from Marino in Dublin, served in No.500 Squadron which was equipped with Baltimores and involved in night-interdiction operations against German traffic in northern Italy. The 21-year-old was in one of two Baltimores lost on the night of 1/2 April 1945. His aircraft, G-George, 'disappeared without trace'.[62]

Warrant Officer Kingsmill Williams, aged 23, from Mallow, County Cork, served with No.72 Squadron which flew Spitfire IXs from Ravenna.[63] Kingsmill Williams took off at 1040 on 10 April 1945 for an armed reconnaissance between Ferrara and the Po. The 10th was the first full day of Eighth Army's Operation BUCKLAND and Allied ground troops were in a determined advance on the ground between the Senio and Santerno. Although German forces had taken massive punishment the previous day, they remained defiant with their AA gunners as effective as ever, although many of their guns had been destroyed. Allied aircraft over the battlefield faced a storm of AA fire, from light weapons up to heavy AA guns. Against low-flying fighters, such as Kingsmill Williams' Spitfire, the most likely weapons to be deployed were 20mm, 37mm and 40mm guns, some of them multi-barrelled and capable of creating a blizzard of shells; the 20mm four-barrelled *Flakvierling* 38 had a theoretical rate of fire close to 2,000 rounds per minute. At 1120, forty minutes into his mission, Kingsmill Williams' Spitfire was hit by AA five miles north of Portomaggiore. The aircraft was brought down and Warrant Officer Williams was killed.[64] He was interred in Padua war cemetery. Later that day, another Spitfire from No.72 Squadron was engaged in strafing enemy artillery when it was hit by AA rounds. It crash-landed but struck a tree, killing the pilot, Flight Lieutenant King.[65]

Chapter 11

Ruling The Waves

The Royal Navy has long been regarded as the 'Senior Service' with its history predating by centuries the creation of a national army. It protected the Empire's sea lanes and, thus, trade. It also ferried the Army to foreign fields in times of war and plucked it from danger, as with Moore's forces in the Peninsula, the force at Gallipoli and, more recently, from Dunkirk, Greece and Crete while, at great cost, it had kept the garrison of besieged Tobruk supplied in 1941.

Admiral Sir Andrew Browne Cunningham, known as ABC, had been appointed Commander-in-Chief Mediterranean Fleet in June. Born in Rathmines, Dublin in 1883 – his Scottish father was professor of anatomy at Trinity College – Cunningham was educated in Dublin and Edinburgh and chose a career in the Royal Navy.[1]

On 6 June 1939, Cunningham became C-in-C Mediterranean Fleet with his HQ in Alexandria, Egypt where it had been moved from Malta, considered to be at too much risk due to its proximity to Sicily. With Italy neutral, most of Cunningham's ships were transferred to other commands. By the time Italy entered the war in June 1940 his fleet had not been restored to its September 1939 strength.[2] Nonetheless, Cunningham proved a master and the aerial raid on Taranto harbour on 11 November 1940, Operation JUDGEMENT, crippled the Italian fleet, forcing the *Regia Marina* to move its main base. Among the pilots of the Swordfish torpedo-bombers that struck from the aircraft-carrier HMS *Illustrious* was Lieutenant Michael Torrens-Spence from County Antrim whose torpedo struck the battleship *Littorio.* Torrens-Spence was awarded the DSC and was later appointed DSO for his part in the Battle of Cape Matapan in which Cunningham outfought the Italian fleet and established Royal Navy supremacy in the Mediterranean.[3] Cunningham remained in post until October 1943 when he was appointed First Sea Lord. He was transferred temporarily to oversee naval arrangements for Operation TORCH, the landings in French North-West Africa. His HQ planned and executed Operations HUSKY, BAYTOWN, AVALANCHE, SLAPSTICK and SHINGLE. When Mark Clark lost his nerve at Salerno and wanted to lift

Fifth Army off the beaches, Cunningham informed him that there would be no evacuation.

Although many Irish men, and a few women, served in naval uniform in Italy, very few are numbered among the campaign's casualties. On 18 February 1944, the Arethusa-class light cruiser HMS *Penelope*, known as HMS *Pepperpot*, from the many holes in its hull and superstructure caused by enemy action during earlier service in Malta, was west of Naples steaming for Anzio at 26 knots when it was spotted and torpedoed by *U-410*. A torpedo struck at 0658. Sixteen minutes later, Fenski, the U-boat's captain, launched another and the Belfast-built cruiser sank quickly. Of the crew, 415 were lost but 206 survived.[4] It is believed to be the only case of a ship sailing at such a speed being torpedoed. The dead included Petty Officer Stokers Albert Hutchings of Dublin, aged 27, and Kenneth Hewitt of Londonderry, aged 24; Marine Robert Rock of Bray, County Wicklow, whose brother George had been killed in Tunisia serving with 2nd London Irish; and Stoker 2nd Class Joseph McAvoy of Belfast, aged 19. Able Seaman William Hunter, aged 23, from Ballyclare, County Antrim survived. Also among *Penelope*'s dead was Lieutenant Robert Mcinroy 'Robbie' Robertson from Merchiston, Edinburgh, the ship's paymaster.[5] Robbie Robertson, aged 29, had become engaged to Lieutenant Eveline McGrath, of the QAs, who had experienced the Bari bombing. At her own request, Eveline had been transferred to Torre Annunziata to be closer to her fiancé.[5] Albert Hutchings and Joseph McAvoy are remembered on the Plymouth Memorial while the other three dead are named on the Portsmouth Memorial.

During Operation SLAPSTICK, the landing of V Corps at Taranto in September 1943, the fast minelayer/cruiser HMS *Abdiel* struck a mine whilst swinging at anchor. The ensuing explosion broke the ship's back. Forty-eight naval personnel died in the explosion or drowned as *Abdiel* sank, as well as 120 soldiers of 6th Parachute Battalion, Army Air Corps. Included in the naval dead were two Irishmen: Petty Officer Andrew Dooley, from Castledermot, County Kildare and Able Seaman Hugh Hutchinson of Belfast. Petty Officer Dooley, aged 30, is commemorated on the Plymouth Memorial while Able Seaman Hutchinson, aged 42, is buried in Bari cemetery.[6]

Admiral Cunningham chose to establish an advanced naval HQ in Naples, moving most of his staff there in January 1944.[7] From its new location, the HQ completed the planning and organization of Operation SHINGLE, the Anzio landings. Included in the staff were members of the Women's Royal Naval Service, the WRNS, popularly – and officially – known as Wrens. The WRNS was formed in 1917 and, a year later, a 19-year-old Irish Wren, Josephine Carr, became the first Wren to die on active service: Josephine was aboard the RMS *Leinster* when it was torpedoed en route from Kingstown (Dun Laoghaire) to Holyhead on 10 October. Disbanded in 1919, the WRNS was re-formed in 1939.

Elizabeth Chamberlain, daughter of a Church of Ireland canon, was keen to join the WRNS but the Admiralty refused to accept volunteers from Éire. As a result, Elizabeth and three other young women took advantage of an opportunity to travel to England by becoming volunteers with St John Ambulance in Dublin. All four received basic training that would allow them to become nursing aides in England. The training was organized by Dr Thomas Graham MC, President of the Royal College of Surgeons in Ireland and a driving force in St John in Dublin.

> I wanted to join the Wrens because their uniform was the most attractive. But the WRNS wouldn't accept applicants from the south of Ireland, so I had to get to England. Brenda's father [Dr Graham] made this possible. He was able to arrange jobs for four of us at Chertsey Hospital as nursing aides. So, I went to England to be able to get into the Wrens.[8]

She then applied, using a friend's address, and was accepted and, subsequently, commissioned. Although uncertain of her prospects with the commissioning board, she realized that one of the officers interviewing her had been to school in Dublin with her mother.[9]

Elizabeth also married but her husband, Sub-Lieutenant (Air) Michael Beresford-Jones, was killed when his aircraft crashed off Machrihanish in Scotland on 23 May 1943. He had previously served on *Illustrious* in the Mediterranean.[10]

Third Officer Beresford-Jones, by then a skilled cipher officer, applied for and received a posting to the Mediterranean Fleet in Naples. Travelling by troopship, the SS *Christian Huigens*, from Liverpool to Naples, she met John Kerans, from Parsonstown, County Offaly, who would achieve worldwide fame as captain of HMS *Amethyst* during the Yangtze incident in 1949. (In the film *Yangtse Incident: The Story of HMS Amethyst*, Kerans was played by another Irish war veteran, Richard Todd.)

Disembarking in Naples, she was amazed to meet three friends from Dublin on the Via Roma during her first day. Her accommodation in a large block of flats housed some twenty WRNS officers. On duty she worked with US Navy officers but there was an expectation that Wren officers would share watchkeeping duties and attend dinner parties in Villa Emma, once the home of Lady Hamilton, Nelson's mistress. There she met many senior officers. 'I hate to say it, but I enjoyed the war. You forget all the horrible parts. My time in Liverpool and Skipness was pure hell. Then there was the poverty of Naples, seeing people eating out of dustbins.'[11]

After the war, Elizabeth Beresford-Jones married Captain Andy Parsons MC of the RAMC who had been wounded severely at Anzio. His MC had been earned in North Africa during the advance to Tripoli following the final battle at El Alamein. They had known each other before the war when Andy Parsons, from Athlone, County Westmeath, had studied medicine at Trinity College.[12]

Earlier in this book, Irish chaplains including Alan Buchanan, Victor Pike, Dan Kelleher and Patrick Bluett are mentioned. All served with the Army but the Royal Navy had a chaplain in Italy with a remarkable record. The Reverend Willie Devine had served with the Australian 48th Battalion in France during the Great War, earning both the MC and the French Croix de Guerre. A native of Castlederg, County Tyrone, he had studied at Maynooth, the Catholic Church's national seminary in Ireland, under the future Cardinal Archbishop of Melbourne, Daniel Mannix. When appointed as co-adjutor bishop of Melbourne, Mannix had requested that his gifted student William Devine should join him in Australia. Devine volunteered as a chaplain to the Australian Imperial Force (AIF) and, via the Middle East, arrived in France in 1917. He eventually returned to Ireland and his native Diocese of Derry where he was a curate in Sion Mills, County Tyrone, when war broke out in 1939.[13]

In 1940, Devine began a Catholic chaplaincy to the Royal Navy in Londonderry, soon to be the largest escort base in the UK for transatlantic convoys. His position was regularized in 1941 when he was appointed official RC Chaplain to the Londonderry, or Mid-Ocean, Escort Force. He gained the soubriquet 'the Major' due to his previous service and his soldierly appearance.[14] In 1943, he was transferred to the Mediterranean Fleet's base at Taranto, HMS *Fabius*, having been posted to Egypt (HMS *Stag*, at Port Said) and Malta (HMS *St Angelo*) before arriving in Taranto in January 1944.[15] Father Walter Meyjes, another Catholic Royal Navy chaplain, recalled how he met Father Devine, 'an elderly very charming Irishman who was based … at Taranto' (Devine was 56).[16]

Devine arranged to meet Meyjes to discuss how to divide their workload, deciding that Devine would take the east coast of Italy etc., with Meyjes staying on the west, but with responsibility also for North Africa. Gordon Taylor noted that 'some shore-based Roman Catholic chaplains in wartime had to do much of their work on their own initiative, and that, consequently, much personal responsibility devolved upon them'.[17]

An article on Devine in the *Australian Dictionary of Biography* includes a comment that 'In 1944 the Vatican sent him on a mission to Yugoslavia which he believed compromised his position as a chaplain'. Although no further details of the mission are included, it is likely that Devine felt the mission may have been like Father Bluett's sighting of the German tank in late 1943.[18]

While Willie Devine may not have had the excitement of a chaplain with an infantry or armoured unit, there was little doubt that he served his 'flock' with devotion and care, fulfilling the role of naval chaplain as he had done that of army chaplain a quarter-century earlier.

Chapter 12

Liberating Italy

While the Allies fought their way up Italy they were aided by Italian partisans who had begun resisting the Germans almost as soon as Hitler's forces deployed into Italy, and while both countries were still allies. The first clear example of the effectiveness of Italian resistance was the 'Four Days of Naples', during which Neapolitans rebelled against the German scorched-earth policy in the city – the destruction of major buildings, utilities and national treasures, including a major library with priceless books and documents.[1] So effective was the insurrection that Neapolitans liberated their own city, setting a pattern for other cities, notably Bologna, evicting the Germans before a single Allied soldier arrived.

Of course, there were problems for the Allies with partisans, many of whom had objectives very different from those of Allied commanders and politicians. Against that may be set the effect on the Germans of the partisan groups, requiring deployment of the equivalent of a field army under SS General Karl Wolff, Supreme SS and Police Leader in Italy. Allied support was given to partisans, principally by the UK but also by the Americans. German-occupied Italy fell within the remit of the Special Operations Executive (SOE), to which Churchill had given the instruction 'set Europe ablaze'.

Among SOE operatives in Italy were two Royal Irish Fusiliers, Captains Tony Morris MC and John Keany, the former from Galway, the latter from Cork. Morris had earned the MC during the pre-war Arab rebellion in Palestine. As a captain he was appointed OBE in October 1943[2] but no details of the citation have been found. Contemporaries believed that he had served with SOE in Yugoslavia

John Keany was born in County Cork where his father, District Inspector (Superintendent) Michael Keany of the Royal Irish Constabulary, was serving in Clonakilty. Michael Keany was murdered by the IRA in February 1921 and John's 19-year-old brother, Edward, wounded. DI Keany's widow subsequently moved to England where John was educated. Commissioned in the Royal Irish Fusiliers early in the war, he later volunteered for SOE. An Italian speaker, he was sent as a British Liaison Officer (BLO) to the Piedmont region, parachuting from a USAAF C-47 Skytrain on the night of 4 February 1945 to join the 'Green Flames' group. The SOE team was led by Major Max Salvadori MC with Major Adrian Hope, a South African with a refined English accent as second-in-command. Sergeant Bill Pickering, the group's radio operator, recalled Keany as being talkative and lively with 'a terrific sense of humour'.[3] Their operation was codenamed CHERITON.[4]

With Germans nearby when they landed, Salvadori's team was whisked away by partisans who, even with the threat, gathered the equipment dropped by the C-47. Their Italian guides revealed that the Germans did not like operating at night and did so only under orders. The first destination was a church at Mombarcaro where guns, ammunition and other supplies were concealed in the cellar before the group split up, Salvadori making for Milan by a direct route while guides took Keany and Pickering on a more roundabout one. Pickering recalled that Keany shouted 'See you in Milan' as they turned to depart: 'It was a typically cheerful and positive remark from my Irish pal. Unhappily it was a promise that was not fulfilled.'[5]

Their first stop, having trekked through snow in the dark, was a farmhouse near the village of Monesiglio, home of 'Tal' and Luisa Biestri, a strongly anti-Fascist couple and partisan supporters. Pickering was shocked to learn that they were less than a quarter mile from a base for German and Fascist Italian troops operating sweeps for partisans and SOE personnel. However, their hosts assured them that Monesiglio and the farmhouse were the last places that would be searched, an assurance Pickering found of little comfort. Commenting that he had volunteered for dangerous duties three years before, he was certain that he had not signed up for 'suicide missions with crackpot Italians and a mad Irishman'.[6] In contrast, Keany considered their situation 'a great lark'.[7] Following a meal of stewed steak, bread and wine, they were shown to a hut that would be their home for the next three weeks. Awakening in the afternoon, they observed Monesiglio through binoculars, watching German soldiers in the streets. Keany observed that he and Pickering were 'going to like it here'. To Pickering it appeared that Keany had no fear.[8]

They made their first broadcast that night and received messages for the CHERITON team. Although the Germans could pick up their transmissions, it took at least an hour to 'fix' a location with two radio-direction-finding vehicles. Transmissions were always under sixty minutes and, although made at 2300, no location was used twice. While Pickering operated the radio, Keany maintained watch, armed with a sub-machine gun.[9]

Partisans visited the farmhouse to deliver and receive messages, one even bringing the parachutes Keany and Pickering had left at the church. At night, that partisan took them to a seamstress in Monesiglio who agreed to make them each a dressing gown and two pairs of pyjamas, using any remaining fabric to make underwear for the village women. Monesiglio was also visited to recharge the radio batteries, their hand generator not being strong enough. Keany, a risk-taker, chose to spend an evening drinking in the village. Pickering remained sober enough to stop Keany singing 'Danny Boy' and himself belting out 'Rule Britannia'. There were other narrow escapes as, when moving to a broadcast spot one night, they stepped off the path to answer the call of nature and a German patrol passed by without spotting them. A few nights later, they heard a German patrol searching for the Allied spies they knew were in the area, but it changed direction away from them.[10]

Although the enemy made systematic sweeps, their approach to clandestine warfare was unsophisticated, tending to flood an area but without using dogs, or even deploying covert patrols to trap partisans.[11]

While the Allies supported and armed the partisans, even issuing dyed British battle-dress, they remained wary of pro-Tito groups in north-eastern Italy, especially Venezia Giulia where partisans operated under command of the Slovene Corps of the Yugoslav Army of Nation Liberation, believing that they could try to establish a communist state in that region after the war.[12]

When another agent, Luigi Cavalieri, who used the *nome di battaglia* Roccia, arrived to support Hope, Keany and Pickering had to meet him. Supplies were also dropped with 'Roccia', a Roman lawyer. Shortly afterwards, Keany and Pickering witnessed the ambush by Garibaldini partisans of a German force on a sweep. Some seventy Germans and several Garibaldini were killed. Keany chose not to make his presence known to the Garibaldini whom he did not trust; he was concerned that they might seize power in post-war Italy. German and Fascist Italian activity was increasing, making it more difficult to find transmission spots. Keany decided to make a transmission to Bari to that effect. En route to do so, they exercised 'more caution than usual' which proved wise when their two partisan scouts signalled them to take cover. By doing so, they eluded capture by a Brigata Nera patrol, Pickering recalling his face being inches from Fascist boots. Their final transmission was interrupted by news that a detection vehicle was closing in. Making their escape, Keany deciphered the messages they had received, including one telling them to leave for Milan next day; their mission was complete.[13]

The journey to Milan was made with a partisan escort and a guide, Settino Maggiorino, an Alpini veteran, who knew the region intimately. After a rest at Cisterna, Keany and Pickering set off in peasant guise with a donkey and cart, escorted by partisans. Although intercepted by Garibaldini, Keany bluffed his way through by promising to arrange a weapons and supply drop for them. By 8 March they were some fifteen miles from Brusasco and planning their route there when Pickering spotted Germans below them. As Keany continued planning with the partisan leader, Pickering saw more Germans appear. In two hours over sixty entered a building, but none left. Expressing concern that the Germans knew of their presence, Keany dismissed his fears, arguing that the Germans had a steep incline to climb and were certain to be spotted. He was badly mistaken. Pickering noted that 'those were Keany's last words'.

> I had been standing by his side as we spoke … . For no reason I could ever explain I suddenly felt frightened, vulnerable and exposed. I moved two or three paces away from Keany's left side … . As I did so the German sub-machine guns opened up. I flung myself to the ground and saw Keany's chest neatly stitched with a row of bullets. He was flung backwards without a sound, at least no sound that could be heard above the noise of gunfire.[14]

Four partisans died with John Keany. The others managed to escape, as did Bill Pickering. The partisans later returned to remove the bodies which were buried in unmarked graves at Cinaglio, a local priest conducting the funeral. Today Captain John Keany rests in Milan war cemetery.

* * *

SOE established offices in neutral countries, one of which was Switzerland. In charge of the Swiss office, in Berne, was John McCaffery, an Irishman born in Scotland (his father was a Glasgow policeman) who had been teaching in an Italian university after leaving the seminary where he had been studying for the priesthood.[15] He and his American counterpart Allen Dulles, whom he considered naïve and who later headed the Central Intelligence Agency, were drawn into the frictions within Italian partisan groups and political parties. Although Mussolini had been deposed in July 1943, his proscription of all political parties other than his own Fascists was maintained by the Badoglio government. As a result, the proscribed parties shared a distrust of the government and created a common front, the Committee of National Liberation of Northern Italy (CLN).[16]

However, friction between partisans remained and the Garibaldini partisans established a headquarters in Milan in November 1943 under Luigi Longo and Pietro Secchia. That coincided with the arrival in Switzerland of two non-communist partisan leaders, Alfredo Pizzoni, a Milanese banker, and Ferrucio Parri, later prime minister of Italy, the former a right-winger and the latter a socialist. They met McCaffery in Lugano on 3 November and were assured of supplies of money and arms while McCaffrey learned of the depth of anti-Badoglio feeling permeating the partisan movement.[17]

McCaffery's role as the British government's intermediary with the partisans gave him a central part in a remarkable episode. As Allied armies advanced from Rome in summer 1944, the CLN decided to liberate an area around Domodossola and declare it a Free Republic with no connection to Badoglio's government. Bounded by Lake Maggiore and the Swiss border, the proposed Domodossola Republic had a population of about 82,000 and an area of some 1,600 square kilometres. Its founders planned to extend the area by seizing Valle d'Aosta and Val Comonica.[18]

Partisans had earlier taken control of part of the area between Ascona and Domodossola, but the Germans had mounted a *rastrellamento*, a large offensive, to regain it in May 1944. That had been followed by reprisals against civilians with some 200 partisans killed, including forty-three after being captured. By August, several partisan groups, non-communist and communist, were making plans to seize the Domodossola area and establish the republic. They held large stocks of modern weapons from Allied air drops and believed that they would succeed.[19]

While partisan leaders were confident and keen to proceed, the Allies did not share their enthusiasm: the action was political and outside the guidelines for partisans. Moreover, a violent and bloody response was certain, a *rastrellamento* worse than previous *rastrellamenti*. McCaffery was told to do his utmost to prevent the partisans taking such action. He and Dulles told their governments that the plan could lead to an adverse reaction from the resistance movement generally, but, although unenthusiastic themselves, accepted that the plan was going ahead and agreed to provide money and supplies. They also sent a Canadian liaison officer, Lieutenant George Patterson, who had considerable experience with the Italian resistance, to work with the partisans. The Foreign Office let McCaffrey know of its disapproval.[20]

On 23 August the partisan army struck in Valle Antigore which fell by the 26th. All territory north of Domodossola was in partisan hands in early September with Val d'Ossola and Valtoce following soon after. The German garrison in Domodossola was surrounded and outnumbered by a partisan force. After negotiations with local priest Dom Luigi Pellanda as intermediary, an armistice was signed on 9 September and the garrison began withdrawing. Next day the Free Republic of Domodossola was proclaimed in the town centre, a provisional government appointed and fascist officials removed from office. Neither Badoglio's government in Rome nor Mussolini's Fascist rump government in Salo on Lake Garda was pleased by what had happened.[21]

Professor Tibaldi, a friend of John McCaffery, was appointed president and arrived by train from Rome to take up his post. While arrangements were made for the provision of food and other necessities, the Garibaldini proved an insurmountable obstacle to establishing a sound military structure. When stocks of food ran low, McCaffery and Dulles provided money for supplies from Switzerland, although rationing proved necessary and coupons were introduced. The political parties produced newspapers, and a radio station to counter Mussolini's propaganda station was planned. Schools re-opened with a new, non-Fascist curriculum.[22]

The Swiss government recognized Domodossola's independence. Switzerland and Domodossola shared a land frontier with two railway lines crossing the border, Domodossola town sitting on the Geneva-Milan line. A line to Locarno crossed the border at Ascona, through which SOE and the American Office of Strategic Services (OSS) maintained direct contact with the Domodossola government. Some Allied officers crossed the border to advise and assist the partisans, to whom supplies were air-dropped. The UK government continued to let McCaffery know that it disapproved of the new state's existence and instructed him to let Ferrucio Parri know that the Allies were not pleased about the republic's independence from Rome.[23]

The Germans and their Fascist allies were not going to let the new republic prosper. On 13 October, a 3,000-strong force under SS General Tensfeld attacked. The failure to create a firm military command structure was soon felt. Although outnumbering their assailants, the partisans suffered heavy losses and broke off the battle after two days. While some re-grouped near Lake Orta, which remained under their control, most escaped into Switzerland. By 26 October all Italian frontier posts were in Fascist hands.[24]

Although it survived only thirty-four days, the Republic of Domodossola was a 'spectacular and courageous' achievement for the CLN and is unique as the only sizeable area of occupied Europe to seize its independence from Nazi domination, something that official Swiss recognition proved.[25] McCaffery understood concerns in the Allied command about what might happen in post-war Italy when the Germans had been defeated since he was

> a shrewd observer who understood everything about the Italian political divides, and his reports to the Foreign Office about Domodossola increased the British Government's fear that all-out aid to the partisans might lead to chaos and civil war when the Germans abandoned Italy.[26]

John McCaffery played an important, if unsung, role in the war in Italy. He was rewarded by being appointed OBE after the war.

* * *

Perhaps the best-known non-combatant Irishman in Italy was Monsignor Hugh O'Flaherty, the 'Scarlet Pimpernel of the Vatican'. An adopted Kerryman, although born in County Cork, and an avid supporter of Kerry's Gaelic football team, he played golf, handball and hurling, as well as being a boxer. The subject of several books, a novel, two plays, a TV documentary and a feature film, *The Scarlet and The Black*, in which he was played by Gregory Peck, O'Flaherty, in common with John Keany and John McCaffery, was a policeman's son.

Monsignor O'Flaherty became the central figure in an organization helping Jews escape the Germans and assisting escaped Allied prisoners to freedom.[27] He had a strong network of supporters, including several Irish people, notably singer Delia Murphy, wife of Ireland's envoy to the Holy See, Dr Thomas Kiernan, and their teenaged daughter, as well as priests and nuns. However, O'Flaherty's importance was emphasized in Sam Derry's book *Rome Escape Line*, published in 1960 when the prelate was still alive. In his foreword, Derry commented that he had written the book unknown to Monsignor O'Flaherty, 'one of the finest men it has been my privilege ever to meet. Had it not been for this gallant gentleman, there would have been no Rome Escape Organisation'.[28]

Major Sam Derry, a Royal Artillery officer, was captured in North Africa in early 1942 and incarcerated in a prison camp in Chieti in Italy. Facing transfer to a camp in Germany, he escaped from a train taking him to Rome and went into hiding with the aid of Italian civilians, eventually being put in contact with Monsignor O'Flaherty in the German College in Rome. In turn, O'Flaherty introduced Derry to a young woman, Blánaid Kiernan, known as Blon, daughter of the Irish minister to the Vatican. So began the co-operation between Derry and O'Flaherty that was to result in helping not only prisoners of war, but as many as 5,000 members of the Jewish community in Italy. One of O'Flaherty's biographers notes that, when Rome was liberated in June 1944, almost 4,000 Allied escapees were being sheltered by the organization.[29]

Everyone involved in the organization took enormous risks and the Gestapo chief in Rome, Herbert Kappler, was determined to capture O'Flaherty. It was Kappler who described him as the 'Scarlet Pimpernel of the Vatican' and Kappler who had a white line painted on the border between the mini-state and Rome. Should O'Flaherty step over that line, German personnel were authorized to shoot him. To hide his 'guests', O'Flaherty used various Vatican properties throughout Rome, all officially part of Vatican City, while churches also housed them; Jewish Sabbath services were conducted in Catholic churches. Derry 'lodged' with O'Flaherty and was impressed not only by his courage, energy and ingenuity, but also

> his ability to see the best in people, even the vilest creatures who were capable of terrible deeds, he would feel there must be some good in them somewhere. He was quite incapable of feeling spite or a wish for revenge.[30]

Father Michael Keaveny, from Moville in Donegal and a priest of the diocese of Derry, was a student in the Irish College shortly after the war and has positive memories of Monsignor O'Flaherty. One, in particular, stood out. The Monsignor took no nonsense from anyone and seminarian Michael Keaveny was eyewitness to a prime proof of that. In post-war Italy there was considerable pro-communist and anti-clerical feeling with priests on the streets often being verbally abused. One day, Michael Keaveny saw Monsignor O'Flaherty on the other side of the street and noticed an Italian man approach the Kerryman. As the two closed, the Italian spat at O'Flaherty and shouted 'Scarabeo nero' (black beetle), a typical insult. Suddenly the Italian was lying flat on the ground: O'Flaherty, the boxer, had punched him.[31]

A very modest man, Hugh O'Flaherty was appointed CBE by the UK government in 1945. He was also appointed a papal domestic prelate by Pope Pius XII.

Among the Irish involved in the escape organization were priests, brothers and nuns of various orders. Brother Humilis, a Franciscan (but not a 'monk' as noted in some accounts; ordained Franciscans are *friars*), was one and there were nuns of the Missionary Franciscan Sisters (one of the author's maternal aunts had been professed in that Order in Rome in April 1939 but had been sent to Alexandria in Egypt), and diocesan priests 'trapped' in Rome, some of whom were enlisted into the Royal Army Chaplains' Department by Father Dan Kelleher MC – Fathers Louis Madden, Achonry and Kevin McCabe, Kilmore; Fathers Sean Quinlan and John Shortall followed later. Other priests included Fathers Tom Tuomey from Tralee, Ben Forsythe from Fermoy, John Buckley, known as 'Spike', from Mayo, John Claffey from Westmeath and Vincent Treacy from County Galway, the last a member of the Congregation of the Priests of Saint Mary.[32] The Church Militant was very much in evidence.

* * *

Delia Murphy has been referred to already, as has her daughter Blon. Both were important members of O'Flaherty's organization and displayed considerable courage in their work. Indeed, Delia had demonstrated that courage in Belfast's Ulster Hall in April 1941. As she was singing, German bombers were attacking the city and many in the audience were terrified. 'Miss Murphy, however, remained perfectly cool, and kept singing continuously, asking those present to join her.'[33]

Not long after arriving in Rome, Delia Murphy met O'Flaherty and thus began her support for his efforts, although at first she had pondered her course of action.

> A voice inside me said charity was something God intended for all humanity, in war and peace. I remembered the words of St Paul: Now abideth faith, hope and charity, these three; the greatest of these is charity. What else could it be but charity to help those in trouble with the Nazis.[34]

That she truly believed in charity was shown by her helping a German soldier who had been found close to one of the city bridges. Exhausted, the man claimed to be a priest fasting in the hope that he would be able to celebrate Mass. Introducing the German to Monsignor O'Flaherty, his claim was verified and arrangements made for him to celebrate Mass.[35]

Among risks she took was using her husband's official car to transport a British soldier suffering from appendicitis to hospital, later repeating the journey to return him to his hiding place.

Pius XII appointed her to a papal damehood in the Order of the Holy Sepulchre while the UK ambassador to the Holy See, Sir D'Arcy Osborne, wanted the UK government to recognize her efforts but was thwarted by protocol although he presented her with a Ming vase.

* * *

Dubliner Denis Johnston was a war correspondent who had been a protégé of Yeats and Shaw and a friend of O'Casey. Since becoming a war correspondent for the BBC, he had been at El Alamein and through much of the Italian campaign with Eighth Army, under both Montgomery and Leese. There was also a trip to Yugoslavia that did not have formal approval but which earned him the Yugoslav Partisans' Medal while he was appointed OBE and Mentioned in Despatches.[36]

In North Africa and Italy, Johnston was among the first BBC correspondents to use what were called 'midget recorders', allowing them to record on discs that were flown back to the UK for use in BBC programmes.[37] Revolutionary at the time, the term 'midget' would be considered a misnomer today.

Johnston arrived at the Irish legation in Rome on 5 June 1944, the day after the liberation and met Delia Murphy Kiernan, of whom he enquired how she first became aware that the city had been liberated.

> She tossed her head of black curls, and smiled the smile that must have baffled many an Axis official. 'They call me your Excellency here. It is the way they have in the Diplomatic, d'ye know. Well, I was out taking a walk in the morning to see what was going on. And there was … lads in uniform lying on the pavement in front of the railway station, taking a rest … . And I thought they were Germans, until suddenly one of them sat up and said: 'Say sister. Come and park your arse beside me.' So then I knew I was liberated.[38]

Johnston later moved to north-west Europe, reporting on the war there. His reportage later formed the basis for his book *Nine Rivers from Jordan*, published in 1953.

In James Holland's *Italy's Sorrow*, the reader encounters Iris, wife of the Marchese Antonio Origo, who lived in a palazzo in Val d'Orcio in Tuscany. Iris, although born in England to an English mother and an American father, had Irish grandparents and holidayed in Ireland. Early in the war she had joined the Italian Red Cross. Her experiences during the fighting in that region and its effects on the population are recounted by Holland; after the war Iris became a historian and a writer.[39]

There might never have been an Italian campaign, nor a North African campaign, had it not been for the Italian dictator, Benito Mussolini. He it was who thrust his country into an alliance with Hitler's Germany and conflict with the UK and France, declaring war on both when he thought they were beaten. France had been, the UK remained defiant and continued to fight Germany and Italy.

In 1953, Luigi Barzini published his book *The Italians* in which he explained his fellow countrymen and women to a wider audience. His comments on Mussolini emphasize the man's ego: his indolence (he would look out his office window, see his driver standing smoking by his limousine and stroll down for a casual conversation); his failure to properly equip the armed forces (a regiment of light tanks looked much more impressive than a squadron of mediums, and the navy was denied aircraft carriers); and his cruelty (many who opposed fascism were murdered).[40] And yet there was another side to Il Duce. Lucia Bedeschi, in the same class as Mussolini's daughter, recalled occasions when a knock at the classroom door heralded the arrival of *Il Duce* to collect his daughter.[41] There can have been few world leaders who have made the school run. This was the man whose vanity plunged his country into war and suffering.

However, had an Irish woman been a better shot on Wednesday 7 April 1926, Mussolini would have died that day. Violet Gibson, a daughter of the nobility, shot him outside the Palazzo dei Conservatori, her first round grazing the bridge of the dictator's nose. Violet's second attempt failed when her Lebel revolver jammed. Mussolini, realizing that he was still alive, dismissed the wound as 'a mere trifle'. Embarrassment led to Violet being deported to the UK, since she was a British citizen, Ireland then being a Dominion, where she was committed to an asylum for the rest of her days.[42]

Epilogue

Eight decades after victory in Italy, there are few surviving veterans of the campaign. Some left memoirs, collections of memories or brief accounts of an incident or short period of action. Many left photographs, generally of groups of friends. Few spoke to family or friends of their experiences, although many could recall pleasant experiences amidst the horror of war.

Now and again, a hint of the horror broke through. Joe Robinson of 2nd Irish Rifles once told me of a fellow rifleman who found a flushing toilet in an abandoned house. Determined to use it, against advice, there was an explosion when he did so. He died instantly. The cistern had been booby-trapped.

In contrast, Joe told me of being discharged from hospital to spend some time in a convalescent centre, a former Italian army barracks. Most men there awaited return to their units, or a posting, but were exasperated by the routine which involved an early morning parade and inspection by the commandant. One morning, the men assembled, right markers took their places and the soldiers in transit fell in, all with a sense of anticipation. The RSM marched on to the square, turned smartly and loudly to face the ranks. He then swore even more loudly, face red with anger, demanding to know which 'blanking blank did that on my blanking wall??' 'That' was a perfectly-formed set of white footsteps ascending the wall. Many knew the answer but nobody could tell the RSM or the commandant who had climbed a ladder during the night with a bucket of whitewash and a pair of army boots to leave the imprints as a work of art to be admired by anyone other than the RSM and commandant. The culprit? It was Sligo's finest, Lance Bombardier Terence Milligan MiD, later known to the world as Spike Milligan. Born in India, the son of a gunner from Sligo and grandson of a gunner in the Sligo Militia Artillery, Milligan was serving in 56th Heavy Regiment, Royal Artillery.

Many who served in Italy had fond memories of the country and its people. Robert Hamilton, 24 HAA Battery, recalled the friendliness of local people, especially when they realized that Robert's regiment was Irish. However, they were puzzled by the fact that Robert was not a Catholic, but a Protestant: they had believed there were no Protestants in Ireland. Decades later, Robert could still wonder at the friendship shown by Italian civilians, 'even when we destroyed their crops to build gun emplacements'. Early in the campaign, while stationed in Naples, the Derry Boys provided local people with salt which was in short supply. My father had souvenirs of Italy, including prayer cards commemorating the First Communion and Confirmation service for a child with whose family he had become friendly. I am also the possessor of guidebooks (in English) to Naples and Rome collected by Gunner J.J. Doherty.

There were other legacies of the campaign in the form of marriages. Brenda Graham, whom we met in Chapter 11, had gone to England with Elizabeth Chamberlain to become a VAD. Later, she was posted to Italy to serve in military hospitals and met Brian Clark, adjutant of 1st Royal Irish Fusiliers. The pair married in Austria and, when Brian retired from the Army in 1967, they settled in County Wicklow in the shadow of the Sugarloaf. There were many other marriages. Lucia Bedeschi, who had been a classmate of Mussolini's daughter, met Signalman Joe Radcliffe of the Royal Corps of Signals and married him in St Patrick's Church on the Via Boncompagni in Rome on 6 October 1946. Their first child, Marina, was born in August 1947 and the Radcliffes were my next-door neighbours from October 1949 until September 1958. John Logue, who drove his DUKW ashore in Sicily and Anzio, continued driving it until the end of the campaign when he was posted to Venice to transport civilians working in prisoner-of-war camps. One of his passengers was a young woman called Edera Santin who later became his wife, in spite of initial misunderstandings caused by the language barrier.

The Italian campaign became overshadowed by the campaign in North-West Europe after June 1944 and has never attracted the same attention of popular writers, or Hollywood, as the fighting in France, the Low Countries and Germany. But it included some of the war's most brutal fighting in Europe and the finest example of manoeuvre warfare by the western Allies in Operation GRAPESHOT in April 1945. It deserves to be remembered, as do those who served there and, especially, those who died liberating Italy.

British Army deaths in North-West Europe from 6 June 1944 to the end of the war totalled 34,226, of whom 798 were Irish, 2.3 per cent of the total. In the Italian campaign 24,080 British Army personnel died, of whom 764 were Irish, almost 3.2 per cent of the total. Those figures emphasize the scale of Irish involvement in the campaign. Even in April 1945, the last month of fighting in Italy, over 900 British soldiers died (almost half of 1,882 deaths in 1945). Twenty-six were Irish, a seemingly insignificant figure but 2.7 per cent of the total, in spite of the fact that the number of Irish units had reduced with the departures of 9th (Londonderry) HAA Regiment, 1st Irish Guards and the disbandment, re-roling or transfers of 66th and 117th LAA Regiments and 6th Royal Inniskilling Fusiliers.

It is important to remember. Those who perished gave all for freedom while those who survived gave the best years of their lives. They deserve to be remembered across Ireland as they *are* in Italy. Remembering should be simple, but perhaps Clausewitz had it right when he suggested that 'Everything is very simple in war, but the simplest thing is difficult'. Is remembering the simplest thing?

Notes

Chapter 1: Sicily

1. Hogg & Weeks, *The Illustrated Encyclopedia of Military Vehicles* p.310
2. Alexander, *Despatches: The Conquest of Sicily,* p.1013
3. NA Kew, ADM196/93/115; The baronetcy in the County of Meath was created in 1886 in the UK peerage for Edward Gibson, Lord Chancellor of Ireland
4. Roskill, *The War at Sea, Vol.III,* p.131
5. NA Kew, WO169/10178, war diary 1st Black Watch
6. Abbatiello, in Jennings & Steele, *The Worst Military Leaders in History,* p.165
7. Molony, *The Mediterranean and Middle East, Vol.V,* p.51
8. Booth & Spencer, *Paratrooper, The Life of General James Gavin,* p.22
9. Molony, op. cit., pp.79–81 & 95–6
10. Ibid., p.54., p.54
11. Horsfall, *Say Not The Struggle,* p.20
12. Connell is commemorated on the Cassino Memorial; Hill is buried in Syracuse
13. Truesdale, *Brotherhood of the Cauldron,* pp.47–8
14. Army Roll of Honour (hereinafter RoH)
15. Truesdale, p.72
16. NA Kew, WO169/8837, war diary 1 Para Bde, 1943
17. Truesdale, p.72
18. Ibid., pp.72–3
19. Richardson, *Dark Times, Decent Men,* pp.120–2
20. Molony, op. cit., p.81; McClean, *SAS: Special Raiding Squadron,* p.33
21. Rostron, *Dempsey,* p.1
22. Aris, *The British Fifth Division,* pp.111–12
23. Ibid., p.112
24. Molony, op, cit., p.54
25. Ibid., p.55
26. Hogg & Weeks, op. cit., p.310
27. Logue, interview Nov. 1988
28. Molony, op. cit., p.61
29. Roskill, op. cit., p.131
30. Clay, *The Path of the 50th,* p.158
31. Fox, Sir Frank, *The Royal Inniskilling Fusiliers in the Second World War,* pp.71–2
32. Molony, p.82; Bolton, *With 11th (HAC) Regiment, RHA,* pp.61–2; NA Kew, WO373/3, Goodbody
33. WO373/3/398, Fraser
34. Ibid., WO373/3/505, Lidwill
35. Messenger, *The Commandos,* pp.198–9; RoH
36. *London Irish at War* (hereinafter *LIR History*), pp.73–4

37. Ibid., p.74; WO373/3/384, Good
38. *LIR History*; CWGC Register
39. *LIR History*
40. Fox, op. cit., p.74
41. Ibid.
42. Ibid.
43. Cole, *Rough Road to Rome*, p.34
44. Fox, op. cit., pp.74–5; Cole, pp.48–9
45. WO373/3/509, O'Brien-Twohig
46. Ibid.; WO373/3/511, Christie
47. Cole, p.97
48. Ibid.
49. WO373/3/542, Bradley
50. WO373/3/ 624, Moore, T.J.
51. Fox, p.75
52. Ibid., p.76; WO373/3/222, Moore, W.
53. Fox, p.76
54. Simms, interview with author
55. WO373/3/497, Sheil
56. NA, WO169/10002, war diary 66 LAA Regt
57. Ibid.
58. Ibid.
59. Frederick, *Lineage Book of British Land Forces*, p.838
60. WO169/10019, war diary 117 LAA Regt
61. Doherty, *Clear The Way!* (hereinafter *CTW*), pp.10–11
62. Ibid., p.65
63. Ibid.; WO169/10234, war diary 6 INNISKS
64. *CTW*, op. cit., pp.68–71
65. WO373/3/122, Crocker
66. WO373/3/76, McClinton
67. WO373/3/218, Phillips
68. WO373/3/220, Apling
69. *CTW*, p.72
70. Baxter to author
71. *CTW*, p.72
72. Ibid.
73. Ibid.
74. Russell
75. Ibid.
76. WO373/3/200, Donaghy
77. WO373/3/221, Shaw
78. WO373/3/67, Butler
79. CWGC Register; David Marshall
80. CWGC Register; Russell
81. Russell
82. WO373/3, Goodbody
83. *CTW*, pp.77–8
84. CWGC Register

85. *LIR History*, p.88; WO373/3, Seymour; WO373/3, White
86. Fox, p.77
87. *LIR History*, p.91; WO373/3/347, Byrne
88. *LIR History*, p.93

Chapter 2 Italy: Tough Old Gut

1. Graham & Bidwell, *Tug of War*, pp.47–52
2. NA, WO169/8520, HQ Eighth Army GS1, IntSum 544
3. WO373/4/310, McCormack
4. WO373/6/534, McCormack
5. WO373/7342, Joyce
6. WO373/4/910, O'Brien
7. Hamilton, interview with author
8. Doherty, *Wall of Steel* (hereinafter *WoS*), p.131
9. Hamilton, interview with author, Jan. 1989
10. Taylor, interview with author, Jan. 1989
11. Canning, interview with author, Jan. 1989
12. *WoS*, pp.131–2
13. Ibid., p.132
14. Ibid., p.133
15. McCready, interview with author, Jan. 1989
16. *WoS*, p.131
17. WO170/1128, war diary RHQ 9 HAA Regt; WO170/1161, war diary 25 HAA Battery
18. *WoS*, p.134
19. CWGC Register
20. WO169/10002, war diary, 66 LAA Regt
21. Ibid.
22. *CTW*, p,85; Ray, *Algiers to Austria*, pp.85–7
23. Ibid.
24. NA, WO169/8836, war diary 56 Recce; Chavasse, *Some Memories*, p.74
25. Kesselring, *Memoirs*, p.188
26. McKenzie, quoted in Ford, *Battleaxe Division*, p.90
27. Russell
28. Ray, op. cit., p.89
29. Ibid., pp.90–1
30. Chavasse, pp.74–5
31. Ray, p.90; Russell
32. Russell
33. Linklater, *The Campaign in Italy*, p.99
34. *CTW*, p.86
35. Russell
36. *CTW*, p.86; WO373/4/354, Proctor
37. Perhaps the worst example appears in a gazetteer of the SAS which claims that a 'detachment of Royal Irish Rangers' with some Canadian tanks saved the day. The Royal Irish Rangers were formed on 1 July 1968.
38. Doherty, *Only the Enemy in Front*, pp.32–69
39. REMNI, 5 Oct. 2024; CWGC Register

40. Fox, op. cit., pp.85–6; WO373/68/224, Crawford
41. Fox, pp.86–7
42. Ibid., p.87; WO373/4/495, Crawford
43. Fox, p.87
44. *LIR History*, pp.98–101
45. The comment became common amongst Allied soldiers
46. *LIR History*, p.102; WO373/5/23, Crocker
47. *LIR History*, p.102
48. Ibid., pp.102–3
49. Ibid., pp.103–4
50. Fox, p.102; WO373/4/494, Christie
51. *WoS*, op. cit., pp.139–40
52. Ibid., pp.140–1
53. Ibid., p.141
54. Ibid., p.143
55. Hamilton & Ormsby, interviews with author, April 1987
56. *WoS*, pp.143–5
57. Ibid., p.143
58. Ibid., pp.145–6
59. Ibid., pp.146–7
60. Ibid., pp.147–9
61. Clarke, interview with author
62. Routledge, *Anti-Aircraft Artillery, 1914–1955*, pp.274–5
63. Clarke, interview with author
64. Dungan, *Distant Drums*, p.116
65. Doherty, *Irish Volunteers in the Second World War*, p.38
66. Stewart, Paul, 'Little Pearl Harbour', *Scope*, Vol.3, No.5, Nov/Dec 2010, pp.32–6

Chapter 3: The Slog Continues

1. Aris, op. cit., pp,159–60
2. Ibid., p.159
3. Fox, p.102
4. WO373/5/39, Duane
5. Aris, pp.172–3; Fox, p.103
6. Brookes, *Montgomery and the Eighth Army*, p.328. The book was written but as *Alamein to the River Sangro*
7. *Cross on the Sword*, p.215; WO373/5/49, Bluett
8. *LIR History*, p.113
9. Williams, *The Black Cats at War*, p.68
10. *LIR History*, p.114
11. Ibid., p.115
12. Ibid., p.116
13. Williams, p.69; RoH; CWGC Register
14. Walmsley, *Londonderry's City Cemetery*, p.242
15. WO373/4/431, Mordaunt
16. *CTW*, pp.114–15; Martin Cassidy and George Mills for information on Kendrew
17. Russell; *CTW*, p.91
18. Ibid., pp.91–2

19. Woods, Account of Service with H Company 2 LIR
20. Ibid.
21. Russell
22. *CTW*, p.93
23. Ibid., p.94; *LIR History*, pp.107–8; Woods, op. cit.
24. Russell
25. *CTW*, p.96; war diary 1 RIrF
26. *CTW*, p.96
27. WO373/4/369
28. *CTW*, p.97
29. Ibid. pp.97–8
30. Russell
31. Fox, p.97; WO373/5/297, Chatburn;/5/299, Madden;/5/301, Powell
32. Moloney, op. cit., p.488
33. Woods, op. cit.
34. *LIR History*, p.110
35. Ibid., *CTW*, pp. 98–9; RoH; CWGC Register
36. *CTW*, pp.100–3
37. Russell
38. WO373/5/300, Milligan; *CTW*, pp.103–4
39. *CTW*, pp.104–5; Russell
40. Mowat, *And No Birds Sang*, p.167

Chapter 4: More Mountains, More Rivers – and Anzio

1. Moloney, pp.596–7
2. Ibid., p.589
3. Ibid., p.590
4. Fitzgerald, *History of the Irish Guards in the Second World War*, pp.197–8
5. Williams, op. cit., p.78
6. Moloney, pp.612–13
7. Williams, p.80; *LIR History*, pp.126–7; RoH; CWGC Register
8. *LIR History*, p.127
9. Fox, p.105
10. Ibid., pp.106–8; WO373/6/423, Banton
11. Fox, pp.108–9
12. Cole, *Rough Road to Rome*, pp.19–20
13. Fox, p.109; WO373/6/422, Boak
14. Fox, p.109
15. WO373/6/421, Anderson; /6/427, Stranex
16. Fox, pp.111–12; WO373/6/278. O'Brien-Twohig
17. Fox, pp.112–13; CWGC Register
18. Fox, p.113
19. Ibid., p.115
20. Moloney, p.788; RoH; CWGC Register
21. *LIR History*, pp.127–8
22. Ibid., pp.128–9
23. Fox, pp.116–17
24. Ibid.; war diary 2 INNISKS

25. Fox, p.117; Cole, p.213
26. WO373/2/46, Moore
27. Logue, interview with author
28. Ibid.
29. Moloney, pp.650–2; Clarke, *Anzio*, pp.46–8
30. Fitzgerald, op. cit., p.215
31. Ibid., p.221
32. Clark, p.114
33. Moloney, pp.668–9
34. Clarke, cit., p.130
35. Ibid., pp.130–3
36. Aris, p.207
37. Mahon et al, *Irish Guards, The First Hundred Years*, p.104
38. Brookes, *Father Dolly*, p.152
39. Verney, *The Micks*, pp.145–6; Fitzgerald, pp.234–5
40. Fitzgerald., p.235
41. RoH
42. Ibid.
43. Moloney, p.670
44. Ibid., p.671
45. WO373/6/72, Young
46. Ibid.
47. Mills, account from Fitzgerald
48. Ibid.
49. Ibid.
50. WO373/3/163, Montgomery
51. Ibid.
52. WO373/6/222, Taylor
53. WO373/6/159, Dunne
54. WO373/6/119, Kennedy; Fitzgerald, pp.236–49
55. WO373/9/159, Banks
56. WO373/6/156, Moriarty
57. WO373/7/224, Dodds
58. WO373/6/218, Cross
59. Ibid.
60. WO373/6/88, Gordon-Watson
61. WO373/14/485, Fitzgerald, G.
62. WO/373/7/176, Combe; /6/120, Keigwin
63. Jocelyn, *Major D.M. (John) Kennedy*, pp.132–3; WO373/7/225, Fahy
64. Fitzgerald, p.354
65. WO373/7/225,. Fahy
66. Quoted in Fitzgerald, p.356
67. Verney, p.160
68. Ibid., p.146
69. Brookes, op. cit., p.150
70. Ibid.
71. WO373/9/57, Brookes
72. Quoted in Doherty, *The British Reconnaissance Corps*, p.19

73. *LIR History*, pp.134–5
74. Ibid., p.136
75. Ibid., p.137
76. Ibid., p.138
77. Ibid., p.139
78. Ibid.
79. Ibid., p.140; WO373/6/323, Haigh
80. *LIR History*, p.140
81. Ibid., pp.140–1
82. Ibid., p.142
83. Ibid.
84. Ibid.
85. Quoted in Moloney, p.739
86. Moloney, pp.744–5
87. *LIR History*, p.146
88. Ibid., p.148
89. Cassidy, interview with author, Feb. 2008
90. *LIR History*, p.151
91. Ibid., pp.151–2
92. Logue interview, op. cit.
93. WO373/6/643, Donaghy
94. Fox, p.119
95. 2 INNISKS, war diary
96. Aris, op. cit., p.209
97. Scott, Col Bobby, 'Anzio to Rome 23rd May-4th June 1944' (hereinafter Scott)
98. Aris, p.209
99. 2 INNISKS, war diary
100. Aris, p.208
101. Fox, p.119
102. Ibid.
103. Ibid.
104. Aris, p.210
105. Fox, p.119
106. Ibid.
107. 2 INNISKS war diary
108. Fox, p.119
109. Ibid.
110. Scott
111. Ibid.
112. Ibid.
113. 2 INNISKS war diary

Chapter 5: The Road to Cassino

1. Ray, *Algiers to Austria*, p.107
2. Ibid., p.106
3. Russell
4. Ibid.
5. *CTW*, p.109–10

6. Woods, op. cit.
7. Elwood, letter to author; RoH; CWGC Register
8. Chavasse, p.75
9. NA, WO170/605, war diary HQ 38 Bde
10. *CTW*, p.110; 6 INNISKS, war diary
11. Russell
12. Ibid.
13. *CTW*, p.113
14. Ibid.
15. Ibid.
16. Brig. Scott
17. 6 INNISKS, war diary
18. Scott, op. cit.
19. Ibid.
20. *CTW*, pp.121–3
21. Ibid., 123
22. Gunner, *Front of the Line*, p.81
23. WO373/7/185, Kelleher
24. Gunner, p.82
25. Trousdell notes to author
26. Brig. Scott
27. *CTW*, p.126
28. Jack Broadbent, letter to author
29. NA Kew, WO170/825, war diary 16/5L
30. Ford, op. cit., p.130
31. Brian Clark to author
32. Horsfall, p.45
33. *CTW*, pp.126–7
34. Ibid., p.132
35. WO373/7/239, Ford
36. WO373/11/247, Clark
37. WO373/8/16, Ponsonby
38. WO373/71/156, Kirwan
39. Horsfall, p.45
40. Doherty, *Monte Cassino*, pp.274–6
41. *CTW*, p.136; RoH
42. Ibid., pp.136–7
43. Woods, op. cit.
44. Ibid.
45. Ibid.
46. Ibid.
47. Davies, notes
48. Doherty, *Monte Cassino*, pp.278–9
49. *CTW*, RoH; Trousdell, notes
50. RoH
51. Trousdell, notes
52. *CTW*, p.142
53. ffrench-Blake, *A History of the 17th/21st Lancers, 1922–1959*, pp.160–8

54. *CTW*, p.142
55. Brig. Scott; *CTW*, p.142
56. Brig. Scott; *LIR History*, p.161
57. *CTW*, p.144
58. Brig. Scott
59. Ibid., *CTW*, pp.147–8

Chapter 6: Breaking the Hitler Line

1. Molony, Vol.VI, Pt I, pp.180–8
2. Strickland, *Strick*, pp.169–71; Doherty, *The North Irish Horse* (hereinafter *NIH*), p.128
3. *NIH*, p.133
4. Ibid., p.136; RoH; GWGC Register
5. Ibid., RoH; CWGC Register
6. RoH
7. WO373/7/211/, Maxwell
8. *NIH*, p.140; WO373/7/162, Griffith; RoH
9. Farmer, quoted in *NIH*, p.139
10. WO373/7/204, Neilson; *NIH*, pp.140–1
11. WO373/8/414, Strickland; *NIH*, pp.142–3
12. *Northern Whig*, 12 Jul. 1944
13. *NIH*, pp.144–5
14. Doherty, *Only the Enemy in Front* (*OTE*), pp.129–30
15. Scott, Col Bobby, 'Anzio to Rome'
16. Ibid.
17. Ibid.
18. Ibid.; RoH; CWGC Register
19. Scott, Bobby, op. cit.
20. Ibid.
21. Fox, p.120
22. Scott, Col Bobby; WO373/7/448, Long; /11/270, Nolan, /7/501, Godber
23. Scott, Col Bobby
24. Ibid.
25. *CTW*, p.148; RoH; CWGC Register
26. *CTW*, pp.148–9
27. Davies, notes
28. *CTW*, pp.152–3
29. Brig. Scott
30. CTW, pp.156–7
31. *WoS*, op. cit., p.159
32. Information from J.J. Doherty, Joe Robinson & Jim Hamilton MM
33. Brig. Scott
34. Kendal Chavasse to author
35. Brig. Scott
36. *CTW*, pp.160–1
37. Ibid, p.161; Horsfall, op. cit., pp.132–3
38. Palmer to author
39. *CTW*, p.162
40. Ibid.; WO373/8/572, Manson

41. Brig. Scott
42. *CTW*, p.163
43. Durney, *Far from the Short Grass*, p.186; RoH; CWGC Register
44. Ford, op. cit., pp.162–4
45. Horsfall, *Fling*, p.137
46. Brig. Scott
47. *CTW*, pp.166–7
48. Horsfall, pp.150–2
49. Woods, op. cit.
50. Ibid., *CTW*, p.168
51. *CTW*, PP.169–70
52. Ibid., p.170; Horsfall, pp.156–7
53. Trousdell, notes to author
54. Ibid.; *CTW*, p.175; WO373/8/765, Hobden
55. Brig. Scott
56. Ibid.
57. Ibid.; Clark to author
58. *CTW*, p.179
59. Ray, op. cit., p.150
60. *CTW*, p.181
61. Brig. Scott
62. Ibid.

Chapter 7: The Road to Florence and the Road to Rome

1. *NIH*, pp.148–51; RoH
2. Ibid., pp.152–4
3. Ibid., pp.155–7
4. Ibid., p.156
5. Ibid., pp.156–7
6. Ibid., p.161
7. Ibid., p.161; *Remembrance NI* (REMNI)
8. *NIH*, p.162
9. NA Kew, WO204/7268, 25 Tk Bde operations
10. Doherty, *Ireland's Generals in the SWW*, pp.176–81
11. *LIR History*, p.172
12. Ibid.
13. Ibid.
14. Jackson, *The Mediterranean and the Middle East, Vol.VI, Pt.II*, p .126
15. *WoS*, pp.150–1
16. Ibid., p.153
17. Ibid., pp.153–4; NA Kew, WO WO170/, war diary 25 HAA Bty, 1944
18. *WoS*, pp.154–6
19. Ibid., p.156
20. Ibid., pp.98–100
21. Tom Patton to author, 16 Jun 1964; interviews with 25 Bty veterans, Jun 1986
22. *WoS*, p.157

Chapter 8: The Gothic Line

1. *LIR History*, p.172
2. Doherty, *Eighth Army in Italy* (*EAIt*), p.131
3. Jackson, op. cit., p.21
4. Ibid., p.232
5. Ibid.
6. Joslen, *Orders of Battle*, p.14
7. Jackson, pp.234 & 240
8. *EAIt*, p.140
9. *NIH*, p.174
10. Ibid., pp.174–5
11. Ibid.
12. Ibid., p.175
13. Ibid.
14. Ibid.
15. NA Kew, WO170/617, war diary HQ 128 Brigade, Jul-Dec 1944
16. *EAIt*, p.114 M
17. Joslen, p.148
18. Williams, p.100
19. *LIR History*, p.174
20. Ibid., p.175
21. Ibid.; WO373/9/429, Henry
22. WO373/9/430, Martini
23. *LIR History*, p.175
24. WO373/9/360, McDaid
25. *LIR History*, pp.175–6; WO373/9/432, McDonald
26. Ibid.; WO373/9/279, Smith
27. *LIR History*, p,176; WO373/10/205, Gamble
28. Williams, op. cit., p.101; *LIR History*, pp.176–7
29. *LIR History*, p.177
30. Ibid., pp.177–8
31. Ibid., p.178
32. Ibid., p.179
33. Ibid., pp.179–80
34. Ibid., p.180
35. Ibid.
36. Ibid., pp.180–1
37. Ibid.
38. Ibid., p.181
39. Ibid., p.182
40. *NIH*, p.180
41. Jackson, op. cit., pp.256–64
42. *NIH*, pp.181–2
43. Ibid., p.184; WO373/13/277, King
44. Ibid., p.186; WO373/12/263, McAughtry
45. *NIH*, p.187
46. *WoS*, pp.160–1
47. Ibid., p.161
48. Ibid.

49. Ibid.
50. Ibid., pp.161–2
51. Ibid., pp.162–3
52. Ibid., p.163
53. Ibid., pp.163–4
54. Ibid., p.166
55. Ibid., p.165
56. Hamilton, interview with author
57. Smyth, interview with author
58. Hamilton, interview with author
59. *WoS*, p.168
60. Ibid.
61. Brig. Scott
62. Ray, op. cit., pp.160–1; *CTW*, pp.189–90
63. Brig. Scott; *CTW*, pp.190–1
64. *CTW*, p.192
65. Horsfall, op. cit., pp.198
66. *CTW*, p.192–3
67. Ibid.; Horsfall, pp.198–9; WO373/10/540, Robinson
68. Horsfall, p.199
69. *CTW*, pp.193–4
70. Horsfall, p.201
71. Ibid., p.203
72. Ibid., p.204
73. *CTW*, pp.196–7; RoH
74. *CTW*, p.197; RoH
75. Brig. Scott
76. Ibid.
77. Bredin, interview with author
78. Ibid.; RoH
79. *CTW*, pp.198–200
80. WO373/10/604, Strainger
81. *NIH*, pp.190–1
82. Ibid., p.193; RoH
83. *NIH*, pp.193–4
84. RoH; CWGC Register
85. *NIH*, p.199
86. Ibid., pp.199–200
87. Ibid., p.202
88. Ibid., pp.204–5; RoH
89. Ray, op. cit., p.176
90. Brig. Scott; Trousdell, notes to author
91. *CTW*, pp.204–5
92. Horsfall, pp.212–13
93. Trousdell, notes to author
94. Ibid.
95. Horsfall, p.213
96. Brig. Scott
97. Ibid.

98. Trousdell, notes to author
99. Horsfall, p.213
100. Ray, p.177
101. *CTW*, p.214
102. Brig. Scott
103. Trousdell, notes to author; Clark to author
104. *LIR History*, pp.187–8; WO373/12/575, Montgomerie
105. Brig. Scott
106. *NIH*, p.209
107. Ibid., p.210
108. Ibid., pp.211–12; WO373/11/93, Barbour
109. Ibid., pp.213–14; WO373/11/92, Donaghy
110. Doherty, *Victory in Italy* (hereinafter *VicIt*), pp.41–2; Bigger, *The Royal Engineers Journal*, Vol.138, No.1, pp.80–5
111. *NIH*, p.215
112. Ibid., p.217
113. Ibid., pp.219–19
114. Ibid., p.219
115. Ibid., pp.219–21; RoH
116. *NIH*, pp.220–21; WO373/11/679, Verso
117. *VicIt*, p.42; *NIH*, p.223

Chapter 9: 1945: The Last Battles

1. *LIR History*, pp.190–1
2. Ibid., p.191; Brig. Scott
3. Ibid., p.190
4. Ibid., pp.190–1; WO373/12/624, Wardle
5. Ibid., pp.190–1; WO373/13/662, O'Connor
6. *NIH*, p.223; WO373/13/10, Reid
7. *NIH*, pp.224–5
8. Ibid., pp.225–6
9. Ibid., pp,226–7
10. Ibid., p.227
11. Brig. Scott
12. *CTW*, pp.219–20
13. Ibid., p.221
14. Ibid., p.223; *VicIt*, op. cit., pp.56–7; WO373/13/61, Doherty
15. Robinson, notes to author
16. Brig. Scott
17. *CTW*, pp.224–6; Brig. Scott; WO373/13/23, Salter
18. Robinson, op. cit.
19. Ibid.
20. Brig. Scott; Palmer, interview with author
21. Brig Scott; *VicIt.*,
22. *LIR History*, pp. 195–9
23. Ibid., p.199
24. Ibid., pp.199–201; WO373/13/306, Satchell; /13/367, McClelland; /13/613, Boswell
25. NA Kew, war diary Eighth Army
26. *VicIt*, p.xxiii

27. Ibid., pp.102–3
28. Harpur, information on jacket
29. Ray, op. cit., p.201
30. *VicIt*, pp.118–19
31. *CTW*, p.236
32. WO373/14/472, Harpur
33. Duane, notes to author
34. *CTW*, pp.239–40
35. WO373/14/7, Palmer
36. Bredin, notes to author
37. Ibid.
38. Ibid.
39. Brig. Scott
40. Ibid.
41. *CTW*, p.241
42. Ray, op. cit., p.209
43. WO373/14/92, Bell
44. Ibid.
45. WO373/14/5, Shaw
46. RoH; CWGC Register
47. *CTW*, p.243; WO373/14/83, Howard
48. Brig. Scott
49. Bredin
50. *CTW*, pp. 244–5
51. *VicIt*, pp.149–50
52. Brig. Scott
53. Duane, notes to author
54. Ray, op. cit., p.216
55. Brig. Scott
56. *LIR History*, pp.207–8
57. *CTW*, pp.250–1
58. Ibid.; Bredin
59. Brig. Scott; Bredin
60. Ray, pp.222–4
61. Brig. Scott
62. *VicIt*, Ch.12 passim
63. *LIR History*, p.210
64. *NIH*, pp.229–30; WO373/13/276, Bexon; /14/383, Maguire; /13/306, Ballard; /13/8, Foott
65. *NIH*, pp.231–2; WO373/13/277, King; /13/275, Sidebottom
66. *NIH*, p.233
67. Rea, *The Best is Yet to Come,* passim; WO373/73/413, Rea
68. McCorkell, interview with author
69. Lunt, *The Scarlet Lancers*, p.135
70. ffrench-Blake, notes to author; RoH; CWGC Register
71. *Leinster Leader*, 3 Jly 1945, via James Durney
72. WO373/13/217, ffrench-Blake
73. Woods, op. cit.

Chapter 10: In The Air

1. Webster Browne, Notes on Tony Lovell
2. Ibid.; The Battle of Britain London Monument (BBLM), accessed Feb. 2024
3. Webster Browne, op. cit.
4. BBLM
5. Ibid.
6. Ibid.
7. Ibid.
8. *London Gazette*, 20 Apr. 1945
9. BBLM
10. Ibid.
11. Ibid.
12. Ibid.
13. Ibid.
14. McAughtry, *The Sinking of the Kenbane Head*, passim.
15. Dungan, *Distant Drums*, p.108; McAughtry, interviews with author
16. The Soldier's Medal is awarded to any member of the US armed forces or of a friendly foreign nation who, while serving in any capacity with the US Army, distinguished himself or herself by heroism not involving conflict with an enemy.
17. CWGC Register
18. to 28. Ibid.
29. Halley, pp.150–1
30. Shores et al., *A History of the Mediterranean Air War*, Vol,4, p.475
31. CWGC Register
32. Ibid.
33. Shores et al., op. cit., p.234
34. Ibid., Vol.5, p.273
35. Ibid., p.364
36. Ibid., Vol.4, p.114
37. Ibid., p.37
38. Ibid., p.427
39. Ibid.
40. CWGC Register
41. Shores et al., Vol.4, p.408
42. Ibid., Vol.5, p.198
43. Ibid., Vol.4, p.519
44. Ibid., Vol.5, p.140
45. Ibid., p.240
46. Ibid., pp.328 & 339
47. Airmen Died; CWGC Register & RIrF info
48. Halley, op. cit., *The Squadrons of the Royal Air Force*, p.242
49. Shores et al, Vol.4, p.591
50. Airmen Died & CWGC Register
51. Ibid.
52. Ibid.
53. Ibid.
54. Shores et al., Vol.5, p.383
55. Ibid., Vol.4, 240

56. Airmen Died & CWGC Register
57. Ibid., Vol.5, p.346
58. CWGC Register
59. Shores et al., Vol.5, p.106
60. Airmen Died & CWGC Register
61. Ibid.
62. Shores et al, Vol.5, p.403
63, Ibid., p.414
64 Airmen Died & CWGC Register
65. Shores et al, Vol.5, p.414

Chapter 11: Ruling the Waves

1. Simpson, M., in *Oxford Dictionary of National Biography*, online edtn, accessed Feb. 2024
2. Roskill, op. cit., Vol.1, p.49
3. Doherty, *In the Ranks of Death*, pp.102–5
4. Kemp, *The Admiralty Regrets*, p.228; Kemp states only 85 survived but U-boat.net provides the accurate figure and a list of the dead.
5. U-boat.net: accessed Feb 2024
6. CWGC Register; *EAIIt*, p.8
7. Roskill, Vol.3, p.299
8. Elizabeth Dobbs, interview with author
9. Ibid.
10. CWGC Register
11. Dobbs, interview with author
12. Ibid.
13. Daly & Devlin, *The Clergy of the Diocese of Derry*, p.54; Daly, interview with author
14. Former Wren Maeve Kelly, interview with author
15. www.unithistories.com RN Officers 1939–45, accessed Feb 2024
16. Taylor, *The Sea Chaplains*, p.444
17. Ibid., p.445
18. McKenna, Michael, *Australian Dictionary of Biography*, Vol.8, 1981, transferred online 2006, accessed Feb 2024

Chapter 12: Liberating Italy

1. Lowe, *Naples 1944*, pp.237–78
2. *London Gazette*, 14 Oct. 1943
3. Royal Irish Fusiliers' Museum; Pickering, *The Bandits of Cisterna*, p.3
4. Pickering, p.4
5. Ibid., p.26
6. Ibid., p.27
7. Ibid.
8. Ibid., pp.27–8
9. Ibid., p.30
10. Ibid., p.323–4
11. Ibid., pp.43–4
12. Stafford, *Mission Accomplished*, p.264
13. Pickering, pp.47–8

14. Ibid., p.67
15. Stafford, op. cit., p.91
16. Doherty, *Irish Volunteers in The Second World War* (*IrVol*), pp.95–6
17. Ibid.
18. Ibid., p.96
19. Ibid., p.95
20. Ibid., p.96
21. Ibid.
22. Ibid.
23. Ibid., pp.96–7
24. Ibid., p.97
25. Ibid.
26. Lamb, *War in Italy*, p.221
27. Derry, *Rome Escape Line*, p.4
28. Ibid.
29. Fleming, *The Vatican Pimpernel*, p.191
30. Derry, quoted in Fleming, p.190
31. Revd Michael Keaveny to author, June 1983
32. Information from the late Bishop Edward Daly, Msgr Sean Quinlan and the Revd Louis Madden
33. *Irish News*, quoted in Fleming, p.11
34. Quoted in Fleming, p.71
35. Fleming, p.71
36. Referred to in a Wikipedia article on Johnston and a file in the National Archives, Kew
37. Wills, *That Neutral Island*, p.197
38. Finn & Morgan, *The Irish in the Resistance*, p.90
39. Holland, *Italy's Sorrow*, passim.
40. Barzini, *The Italians*, passim.
41. Lucia Bedeschi-Radcliffe to author, Oct. 2008
42. Stonor Saunders, *The Woman who shot Mussolini*, passim.

Bibliography

Adleman, Robert, and Walton, Colonel George, *Rome Fell Today* (Leslie Frewin, London, 1969)

Alexander, Field Marshal Sir Harold, *Despatch* (on the Allied Armies in Italy during the period from 3 September 1943 to 12 December 1944) (HMSO, Supplement to *London Gazette*, London, 6 June 1950)

——, *Memoirs*, John North (Ed.) (Cassell, London, 1962)

Anon, *The 78th Division in the Final Offensive in Italy* (Naval & Military Press Ltd reprint, Uckfield, nd)

Aris, George, *The Fifth British Division 1939 to 1945 (Being an account of the Journey and Battles of a Reserve Division in Europe, Africa, and Asia)*, The Trustees of the Fifth Division Benevolent Fund, London, 1959)

Ascoli, David, *A Companion to the British Army, 1660–1983* (Harrap Ltd, London 1983)

Barzini, Luigi, *The Italians* (Hamish Hamilton, London, 1953)

Battistelli, Pier Paolo, *Assault on the Gothic Line 1944: The Allied Attempted Breakthrough into Northern Italy* (Osprey Publishing, Oxford, 2023)

Bennett, Richard, Deering, John, Forgrave, William, Hogg, Robin and Scott, Mark, *Globetrotters: The Story of the 2nd Battalion Royal Inniskilling Fusiliers in the Second World War* (The Inniskillings Museum, Enniskillen, nd)

Bolton, Major Kenneth MC, *With the 11th (HAC) Regiment, RHA in World War II* (Naval & Military Press Ltd reprint, Uckfield, nd)

Booth, T. Michael, and Spencer, Duncan, *Paratrooper: The Life of General James M. Gavin* (Casemate Publishers, Haverton PA, 2013)

Brookes, The Right Revd Dom Rudesind, OBE MC TD OSB, *Father Dolly: The Guardsman Monk: The Memoirs of Captain the Right Reverend Dom Rudesind Brookes OBE MC TD OSB, Titular Abbot of Sherborne, sometime Irish Guards, monk of Downside, and Army and Royal Air Force Chaplain* (Henry Melland, London, 1983)

Brookes, Stephen (ed), *Montgomery and the Eighth Army* (The Bodley Head, London, 1991)

Broom, John, *Faithful in Adversity: The Royal Army Medical Corps in the Second World War* (Pen and Sword, Barnsley, 2019)

Caddick-Adams, Peter, *Monte Cassino: Ten Armies in Hell* (Preface Publishing, London, 2011)

Carew, F.A., *The Army Medical Services: Campaigns: Vol. III: Sicily, Italy, Greece (1944–45)* (HMSO, London, 1957; N&M Press Ltd, reprint)

Casey, P.J., Cullen, K.T. and Duignan, J.P., *Irish Doctors in the Second World War* (Merrion Press, Newbridge, Co. Kildare, 2024)

Clark, Lloyd, *Anzio: Italy and the Battle for Rome – 1944* (Atlantic Monthly Press, New York NY, 2020)

Clay, E.W., *The Path of the 50th: The Story of the 50th (Northumbrian) Division in the Second World War, 1939–1945* (np, 1947; Naval & Military Press, Uckfield, nd)
Cleaver, Thomas McKelvey, *Gothic Line 1944–45: The USAAF starves out the German Army* (Osprey Publishing, Oxford, 2022)
Cole, Sir David, *Rough Road to Rome: A Foot-Soldier in Sicily and Italy 1943–44* (William Kimber, London, 1983)
Cunliffe, Marcus, *The Royal Irish Fusiliers 1793–1968* (Oxford University Press, 1952 & 1970)
Daly, Edward and Kieran Devlin, *The Clergy of the Diocese of Derry: An Index* (Fourt Courts Press, Dublin, 1997)
Daniell, A.P. de T. (Tony) OBE MC TD, *Mediterranean Safari March 1943-October 1944* (Orphans Press, Leominster, 2000)
Derry, Sam, *Rome Escape Line* (Harrap, London, 1960)
Doherty, Richard, *Wall of Steel: The History of 9th (Londonderry) HAA Regiment, RA (SR)* (North-West Books, Limavady, 1988)
——, *Clear The Way! A History of 38 (Irish) Brigade, 1941–1947* (Irish Academic Press, Dublin, 1993)
——, *Irish Generals: Irish Generals in the British Army in the Second World War* (Appletree Press, Belfast, 1993)
——, *Only The Enemy in Front: The Recce Corps at War, 1940–46* (Tom Donovan Publishing, London, 1994)
——, *A Noble Crusade: A History of Eighth Army, 1941–1945* (Spellmount Publishing, Staplehurst, 1999)
——, *Irish Men and Women in the Second World War* (Four Courts Press, Dublin, 1999)
——, *Irish Volunteers in the Second World War* (Four Courts Press, Dublin, 2001)
——, *The North Irish Horse: A Hundred Years of Service* (Spellmount Publishers, Staplehurst, 2002)
——, *Ireland's Generals in the Second World War* (Four Courts Press, Dublin, 2004)
——, *Eighth Army in Italy 1943–1945: The Long Hard Slog* (Pen and Sword, Barnsley, 2007)
——, *The British Reconnaissance Corps* (Osprey, Oxford, 2007)
——, *Ubique: The Royal Artillery in the Second World War* (Spellmount Publishers, Staplehurst, 2008)
——, *In the Ranks of Death: The Irish in the Second World War* (Pen and Sword, Barnsley, 2010)
——, *Victory in Italy: 15th Army Group's Final Campaign* (Pen and Sword, Barnsley, 2014)
——, *Monte Cassino: Opening the Road to Rome* (Pen and Sword, Barnsley, 2018)
Dungan, Myles, *Distant Drums: Irish Soldiers in Foreign Armies* (Appletree Press, Belfast, 1993)
Durney, James, *Far from the Short Grass: The Story of Kildare Men in Two World Wars* (Leinster *Leader*, Naas, Co. Kildare, 1999)
——, *'A Good Aul Life.' Mickser Mahon 1921–1997* (Naas Local History Group, Naas, 2021)
Durnin, David and Ian Miller (eds), *Medicine, Health and Irish Experiences of Conflict 1914–45* (Manchester University Press, Manchester, 2017)
ffrench-Blake, R.L.V., *A History of the 17th/21st Lancers, 1922–1959* (Macmillan & Co. Ltd,, London, 1962)
Finn, Clodagh, and John Morgan, *The Irish in the Resistance: The Untold Stories of the Ordinary Heroes who resisted Hitler* (Gill Books, Dublin, 2024)

Fitzgerald, Desmond, *History of the Irish Guards in the Second World War* (Gale & Polden, Aldershot, 1949)
Fleming, Brian, *The Vatican Pimpernel: The Wartime Exploits of Monsignor Hugh O'Flaherty* (The Collins Press, Cork, 2008)
Ford, Ken, *Mailed Fist: 6th Armoured Division at War, 1940–1945* (Sutton, Stroud, 2005)
Fox, Sir Frank, *The Royal Inniskilling Fusiliers in the Second World War, 1939–45* (Gale and Polden, Aldershot, 1951)
Graham, Dominick and Shelford Bidwell, *Tug of War: The Battle for Italy: 1943–45* (Hodder & Stoughton, London, 1986)
Halley, James J., *The Squadrons of the Royal Air Force* (Air-Britain Historians Ltd, Tunbridge, 1980)
Harpur, Brian, *The Impossible Victory. A personal account of the Battle for the River Po* (William Kimber, London, 1980)
Hewitt, John C., *Ireland's Aviator Heroes of World War II* (Hewitt, Belfast, 2003)
——, *Ireland's Aviation Heroes of World War II*, Vol. II (Mercier Press, Cork, 2016)
Hogg, Ian V., and Weeks, John, *The Illustrated Encyclopedia of Military Vehicles* (New Burlington Books, London, 1980)
Holland, James, *Italy's Sorrow: A Year of War, 1944–45* (Harper Press, London, 2008)
——, *Sicily '43: The First Assault on Fortress Europe* (Bantam, London, 2021)
——, *The Savage Storm: The Battle for Italy 1943* (Bantam, London, 2023)
Horsfall, John, *Say not the Struggle …* (Roundwood Press, Kineton, 1977)
——, *Fling our Banner to the Wind* (Roundwood Press, Kineton, 1978)
Jackson, General Sir William, *The Mediterranean and Middle East. Vol. VI, Victory in the Mediterranean, Pt I – 1st April to 4th June 1944* (HMSO, London, 1986)
Jennings, Christian, *At War on The Gothic Line: Fighting in Italy, 1944–1945* (Osprey, Oxford, 2016)
Johnstone, Tom and James Hagerty, *The Cross on the Sword: Catholic Chaplains in the Forces* (Geoffrey Chapman, London, 1996)
Junier, Alexander and Smulders, Bart, with Joop Korstloof, *By Land, Sea and Air: An Illustrated History of the 2nd Battalion The South Staffordshire Regiment 1939–1945* (R.N. Sigmond Ltd, 2004)
Kemp, Paul, *The Admiralty Regrets: British Warship Losses of the 20th Century* (Sutton, Stroud, 1999)
Kennedy, Jonathan, *Pathogenesis: How Germs made History* (Torva, London, 2023)
Lamb, Richard, *War in Italy 1943–1945: A Brutal Story* (DaCapo Press, Indiana, 1996)
Linklater, Eric, *The Campaign in Italy* (HMSO, London, 1959)
Love, Keith, *Naples 1944: War, Liberation and Chaos* (Collins, London, 2024)
Lunt, James, *The Scarlet Lancers: The Story of 16th/5th The Queen's Royal Lancers 1689–1992* (Leo Cooper, London, 1993)
McClean, Stewart, *SAS: The History of the Special Raiding Squadron: 'Paddy's Men'* (Spellmount, Stroud, 2006)
Mahon, Sir William Bt, Robin Bullock-Webster, Peter Verney and Sir Anthony Weldon, *Irish Guards: The First Hundred Years, 1900–2000* (Spellmount, Staplehurst, 2000)
Mead, Richard, *The Last Great Cavalryman: The Life of General Sir Richard McCreery, Commander Eighth Army* (Pen & Sword, Barnsley, 2012)
Messenger, Charles, *The Commandos: 1940–1946* (William Kimber, London, 1985)
Molony, Brigadier C.J.C., *The Mediterranean and Middle East. Vol. VI, Victory in the Mediterranean, Pt I – 1st April to 4th June 1944* (HMSO, London, 1986)

Mowat, Farley, *And No Birds Sang* (Douglas & McIntyre, Toronto, 1980)
Moyes, Philip, *Bomber Squadrons of the RAF and their Aircraft* (Purnell, Abingdon, 1976)
O'Connor, Steven, *Irish Officers in the British Forces, 1922–45* (Palgrave Macmillan, Basingstoke, 2014)
Pickering, William, with Alan Hart, *The Bandits of Cisterna* (Leo Cooper, London, 1991)
Rea, Kathleen, *The Best Is Yet To Come: Fifty Years in Zimbabwe* (Munn, Harare, 1992)
Richardson, Neil, *Dark Times, Decent Men: Stories of Irishmen in World War II* (The O'Brien Press, Dublin, 2012)
Roskill, Captain S.W. DSC RN, *The War at Sea 1939–1945: Vol. III, The Offensive Pt I 1st June 1944–14th August 1945* (HMSO, London, 1960)
——, *The War at Sea 1939–1945: Vol. III, The Offensive Pt II 1st June 1944–14th August 1945* (HMSO, London, 1961)
Rostron, Peter, *The Military Life of General Sir Miles Dempsey GBE KCB* DSO *MC, Monty's Army Commander* (Pen & Sword, Barnsley, 2010)
Routledge, Brigadier N.W., OBE TD, *Anti-Aircraft Artillery, 1914–55* (Brassey's, London, 1994)
Sherrard, William, *The War Diary of William Sherrard, 9th (Londonderry) Heavy Anti-Aircraft Regiment Royal Artillery (SR)* (North-West Archaeological and Historical Society, Londonderry, 2005)
Shores, Christopher and Giovanni Massimello with Russell Guest, Frank Olynyk, Winifried Bock and Andrew Thomas, *A History of the Mediterranean Air War 1940–1945: Vol. 4: Sicily and Italy to the Fall of Rome: 14 May 1943–5 June 1944* (Grub Street, London, 2018)
——, *A History of the Mediterranean Air War 1940–1945: Vol. 5: From the Fall of Rome to the End of the War 1944–1945* (Grub Street, London, 2021).
Smith, E.D., *The Battles for Cassino* (Ian Allan, London, 1975)
——, *Even the Brave Falter* (privately published, London, 1978, 1980 & 1993)
Snape, Michael, *The Royal Army Chaplains' Department: Chaplains under Fire* (Boydell Press, Woodbridge, 2008)
Stafford, David, *Mission Accomplished: SOE and Italy 1943–1945* (The Bodley Head, London, 2011)
Stonor Saunders, Frances, *The Woman Who Shot Mussolini* (Faber and Faber Ltd, London, 2010)
Strawson, John, *General Sir Richard McCreery* (published privately by Lady McCreery, 1973)
Strickland, Tim, *Strick: Tank Hero of Arras: The Making of an Extraordinary Soldier* (Casemate Publishers, Haverton PA, 2021)
Taylor, Gordon, *The Sea Chaplains: A History of the Chaplains of the Royal Navy* (Oxford Illustrated Press, Oxford, 1978)
Truesdale, David, *Brotherhood of the Cauldron: Irishmen in the 1st Airborne Division from North Africa to Arnhem* (Redcoat Publishing, Newtownards, 2003)
Verney, Peter, *The Micks: The Story of the Irish Guards* (Pan Books, London, 1973)
Williams, David, *Black Cats at War: The Story of the 56th (London) Division, TA, 1939–1945* (Imperial War Museum, London, 1995)
Williamson, Hugh, *The Fourth Division, 1939 to 1945* (Newman Neame, London, 1951)
Wills, Clair, *That Neutral Island: A Cultural History of Ireland in the Second World War* (Faber & Faber, London, 2008)

Unpublished

Anon, *Two Five* (25 HAA Bty, 9th Londonderry HAA Regiment)

Chavasse, Col K.G.F. DSO* MiD, *Some Memories of my Life*

Davies, Maj. Sir Mervyn MC, An account of E Coy 2LIR in Italy

Duane, Maj. John MC, Notes on his service in Italy with 2nd Royal Inniskilling Fusiliers.

Ormsby, John, 'Journal' (25 HAA Bty)

Russell, Brig. N. DSO MC, Narrative of 38 (Irish) Brigade to Feb. 1944

Scott, Col Bobby, 'Anzio to Rome 23rd May-4th June 1944'

Scott, Maj. Gen. T.P.D. DSO, Narrative of 38 (Irish) Brigade, Feb. 1944-May 1945

Webster Browne, R.G. Lovell, Notes on Tony Lovell DSO* DFC* DFC (US) MiD

Woods, Col A.D. MC*, An Account of his service in Italy as OC H Coy, 2 LIR

Articles

Bigger, Col (retd) D.L.D. MInstRE, 'Spring 1945: Advance to the River Po and the Formation of 25 Armoured Engineer Brigade' *The Royal Engineers Journal*, Vol.138, No.1, April 2024, The Institution of Royal Engineers

Stewart, Dr Paul, 'Little Pearl Harbour', *Scope*, Vol.3, No.5, Nov/Dec 2010, Med Media, Dun Laoghaire

UK National Archives, Kew

Although many files were consulted, space precludes a full list: those used are listed in the notes where appropriate.

Other sources

www.irishbrigade.co.uk A website dedicated to 38 (Irish) Brigade in the Second World War, including war diaries and photographs as well as personal accounts and recollections

www.royal-irish.com A Virtual Military Gallery website dedicated to the history of the antecedent regiments of the modern Royal Irish Regiment

wartimeni.com Northern Ireland during the Second World War

remembranceni.org A daily blog commemorating Northern Ireland people in both world wars

Northern Ireland in the Second World War Facebook page

Airmen Died in the Second World War 1939-45: The Roll of Honour of the British, Commonwealth and Allied Air Services DVD-ROM constructed by the Naval & Military Press Ltd, Uckfield

Army Roll of Honour: Soldiers Died in the Second World War 1939-45 CD-ROM constructed by the Naval & Military Press Ltd, Uckfield

Index

Military, Naval and Air formations, units, etc.

Individuals

General